Germany

Austria

• Innsbruck

• Davos

• St Moritz

Monte Pelmo ▲   • Cortina

z ▲▲ Piz Palü

ina

Marmolata ▲

Monte Disgrazia

Brenta   • Trento
Alps

• Lake Garda

• Venice

Italy

N

NW   NE

W   E

SW   SE

S

IN SEARCH OF

PEAKS, PASSES & GLACIERS

IRISH ALPINE PIONEERS

This book is dedicated to my grandson, Hugh Gavin Christopher.
May he come to know and love the hills and wild places.

IN SEARCH OF

PEAKS, PASSES
& GLACIERS

IRISH ALPINE PIONEERS

Frank Nugent

The Collins Press

First published in 2013 by

The Collins Press

West Link Park

Doughcloyne

Wilton

Cork

© Frank Nugent 2013

A CIP record for this book is available from the British Library.
ISBN: 978-1-84889-178-4

Design and typesetting by Bright Idea
Typeset in Minion Pro
Printed in Italy by Printer Trento

Contents

Foreword

In Search of Peaks, Passes & Glaciers tells the story of Irish alpinism from the middle of the nineteenth century until 1921, when the first Everest reconnaissance expedition was led by Charles Howard-Bury. It might accurately be subtitled 'a history of the Irish members of the Alpine Club', as most of those featured in the book are distinguished by their membership of that august body or indeed by their being blackballed from joining it. The one exception to this rule was Elizabeth Hawkins-Whitshed, an Irish aristocrat who climbed as well as any man and was a founder of an alternative club for women mountaineers.

Few of the Irish mountaineers' names are well known in Ireland and many that are known internationally for their climbing achievements are often labelled British or English in other mountain histories. Collectively, their contribution to the exploration and mapping of the Alps, the Pyrenees, the Southern Alps, the Selkirk range of the Canadian Rockies and the approaches to Everest is impressive. It is the author's hope that this book will ignite renewed Irish interest in alpinism as a source of limitless adventure and lifelong enjoyment.

Quotations and excerpts throughout this book are faithfully transcribed from diaries, books and journal articles; misspellings or grammatical errors within original passages have not been altered. A glossary of mountaineering terminology is appended for non-mountaineering readers.

Facing page: Cima Tosa in the Italian Brenta Dolomites: an etching by F. F. Tuckett in *The Italian Alps* by Douglas Freshfield (1875). The mountain was first climbed by John Ball from Dublin and W. E. Forster on 1 August 1865 with a local man named Nicolussi. However, an Italian, G. Loss, later claimed to have climbed it twelve days earlier.

Acknowledgements

THIS WORK HAS BEEN a work of love that has engaged me for over eight years, since the publication in 2003 of my first history of Irish exploration, *Seek the Frozen Lands: Irish Polar Explorers, 1740–1922*. It has proved a much more difficult task of research to uncover the lives and achievements of the Irish mountaineers than the Polar explorers. Polar exploration during that period was largely organised in cooperation with the navy, bringing the attendant benefits of official accounts and logbooks that were written and properly archived by the authorities. Mountaineering, on the other hand, has always largely been organised and executed by individuals whose accounts and diaries are much more difficult to source. Happily, the prime movers in early Irish alpinism (Ball, Tyndall, Reilly, Russell, Mrs Le Blond, Green, Bryce and Howard-Bury) all produced books, articles for journals, or maintained diaries related to their mountain adventures. To uncover their climbing lives I have primarily drawn on the resources of the National Library of Ireland, the National Achives and the library of the Royal Irish Academy (all in Dublin), as well as the records and archives of the Alpine Club in London. Ron Barrington of Greystones provided access to his family's own private papers and to images of both Charles and Richard Manliffe Barrington; the Library of the Society of Friends, Dublin, also provided information on both men and their times. William Spotswood Green's papers were sourced and visited at Alexander Turnbull Library, Wellington, and the papers of T. Graham Brown (which include much information about Valentine Ryan) were sourced at the Scottish National Library in Edinburgh.

Special mention must be given to Con Collins who accompanied me in 2005 when following the Adams-Reilly route on Mont Dolent, the Burnaby Ridge on the Bishorn in Switzerland, and John Ball's line up Monte Pelmo in Cortina. Paddy O'Brien and Harry Connolly were enthusiatic partners in ascents of Higravstinden and Paddy Barry on Trollfjordtinden in Lofoten in 2009. Both expeditions were nice pieces of action research. It would be remiss of me not to mention earlier climbing partners, such as Harry O'Brien with whom I first went to the Alps in the late 1960s when among other routes we climbed Fowler's Aiguille du Chardonnet and later in 1990 made an ascent of the wonderful Ryan-Lochmatter east ridge of Aiguille du Plan. It was another Dubliner, Shay Nolan, with whom I climbed Reilly's Aiguille d'Argentière. Those enjoyable days are all the more memorable in retrospect. In 1987 the late Joss Lynam AC provided the first opportunity for me to explore the Rongbuk Glacier first tramped by Charles Howard-Bury, Edward Oliver Wheeler, Mallory and Co. in 1921; to Joss and all the Changtse team, I am eternally indebted.

I am fortunate to have had access to the quality work of other Irish mountain historians, particularly to Kevin Higgin's work on Adams-Reilly, Valentine Ryan and A. O. Wheeler and to Marian Keaney's work on the mountain travels of Howard-Bury. The high standards they achieved have set a benchmark for my work. Archivist Glyn Hughes and librarian Tadeusz Hudowski not only welcomed me to the Alpine Club library in London, but over many years have provided invaluable assistance in my pursuit of the diaries, records and publications of

Facing page: A close-up of the Hörnli Ridge of the Matterhorn, the route taken on the first ascent in 1865. Its conquest marked the end of the golden era of alpinism.

the Club's Irish pioneer members. The *Alpine Journal* available at the National Library of Ireland (NLI) in Dublin has proved an invaluable and true source of information on alpine and world mountaineering history since 1860; may it continue to annually record mountain endeavour in whatever format supports future generations of climbers. To all the staff at the NLI and Café Joly thanks for making the reading room such a wonderful space where this labour of love has been completed. Sofia Evans at the RIA library helped me source the scientific work of Ball, Green, R. M. Barrington, Hart and Tyndall. I acknowledge the professionalism of those responsible for the editing, design and publication of this book, particularly Cathy Thompson (editor), Cathal Cudden (designer) and all at The Collins Press who have given support to many authors of books relating to Irish polar and mountain exploration history.

To my wife, Carol: as ever thanks for your continued support and encouragement of my climbing and writing activity; thanks to Ciarán and Cathy for their patience and encouragement and to Eoin for reading the draft manuscript.

Introduction

Who can truly rejoice on the loftiest pinnacle of a great peak if it cost him neither trouble or fatigue nor difficulty to get there? Who cares to triumph over a foe that shows no fight? The exhilaration of the struggle – that is what makes life worth living.

Mrs Aubrey Le Blond, *Mountaineering in the Land of the Midnight Sun, 1908*

WHAT IS CALLED the 'golden age' of alpinism is considered to have started in 1854 with the first ascent of the Wetterhorn in Switzerland and continued in a frenzy of exploration and peak bagging until the summer of 1865, when the summit of the sublime Matterhorn was won after years of competitive exploration to reach its lofty roof. The first ascent ended in tragedy and brought public anger on those who survived. The early climbers were mainly English artists, scientists and clergymen of the Victorian era, who hired experienced local chamois hunters or crystal collectors to act as guides and porters in their service.

The Alps became part of the itinerary of the 'grand tour' undertaken by many wealthy and upper-class people at this time; in small towns such as Chamonix, Grindelwald and Zermatt the numbers of tourists who wanted to be brought to walk onto a glacier, to cross a high mountain pass, or to climb to the summit of an alpine peak grew so quickly that in 1821 the first organisation for mountain guides was established in Chamonix. It occurred in a period when comparative peace reigned in Europe, particularly between France and Britain. As a result the expanding middle-class elite, prospering during the Industrial Revolution, took advantage of the improved transport systems that unlocked the continent to mass tourism.

However, the significant Irish contribution to the development of alpinism is not very well known or acknowledged. Few know that the first ascent of stunning Weisshorn in Switzerland was completed by John Tyndall from Carlow, or indeed that conquest of the notorious Eiger was lead by Charles Barrington, a young man from Bray, County Wicklow.

The British are rightly credited with the development of alpine mountaineering in the latter half of the nineteenth century. However, a close examination of the Irish contribution to that effort reveals that, few as Irish mountaineers were in number, their achievements were very significant. Tyndall was one of the most daring climbers and popular mountain writers of the age.

John Ball (first president of the Alpine Club) was responsible for the drafting and publication of a magnificent series of well-researched guidebooks to the full Alpine range; a skilled geologist and botanist with an easy writing style, he was one of the earliest and most experienced of the Victorian alpine explorers. He instinctively knew what information travellers needed. He and Tyndall were prominent among the ranks of intellectuals who joined the newly formed Alpine Club and both were very active in alpine exploration. The surveying and drafting by Anthony Adams-Reilly from County Westmeath of the first reliable map of the Alps' highest and most important massif, Mont Blanc, addressed another very significant need for visitors. John Ball, through his political support for the Palliser expedition that explored Canada in 1854, started a chain of Irish involvement in the development of Canadian mountaineering that involved not only Palliser himself, but would later engage the passions of Henry Swanzy from Cork, Richard Manliffe Barrington from Bray, William Spotswood Green from Youghal, and lastly Arthur Wheeler from Kilkenny who surveyed and mapped the Canadian Rockies and was a founder of the Canadian Alpine Club.

The 'silver age' of alpinism (when more difficult and aesthetic routes were ascended on many of the previously climbed mountains) is considered to have started with Tyndall's first traverse of the Matterhorn in 1866 and lasted until near the turn of the century when modern unguided mountaineering commenced. During this period Elizabeth Hawkins-Whitshed from Greystones, County Wicklow (better known as Mrs Aubrey Le Blond after she married her third husband), was not only one of the leading climbers of the period but was also a major pioneer of winter climbing, author of many books on her own alpine experiences, one of the founding members of the first women's climbing club in England (the Pinnacle Club), and was elected first president of the Ladies' Alpine Club when it was formed.

At about that time in New Zealand an Anglican priest from County Cork, William Spotswood Green, made a single visit to the Southern Alps and reached the summit plateau of the range's highest peak – the unclimbed Mount Cook – in difficult conditions. In the early years of the new century Captain Valentine Ryan from Johnstown near Birr, County Offaly, formed a swashbuckling young team with a pair of Swiss guides, Franz and Joseph Lochmatter, to blaze a trail of daring new routes across the Alpine chain. Viscount James Bryce MP from Belfast, who was Chief Secretary for Ireland for a short period in 1905, was the second Irish Alpine Club president. Foreseeing the need for such legislation in 1882, he introduced the first Access to Hills Bill in the House of Commons. Charles Howard-Bury, who lived in the county with the lowest elevation in Ireland, was chosen by the Royal Geographical Society to be leader of the first Everest reconnaissance expedition in 1921, which discovered and mapped the northern approach route to the mountain.

All of these Irish alpine pioneers are largely unknown and unheralded today in their native country and their Irish lives and identities are not linked in international mountaineering historical publications. The objective of this volume is to redress this historical oversight.

The author is a modern Irish mountaineer and polar traveller with many seasons spent in the Alps since 1967 when, in his late teens, he made his first Alpine ascents. He has four Irish expeditions to the Himalaya under his belt and was deputy leader of Dawson Stelfox's expedition that made the first Irish ascent of Everest in 1993. He followed the footsteps of Irishmen Ernest Shackleton and Tom Crean across the island of South Georgia in 1997 and was among the crew of the 50-foot sailing boat *Northabout* in 2001 when she completed the first Irish sailing of the Northwest Passage. He is the author of *Seek the Frozen Lands: Irish Polar Explorers, 1840–1922* (Cork, The Collins Press, 2003), which detailed the substantial Irish contribution to the exploration of the Arctic and Antarctica.

In this companion volume the author sheds light on the significant Irish mountaineering achievement in the European and New Zealand Alps, the Pyrenees, the Canadian Rockies and the first reconnaissance of Everest with a cast of Irish characters. But the diverse social, political and scientific backgrounds of each of these great climbers (and the roles they played in wider society, to which each also made a considerable contribution) provide an interesting insight into the many facets and perspectives that characterised nineteenth-century Anglo-Irish society. The author explores the relationship of each person with the country of their birth in a period of political and social upheaval that followed the Great Famine and coincided with the golden era of alpine exploration. The author respects the part played by the local mountain guides who supported the Irish climbers, for they number among the best and finest of the period. Names such as Michel Croz, Christian Almer, the Lochmatter brothers and Melchior Anderegg must rank surely amongst the finest professional climbers of the age. Their characters, achievements and sacrifices are an essential component of this story.

The Irish contribution to the Victorian and Edwardian age of alpine exploration is detailed for the first time in this book. It is an impressive record of individual industry and achievements, deserving of both domestic and international recognition and acclaim.

1

The Origins of Alpinism

Great excitement was caused in the town of Chamounix on Wednesday the 28th by the departure of Mr Gretton, late of the 5th Fusiliers and Mr Richards, of County Wexford, for the purpose of ascending Mont Blanc . . . About eleven o'clock, the clouds clearing away from the summit of the Father of the Alps, the little band was seen to be slowly approaching the top, and a few minutes after the report of the cannon in Chamounix announced the undertaking to be successful.

The Times, London, 9 September 1850

THE FIRST ASCENT of the highest peak in the western Alps was made by two local men on 8 August 1786. Dr Michel-Gabriel Paccard (1757–1827), a local doctor from Chamonix, the village nestled at the foot of Mont Blanc, and Jacques Balmat (1762–1834), a local crystal hunter, made up that historic party. Paccard had spent three years probing possible ascent routes before he made his historic climb. He was motivated partly by science (for the distinction of making the first barometric and temperature readings from the summit) and partly by his ambition to be first to make the ascent of the great mountain. Conversely, Balmat's motivation was mainly to collect the prize money offered to the first ascent party. The ascent proved to be technically straightforward, however, the equipment used was quite basic: an alpenstock (a stout pole with a metal spike), some food, a single blanket and scientific apparatus. The climb involved an overnight bivouac in rocks below the snowline, a dawn start, and a long snow walk up past the rocks known as the Grands Mulets to reach a ridge leading to the summit plateau before reaching the summit at 6.25 p.m. Overtaken by darkness during the descent, they continued in moonlight, stopped at midnight out in the open at a place known as Montagne de la Côte, resting at the rocks wrapped in just a blanket. At first light they descended safely to Chamonix, to be greeted by the rejoicing villagers who had observed them on the summit the evening before. Paccard suffered badly from snow blindness during the descent and was quite exhausted when he reached the village at the foot of the mountain. Shortly afterwards, Balmat travelled to Geneva to collect the monetary reward offered by Professor Horace-Bénedict de Saussure to those who would achieve the summit first.

Saussure, a Swiss professor of natural science, made the second ascent of the great mountain a year later. He could see the great white summit on a clear day from his base in Geneva.[1] He was an important early alpine traveller whose geological and botanical investigations motivated his many crossings of the main Alpine chain by different passes. He once spent seventeen days in residence on the Col du Géant, a mountain pass above 3352.8m, in observation of the mountains.[2] De Saussure's interest was mainly scientific, but in offering a bursary to the first person to make an ascent of Mont Blanc he had stimulated a wider interest in alpinism.

The advent of British mass interest in the Alps and mountaineering is mainly attributed to James David Forbes (1809–1868), Professor of Science at the University of Edinburgh. He provides a direct link between Saussure and the activities of British Victorian mountaineers. Indeed, the earliest Irish alpine pioneers can be divided into supporters of Forbes' theories on the movement of glaciers or those who disputed his theories. The English mountaineering historian Ronald Clarke wrote of Forbes, 'He came to study and stayed to worship.'[3] Forbes completed his first European grand tour when he was just sixteen years of age, visiting Innsbruck, Vienna, Rome, Naples and Chamonix.

In 1842 Forbes conducted some experiments with the aid of local guide Auguste Balmat, taking measurements on the Mer de Glace, the great glacier that terminated at Chamonix. His observations proved three important things: glaciers move steadily, they move both by night and by day, and they move faster at their centre than at their sides. He published his observations in his seminal book of 1843, *Travels through the Alps of Savoy*, a publication which is a pure pleasure for any mountain lover to read. Its creator in one passage reflects on his daily practice when visiting the Alps, writing of mornings of active exercise followed by evenings of quiet thought and speculation which 'give a sense of living twice over'.[4]

Facing page: Statue to Horace Benedict de Saussure in the Town Square, Chamonix. (Author's photo)

Below: Professor James David Forbes (1809–1868). (*Alpine Journal*)

He was lyrical in recording his thoughts when setting out for a summer in the Alps: 'Happy the traveller who starts on his first day's walk amongst the Alps in the tranquil morning of a long July day, brushing the early dew before him, and armed with his staff makes the hill top when he sees the field of his summer campaign spread out before him, its wonders, its beauties and its difficulties, to be explained, to be admired and to be overcome.' Forbes crossed the principal chain of Alps twenty-seven times, generally on foot, by twenty-three different passes, and had intersected the lateral chains in very many directions. In *Travels through the Alps of Savoy* he lists the passes and direction he travelled from starting location to destination.[5]

In the course of his travels and studies he met the Swiss geologist Louis Agassiz in August 1841 and spent nights with him in a bivouac on a rock island in the middle of the Unteraar Glacier. Agassiz's major work, *Études sur les Glaciers,* provided observations on the formation and movement of glaciers. Forbes in his publication respectfully acknowledged the research of those whose work and theories preceded his own, including Saussure, Agassiz and another glaciation theorist, Bishop Rendu, writing that 'it is the duty which every one who writes owes to the public and to himself, to be informed, generally at least, of the labours of his predecessors, that he may not, even involuntarily assume to himself credit for that which belongs to another, nor invite attention to that which is already well known.'[6] Having stated his ethical position at the outset, he went on to relate the published scientific work on glaciation theory (including that of Saussure) and then proceeded to criticise the extent and methods of observation and the lack of accurate data collection of some of his contemporaries, including Bishop Rendu and Louis Agassiz.

Despite his acknowledgment of other theorists Forbes was later accused by John Tyndall of having overlooked Rendu's most important observations, while lauding the better-known passages. Tyndall's serious criticism of Forbes' work divided both the scientific fraternity and Alpine Club members into pro- and anti-Forbes factions, a division that became more heated when doubts arising from Tyndall's allegations apparently denied Forbes the coveted Copley medal awarded by the Royal Society. It also divided the Irish alpinists: Adam-Reilly, already an admiring friend of the Scottish scientist, became a fierce advocate for Forbes and a formidable opponent of Tyndall's criticism as a result.

The popularisation and rapid development of alpinism is attributed to a number of factors, including improved transport arising from the rapid establishment of the railways. Long periods of comparative European peace, stability and economic wellbeing along with a general development of tourism were all factors that made it easier for wealthy Victorians to tour Europe and access the Alps. It is notable that amongst the early ranks of Alpine Club members were many scientists and churchmen. The development of mountaineering and the increased numbers of visitors seeking to venture into the mountains brought with it the advent of alpine tourism and the expansion of the transport infrastructure in the Alps, with a demand for reliable local guides, better inns and the provision of new and safer climbing techniques and equipment.

The visitors' book at the Monte Rosa Hotel (the first inn opened in the town of Zermatt at the foot of the Matterhorn, in 1839) contains the following entries: on 11 August 1845, when he crossed the Col de St Théodule, 'John Ball of Dublin: Visp to Milan – disappointed by bad weather'; a later entry on 17 August 1845, which records the first passing by the Dubliner using the Schwarztor Pass, he wrote, 'John Ball, Irlandais – très content de l'auberge et de Jean Baptiste Brantschen.Visp à Gressonnay'. The same records also track the presence of John Hewitt Jellett, then Provost of Trinity College, Dublin, nine days later on 26 August 1845. He recorded his route: 'Chatillion by Mont Cervin to Visp'.[7]

The first recorded Irish ascent of Mont Blanc occurred on 29 August 1850 by a Mr Richards of Wexford, 'an Irish gentleman and a member of Trinity College Oxford.'[8] It was the thirty-third recorded ascent of the peak. Their guide was Jean Payot who had been acquainted with Jacques Balmat. Their feat was recorded in *The Times* of London on 9 September.

> Great excitement was caused in the town of Chamounix on Wednesday the 28th by the departure of Mr Gretton, late of the 5th Fusiliers and Mr Richards, of County Wexford, for the purpose of ascending Mont Blanc. Crowds assembled to witness the start, as the arduous nature of the adventure was well known, the guides having left their watches and little valuables behind, and the two gentlemen made their will and prepared for the worst. Great anxiety was expressed on many a face as the little band headed by our two countrymen disappeared in the forest at the foot of the mountain . . . At three o'clock the report of the cannon at Chamounix announced that our adventurous countrymen had gained the Grands Mulets, the rocks on which they were to take up quarters for the night. The next day was all excitement – nothing else was thought of in the town. The Flégére and the Brévent were crowded with anxious observers. About eleven o'clock, the clouds clearing away from the summit of the Father of the Alps, the little band were seen to be slowly approaching the top, and a few minutes after the report of the cannon in Chamounix announced the undertaking to be successful. The clouds however soon obscured them from our view, and we saw nothing more of them till half-past seven p.m. when, preceded by the best music Chamounix afforded, and carried on the backs of some enthusiastic Frenchmen, they were receiving at the Hotel de Londres with loud cheers, firing of cannon, and expressions of delight at their safe return. The guides gave great praise to both gentlemen for the coolness and courage they displayed.[9]

It is interesting to note that this ascent was one year before Albert Smith's famous ascent on 19 August 1851. Smith's subsequent highly publicised illustrated lectures recounting his ascent are given credit for the increased popularisation of alpine climbing among the middle classes in England in the years that followed. Smith wrote for *Punch* and *The Illustrated London News*. He famously travelled to the Middle East in 1849 and on his return presented a public entertainment about his travels called *The Overland Mail*. In 1851 he went to Chamonix and with three other ascentionists he bivouacked at the Grands Mulets rocks from where they climbed to enjoy a good view from the summit. They made a safe descent and on arrival in Chamonix they celebrated with a party hosted by Sir Robert Peel.

Not everybody was happy, however, as the following quote from the *Daily News* in London illustrates: 'The aimless scramble of the four pedestrians to the top of Mont Blanc, with the accompaniment of Sir Robert Peel's orgies at the bottom, will not go far to redeem the somewhat equivocal reputation of the herd of English tourists in Switzerland, for a mindless and rather vulgar redundance of animal spirits.'[10] Despite that report, Smith's popular presentation of a magic lantern show on his climbs did much to publicise the new sport.

As mentioned earlier, the commencement of the golden age of alpinism is generally regarded to coincide with the ascent of the Wetterhorn in Switzerland by Englishman Alfred Wills. Wills, a barrister at law, is perhaps best known in Irish context as the judge who found Oscar Wilde guilty of gross indecency and who sentenced the great writer and dramatist to imprisonment for two years with hard labour.[11] The importance of Wills in Victorian mountaineering, however, is linked to his development of working relationships between local alpine guides and the English gentlemen who engaged them. The publication of his book *Wanderings among the High Alps* inspired many young wealthy men to travel to the Alps in search of high adventure.

Guido Rey, an accomplished Italian mountain guide who wrote a history of the Matterhorn (or Monte Cervino as it is called on the Italian side), accurately reflected the changes then occurring in alpinism:

> The army of students and poets was now about to be succeeded in the tourney at Cervin's feet by the company of the real climbers, the knights errant girding themselves up for the conquest of the fair virgins of the Alps; they were not urged by the love of science or of art alone, but also by an inexplicable passion whose fascination, whose very existence lay in the difficulty of the struggle. They entered the lists brandishing their new weapon, the ice axe, and followed by their faithful esquires, the new guides.[12]

Despite the fact that the early Irish alpinists came from backgrounds of comparative wealth, their individual life stories and experience reflect the confusing milieu that was Irish society in the nineteenth century. The social and political background to their lives included post-Famine mass poverty and emigration, violent politics, religious bigotry, land and tenant rights agitation and the acrimonious passage of Catholic Emancipation and Land Acts. John Ball, an Irish Catholic politician and first president of the Alpine Club, arguably had the greatest single impact on the growth and organisation of alpinism into a respected recreational activity and sport. Ball, an independently minded Catholic of great integrity, was mauled in his pursuit of Irish politics; so much so that he retired from politics permanently when invited to take the reins of the newly founded Club. That he did so was to the benefit of mountaineers worldwide to this very day.

Later in the century winter sports such as skating, tobogganing and skiing were developed as wealthy British tourists in pursuit of outdoor recreation took up residence year round in the alpine valleys. Indeed many engaged in winter mountaineering. Mrs Elizabeth Burnaby née Hawkins-Whitshed (later Mrs Main and Mrs Aubrey Le Blond) from Greystones in County Wicklow was to become prominent in the vanguard of that second wave of alpinists. She made many first winter ascents and was also an enthusiastic winter sports pioneer and photographer.

Other Irish pioneers such as Anthony Adams-Reilly and William Spotswood Green surveyed and produced accurate maps of the Alps, Mount Cook in New Zealand, the Selkirk range of the Canadian Rocky Mountains and later Charles Howard-Bury and Edward Wheeler the approaches to Everest; others like Tyndall and Ryan made many important first ascents and competed with the elite of British climbing in the ongoing raising of standards and mountain achievement.

Glacier Table on the Mer de Glace. (Forbes, *Travels through the Alps of Savoy* (1843))

2

John Ball:
Encyclopaedia Alpina

I venture to state with the utmost confidence that no man has ever possessed a wider and more thorough knowledge of the entire chain of the Alps, than Mr Ball.

W. A. B. Coolidge, Obituary for John Ball in *The Alpine Journal*, 1889

THE IRISHMAN who, arguably, made the most significant and important contributions to the formal development of alpinism during the golden age was John Ball. He was perhaps best known to his peers because of his extensive pioneering exploration and his encyclopaedic knowledge of many Alpine districts, assimilated over many years. He was admired for the sheer number of passes he crossed and peaks he climbed in his travels. It was this knowledge and experience that caused him to be head-hunted by the Club's founders to become the first president of the newly formed Alpine Club in 1858. He is universally acknowledged for his personal initiative and his expert work as the editor of *Peaks, Passes and Glaciers*. First published in 1859, it was the collective record of the excursions of leading Club members and also the blueprint for that other invaluable source of information for contemporary mountaineers, *The Alpine Journal,* which has been published annually by the Alpine Club ever since.

The most important single act in the popularisation of alpine climbing as a leisure activity may have been the publication, between 1863 and 1868, of the first series of climbing guidebooks to the Alpine chain. This was because the original publications not only met the growing demand for such guides, but because the high standard and detail achieved in the first edition was both optimal and appropriate and set standards for all subsequent climbing guidebooks. Ball's detailed

John Ball, 1818–1898

- Dublin-born naturalist and botanist
- Educated at Jesuit College, Oscott, Birmingham, and at Cambridge
- An early and extensive pioneer of the Alps from 1840
- Appointed a Poor Law commissioner during the Great Famine
- Elected MP for County Carlow in 1852
- Appointed Under-Secretary of State for the Colonies
- First crossing of the Schwarztor, a high mountain pass between the Swiss village of Zermatt and Val d'Ayas in Italy
- First ascent of Monte Pelmo (a rock tower in the Dolomites), 9 August 1857
- Elected first president of the Alpine Club, 31 March 1858
- Editor of *Peaks, Passes and Glaciers* (forerunner to *The Alpine Journal*), still produced annually by the Alpine Club
- Editor of the first series of Alpine guidebooks (1860–1865), updated by the Alpine Club ever since
- Completed a botanical survey of Morocco with Joseph Dalton Hooker
- Buried at St Thomas' Church, Fulham, London

Facing page: John Ball, one of the most travelled of the early Alpine pioneers, and industrious first president of the Alpine Club. (Rev. William Ball Wright, *Ball Family Records*)

knowledge was such that he was acknowledged to be a veritable human *Encyclopaedia Alpina*. Responsibility for the subsequent publication and updating of Alpine guidebooks has provided the Alpine Club with perhaps the most important and meaningful service it has given to generations of climbers in its long and distinguished history.

When he wrote Ball's obituary for the *Journal* in 1889, W. A. B. Coolidge accurately captured the man's substantial contribution: 'it is impossible to send forth this number without a few words to the honour and praise of a man whose work in the Alps may perhaps be more fitly characterised as that of the chief pioneer of mountain exploration, whether in its scientific, its practical or its literary aspects.'[1] He also ventured to state with the utmost confidence 'that no one man ever possessed a wider or more thorough knowledge of the entire chain of the Alps than Mr Ball.' Coolidge's opinion had previously been endorsed by no less an authority than the editorial board of *Encyclopaedia Britannica*, which chose Ball to articulate the geography of the European Alps.

But John Ball was more than just a well-travelled mountaineer; he was a humane public administrator whose first 'proper' job was as an assistant Poor Law commissioner in Ireland during the Great Famine. He became an articulate champion for Catholic emancipation and land reform and, when elected MP for Carlow, he proved a competent politician and government minister. However, primarily he must be acclaimed as a highly accomplished and significant botanist and geologist. It is interesting to note that among his climbing companions and close friends were Alfred Wills whose first ascent of the Wetterhorn in 1854 is considered to be the first purely sporting alpine climb.[2] C. E. Mathews, one of the founders of the Alpine Club, wrote of Ball after his death:

> Probably few of the many men of intellectual eminence who have found their best form of recreation in the Alps have been as many-sided as the late John Ball. He was a mountaineer and a statesman, a man of the world and a man of science, a traveller in many countries and appreciated in all . . . His early exploits date back to what seem pre-historic times, for it was in the year 1845 that he made the first passage of the Schwarz Thor from Zermatt to San Giacomo d'Ayas, accompanied, or rather impeded by a Zermatt peasant, in days when regular guides in that region were unknown.
>
> He edited the first series of that remarkable work 'Peaks, Passes and Glaciers' first published in 1858, and between 1863 and 1868 brought out 'the Alpine Guide' . . . Probably no guidebook was ever more clear in its grasp or comprehensive in detail, more stored with general and special knowledge; the whole being lighted up on almost every page by a graceful and charming literary style.[3]

John Ball was born in Dublin on 20 August 1818 into a family tradition with strong legal and political connections that supported the Catholic emancipation politics of Daniel O'Connell and the English liberals. John Ball's father, Nicholas Ball (1791–1865), had been educated at Stoneyhurst and matriculated at Trinity College, Dublin, in 1808 where he took the degree of BA in 1812, entering Lincoln's Inn the same year. When he was called to the Irish Bar in 1814, his wealth saved him from the struggles which many young barristers had to undergo. After being elected MP for Clonmel in 1836, he was made Attorney General for Ireland in 1838 and appointed a judge of the Court of Common Pleas (Ireland) the following year. His son would display an early passion for scientific reading, observation and experiment, which was to lead to his interest in the Alps and particularly in the study of glaciology and botany.

The young John was precocious and described the streets of Dublin where he took his daily walks as being 'of excessive dullness';[4] nonetheless he managed to discover pyrites and other minerals among stones broken for wall mending, along with wild flowers he identified with the aid of a children's book on botany. He drew his own map of the stars at that age and gathered a stock of philosophical apparatus. His reading was not confined to science as he took delight in *Don Quixote*.

His interest in mountains was first aroused when, as a small child, he was taken up to Cave Hill, the mountain which overlooks Belfast, to see Belfast Lough.[5] A year later his voracious appetite for physical science was whetted further when his father presented him with a mountain barometer, which prompted his pursuit of

Alfred Wills. (*The Alpine Journal*)

measuring every hill around. This he combined with collecting minerals, shells and fossils, which he endeavoured to learn about from books. He appears not to have had much formal primary education, apart from benefiting for a short time from access to a tutor for classics. Neither was he involved in any boyish sports; instead he pursued his private interest in physical science and natural history, managing to write an article called 'Elements of Chemistry' and to make tolerable geological sections, and tried to establish the identity of the galvanic pile and solar spectrum.[6]

His first visit to the Alps was in 1827, when he was nine years of age and experienced his first view of the Alps from Faucille in the French Jura. He recorded the experience in a journal which he kept:

We reached the top of the Col de la Faucille just before sunset. The sky was almost cloudless. We all got out. I managed to get a little apart from the others, and remained fixed for almost half-an-hour. The light gradually stole upwards from the lake over the nearer mountains, and then over the Savoy Alps, and finally the peak of Mont Blanc alone remained illuminated. One little cloud only hung over the peak. As the peak also became dim, the cloud remained like a glory over his head. For long years that scene reoccurred constantly to my mind, whether asleep or awake, and perhaps nothing has had so great an influence on my entire life.[7]

He went on to Chamonix and to the Montanvert from where he observed the great Mer de Glace glacier and, while in Geneva, he ascended the Salève, which at 1380m provides a magnificent panorama of the Mont Blanc massif.

Both his parents were staunch Catholics who, despite their declared religious convictions, were wealthy members of the legal and political establishment; in 1831 they sent John to Birmingham to attend St Mary's Jesuit College, Oscott. Here he learned classics, a smattering of mathematics and some chemistry, which he said was pursued under every discouragement.[8] In Dublin during the summer of 1835 he attended a meeting of the British Association for the Advancement of Science as a juvenile member. At the close of this conference he went on a natural history tour of Galway and Connemara under the charge of a Professor Babington, during the course of which they studied and observed the natural history of the west of Ireland; an account of the tour is given in the *Magazine of Natural History*.[9] Some of the geological passages in this account were written by the precocious young Ball.

He progressed to Christ's College, Cambridge, on 23 June 1835, where he spent the next four years studying natural science; amongst his teachers were Sir George Airy (astronomy), Sir John Stephens Henslow (a botanist and Charles Darwin's mentor) and Adam Sedgwick (geology). In his free time Ball socialised with Henslow's family, providing vocals and accompaniment on the piano. He was also a keen chess player. One of Henslow's daughters would later marry a friend of Ball's, Joseph Dalton Hooker, the eminent botanist. He is reported to have completed a brilliant degree course, but because of his Catholic religion he left Cambridge that year without being conferred. There was, however, some recognition for his academic prowess and competence when he was elected to membership of the Royal Irish Academy the following April and, even more significantly, fifty years later in 1888 he was elected an Honorary Fellow of Christ's Church College, Cambridge. He was admitted as a student of the Middle Temple in 1857 and he was called to the Irish bar in 1845, but he was never to practise law as he had no real interest in it and his family wealth did not require it. He developed his interest in natural science and botany, which led him to travel extensively in Europe and to become, by his private and self-financed activities, a distinguished scientist, botanist and pioneering mountaineer.

His early travels included visits to Sicily in pursuit of botany and to Zermatt to study glaciers. These visits were made more interesting to a man of science by J. D. Forbes' *Travels through the Alps of Savoy*. which was published in 1843. Interest, discourse and differences of opinion relating to the exact theories of glaciology animated the relationships between Ball's Irish mountaineering peers, John Tyndall, the Carlow-born physicist, and the mapmaker Anthony Adams-Reilly, who was a passionate supporter of Forbes in his lifetime and one of his joint biographers after the death of the great Scottish scientist. Reilly was openly hostile to Tyndall because of the latter's attacks on the originality of Forbes' esteemed work and, while Ball supported some of Tyndall's discoveries and modified theories, he made it clear he was not satisfied that Tyndall had fully developed his theories. Ball's own competence in this area, and indeed his familiarity with his native Irish hills, is clearly illustrated by a paper published in the Geological Society of Dublin journal in 1849 in which Ball observed the existence of extinct glaciers in the vicinity of Brandon Head in County Kerry.[10]

Ball's serious climbing activity commenced in 1840 when, among his activities, is the first recorded ascent of the Grauhaupt[11] while completing a traverse from the Italian Aosta Valley via the Val de St Barthelemi over the Col de Jon and Brussone to the Val d'Ayas, and from there over the Col de la Ranzola to Gressonay,[12] and from there via the Col de Val Dobbia to Sesia.[13] He seems to have explored every valley and recorded where there were good mule tracks and the location of inns suitable for travellers. His description of his route from the village of Champolien to the summit of the Grauhaupt is not only concise, accurate and descriptive of the terrain and the panoramic view to be found from the summit, but also lists in Latin the flora he found near its summit:

> At the last named hamlet commences the ascent of the *Pinter Joch* or *Col de Cunéa*, crossing the range between the valleys of Ayas and Lys, immediately to the S of the Grauhaupt. The pass may be effected in 6 hrs. or even less; but a traveller, favoured by tolerable weather, should not omit the ascent of the adjoining peak, which commands the finest view of the S. side of Monte Rosa. The greater part of the ascent from Champolien to the Col is easy enough commanding at intervals fine views of the Matterhorn, but after about 3 hrs the way becomes steep, and difficult to find. It lies along the l. bank of a waterfall, and in ¾ hr farther leads to the crest of the Col. The summit is probably about 8,200 ft. in height. It has a wide view to the W., which includes Mont Blanc and the higher peaks of the Cottian Alps, but is shut out from the Monte Rosa by the adjoining peak of the Grauhaupt, or Graues Haupt, which may be attained in 2 hrs. The ascent is rough, lying in great part over and amidst large loose blocks; but except close to the top, where the rocks become steep, it presents no difficulty. The height is 10,702 ft overtopping all the near summits, and the parorama is one of the finest on the S side of the Alps. *Campanula cenisia, Eritrichium nanum, Linaria alpina, Carex curvula* and a few other flowering plants, have been found close to the summit.[14]

He ascended Mount Etna, the 3,329m-high active volcano in Sicily, in the early May of 1841. His interpretation of the geology and botany and advice to travellers flow easily from his description of the scene:

> Trusting to my legs, I took no mule, and but a light coat to wear on top of the mountain over the cotton dress in which I made on foot much of the tour of Sicily. During the night a passing storm drenched us; the snow, which lay deep enough to cover all but the roof of the Casa degli Inglesi, was very soft for a great part of the way. Towards morning the cold became severe, and when we reached the top, an hour before sunrise, my coat, which had been strapped to a provisions basket, was frozen so hard that I could not put it on. I was glad to find some snow with which to rub two fingers which had become insensible. The great crater, a league in circumference, which was, I believe, much altered during the eruption of the following year, presented a grand and extraordinary appearance. In a few places arose columns of steam, from fissures in the lava, but elsewhere snow remained unmelted, wherever a ledge or crag allowed it to rest. The glories of sunrise from Ætna have been often described. I will merely say that they soon dispelled all thoughts of fatigue and discomfort.[15]

He recommended solid shoes or a second pair in reserve on account of the razor-sharp lava that cut his boots to pieces and to cope with the fierce mountain vegetation, such as 'the dense tufts of the spiny *Astragalus siculus*, varying in size and shape from a large hedgehog to a hunch 5 feet (1.52m) long and 2 feet (0.61m) high, compared to which forcing one's way through the stoutest furse bush or quickset hedge is but child's play.'

In 1845 Ball made the first passage of the Schwarztor from Zermatt in Switzerland to Ayas in Italy; it was the highest pass to be crossed in the Alpine range at that time.[16] He faithfully recorded the crossing of the highly crevassed glacial pass from Zermatt in the vicinity of the twin conical snow domes of Castor and Pollux to Gressonay; his motivation was to establish communication between Zermatt and the Italian side of the range. He compares the height of the pass with the neighbouring rock summit of the Breithorn. His first task was to find a companion in the undertaking for, as he explained, 'It is an indefensible piece of rashness to travel alone in the upper regions of the glaciers; no amount of skill and experience can avert the almost certain consequences of the yielding of the snow coating that covers a concealed crevasse. But I have always thought that two practised mountaineers may safely undertake any expedition, and that they are just as likely to succeed as a larger number.' He observed the change from moonlight to daylight and tried to catch the moment when daylight overtakes the nightlight.

His companion, named Mathias Tangwald, was reputed to have been one of the best chamois hunters in the valley. Ball observed his heavy countenance, which to him 'denoted neither energy nor enterprise'. He transpired to be an unwilling and inexperienced mountain guide, particularly when they were climbing over ice pinnacles and snow bridges that collapsed under their weight. Ball, from experience, carried in his own knapsack a woollen waistcoat with long sleeves and a Scotch plaid (blanket); strapped to the knapsack he had a 30-foot length of stout rope and an umbrella to protect him from the hot sun. He also carried a couple of thermometers, a prismatic compass, a good opera glass, a sketchbook and a single volume edition of Shakespeare as a resource for a wet day. He brought a tin box for plants and 'a geological hammer of a form available for occasional use as an ice axe'. His guide carried three pieces of iron that could be attached to convert the long alpenstock each of them carried into a short ladder for crossing snow bridges, but was more often used to help Ball reach plants on steep walls. The guide carried the provisions and a small wooden keg of wine for his own use. They walked from Zermatt to a group of chalets at 2,134m, at a place called Augstkumme in the direction of the Riffelhorn and the Gornergrat. There they slept in the barn until called for breakfast. Ball's determination and surefootedness saw them through safely as he later recorded.

He and his companion set out at three o'clock from Augstkumme after a fine breakfast, to which he was able to do full justice, thanks, he claimed, to the vigorous health that rewards active life in the mountains. Just before sunrise they reached the steep slope that looks over the Görner Glacier and the full range of Monte Rosa came into view. He followed a line of snow bridges to trace his way through a great mass of ice cliffs. Ploughing through the soft snow on the other side, he erected his umbrella at midday to defend against the sun. On nearing the top of the pass, Tangwald was particularly upset when Ball started to descend a steep ice slope at an angle of not less than 60°. Ball explains: 'I was most afraid of his being unnerved, if his eyes were to wander down the dizzy slopes into the yawning crevasses of the glacier that lay far beneath us, and I ordered him to keep his eyes constantly fixed upon the spot where he was to place his foot.' He repeated this three or four times before the difficulty was surmounted and they reached the top of the glacial plateau and, an hour later, the top of the pass, which Ball claimed was 'certainly by far the highest pass which has yet been effected in the chain of the Alps'.

It was 1.15 p.m. when they reached the ridge to discover on the Italian side 'a vast boundless sea of fleecy clouds' towards Val d'Aosta. They encountered more difficulty in descending the glacier on the other side, finding the only possible route was down an avalanche-prone but easily angled couloir. The botanist fixed his location when on rocks 'perhaps never visited by traveller or botanist' by using his sightings of rare plants; for example, he was able to use *Senecio uniflorus* in this way 'as it is peculiar to the southern valleys of Monte Rosa'. Finding a cattle track, they soon were in a pasture and a lift in the clouds revealed a small chalet where they met a herdsman who was unable to speak either German or Piedmontese. An hour later they were in a small village named San Giacomo d'Ayas – the highest village in the valley of that name – and not in Val de Lys, which Ball had expected.

In 1846, when Ball was aged twenty-seven, he took up his first proper job: he was appointed an assistant Poor Law commissioner as a part of the government's response to the trauma of the Great Famine in Ireland. The Poor Law Commission was the body established to administer poor relief under the provisions of the 1834 Poor Law Amendment Act; it was the job of the assistant commissioners to establish local 'unions' or committees that would analyse conditions and respond to local hardship, reporting back to the Custom House, Dublin, where Poor Law Commissioner Edward Turner Boyd Twistleton was based.

Ball's extensive, handwritten reports to the Commissioner's office outline in meticulous detail his assessments and his meetings with clergy, landowners and farmers to identify individual families in distress and to decide on useful local project relief work. From Westmeath he reports: 'As far as I can judge from a hurried visit I would suppose that the employment afforded by the work proposed within the town, and that given by the contemplated drainage, should both undertakings be carried into effect within a sufficiently short period, will relieve the wants of the most distressed part of the population.' He goes on:

> I should mention that on the road from Mullingar to Ballymore about 3 miles east from the latter place, I passed some very wretched cabins inhabited by tenantry of the same estates. The potatoes which they were taking out of the pits where they are stored were quite unfit for human food; – amongst the worst I have ever seen. These cabins were situated on either side of a running stream which passes through a considerable tract of land almost worthless for the want of draining. Considering that some immediate measures are desirable with respect to the condition of the suffering population, I have thought it better not to lose a day's post, and have drawn up this hurried statement, whilst yet upon my journey, within a few miles of the locality referred to.[17]

Later, reporting to Twistleton from Tralee, Ball suggests two public works projects: the building of a new road from Ballyheigue to Lixna (for which an application to the Lord Lieutenant of £3,000 was made), and the drainage of the River Brick under the Drainage Act, as advocated by local landowners. Ball believed that if this work was under way and putting money in local pockets (10 pence per day was suggested as remuneration), and if the government ensured delivery of a large quantity of cheap Indian meal to Tralee, then local farmers (particularly those in the less affected uplands) would be forced immediately to lower the price of the considerable quantity of provisions they were known to have in store – including quantities of sound potatoes.[18] The care that he took to record the exact numbers and condition of the suffering inhabitants proves him ever diligent, honest and suitable for his judicious position, but it also showcases the interests and skills that were to prove immeasurably useful in other areas of his life: his genuine desire to make records that would accurately describe a situation; the scientific education that enabled his forensic analysis of the condition of the potato itself; and his effectiveness as a communicator and administrator in offering practical suggestions for reducing food prices.

The stress of this work and the continuous travel it involved affected Ball so badly that his health was soon threatened, causing him to resign and go abroad to recuperate within a year of his appointment. However, his experience as an assistant Poor Law commissioner had undoubtedly whetted his interest in politics, for he went on to write and publish a pamphlet entitled *What is to be Done for Ireland?*, which criticised the British government's handling of the crisis and took particular issue with Trevelyan's Labour Rate Act and its negative effects in attempting to address the consequences of the potato failure of 1845–1846. He criticised the Act on many grounds: the impossibility of effectual superintendence of the public works; the hardship and demoralisation caused by the assembling together of the applicants, whether able-bodied, infirm or diseased; the requirement to make applicants work outdoors in inclement season; and, lastly, the permanent injury to the habits of the labouring class when they became familiar with a system of 'sham' work and lost every incentive to earnest industry.[19]

Ball asserted that significant improvements in agricultural technique had already been witnessed in the Irish countryside during the years just prior to the Famine, and he disputed Trevelyan's assertion that the Labour Rate Act was calculated to induce – or even to permit – an increased expenditure of capital upon the cultivation and improvement of land. The pamphlet attempted to reconcile the perceived incompatibility between securing (on the one hand) adequate security for the investment of capital in agricultural improvement and (on the other) freedom in the relations between the employer and the labourer. In a mainly agrarian economy where property ownership and access to power was enshrined, this was always going to be a tall order. Ball was trying to address what he called the two main evils of property 'rating' (evaluation): the increased financial temptation for landlords to clear property and the gradual approach to a compulsory labour system in order to obtain relief.

In presenting his own proposals for addressing these issues, he freely acknowledged the impossibility of satisfying all concerned, but he suggested that it be made impossible for an 'exterminating landlord' to shift from himself the burden of supporting his own poor, unless they were to be provided with the means to support themselves for eighteen months after they ceased to reside upon his estate. His philosophy was simple: 'those who possess the chief control over the condition of the working classes, should in the first place be responsible for their support; but that as soon as a permanent surplus [population] is ascertained, the community should become interested in the means of relieving their destitution.'[20]

His final point relates to England's errors in imposing the series of iniquitous penal laws; although Catholic emancipation had largely been achieved with the Catholic Relief Act (1829), in Ball's view further legislation was essential in order to in order to fully restore justice. He wrote:

The false principles by which the Government of Ireland has long been guided, and from which the entire empire has reaped such bitter fruits, have been for the most part abjured and abandoned; but if England will not continue to suffer from her misdeeds, she must complete the work of justice. That great reparation which was commenced in 1829, must be followed on to its legitimate conclusion; perfect equality of legal rights and religious faith must be thoroughly and practically acknowledged; then, and not till then, that progress towards prosperity and contentment can commence, which Time, the healer of evils of the past, alone can lead to the desired consummation.[21]

It was clear that Ball was now ready to enter political life and that religious equality and land reform were fundamental to his politics. But it is also noteworthy that he does not discuss or consider Home Rule or independence for Ireland and clearly was happy with the Union. He was soon to discover that politics, and particularly Irish politics, is no place for the timid or faint-hearted. His future constituents would prefer their representatives to be of the partisan variety, and that was not his nature.

To the majority of the Irish the 1801 Act of Union had proved a great disappointment, since it was evident that most of impoverished Ireland's problems were ignored by a government pursuing an uncaring and ruthless economic policy. Advocates of the Act were in the minority; they came mainly from the Protestant landlord class who supported the Conservatives in parliament and were, by and large, as opposed to land reform as they were to the repeal of the Act of Union. Irish liberals supported the Whigs in embracing these issues and were led, in the pre-Famine years, by Daniel O'Connell, the darling of Ireland for his efforts in achieving a repeal of the penal laws and many measures of Catholic emancipation in the first half of the century. But with the trauma of the Great Famine his campaign ran out of energy and mere survival took precedence over politics.

The Whig Party (which was only officially to become the Liberal Party after 1859, but whose adherents were increasingly referred to as 'Liberals' in the decades before) was supported in Ireland by many native Catholic voters, but there were some issues where Irish and English liberals differed sharply. Many Irish liberal MPs during the period were committed to 'the pledge': in other words, they would support a Whig government in the introduction of legislation that was not detrimental to Irish interests, but they would not accept ministerial office. Irish liberals were also in support of the Papal States' muscular opposition to the struggle for the unification of Italy (known as 'il Risorgimento') in an attempt to maintain both the civil and religious authority of the Papacy. Ball was out of line with his Irish liberal colleagues on both of these issues. He felt himself unable to take the pledge because he felt that to fight from the inside for any small improvement in Ireland's plight was better for her people than the principled non-participation of her politicians. As to the Papal States, although he was a Catholic, he was quite clear in his own mind about the difference between temporal and divine authority and where that line should be drawn. As a result when he arrived on the hustings in Sligo, Carlow, and later in Limerick, he found many hostile clerical opponents, some of whom used the pulpit to full advantage in advising their flocks which candidates they ought to vote for and which were to be shunned. It should be said that in Carlow this worked in Ball's favour, but it was to work against him when he sought to be elected in Sligo and Limerick.

Ball's first electoral campaign took him to Sligo in 1848, where he polled well as a first-time candidate and a largely unknown outsider. It was here he learned the practicalities of getting elected and also discovered some of the many trials that beset those seeking public office. The election arose when the sitting Whig member, Charles Towneley, was unseated following a successful petition to a House of Commons committee due to some irregularities being proved in his election campaign. The petition had been prosecuted by Mr Somers, a former MP, who had represented the borough's Whig voters prior to Towneley's election.

Ball's manifesto proposed a measure of tenant's rights and the holding of one session of parliament in Dublin each year, the latter being easily misinterpreted by his rivals to the voters as evidence that he was 'soft' on the repeal of the Act of Union. Two post-election letters from Ball in July to the local liberal newspaper, *The Champion* (later to become *The Sligo Champion*), illustrate the dirty tricks used against him during the campaign by his main opponent. Ball, in a letter dated 18 July, complains that at a public meeting Mr Somers (who won the election) stated maliciously that Ball had solicited pecuniary aid from the government to contest the borough of Sligo. Another letter by Ball claimed that at the meeting to nominate and elect candidates on 12 July he was reported in the *Evening Mail* as showing a good deal of hesitation in reply to a question put to him by Mr Somers, as to whether he was an advocate for the repeal of the Union. Ball asserted that this was a misrepresentation of his position, claiming he instantly replied 'I am not', but owing to the noise at that moment his words were only heard by those near him. In his letter he repeated his alternative desire for 'an annual meeting of the imperial parliament in Dublin.'[22]

The election was lost when a third Whig candidate from Sligo, a wealthy Mr Hartley, was nominated and supported by former Towneley supporters. Ball had to defend his father's parliamentary record when Somers asked in his address to electors 'what did Mr Justice Ball do for Ireland?' He responded that 'his father's name could be found in almost every page of the proceedings of the committee, which worked on the wording clause by clause of the Corporation Bill and other bills that gave us our share of Liberty'. He brought great cheers when he added that Mr Somers' name would not be found on any such proceedings. The final vote was split three ways, leaving Somers ahead with 102 votes to Hartley's 90 and Ball's 87.[23]

In 1849 Ball returned to the Poor Law Commission, this time as second commissioner, a post he held for two years, when he stood again as a Liberal candidate for Carlow in the election of 1852. This time he clearly presented himself as a more partisan candidate in a blatant appeal to the majority Catholic voters, many of whom supported by choice (or were coerced into voting for) the local gentry and landlords to maintain favourable relations and rents. Appealing to the Irish Catholic vote to turn its back on its landlords and their Tory affections, he made good use of Irish anger at the anti-Catholic feeling that had erupted into violence in England during the Stockport Riots of June that year.[24] Ball ran for the Whigs with a running mate, John Henry Keogh of Kilbride, County Carlow. Their target was to win the two seats for the Whig cause, and it is evident they were well supported from the pulpit by the Catholic clergy. The other candidates were Colonel Bruen and William Bunbury McClintock, Esq. At the close of poll the numbers stood as follows: Ball, 893; Bruen, 891; Bunbury, 878; and Keogh 875. John Ball had headed the poll and he and Colonel Bruen were elected in a very close-run affair with only eighteen votes separating the first and last candidates. The election results from seven baronies indicate the strength of support Ball and his running mate received from the voters of Rathvilly, who, urged on by their Catholic clergy had contributed a third of both men's votes.[25]

In September that year Ball travelled to Zurich and, in poor weather, made his way to the Grimsel

Hospice where he fell into company with two old friends, an American and a German. Finding them arguing over glacial theories, he invited them to come with him across the Strahleck Pass to Grindelwald.[26] Their guides were the son of the hospice owner, Vater Zybach, and an older local man. They left the Grimsel at 4.30 a.m., the old guide leading the way with a lantern to the sound of water rushing everywhere after the recent prolonged rain to the foot of the Lower Aar glacier. At first light the higher summits glowed in the light of the rising sun so they marched towards the junction of the Lauteraar and the Finsteraar glaciers. On reaching the névé, Ball observed no fresh snowfall had occurred and concluded that the weather had been so warm that rain instead of snow had fallen, making the underfoot conditions favourable for their crossing. They headed towards the Finsteraarhorn, which towered above them, until they rounded a projecting spur from the Schreckhorn where the valley turns abruptly right and where the peak presented 'one of the grandest objects to be found in the Alps' or, as Ball further contended, 'in the world'. 'The impression that arises is that of some landlocked fiord in a tideless frozen sea, over which broods forever the shadow of the Peak of Darkness.'

They climbed close to the crags of the Schreckhorn, where it became apparent that the pass lay over a steep ridge of snow that separated a continuous wall of rock. The angle of the slope approached a very formidable 60 °, however, no step-cutting was required due to the soft snow conditions. Ball took the lead of the roped party, thrusting the handle of his alpenstock into the snow horizontally as he kicked high steps, crossing a single crevasse to reach steep but easy rocks that led to the ridge of the Strahleck. It was eleven o'clock. 'It is altogether a scene of the ice world,' he wrote, his attention being absorbed immediately by surrounding mountains, 'which are scarcely to be exceeded for wilderness and grandeur.' He was struck by the great ice basin from where the lower Grindelwald Glacier descended 'overhung as it is by the Walcherhörner and the ridge which connects it to the Mönch and Eiger'.

They had lunch nestled in a sheltered corner where Ball related to his party the explanation for the name of the pass (Strahleck), which translates as 'sunbeam corner'. He explained that the name had first been used by shepherds who noted that the first rays of sunlight in the summer on the meadow at Zäzenburg reached their flocks over the ridge of the Strahleck. Each climber held a freshly lighted cigar, offered by Ball as they commenced the steep, roped descent; they had no incident until they came to a place on the glacier where rock changed to steep ice. Here the young, athletic guide found a way down through the smooth ice and crawled out on the glacier from under a cavernous crevasse. He cut steps back up the ice to aid the others down. They made their way from there without a stop to Grindelwald; the outing had taken fifteen hours. Ball rejoiced in what he called 'one of the brightest and most glorious days he ever enjoyed' snatched 'from the very midst of the destructive inundations of September 1852.'

Once elected, Ball made his presence felt immediately and actively participated in House of Commons debate, proposing what then appeared to be an advanced land programme and opposing all interference in Catholic convents. Surprisingly, he supported Gladstone's 1853 recommendation that income tax be extended to Ireland. This support for Gladstone's government was used against him when he next sought re-election. Meanwhile that same summer he visited the Dolomites for the first time and commenced his exploration of the eastern Alps. During this visit he discovered and made the first crossing of the Bocca di Brenta in the Brenta Group. This was the first of his many visits to the Dolomites where he was an early pioneer.

His political ability was acknowledged in 1855 when, on the formation of Lord Palmerston's government, he was offered ministerial office. He accepted after due consideration and was confirmed as Under-Secretary of State for the Colonies. This meant he had ignored 'the pledge'. While he was in ministerial office in 1856, Ball married Eliza Parolini, daughter of Nobile Alberto Parolini (1788–1867), a distinguished Italian naturalist and oriental traveller. They had two sons: Nicholas Albert, who was born in London on 3 March 1858, and Albert John, born in Pisa on 7 December 1861. When Ball's wife died in Florence on 12 June 1867, he inherited her father's estates near Bessano, which had become his base during his many Alpine seasons.[27]

During his two-year term of office he created much official interest in the pursuit of science and in this respect his opinion was also later sought and acted upon by government. His passion for botany made him instrumental in gaining financial backing for Sir William Hooker's project to encourage and enable colonial governors to publish inexpensive flora surveys of all the British colonies. He also urged the importance of an expedition to discover the best railway route across the Rocky Mountains in Canada, requesting that William Hooker and his son, Joseph, accompany him to meet the then Financial Secretary to the Treasury, James Wilson, in order to persuade him of the importance of such reconnaissance. Wilson showed great interest listening to Ball's exposition of the advantages that would accrue from it and promised to give the proposal full consideration; he also complimented Ball, saying, 'Well, if all the applicants to the Treasury would give their reasons for coming with the knowledge, completeness, and lucidity that you have, we would have little difficulty in considering what to grant and what to refuse.'[28]

He was therefore largely responsible for securing treasury funding for the Palliser expedition, which set off in 1857 led by the Dublin-born wealthy landowner John Palliser, whose home was Comeragh House near Kilmacthomas, County Waterford.[29] Palliser, part-educated at Trinity College, Dublin, had spent eleven months in 1847 hunting and living off the land in the unsettled prairies and mountains of Upper Missouri and Yellowstone County. The fact that his expedition was manned by an expert scientific staff that surveyed much of the Canadian Rockies and whose report laid down the route followed later by the transcontinental Canadian Pacific Railway can be largely attributed to Ball's support and advice. Ball made a strong case for Palliser on the basis that although he was independent of the Hudson's Bay Company he was not hostile to its long-standing interests in the region. Palliser's first letter to Ball indicates that Ball was personally known to Palliser, addressed as it was to 'My dear Ball'.[30]

The expedition thus became a government expedition and not, as was originally proposed, under the direction of the Royal Geographical Society. Eventual expenditure totalled £13,000, as opposed to the original £5,000 that had been voted by parliament, as a result of two extensions of time and the exploration of additional territories and other unforeseen and inflated costs. Palliser was the first of a list of important Irish explorers and mountaineers who made significant contribution to the exploration and development of Canada's mountain regions and Canadian mountaineering. Palliser's thanks to Ball and Hooker were to name two peaks in the Rocky Mountains in their honour.

Ball held office until the general election in April 1857, when he chose not to seek re-election in Carlow, but opted instead to run in the Sligo Borough. Why Ball chose not to run again in Carlow he explained himself at a public meeting when challenged by a voter to give his reasons: 'Because, after one of the most desperate contests fought in the year 1852, the Tory landlords of the county of Carlow treated their tenants with such cruelty, that it was the opinion of the Liberals in the county that it would not be fair to the people to expose them to such hardships.'

Another elector asked: 'Did not you go into Parliament pledged to Independent Opposition?' Ball answered: 'I did not. I went in as the supporter of a fair Tenant's Rights Bill. At the great meeting, held in Dublin after the general election, I said publicly, that I was not prepared to support any clauses of Sharman Crawford's bill.'[31] It is clear that Ball knew that the electors of County Carlow had punished John Sadleir MP in 1853 for taking ministerial office contrary to his pre-election adherence to 'the pledge' and expected a similar outcome himself.

Ball chose to run again for the Whigs, but on the evening before nominations closed he was confronted with a list of electors who demanded payment for their votes and he immediately withdrew from the election on principle. In light of the Sadleir episode in 1854 it is easy to understand Ball's quick decision.[32] However, *The Sligo Champion* thought Ball had over-reacted and reported his decision as follows: 'Mr Ball was scared from the Borough by the absurdist reports invented by knaves and circulated by fools. Mr Somers was in the last moment of despair adopted by the Liberal party in the Borough. Mr Ball fell back on the County (where he ought to have gone at first), and all three seats were lost to the Liberal and Catholic cause.'[33] The election returns show the three seats in both city and borough were won well by the Conservative party, whose landlords where able to bring out the vote from their own estates. One of those elected was Robert Gore-Booth.[34]

Returning to the Alps for the summer on 9 August 1857, Ball made the first ascent of one of the great Dolomite rock towers. Again his local guide was found to be wanting and Ball had to complete the climb to the top of the rocky ridge alone, but Ball makes no attempt to talk up his achievement. The author made an ascent of this route in August 2005 and found he still had to crawl 'reptile fashion', as Ball described, to pass the ledge where an overhanging roof forces the climber to move horizontally along the ledge. Ball writes:

> Monte Pelmo (10,377ft), from whatever side it can be seen, but especially from the E. and S., shows as a gigantic fortress of the most massive architecture, and fretted into minarets and pinnacles, like most of its rivals, but merely defended by huge bastion outworks,

The Monte Pelmo traverse.
(Douglas Freshfield, *The Italian Alps* (1875))

whose walls in many places fall in sheer precipices more than 2,000 ft. The likeness to masonry is much increased by the fact that, in great part, the strata lie in nearly horizontal courses, and hence it happens that many of the steepest faces of the mountain are traversed by ledges wide enough to give passage to chamois and to their pursuers. As chamois-hunting seems to be a favourite pastime in Val di Zoldo, the hunters gradually become well acquainted with the network of narrow ledges that cover the greater part of the mountain, and thus in time they have found out not merely one, but four different ways to reach the top most plateau. As the most practiced mountaineer is not likely to hit upon any of these without a guide, it suffices to say that the two best routes are commenced from the south side of the mountain, or from Zoppé. The writer ascended from Borca by the East face of the mountain with a chamois hunter who professed to discover the course which they followed. At the comparatively low level (less than 7,000 ft.) a ledge was gained which had to be followed horizontally along the face of the precipices that show so boldly on the side of the Ampezzo road. Three deep recesses were rounded in succession. In two places the ledge had been broken away, but it was found possible to clear the gap thus created. The most eccentric obstacle was encountered at a place where the overhanging rock came down so low as to leave a space of only 18 inches (45.7 cm); far too little to make it possible to creep on hands and knees. The guide, who had hitherto gone first, declared the breaking away of a projection of rock that overhung the precipice on the L hand, had made the passage impossible. Unwilling to be baulked, the writer contrived to crawl along the narrow ledge in reptile fashion, and was followed by the guide. Soon after a place was reached from which the ascent to the topmost plateau is merely a long and steep, but not difficult, scramble.

In addition to the characteristic species of the Dolomite Alps, *Valeriana repens*, *Campanula morettianna*, and *Androsace hausmanniana* were gathered on this side of the mountain. Whatever course the traveller may take, he finds with surprise a not inconsiderable glacier lying on the broken plateau which is surrounded by the topmost ridges of the mountain. On a small rock-terrace above the upper end of the glacier, the writer was told that they had reached the top, and on his pointing to the shattered ridge above, was assured by the guide that this being all 'croda morta' – disaggregated rock loosened by weathering – the further ascent was totally impracticable. It required some time and some caution to loosen with the Alpenstock considerable masses of rock, still hanging together, but detached by slight effort, before the real topmost ridge was reached by the writer, without his guide. No token or stone man was seen, and it is not unlikely that the barometer observation recorded by Fuchs was made some way below the true summit. The height must be about the same as the Civetta and can scarcely be 200 ft. below that of Antelo. Melchior and Luigi Zugliani of Selva, near Caprile, are recommended as guides for the Pelmo; but there must be several competent men in Val di Zoldo.[35]

If the Sligo election had not put Ball off politics, his experiences in Limerick the following year surely completed the process; the vitriol that was directed against him during the course of the two campaigns he fought must at times have been frightening for a man of his tender upbringing. His obituary in *The Times* reminded readers of the importance that a major European event had played in his Limerick defeat: 'At that time, however, a cloud was rising on the horizon, which gravely disturbed the Catholic constituencies, though the rest of the world knew little of it yet. This was the Italian question. The Irish priests foresaw the coming struggle and demanded that their candidates should take sides with the Papacy and the Duchies against Piedmont and the revolution.' *The Times* maintains Ball refused to give the Limerick clergy an undertaking that he would support the Papacy and Duchies against Piedmont and the revolutionaries; he was therefore opposed by the priests and, after a hard struggle, was defeated.[36]

The newspaper reports of the time show that when Ball was narrowly defeated in the first Limerick election, he filed a petition in the House of Commons against the return of his opponent, Major Gavin, on Friday 13 March, protesting the results on the grounds of elector intimidation and bribery. The ensuing committee proceedings resulted in the unseating of Major Gavin, as a consequence of the bribery of electors by his agents. Ball returned to Limerick city by train a few days later to be met by a large, cheering crowd of supporters and published a letter of thanks to them, with an appeal for their continued vote. The same edition of the newspaper carried an advertisement from a group of his supporters calling themselves 'Roman Catholic priests and Electors of the city and liberties of Limerick' and deploring the idea that anyone other than a Catholic should be returned to represent the city.

However, as Gavin's supporters searched for a replacement candidate, it became clear that Ball had some fierce adversaries in Limerick even amongst his co-religionists. In April the *Limerick Chronicle* reported as follows:

> Major Gavin's committee should give support to any man likely to succeed against Mr Ball irrespective of his religious opinions and totally regardless of his qualifications for the responsible office of representing this city in parliament . . . The British parliament refuses to admit Jews to a seat in the Legislature, but the Catholic clergymen and laymen of Major Gavin's committee openly profess that they will

Monte Pelmo from the valley in 2005.
(Author's photo)

Monte Pelmo traverse ledge in 2005. (Author's photo)

have Moravian, Socissian, or Jew – even Pontius Pilate himself – before Mr Ball.[37]

The replacement candidate selected by Major Gavin's supporters to oppose John Ball was a successful local businessman and shipowner, James Spaight, a Protestant.

Ball's support for Italian unification flew in the face of public opinion in an Ireland that was overwhelmingly in favour of the Pope's army; indeed, over 1,000 Irish volunteers would fight with the Papal army against Garibaldi in 1860. In Limerick Ball's position played into his enemies' hands and the second electoral struggle proved more violent than the first. At one stage of the campaign opposing mobs had to be kept apart by the constabulary and extra troops were drafted in to maintain peace. In the end Ball not only lost the second election, but narrowly escaped an angry crowd with his life. He immediately withdrew from public life and, despite being a man of middle age, he flung himself with great enthusiasm into his scientific and mountaineering pursuits.

His final political setback in Limerick coincided with the formation of the Alpine Club. The idea for the club had arisen during a discussion between William Mathews and E. S. Kennedy while they were engaged in an ascent of the Finsteraarhorn in Switzerland on 4 August 1857. To initiate the Club, Mathews hosted a dinner at his home in Worcestershire on Friday 6 November 1857; it was attended by Kennedy, Mathew's son, St John Mathews, and his nephews William and C. E. Mathews.[38] The time was clearly right for the establishment of a club or society of those who enjoyed exploration and climbing in high mountain regions. The numbers of mountaineers had become considerable; railways were providing easier access to the Alps and mountaineering was promoted by publications and public lectures that recounted exciting ascents of mountains previously believed inaccessible. The Alpine Club idea was simple: it was thought that many of those who travelled and climbed would be willing to meet occasionally to exchange information on their exploits and to plan new achievements. A list was made up of men likely to join; it included many Cambridge graduates known to the initiators, including Ball. Kennedy and Mathews sent out a letter to prospective members calling them to meeting at Ashley's Hotel, Covent Garden, on Tuesday 22 December 1857.

One of those invited to join was Carlow man John Tyndall, who received the following communication from William Mathews Jnr on 27 November:

> I am sorry that the Birmingham Institute will not have the advantage of a lecture from you, but thank you very much for your kind offer of your paper which I am very anxious to see. I write today on a different subject. You will see from the enclosed prospectus that several active mountaineers are about to form 'an alpine club'. Do you feel disposed to join us? We should be extremely glad of your co-operation and I have no doubt of the success of the project – rule VII appears to me questionable. I am not answerable for it. Did Mr Huxley accompany you in the ascent of Mont Blanc?[39]

Tyndall did not accept the invitation to join or attend the next meeting of the Club on 19 January 1858. The rule vii referred to in the letter stated: 'A candidate shall not be eligible unless he shall have ascended to the top of a mountain 13,000 feet in height.'[40] This rule was not adopted at the inaugural meeting. The meeting discussed and amended the draft rules of membership and supported the idea that new applicants for membership would be decided on the basis of each applicant's list of expeditions without strictly defining any necessary height or route difficulty. Admission was simply to be decided by the vote of the general body of members. The original members included Albert Smith (who did much to popularise alpine climbing with his public lectures on his early ascent of Mont Blanc), William Longman (the publisher), T. W. Hinchcliff, and Alfred Wills (whose book *Wanderings Among the High Alps* was published in June 1856). Wills was grandfather of Edward Norton who led the 1924 Everest expedition on which Mallory and Irvine died. He had a home in the Alps and was a judge of the High Court.[41]

The next meeting took place on 19 January 1858 and was again held at the Ashley Hotel, followed by the first Club dinner at the Thatched House Tavern, St James' Street on 3 February. By this stage the Club was established and a vice-president, honorary secretary and five other committee members had been elected. Kennedy was chosen as vice-president and T. W. Hinchcliff as secretary. The only vacant post was that of president. Subsequent committee meetings were held at Mr Hinchcliff's chambers, 3 Stone Buildings, Lincoln's Inn. At the next meeting on 31 March it was agreed that the Club would hold one dinner in summer and one in winter; at the other meetings papers of topographical and geographical interest would be read.

It can be seen that Ball was not involved in the early deliberations; he clearly was occupied by the Limerick election and was not one of the Club's founders. Neither is there a record of his election to ordinary membership, nor was he involved in the election of the other committee members at the meeting on 3 February. Curiously, the position of president was left vacant at that meeting. Ball was defeated at Limerick on 15 February and was elected president of the Alpine

Club at its meeting on 31 March. It is likely that his acceptance of the position was contingent on the decision of the electors of Limerick. Limerick's loss was clearly a gain for generations of mountaineers and the future of the Alpine Club was in safe hands.

His choice as president was undoubtedly due to the respect in which his peers held him, not only as one of the most experienced of all alpine travellers, but also as an esteemed scientific observer and public servant. He was not noted for his boldness or dramatic ascents, but he had travelled throughout the Alps each year for nearly twenty years up until the time of his election. He had crossed the main chain forty-eight times by thirty-two different passes and had traversed nearly a hundred of the lateral passes. The thoroughness of his exploration, coupled with his inquisitive nature and articulate memory, made him a reliable source of valuable information. His personal wealth, charming disposition, interest and breadth of knowledge across many fields of natural science and geology, articulate style of presentation, administrative ability, not to mention his recent retirement from politics – all made him an ideal choice for the post. He wrote fluently in Latin, English, French, German and Italian, contributing articles to many scientific journals.[42] Ronald Clarke in his history of Victorian mountaineers explained the reasons why Ball was invited to become president: 'it was also not only Ball's Alpine record but the feeling that his particular brand of knowledge would enrich the Club, arising as it did from his practice in the orderly, logical presentation of facts.'[43]

The rationale for the world's first alpine club was simple: it was to be sociable and its services were to be useful to mountaineers. The objects of the Club were the promotion of good fellowship among mountaineers, the encouragement of mountain climbing and mountain exploration throughout the world, and to share a better knowledge of the mountains through literature, science and art. Ball took the chair on 15 June at the first summer dinner. 'So great was now the anxiety of mountaineers to join the Club, and attend the proposed dinner, that it was deemed necessary to pass a resolution allowing candidates approved by the committee to dine with the Club on the same terms as members.'[44] The dinner was a great convivial success, with invited guests in the form of the Schlagintweit brothers who were well known Asiatic travellers.

At a meeting on 27 November 1858 twenty-one new members were elected, including two opinionated intellectuals – John Tyndall, a scientist, and Leslie Stephen, a literary critic – both of whom would figure on the list of the greatest climbers of the golden age, but whose disposition and attitude to climbing were as different as chalk from cheese. A resolution was adopted that was destined to have an immense effect on the future of mountaineering: 'that members should be invited to send the Honorary Secretary a written account of any of their principle expeditions, with a view to the collection of an interesting set of such documents for the general information of the Club.'[45]

Interestingly, more than a quarter of the early members of the Club were clergymen; Ronald Clarke observed that among the clergymen who played a major part in early alpine history was Hereford George, the first editor of the *Alpine Journal*, who was ordained after his editorship. Another, Leslie Stephen, relinquished holy orders three years after his editorship and W. A. B. Coolidge, the fourth editor, took holy orders while in office. The Club's membership grew quickly and by 1859, when Forbes was made an honorary member, there were already 134 ordinary members.[46]

It was not long before Ball proved his real worth as a proactive president. To communicate with non-members and to establish a way of working within the Club, he proposed to publish a periodical contributed to by the active members. He outlined his idea in the following letter to publisher William Longman, one of the Club's original members. The letter is dated 25 November 1858:

My Dear Mr Longman,

Though I hope to see you at the Alpine Club meeting on Saturday, I anticipate that opportunity by writing to make you a suggestion which has lately occurred to me as worth your consideration. Among the crowd of tourists who leave England every year a good many visit places of interest in the Alps and elsewhere, that are nearly or quite unknown to the reading public. A fair proportion of them are capable of writing an intelligible and even interesting account of what they have done and seen, but with limited materials it is neither reasonable nor desirable that each should write a book. What would you say to bringing out an annual volume, made up of contributions of travellers? If carefully selected I should say the volume would be generally interesting, and secure of a large sale. Unlike the books of most travellers, the writers would have no occasion to stuff their articles with additional matter taken out of libraries; there would be room for small contributions to science, especially Natural History, but in that department especially I would advise you (if you should adopt the idea and undertake the editing) to use much stricter restraint than most book-writing travellers exercise over themselves. People of limited information are apt to record facts which are either well-known and familiar to men of science, or else wanting in the needful precision and accuracy. A little previous communication with the writers might sometimes convert a loose statement into a useful fact.

You can judge of the details of such a project. My own notion would be that illustrations from tolerably good sketches – when available – would much increase the interest of the book. I believe that few things worth having can in these days be obtained for nothing, and therefore suppose that the authors of accepting contributions should be fairly paid; but on this and other points you are the best judge,

Very truly yours,

John Ball[47]

Longman agreed and the result, *Peaks, Passes and Glaciers*, appeared in early 1859.

Many of the contributors were the stars of this golden age of alpinism. Amongst the contributors was his countryman John Tyndall who wrote 'A Day Among the Seracs of the Glacier du Géant'. Ball himself contributed four articles: 'The Schwartz Thor', 'Passage of the Strahleck', 'Suggestions for Alpine Travellers', and 'A Table of the Heights of the Chief Mountains in the Chain of the Alps'. Longman wrote, 'The volume, edited by Mr Ball was published in the following spring. Its success was marvellous. Edition after edition was rapidly called for, and four editions, consisting of all of 2,500 copies, were printed before the end of the year.'[48]

Ball, and later E. S. Kennedy, brought out two more volumes of the members' journal known as *Peaks, Passes and Glaciers* in 1859 and 1862. Then, in 1863, *The Alpine Journal* began to appear regularly; its first editor was H. B. George. It never ceased publication in spite of two world wars. Its importance in the history of mountaineering cannot be overstated as it has provided climbers with up-to-date and well-informed details about every region and aspect of mountaineering from that time.

The journal's subtitle ('a record of mountain adventure and scientific observation')

summarises the direction in which mountaineering was to develop, as it increasingly put mountain adventure first, ahead of other more academic objectives. 'The early climbers attracted a good deal of rather unpleasant notoriety at the hands of a public who regarded them as a mild kind of lunatics,' explained Lord Conway in 1932. He considered *Peaks, Passes and Glaciers* as their apologia, since it breathed 'such a spirit of wholesome enjoyment and mild adventure as could not fail to attract many recruits of an unusually high order of general intelligence.'[49] It became accepted to declare one wanted to climb for sheer enjoyment or adventure, while reserving space for those who wished to record articles of a scientific nature.

The development of the member's journal is surely one of Ball's greatest legacies to mountaineering, only exceeded by his next innovation: a set of climbers' guides to the Alps. Ball was never a mere committee man or administrator; he understood the needs of active alpinists for he was one of the first of the kind. At the meeting of the Club on 4 June 1861 Ball called attention to the need for a guidebook capable of dealing with the whole chain of the Alps, irrespective of political boundaries; its focus was to address the particular needs of mountaineers. He set about producing a comprehensive practical and topographical guide, with special attention to botany and geology, of the main chain from the Col de Tenda in the Maritime Alps near Nice to the Semmering Pass in lower Austria and Styria. By 1863 he had made forty-eight complete crossings of the main chain, collecting 150 lateral passes on the way. In the introduction to the guide he made 'no claim to a brilliant share in the adventurous performances of his friends and fellow members of the Alpine Club', saying that his qualifications to do this job 'arise rather from a somewhat prolonged and extensive acquaintance with the greater portion of the Alps.'[50]

The work engaged and absorbed him for several years after his retirement as president of the Alpine Club in 1860. First to be published in 1863 was the book covering the western Alps, then the central Alps in 1864, and finally the volume dealing with the eastern Alps in 1868. In the course of his research in 1865, Ball with W. E. Forster made a number of important ascents including Cima Tosa (3,135m) in the Italian Brenta Alps. In 1860 with J. Birkbeck and guide Victor Tairraz he had made the first ascent of Marmolata di Rocca (3,309m). The last volume was probably his most important work, a comprehensive study of the geography, geology, and botany of the largely unknown region.[51] By the time he had completed the guidebook series Ball was indisputably the greatest 'pass bagger' of his era. In its accuracy, sketches, layout and concise descriptions, the series set the standard for mountaineering guides to this day. In the preface he explained the need for the books: 'The day is past when it could be thought necessary to apologise for or to explain the prevalence of a love of mountain travelling. It is a simple fact that, especially in our own country, thousands of persons have learned to regard this a sovereign medicine for mind and body, and to feel that the weeks and months devoted to it are the periods of life most full of true enjoyment, and those that leave the most abiding impressions. The fact that the scenery of the Alps is unsurpassed elsewhere in the world for the union of grandeur, beauty and variety, and that it is accessible with a trifling expenditure of time and money, naturally accounts for the constantly increasing influx of strangers.'[52]

The three volumes of the guide each recommended a number of different types of tour for different types of alpine traveller. For example, the guide to the western Alps recommended the following: 1. a thirty-day carriage tour, using carriages, rail and occasional boats (with thirty stops, it was designed for those who just wanted to see alpine scenery); 2. a tour of three months for moderate pedestrians or ladies able to ride (with fifty-four stops, it was designed for those wishing to walk or ride over the mountains); 3. a pedestrian tour of two months in the Alps of the Dauphiné, south Savoy and western Piedmont, occasionally putting up with very bad accommodation (with forty-one stops and including ascents over glacial passes and climbing peaks); and 4. a pedestrian tour of two months in the Pennine Alps (with forty-five stops and including many classic peaks and passes. This tour required a guide acquainted with the country).

Ball married Julia O'Beirne, daughter of Francis and Winefred O'Beirne of Jamestown, County Leitrim, in 1869.

In June 1879 Ball presented a masterly lecture to an evening meeting of the Royal Geographical Society, entitled 'On the origin of the flora of the European Alps'.[53] It was a lecture that fully demonstrated his scholarly and practical understanding of mountain flora and geology. Present in the audience was Sir Joseph Hooker, the first public figure in the scientific world to support Darwin's theory of natural selection in his own botanical writings. Hooker declared at the meeting that he believed Ball's knowledge could not be equalled by anybody in Great Britain, if by anybody in Europe. That Ball was a disciple of Darwin and Hooker was evident. Speaking of dominant plant families and plant distribution, he described the three zones at which he had observed plants growing in alpine regions: the lower zone that extends up to the limit of deciduous trees, the upper zone, including the higher pine forests and alpine pastures; and the glacial zone, where patches of snow remain through the summer. His own meticulous and extensive records of temperature variations observed at altitudes from 4,000 feet (1,200m) to 14,000 feet (4,300m) were offered in support of his observations on plant distribution, but he declared that the real check to the extension of many species of plant was not only climatic, but the want of suitable soil and situation.

He explained that the relatively rich flora of some mountain ranges is due to the fact that they are ancient continental masses which have never been submerged, and the poverty of other ranges is a consequence of their comparatively recent raising from the oceans. Ball gave an illustration of the value of a mountain traveller's observations to the cause of science when he cited three new sightings of a plant in diverse alpine locations that had blown the theory of an eminent naturalist. The scientist had contended that the plant in question (previously found only in Scotland, Scandinavia and the Swiss Alps) must have been carried to the Alps during the glacial period, but the new sightings by mountaineers had caused a rethink on the origin of the species, so that it was no longer considered an intruding newcomer in the Alps, but a member of an ancient family suffering from unfavourable circumstances and in danger of extinction. As he finished, he exhorted members of his audience who visited new and little-explored parts of the earth to observe the flora of those lands, particularly the plants that dwelt in the highest places. Later that year he went to Morocco and the Great Atlas mountains with his close friend Joseph Hooker and Mr George Maw to observe the flora. The journal of this famous journey was written largely by Ball; it included the identification of many new species, whose descriptions were communicated to the Linnean Society under the title *Spicilegium Florae Maroccaae*. Ball had clearly established himself as an independent authority on geology and botany through his own private work and travels, although he was not attached to any institution or university.

His visit in 1882 to the coast of South America produced similar outcomes: he went to the West Indies, crossed the Isthmus of Panama and visited Guayaquil, Callao, Lima, the lower Andes,

Valpariso and various parts of Chile, Patagonia, Montevideo and Brazil. His *Notes of a Naturalist in South America* (1887) contains an appendix on the 'Fall of temperature in ascending to heights above sea-level', as well as his botanical observations of North Patagonia and western South America. His last contribution to Alpine physics was a paper presented to the Royal Geographical Society in 1888, entitled 'Measurement of heights by the barometer', which was based on the observations of many scientists and climbers in the Alps and Himalaya and included Whymper's observations in the Andes.[54]

Trouble with his throat took him to winter in Tunisia, Algeria and the Canary Islands during his later years. When in the Engadine during the summer of 1889 he became ill and was taken home to London where he underwent surgery. He died at midnight at his home at 10 Southwell Gardens, South Kensington, on 21 October and is buried in the Churchyard of St Thomas, Waltham Green.

Christian Lauener, 1826–1873

Although John Ball engaged many local guides in the course of his travels, it appears that he had no favourite. He did, however, once comment favourably on the Oberland guide Christian Lauener who, like Ball, spent much time in the Dolomites.

Lauener was born at Lauterbrunnen in 1826.[55] His brother Ulrich was also a very competent guide. John Tyndall described him as follows: 'Lauener is more than six feet high, and was mainly a mass of bone; his legs are out of proportion, longer than his trunk and he wears a short tail coat which augments the apparent discrepancy.'[56] The Laueners were passionate chamois hunters; another brother, Johann, was killed on the Jungfrau while they were hunting. His many clients included Francis Fox Tuckett, with whom he had guided in the Tyrol where they climbed the Marmolata and Cima di Brenta by new routes. Tyndall made his first ascent of the Monte Rosa with Lauener, as well as the first ascent of the Lauwinen-Thor in 1860. John Ball referred to Lauener as 'a first-rate guide, good tempered and obliging'. In 1873 he made the first ascent of the Schallhorn from the Moming Pass; and in 1874 he ascended the Dent Blanche by a new route and made the first ascent of the Aiguille de Blaitière with a Mr Whitwell. He survived his guiding career uninjured to open a small *wirtshaus* (alehouse) in the outskirts of his native village.

3

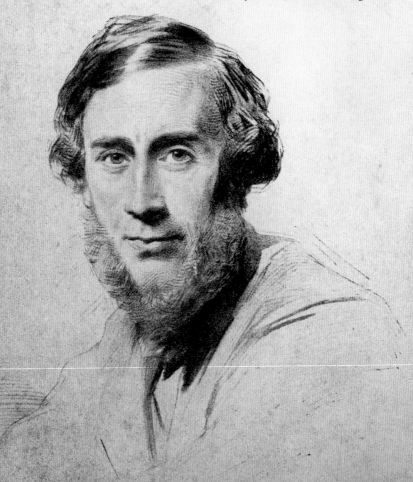

John Tyndall: the Race for the Matterhorn

On the 16th of August 1856 I received my alpenstock from the hands of Dr Hooker, in the garden of Pension Ober, at Interlaken. It bore my name, not marked, however, by the vulgar brands of the country, but by the solar beams which had been converged upon it by the pocket lens of my friend.

John Tyndall, Mountaineering in 1861

CARLOW-BORN AND REARED John Tyndall ranks among the greatest pioneers of alpinism. In 1861 he made the first ascent of the Weisshorn (at 4,506m one of the most beautiful of the higher peaks in Switzerland) and later rivalled Englishman Edward Whymper in his bid to be the first to conquer the Matterhorn. Whymper's ascent of the Matterhorn in July 1865 signalled the end of the golden age of alpinism; however, Tyndall made the seventh ascent and first completed traverse over the summit three years later, from Breuil on the Italian side, to summit and descend into Zermatt on the Swiss side. This traverse provided a significant event that heralded the beginning of the silver age of alpinism, when more difficult routes up previously climbed mountains were accomplished.

Tyndall came to prominence as a physicist as a result of his study of diamagnetism in 1850 and later for his work on thermal radiation and discoveries concerning the earth's atmosphere. His public lectures and the demonstrations of his experiments at the Royal Institution became sell-out events that introduced physics to the wider public. W. T. Jeans in the *Lives of the Electricians* wrote: 'There are men who have made greater and more useful discoveries in science, but few have made more interesting discoveries. There are men whose achievements have been more highly esteemed by the devotees of pure science, but rarely has a scientific man been more popular outside the scientific world.'[1]

John Tyndall, 1820–1893

- Physicist, born 20 August 1820 at Leighlinbridge, County Carlow

- A life-long adult learner, he progressed from parish school to work as a railway surveyor and then became a vocational teacher

- Completed an MA at a German university using money from his own savings and went on to become an eminent research physicist and lecturer at the Royal Institution

- A study to understand the movement of glaciers led to his induction into the thrills of alpine climbing

- He made the first ascent of Weisshorn with the Swiss guide Johann J. Bennen of Laax in 1861

- Made a solo ascent of Monte Rosa

- Made two unsuccessful attempts with Bennen to climb the Matterhorn in 1860 and 1862, and on the latter attempt reached a minor peak on the Italian ridge now named Pic Tyndall

- Made the first completed traverse of the Matterhorn from Breuil to Zermatt with the Italian guides J. J. and J. P. Maquignaz in 1868

- Died from overdose of medicine accidently administered by his wife

Facing page: John Tyndall – Ireland's greatest climber of the golden era. This drawing was made in 1864 by G. Richmond R.A. (E. and C. H. Creasy, *Life & Work of John Tyndall* (1945))

However, Tyndall's strong public views on many subjects often made him a controversial figure. He championed Darwin in the debate regarding the division between science and religion and politically he was fiercely against Gladstone's Irish Home Rule proposals. His life story provides an exemplary model for vocational development and the value of lifelong learning. Tyndall sandwiched his education between full-time jobs throughout his career: from post-primary student to surveyor who attended night classes to broaden his education, he then became a teacher in a public school, saving his money to self-finance further study as a mature university student, and later became one of the great public disseminators of science through his lectures, textbooks and science columns in a number of periodicals. He succeeded in publishing seventeen science books, mostly written for the general public. It was his interest in the study of glaciology that first brought him to the Alps and the skills he developed working and travelling on glaciers gave him the confidence to become one of the great climbers of the golden age. His articulate and insightful mountain writings contributed to the popularity of alpinism and made him one of its best known exponents.

Tyndall was born in Leighlinbridge, County Carlow, on 2 August 1820. The descendant of a family of small landowners from Gloucestershire, some of whom had settled in the southeast of Ireland in 1670, he believed himself to be distantly connected with the Tyndale (or Tindale) who had first translated the Bible into English from Greek and Hebrew texts:

> I was distantly connected with one William Tyndale, who was rash enough to boast and to make good his boast, that he would place an open bible within reach of every ploughboy in England. His first reward was exile, and then a subterranean cell in the Castle of Vilvorden. It was a cold cell, and he humbly, but vainly, prayed for his coat to cover him and for his books to occupy him. In due time, he was taken from the cell and set upright against a post. Round neck and post was placed a chain, which being cunningly twisted, the life was squeezed out of him. A bonfire was made of his body later.[2]

John's father had been disinherited following a family quarrel and he set up his own shoemaking and leather business in Leighlinbridge, although he left it for a time to become one of the first members of the Royal Irish Constabulary.[3] As a result of his straitened family circumstances John the elder was forced to educate himself in various subjects, including history, and he developed a liking for religious controversy. He was passionate in his politics and a committed Orangeman who cherished the possession of a fragment of a flag that had fluttered at the Battle of the Boyne.[4] Like his father, John's Quaker mother set a high value on knowledge and 'cared above all things for the education of her children'.[5]

It is likely that when the young John first began school he was able to attend the school at Ballyknockan run by John Conwill (a former hedge school teacher of high repute). After several years, during which John's father was posted by the RIC to Nurney, County Carlow, and Castlebellingham, County Louth, the young family were able to return to Leighlinbridge and John was then sent by his parents to the national school at Ballinabranagh where he came back under the influence of Conwill, now principal of this new Catholic school. John's father was clearly confident that his son would gain a sound secular education from Conwill, proof that John the elder was no bigot and, indeed, was a sound judge of character. Under Conwill's tutelage he developed a zeal for knowledge and a special love for mathematics and science, demonstrating an ability to mentally picture and resolve complex problems of plane geometry while still young. The strong views of his father, the quality of Conwill's teaching and his mother's Quaker religion shaped an articulate young man with very strongly independent opinions. His father imbued in him a particular love for theological debate and the two were accustomed to debate the points of doctrine that divide the Protestant and the Roman Catholic churches; sometimes the son took the Protestant view and at other times the Catholic side, demonstrating much dialectical skill and theological knowledge.

He stayed at the school until he was nineteen, receiving lessons in the last two years in mathematics, English and surveying. Practical surveying expeditions were part of the curriculum and Tyndall gained a solid grounding in the necessary skills, which enabled him to secure his first job. Joining the Irish Ordnance Survey in Carlow on 1 April 1839 as a civil assistant on a wage of 5 shillings a week, he commenced surveying within his native county. The survey moved to Youghal in County Cork in 1840, where he was paid less than £1 a week; his lodgings and board consumed half of this. It was here that he formed a close friendship with his superior, Laurence Ivers, who advocated and supported Tyndall's systematic efforts towards self-improvement through study in his spare time. Despite his high expenses he was able to send money home to his mother; his letters home to his father reveal his political and religious opposition to Daniel O'Connell and his vehement refutation of arguments published in support of transubstantiation. His work moved to Kinsale and Cork as he became a competent surveyor and draftsman. Under the pseudonym 'Walter Snooks' he wrote a number of short satirical rhymes for *The Carlow Sentinel*.

In May 1842 John Tyndall left Ireland for the first time when he was transferred to Preston to take up a position with the English Ordnance. He took lessons two evenings a week in French at Preston Institute and was proud of his skills as a draughtsman. However, he grew unhappy with the survey operation, complaining of the inefficiency of the administration and, influenced by the growing Chartist movement, he became embroiled in a struggle to redress inequities in the pay and conditions experienced by the civilian assistants reporting to military officers. In a letter to his father he complained, 'The situation was a paltry one. My salary might answer a settled person well, but for one who had to pay for furnished lodgings etc., it was very poor. It is now a little better than £50 a year.'[6]

Despite his father's warning, he took a leading part in a formal written protest addressed to the Master General of Ordnance, Sir Robert Peel, and found himself summarily dismissed with many of his colleagues in November 1843.[7] He wrote to his father unbowed, 'Well, the thunder has flashed and I have been seared but not shivered by the bolt. I am dismissed – dismissed forever from the legions of ordnance surveyors. Thank heaven however I leave it with my character unstained . . . From you I inherit the principle which guided me; if I be wrong you should not have thought me to be honest.'[8] He arrived back home to Leighlinbridge with just a halfpenny in his pocket and his civil service career in tatters.

He was to spend several months unemployed, but he eventually found work in Manchester as a railway surveyor with the engineering firm of Nevins and Lawton, at a salary of 3 guineas a week in the office and 4 guineas in the field. The expansion of railways was at its height and he was soon working day and night to meet deadlines for the submission of competitive bids on the new lines that had begun to trace their way across the English landscape. It was while on railway work that he met Thomas Archer Hirst. Although Hirst was ten years younger than Tyndall, they became great friends and later corresponded actively.

If his actions in defence of his rights as a worker make him appear a radical, his political views on the Irish Famine, which was decimating the Irish population at that time, reveal his pro-Unionist politics. This is reflected in an entry to his journal: 'He is miserably mistaken who fancies in the repeal of the Union is to be found the panacea of all Ireland's disorders.'[9] About this time work on the railways was slackening and he was aware of his need for alternative employment. An old friend advised him of an opportunity arising at a new school at Stockbridge in Hampshire, where engineering, science and farming were to be taught.

Queenswood College had been built by the socialist reformer Robert Owen and his followers. The school was the first in England to adopt practical and laboratory work in the teaching of applied science. Here a more progressive Tyndall was employed to teach mathematics and surveying in both the classroom and the field. He was also required to act as secretary of the school and to keep the books. He proved to be a successful teacher, combining self-improvement as part of his own teaching philosophy; he strongly believed there was need to develop discipline in the education of the young. Edward Frankland was in charge of the chemistry laboratory at that time and, hungry to learn, Tyndall attended all Frankland's lectures on chemistry, geology, botany, hydrostatics and heat (for which privilege he forfeited part of his salary). The two men were soon friends and decided to widen their scientific education together. Frankland had worked for three months with Professor Bunsen at Marburg. Tyndall, using his savings of between £200 and £300, decided to invest in his own education. He studied German part-time to enable him to study in Germany (at that time leading Britain in the advancement of science); then, with Frankland, he gave up his teaching post worth £200 a year to attend the University of Marburg in October 1848, for which he had to pay tuition fees and the cost of his upkeep.

Marburg and its environs held a measure of ancestral and theological resonance for Tyndall, for it was there that his supposed forebear, William Tyndale, had lived for a time. It was also in a castle near there that Luther and Zwingli had held their famous conference on consubstantiation and transubstantiation. For two years Tyndall was a model mature student. From a starting position of basic German and science he worked sixteen hours a day, resting only on Sundays, to complete a doctorate in philosophy. He was motivated by Robert Bunsen and later influenced by Dr Herman Knoblauch, a young physicist who arrived there in Tyndall's second year to study physics. On 8 September 1849 he faced four professors in an oral examination and was instructed to write a mathematical thesis, to be submitted by 30 November.

With his examination over, Tyndall, then aged twenty-nine and in search of recreation, set off with little money to Switzerland to make his first visit to the Alps. He had planned the trip with Hirst, his railway friend from Halifax, but Hirst's mother died just as he arrived at Marburg and he was forced to return to England for her funeral, so Tyndall set out alone. Sometimes he walked and sometimes he went by rail or by river, including a stretch of the Rhine to Heidelberg. The sight of the distant mountains drove him to Basel and inspired him to walk along the roads. He wrote: 'I knew not the distant mountains; the attraction which they afterwards exercised upon me had not yet begun to act.' He walked from Basel to Zürich, along the lake to Horgen, over the hills to Zug, and along the Zugersee to Arth. 'Here on September 26th', he records, 'I bought my first alpenstock and faced with it the renowned Rigi.'[10] Later, it would be the cloud cover and sound of the wind that he remembered most in recalling his alpine ascent of this 1,797.5m mountain in central Switzerland.

He continued his walk, taking a steamer to Flüelen to reach Andermatt and Hospenthal, and on to Realp to get his first sight of Glacier of the Rhone. He walked to Grimsel and from there reached Guttannen – en route he was forced to scramble over rocks to regain the path; he also experienced his first storm in the Alps on the Great Scheidegg. Crossing the Little Scheidegg next day, he 'saw avalanches on the Jungfrau, and heard the warbles of her echoes'. His walk led him onwards to Interlaken and from there he travelled by steamer to Thun and by carriage to Berne, and finally on foot back to Basel by Solothurn. 'The distant aspect of the Alps appeared to be far more glorious than the nearer view'. He described the overall experience in a letter to Hirst: 'Trusting to my legs and stick, repudiating guides, eating bread and milk, and sleeping when possible in the country villages where nobody could detect my accent, I got through amazingly cheap.'[11]

On his return to Marburg he worked on his thesis, which he submitted on the last day of November. It was entitled 'On a screw surface with inclined generetrix and on the conditions of equilibrium of such surfaces'. He was proud of his original work but, failing further funding, knew that he would shortly have to leave Marburg. Fortunately his friend Hirst sensitively came to his financial rescue, allowing Tyndall to stay another year at Marburg, where he conducted experiments into the new field of diamagnetism, first opened up in 1845 by the discoveries of Michael Faraday. The young physicist Knoblauch collaborated with him and supplied Tyndall with all the necessary apparatus. In conducting this series of experiments with the German, he produced his second memoir on the subject of diamagnetism, which linked his work with that of the German scientific community. He moved to Berlin in early 1851 and was provided a working place by the eminent German Professor Magnus, enabling him to continue his investigations on diamagnetism and magne-crystallic action, the results of which were published in the *Philosophical Magazine* in September 1851.[12]

Tyndall's life and career were at a crossroads; he was now a qualified scientist but, despite offers to return to Marburg, he had not the means to continue his studies and needed a job. He chose to return to teach at Queenswood College, determined to work his way out of debt. But there were some hopeful signs of support in the shape of Dublin-born, Colonel Edward Sabine, treasurer of the Royal Society.[13] Sabine developed a high regard for Tyndall's work and successfully applied on his behalf for an apparatus grant of £50 from the Society, also suggesting that he be elected as a fellow. He was elected on the 3 June 1852 and his fellowship enabled him to communicate with Sabine himself, Michael Faraday, William Thomson and Thomas Henry Huxley – in fact, most of the famous scientific men of the mid-nineteenth century.

Tyndall applied unsuccessfully to obtain the chairs or professorships in science and natural philosophy when vacancies arose at Toronto, Sydney, Cork and Galway universities during that year. His work in Germany did, however, open some doors for him in England: he was recommended to Dr Henry Bence Jones, the secretary of the Royal Institution, by one of his German collaborators, Professor Bois-Raymond of Berlin (secretary of the Academy of Sciences in Berlin), who suggested that Tyndall be invited to lecture at the Royal Institution on the subject of his original research into diamagnetism. The lectures were greeted enthusiastically (even by Faraday, although Tyndall had dared to disagree with him in his second memoir) and in May 1853 he was elected Professor of Natural Philosophy by the Royal Institution. The remuneration was not great and, indeed, as a consequence of his new appointment he would be forced to pay for accommodation and expenses while in London. But the attraction of working with Faraday and the opportunity to develop a friendship with the great man was irresistible. To make ends meet he continued his work of translating German scientific papers and sought other streams of income.

On 10 June 1856 Tyndall delivered a lecture at the Royal Institution entitled 'A theory of slatey cleavage different from any previously given', which was a part of his study of the effects of pressure upon the magnetic force. He conferred with Huxley and the two concluded that the new theory might have some bearing upon the laminated structure of ice, as discussed in Professor Forbes' *Travels through the Alps of Savoy*. It was the pursuit of this quest that took him, later that year, to the glaciers of the Oberland in the company of Huxley on a joint expedition to observe the veined structure of ice. As if to formalise his entry to mountaineering, he was presented with an alpenstock by Dr J. D. Hooker in the gardens of the Pension Ober, at Interlaken. It had his name marked on it by Hooker, 'not marked however, by the brand of the country, but by the solar beams which had been converged upon it by the pocket lens of my friend.'[14]

His journey took him to the Guggi on 17 August 1856; this was the first glacier on which he had actually stood. While there he wondered at the avalanches and was later driven off by a thunderstorm. Later in the evening they crossed the pass to Grindelwald. During the next two days, with Christian Kaufmann as their guide, they examined the lower Grindelwald Glacier. On 20 August Tyndall set out alone for the Grimsel Pass, sleeping the first night at Meiringen. There he rejoined Huxley and they set out for Dollfuss Hut on the Unteraar Glacier. When they arrived there, Tyndall, full of vim, continued on towards Abschwung. The next day was spent sheltering from heavy snow at the mountain hut; snow that turned to rain as the party descended to Grimsel. They then descended to the Rhone Glacier, which they examined, and on the way experienced a vision of a Brocken spectre.

The party broke up. Tyndall's destination was Vienna; he stopped on his way at Gepatsch Alp and, with the aid of a local chamois hunter, he crossed the Weissseejoch (2,927m) into the Lantaufer Tal to view its glacier. He met up with his friend Edward Frankland at the Finstermünz Pass, sleeping at Mals; they walked over the Stelvio to Bormio and back, and then by Trafoi and Meran to Unser Frau in the Schnalsthal, and finally crossed the Hochjoch to Fend (Vent), which ended his short visit. During the following thirteen years he visited the Alps at first for the purposes of glacier observation, but increasingly for the added pleasure which he derived solely from the climbing. He presented his first paper on his collaborative study of glaciers with Huxley to the Royal Society in January 1857.[15]

In the summer of 1857 he revisited the Alps with Huxley and Hirst, reaching Chamonix in mid-July. He crossed the Mer de Glace as he ascended to Montanvert, sleeping in a very basic outbuilding for five weeks in preference to staying in one of the rooms at the more comfortable inn, because of the noise of the early morning risers. During that time he studied the great glacier of Chamonix and measured its rate of progress and made many excursions with local guides Eduard Simond and Petit Balmat. He examined its structure, tributaries, crevasses, moraines, moulins and the disintegration of its surface. On one of these outings he climbed the Col du Géant (3,371m), learning from the experience the mechanics of climbing, the thrills of exposure, and the personal satisfaction of overcoming its anxieties and difficulties. He wrote: 'Wherever we turned peril stared us in the face but the recurrence of danger had rendered us callous to it, and this indifference gave us mechanical surety to the step where such surety was the only means of avoiding destruction.'[16]

Shortly after, Tyndall made his first ascent of Mont Blanc, an outing which for many reasons must be considered as a rash and risky expedition. Huxley joined the party on 10 August, with no time to acclimatise or to get into condition for the arduous ascent. Tyndall saw no reason why they needed more than one guide, a position he negotiated with Eduard Simonds whose opening demand was for four. They employed two porters to carry a ladder, their provisions and some rugs. They set out from Montanvert on 12 August 1857 to the cabin located on rocks called the Grands Mulets, collecting firewood en route to Pierre à l'Echelle where they mounted the Glacier des Bossons. They soon found use for the ladders for crossing deep crevasses that led steeply to their resting place. Huxley, exhausted by the time they reached the cabin, fell asleep on a rug laid out upon a plank. The porters, their job done, departed. The wet socks and leggings they wore were dried over the stove and their boots placed round the fire. They were poorly provided for with food and their evening meal comprised only melted snow into which ground chocolate was mixed; the only special clothing consisted of coarse woollen cloth leggings to keep out the snow. They rested on planks laid near the fire, rising to renew the fire and warm themselves, before Tyndall, Hirst and Simond set out at 2.30 a.m., leaving the clearly worn-out Huxley behind to await their return.

Soon the conditions of hard, frozen snow that had prevailed when they set out changed: they sank to their hips in snow, describing the surface as a 'breakable crust' as they climbed the incline towards the Grand Plateau. The guide (who had climbed Mont Blanc only once before) led them too far right, so Tyndall took the lead towards the base of the Rochers Rouges, breaking the surface at every step with his followers complaining behind him at his speed and the difficulty of walking in his wake. At a dangerous crevasse the unsure Simond took over again and led the way across a dangerous snow bridge that led to a slope of bare ice. Still off route, he cut steps until he was exhausted, when Tyndall took over the step-cutting. Each single step took him a minute to cut, and so it took an hour to cut sixty steps before they were back on snow and could stamp their way again towards the base of the Mur de la Côte. Here they left their rope; they had taken twelve hours to get there, twice as long as the usual time for the total ascent. 'Driving the iron claws of our boots into the scars made by the axe, and the spikes of our batons into the slope above our feet, we ascended steadily until the summit was attained, and the top of the mountain rose clearly above us.' They devoured their scant provisions at a rocky ridge called the Petits Mulets. 'We had not a bit of bread or drop of wine left; our brandy flasks were also nearly exhausted.' They had to go to the top of Mont Blanc and back to the Grands Mulets without food or drink. When Tyndall dozed, Hirst roused him. The pace slowed, stopping every fifteen to twenty paces. Tyndall indulged in philosophical thought as the unfit party eventually reached the top. At 3.30 p.m. he clasped hands with Hirst on the summit. He compared the elongated ridge that shaped the summit to the back of an ass: 'It was perfectly manifest that we were dominant over all other mountains; as far as our eyes could range Mont Blanc had no competitor.' They tried eating snow for their thirst as they descended, with gravity in their favour. Once Hirst slipped, pulling Tyndall with him; the pair of them were carried in a mass of snow to the bottom of the slope. They were almost covered by the time they stopped sliding.[17]

They reached the Grands Mulets at 9.20 p.m. to find poor Huxley in a great state of anxiety, having expected them back at 2 p.m. That night was a weary one, and they rose next morning with muscles more tired than when they had lain down. Huxley wrote: 'Next day we came down such a set of dirty, sun burnt, snow-blind wretches as you never saw.'[18] Tyndall had made the first of his three ascents to the summit of Mont Blanc. They returned to Montanvert, spending every available hour on the ice, in observation and research, which contributed to his findings on glacier movement, each day's work being wound up by an evening of perfect enjoyment. 'Roast mutton and fried potatoes were our incessant fare, for which after a little longing for a change at first we contracted a final and permanent love,' Tyndall wrote. They drank some 'capital Sallanches beer cold as a glacier water, but effervescent as champagne' and after dinner gathered round the pine fire. 'I can hardly think it possible for three men to be more happy than we were.'[19] He regarded his guide Simond as intelligent and trustworthy and not lacking in strength or courage. When the season was over and they worked out the accounts, Tyndall found he had insufficient money to pay him. Hirst was sent to Geneva to access funds that Tyndall had there. To tide Tyndall over until the money arrived Simond, in an affectionate manner, offered him a loan of 500 francs, which augmented the kindly feelings that Tyndall had long entertained towards his guide.

In December 1857 Tyndall was one of the recipients of letters sent by original members of the Alpine Club that set out the objectives and proposed rules of the new club. His reply on 16 December was characteristically direct, formal and challenged the draft rules:

> It is very kind of you to send me your circular though I do not belong to the Alpine Club . . . I ask to be excused chiefly for the sake of my pursuits, and I hope that the scientific side of the Alpine question will not suffer by this arrangement. I shall take an interest in your proceedings and if permitted shall be glad to join in from time to time . . . If rule vii is to stand might it not be modified thus 'ascending a mountain 13,000 feet'. It is the elevation I suppose that gives the claim, not reaching the top of the mountain. W Cobueait for example once lost his baton on the Grand Plateau and was obliged to return without reaching the summit of Mont Blanc. Would not this be a sufficient claim upon his part even though he had not afterwards reached the top of the mountain? [20]

Living in London gave Tyndall an opportunity to socialise with many friends from the scientific community and to make many new friends. Among those he sought out were Tennyson and Thomas Carlyle, of whom he remarked 'what I have seen thus far in Carlyle makes me revere the old brute more than ever'. He enjoyed jousting with the historian when their paths crossed at many dinner parties. On 6 April 1858 he went on invitation to meet the Tennysons at their home where he quoted from his poem 'Maud' and talked of the poem with the poet for some time. When dinner was over he accompanied the poet to his sanctum sanctorum upstairs, where Tennyson filled two pipes as they continued to talk of 'Maud' and Tyndall's journey up Mont Blanc. He also met Livingstone, the African explorer, whom he found full of practical sense, and spent a couple of days with Hooker at Kew.

Tyndall made further investigative visits to the Alps during the summer of 1858 and again in 1859 during both winter and summer. From his findings and laboratory experiments arising from his glacier studies, he questioned Forbes' assertion that 'glaciers flowed viscously'. He interpreted the meaning of viscous to be 'the power of being drawn out' and contended that Forbes had not provided any evidence to support his theory, dismissing Forbes' 'viscosity' as apparent, not real. Alternatively, he proposed a modified theory of 'fracture and regelation', in which he supposed that ice is first deformed by breaking and then re-formed by welding itself together in a new configuration.[21] His field work confirmed Forbes measurements, but he claimed a new fact in his assertion 'that the locus of maximum velocity is displaced towards the outside of a bend, when a glacier is curved.' His laboratory work demonstrated 'that a uniaxial pressure produced laminations in the plane at right angles to the axis.' This work provided important supporting experiments.[22]

The argument became more intense and bitter when Tyndall read a memoir written by Canon Rendu (later Bishop of Annecy) in the course of which he compared a glacier flow with that of a river, leading Rendu to suggest (after consultations with mountain guides concerning the flow rates of glaciers) that the centre moved faster than the sides. Because Forbes had heard of Rendu's theory from the Swiss naturalist Louis Agassiz in 1841, and had possession of a written copy of Rendu's memoir before he published his *Travels through the Alps of Savoy* in 1845, Tyndall suggested that the omission of important parts of Rendu's memoir in Forbes' book hid the fact that Rendu had compared a glacier to a viscous stream before Forbes' own conclusions were published. This charge of deliberate omission came at a point when Forbes was under active consideration as a serious candidate for the Royal Society's Copley Medal for 1859. The medal was awarded instead to another candidate, the German physicist W. E. Weber. In his own book, *Glaciers of the Alps* (published in 1860), Tyndall attributes the plastic flow of glaciers theory to Rendu and bemoans the fact that the existence of the bishop's writings was obscured from British discussions on the subject. Forbes, in reply, took credit for bringing Rendu's work to British public notice by referencing it in his book and put its value into context by outlining the lack of evidence presented by Rendu to support his theory.[23]

J. S. Rowlinson (1980) states that the modern view of glaciers is closer to that of Forbes than that of Tyndall:

> ice in common with many other solids, shows [the] 'genuine molecular plasticity' or continuous deformation under stress, ascribed to it by Forbes. It should be added, however that slipping in its bed (the old theory of Saussure) may account for up to half the motion of the upper part of a glacier. Tyndall's 'fracture and relegation' undoubtedly occurs, as in the formation and subsequent healing of crevasses, but it is not the dominant mechanism of flow he supposed.[24]

In 1858 Tyndall was accompanied in his studies and climbing by Professor Ramsay (later Sir Andrew Crombie Ramsay, 1814–1891). Tyndall intended to visit a wide range of glaciers in Switzerland to augment his specific study of the Mer de Glace. He climbed the Finsteraarhorn with a guide named Johann Joseph Bennen from Laax in the Upper Rhine Valley who was attached to the hotel. He was described by Tyndall as aged between thirty and forty years, of middle stature, but very strongly built, with a countenance that was frank and firm, while a light of good nature at times twinkled in his eye. He gave the impression of physical strength combined with decision of character.[25] Tyndall asked Bennen to take him alone to the top of the Finsteraarhorn, making it clear he would follow where Bennen led and would not need the direct assistance of the guide. In order not to overload the guide Tyndall agreed to two porters being engaged to carry blankets, provisions, wood and hay to the cave of the Faulberg, where they would spend the night. Bennen watched Tyndall closely when on the ascent to the cave and while crossing the first ice and a crevasse; his vigilance ended when he concluded that Tyndall could look after himself.

At the grotto supper was prepared and the scientist measured the temperature of the boiling point of water at 196 °F (99 °C) using his apparatus. The fire was gleaming ruddily, the cave was comfortable and the hardness of the ground was countered by a bed of hay. Bennen gave Tyndall the position closest to the fire and most of the bedclothes; however, the tranquillity of the situation was upset when Bennen started to snore, keeping Tyndall awake. He complained, 'Bennen's snores announced to me at once the repair of Bennen's muscles and the doom on my own.' At 2 a.m. they had coffee, packed their provisions and instruments and set out descending to the Grünhorn Glacier's tributary. The sight of the moonlit Jungfrau 'so pure and beautiful' inspired Tyndall to ask Bennen to change their objective; Bennen replied 'if you desire it, I am ready.' On immediate reflection he remembered his original scientific objective: the Finsteraarhorn was higher and better suited for his observation on the effects of altitude on the boiling point of water. They about-turned and made their way towards the Grünhorn saddle: 'The sun had not yet smitten the snows of the bounding mountains, but the saddle carved out a segment of the Heavens which formed the background of unspeakable beauty.'[26]

The Finsteraarhorn sends down a number of cliffy buttresses, separated from each other by wide couloirs filled with ice and snow. They ascended one of the buttresses, picking their way among the spiky rocks, later ascending snow at the edge of the spine and then abandoning themselves to the *névé* of the couloirs, which was deep and required steps to be cut for its safe ascent. The slope was at an angle of 45° and below them a gloomy fissure opened its jaws just as the sun burst upon them with great power, compelling them to don their veils and dark spectacles. Two years previously Bennen had nearly been blinded by inflammation brought on by the glare from the snow, and he thereafter took great care in protecting his eyes. The rocks before them became more manageable and they climbed over them until faced with a vertical wall. Bennen sought a way around by descending onto poor ground; Tyndall followed in the footsteps of his guide and they moved from rock to couloir, following the best line upwards until they reached a smooth snow slope that needed more step-cutting. The experienced guide fell into a rhythm admired by Tyndall, his foot lifting synchronously as his mattock struck the ice to make the next step as they reached the base of the rock pyramid which caps the mountain. 'Our hardest work is now before us,' the guide said before he led the way up through the steep and splintered rocks with protruding spikes before them. The ground began to alternate between ice and snow and at times very steep pure ice forced them back to the security of the rocks; the effect of the wind was felt on the occasions when they passed gaps between the buttresses. Tyndall fulfilled his promise when he reached the summit without any direct help from his guide, including carrying on his back a fair share of the weight of his boiling-water apparatus and telescope.[27]

The scientific party then moved to the Riffelberg and the Görner Glacier, although Ramsay was forced to go home due to the death of a relative. Tyndall joined up with the guide Christian Lauener on 10 August 1858 for an assault on the Monte Rosa, (which Tyndall refers to as the 'Queen of the Alps') but unfortunately the mountain was covered in fog and provided him with no view from the summit. He compared his fitness and performance with the Mont Blanc ascent, realising he was much fitter and had climbed unroped despite the altitude. The excursion had taken eleven and a half hours up and down. When Tyndall awoke on 17 August (having spent the previous days investigating the glaciers of the Görnergrat and explaining and elaborating on a magnetic phenomenon previously observed by Professor Forbes) he found it was a morning 'of unspeakable beauty'. Feeling in exceedingly good condition, he was prompted to attempt the Monte Rosa solo, as Lauener was lent to another party to climb the mountain. He set out alone in his shirtsleeves, without a coat and with just a ham sandwich and half a wine bottle full of tea to sustain his effort. At the bottom of the Kamm he heard the sounds above of the party under Lauener's guidance. 'My head was clear, my muscles in perfect condition, and I felt sufficient fear to render me careful.' On the Kamm he passed the other party coming down and borrowed a handkerchief from Lauener to cover his throat from the cold wind. He reached the top without any difficulty except when he dropped his axe and it fell about 30 feet (9m); he realised it was 'my staff of life' at that moment. This time he enjoyed the magnificent summit view. He caught up with the other party, slowed by someone with a damaged knee, and accompanied the cripple to the Riffelberg. He 'attached himself to the invalid', otherwise he estimated the summit expedition and back would have been completed in a little better than nine hours.[28]

Below: The title page of Tyndall's *The Glaciers of the Alps.* (1860)

THE

GLACIERS OF THE ALPS.

BEING

A NARRATIVE OF EXCURSIONS AND ASCENTS,

AN ACCOUNT OF THE ORIGIN AND PHENOMENA OF GLACIERS,

AND

AN EXPOSITION OF THE PHYSICAL PRINCIPLES TO WHICH THEY ARE RELATED.

By JOHN TYNDALL, F.R.S.,

MEMBER OF THE ROYAL SOCIETIES OF SCIENCE OF HOLLAND AND GÖTTINGEN ; OF THE SCIENTIFIC SOCIETIES OF HALLE, MARBURG, AND ZÜRICH ; OF THE SOCIÉTÉ PHILOMATIQUE OF PARIS ; OF THE NATURAL HISTORY AND PHYSICAL SOCIETY OF GENEVA ; OF THE PHYSICAL SOCIETY OF BERLIN ; PROFESSOR OF NATURAL PHILOSOPHY IN THE ROYAL INSTITUTION OF GREAT BRITAIN, AND IN THE GOVERNMENT SCHOOL OF MINES.

WITH ILLUSTRATIONS.

LONDON: JOHN MURRAY, ALBEMARLE STREET. 1860.

The right of Translation is reserved.

By then Tyndall had developed a level of self-reliance and had demonstrated to himself and his peers his climbing skills, ability and his powers of endurance. In his diary he recorded his attitude to climbing solo:

People blame me for going alone, and I strongly deprecate doing so in dangerous places ... But where your work is clearly within your powers; when long practice has enabled you to trust your own eye and judgement in unravelling crevasses, and your axe and arm

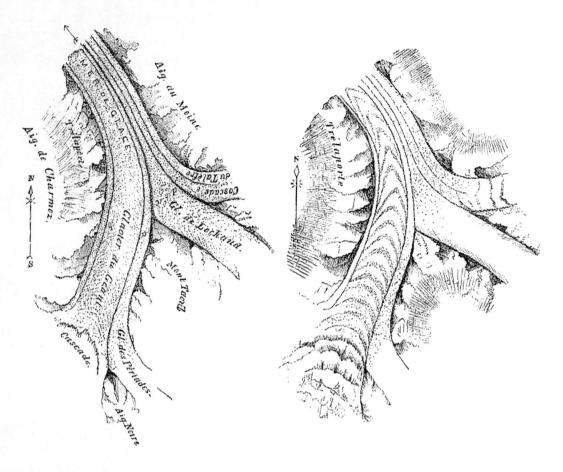

John Tyndall's sketch of the formation of the great glacier, the Mer de Glace, and its medial moraines at and below the junction of the Cascade du Talèfre and the Lechaud, Périades and Géant Glaciers (John Tyndall, *Glaciers of the Alps* 2nd ed. (1896))

in cutting thro' difficulty, it is an entirely new experience to be alone amid these scenes of majesty and desolation. The peaks wear a more solemn aspect, the sun shines with a purer light into the soul, the blue of heaven is more awful. In fact you are raised upon an atmosphere of emotion; your hardness of heart is melted down to an extent which is impossible when you have companions at your side. In places where there is not much danger and which are still beset with possibilities which require a certain amount of strength and skill to overcome, the feeling of self-reliance is very sweet, and you contract a closer friendship with the universe than when you trust to the eye and arm of your guide.[29]

He then visited the village of Saas to explore the glaciers there; a proposed attempt on the Dom with Herr Imseng, the curé, was thwarted by a period of bad weather. Chamonix was his next stop and he brought with him a number of self-registering thermometers destined for the summit of Mont Blanc. The instruments were purchased using a grant from the Royal Society as an encouragement to Auguste Balmat who supported the scheme. Difficulties with regulations at Chamonix regarding the hiring of guides for scientific work delayed the project. With the issue still not sorted and the weather right, Tyndall (in company with Balmat, Alfred Wills and five porters) set out for the Grands Mulets on the 12 September. They were followed by a 'spy' sent by the chief guide to follow them 'who having satisfied himself of our delinquency, took his unpleasant presence from the splendid scene.'[30] They followed the Grands Mulets route and crossed a wide crevasse near to the hut by means of frail snow bridges and a split ladder. They sat out a storm in the damp wooden cabin that was moored to the rock on two sides. The tumult had died down before 1.30 a.m. when they emerged into a starry but moonless night to continue their ascent in deep snow, the porters taking turns to break the steps. The party headed up through avalanche debris with the aid of three lanterns to have their breakfast break upon the Grand Plateau.

The weather was bad during the ascent; clouds were swirling and it was bitter cold when they reached the summit and, while Tyndall lit his boiling-water apparatus and read the temperature, the porters complained of cold and Balmat's hands became badly frostbitten. They dug a hole and planted the thermometers and when he finally got the boiling apparatus working he took and recorded the temperature. Wills had already taken off with Balmat and some of the porters before the scientist, intent on finishing his work, was ready. On the way down it took great efforts from Wills, Tyndall and Balmat himself to restore life into the hands of their faithful guide. Slowly the returning sensation to his hand announced itself by excruciating pain. 'Je souffre!' he exclaimed, words which from a man of his endurance had more than ordinary significance. Thoughts rushed through Tyndall's mind, that he should be in some way responsible for Balmat losing his hands and he even thought of schemes he might devise to support the guide and his family should he lose the use of his hands. At Chamonix with good medical advice Balmat lost six nails but his hands were saved.[31]

On his return to Mont Blanc in the summer of 1859 Tyndall could not find the thermometer that he had buried on the summit the year before. This time he arrived at the Grands Mulets with a party of twenty-six porters carrying a number of wooden poles shod with iron to which minimum thermometers were to be attached; these were placed at five stations located between the bottom of the Bossons Glacier and the summit. Tyndall, Dr Frankland and Balmat, plus two other guides and six porters brought a tent to the summit; it was 10 feet (3.05m) in diameter and they all crammed into it. Disturbed by their novel surroundings, the guides and porters displayed a temper 'very like mutiny', Tyndall wrote.[32] They erected posts at each station buried 6 feet (2m) under and standing 6 feet over the ground. A minimum thermometer was placed in the snow or ice and a maximum/minimum thermometer in the air.

That Christmas Tyndall returned to Chamonix and walked in deep snow up to Montanvert Hotel with Edouard Simond, another guide, and four porters to measure the daily flow rate of movement in winter of the Mer de Glace. They staked out two lines of poles across the glacier, 150 yards (137.2m) apart. The experiment demonstrated that the maximum winter motion of the glacier was half that measured and recorded by him at the same place in summer 1857. He demonstrated his determination and dedication to his work by completing these observations in a blinding snow-storm.[33]

In 1860 Tyndall was halted at the Grands Mulets and prevented by bad weather from reaching the summit, but he discovered that all the lower stations had been destroyed by storms; in

1861 he reported that the summit thermometers were damaged and found useless for observation purposes.[34] August 1861 saw him on his way to meet his guide Christian Lauener at Thun, when he met a fellow alpinist, Mr Vaughan Hawkins, who told Tyndall of his plans and wishes, 'which embraced an attack on the Matterhorn'.[35] Tyndall warmed up by climbing the Faulhorn by a pony track and descending by a more direct route through the pine woods to Grindelwald. The next couple of days he acclimatised by carrying out measurements of the motion of the Grindelwald glacier with the assistance of Hawkins and Lauener. The next route they undertook was the first ascent of the Lauwinen-Thor, which involved climbing up a steep couloir filled with avalanche debris.

Tyndall took to the crags on the right and made good progress until he came to a clear and smooth vertical face where further progress was impossible and any retreat dangerous. He had to call to Lauener for assistance and the guide cut steps to reach him from the couloir. The guide then excelled himself and followed the steep couloir to reach

The ascent of Lauwinen-thor, an etching by Whymper in *Hours of Exercise in the Alps* by John Tyndall (1871). (Courtesy the Alpine Club archives)

the top of the col which the Breithorn overlooks. It took them seven hours from the base of the barrier to the top of the col from where they descended to the Märjelen See and soon found themselves in darkness on the spurs of the Æggischhorn. They lost the track and for a time wandered bewildered until a shout from one of the guides was returned by a local herdsman, who soon undertook the guide's role. Shortly they found themselves under the roof of Herr Wellig, the proprietor of the Jungfrau Hotel. Following this experience Hawkins and Tyndall felt ready for bigger things.

On 18 August rumours reached Tyndall and Hawkins at Breuil regarding an accident on the Col du Géant, which had killed a guide named Tairraz and three Englishmen.[36] Tyndall met the dead guide's brother at Aosta three days later and became determined to find out the facts. He received a written account of the accident and a sketch from the resident French pastor, M. Curie, who had visited the scene and agreed to accompany him back there. They reached the place at the bottom of a rocky couloir where the bodies had come to rest, and found a compass and penknife that belonged to the victims. Tyndall and a local man familiar with climbing the Col followed the furrow that still marked the line of the fatal descent. They found a new ice axe owned by one of the two guides who had survived the accident. Tyndall was convinced there was insufficient reason for this terrible catastrophe, as the snow slope where the accident occurred was only a 45° incline. He contended that at all events a skilful mountaineer might throw himself prostrate on such a slope with perfect reliance on his power to arrest his downward motion. It appears that one of the men had fallen and the momentum of his fall had jerked the man behind him off his feet, causing the other men attached to the rope to hurtle downwards in quick succession. Tyndall was critical of the rope technique employed, by which the guides were not tied into the rope but rather held it looped around one hand with the ice axe in the other. He enquired as to the effort that had been made to check the fearful rush and at what point in descent the two guides had finally relinquished the rope. Which one of them had let go first, he asked? All that was publicly known about the event was that the two guides that had led and tail-ended the party had let go of the rope and escaped – while the three Englishmen and Tairraz fell to their deaths.

He contended that had the guides been tied in they would have been able to use both hands to drive the spiked shaft into the snow before sufficient momentum was exerted by the slip. The lost ice axe and baton of the two guides were evidence, he maintained, that their reaction to the fall had been to grasp the rope with both hands and consequently let go of the axe, the only means of anchoring the party to the slope. He concluded his comment on the disaster: 'Tairraz was in the midst of the party. Whether it was in his power to rescue himself or not, whether he was caught in the coil of rope or laid hold of by one of his companions, we can never know. Let us believe that he clung to them loyally, and went with them to death sooner than desert the post of duty.'[37]

Tyndall had joined the Alpine Club on 27 November 1858 at a Club meeting when twenty-one new members were elected, including Leslie Stephen and Joseph Chamberlain (the industrialist, politician and father of the future British prime minister, Neville Chamberlain). The Carlow man was highly regarded and seen by many in the Club, including Ball, as both a leading climber and a great man of science, personifying the two main aims of the Club. With Ball due for retirement as president in 1860, it was not unreasonable to consider that Tyndall might be his successor. However, his attack on Forbes' glaciation theories in his own book, *Glaciers of the Alps* (published in the same year that Ball retired), militated against his appointment as successor to Ball, a fact that Ball himself acknowledged in a letter to Tyndall, mentioning in his next breath the man who would be elected in Tyndall's stead:

> I merely cease to be President of Alpine Club by virtue of law: having held it for 3 years ... Though I knew it was doubtful whether you could give the little time required my wish was that you might be induced to take my place ... Meanwhile, however, in addition to the doubt whether you would accept, the glacier controversy has waxed hotter (be hanged to it) and though no one who has spoken to me is in the least influenced one way or the other – it was feared that in some quarter or other that might interfere with the thorough cordiality with which the proposition would otherwise have been received by every

individual in the Club. This being the case I am sure that I acted as you might wish your friend to act by advising that the choice should fall on a completely neutral man who will have time to attend whenever wanted. The worthy Kennedy does not care, so long as he has glaciers and peaks to climb, whether the ice moves uphill or down and at the present moment he is the best man we can have. I trust you will not think of leaving the Club.[38]

There is no record of Tyndall's reply but its content may be gleaned from another of Ball's letters, which indicates that Tyndall was contemplating resigning from the Club:

I quite understand that the Alpine Club and its affairs are of infinitesimal importance to you, but as you have joined the body and contributed to its volume and there is in it the promise for future work of a kind that you may turn to real good account, I think it is a pity that you should separate from it. You should not misconceive the feelings of the men in it towards yourself. Several, and those the men whose minds run beyond mere climbing, have spoken or written their wish to see you President both as an honour to the Club and as giving a prospect of future good guidance. Others look on you simply as the boldest and most successful mountaineer and would on that score welcome you as their chief. If you would have taken the place there would certainly have been no opposition but I was led to fear that among a very few who have been affected by recent controversies there might be a want of cordiality instead of the unanimous acclamation that I desired. Perhaps I was wrong.

Be this as it may I am still desirous that you should not leave the Club and especially at the moment when you doing so will be misunderstood. If you are fixed on so doing let me suggest that it would be a graceful thing for you – if not too inconvenient – to come to the dinner on the 13th and propose Kennedy's health. If you can do so I think it would be well, whether you remain or leave the Club especially in the latter case.

Pray send me Rendu. I will return it as soon as you please.[39]

Ball's diplomacy was effective; Edward Shirley Kennedy (one of the Club's founders) was elected president and Tyndall did not resign. The committee meeting on 7 November 1861 altered the Club rules for the express purpose of enabling the members to ensure Tyndall's services as a vice-president; it was proposed to increase the number of vice-presidents to two and that Tyndall should be offered the new office. The proposal being accepted by the Club, Honorary Secretary A. P. Whately wrote to Tyndall on 4 December:

I have great pleasure in informing you that you were last night unanimously elected to the new Vice Presidentship of the Alpine Club. The committee have long been desirous of including you among their number, and have, on more than one occasion, been prevented from requesting you to allow yourself to be put in nomination, only by feeling that your engagements were such as must prevent you from attending the meetings, while the numbers of the committee and officers were not sufficiently large to allow any absent members. This difficulty has at last been met by the creation of a new Vice Presidentship for the express purpose of connecting our more distinguished members more closely with the governing body of the club than has hitherto been possible. And you will I hope understand that though nothing could give us greater pleasure than to see you at the committee meetings (for which you will receive due notice) yet that you are not to be considered as being under any obligation whatever to take any more active part in the club affairs than your own convenience suggests.[40]

Tyndall accepted the office, but never attended a committee meeting. At the winter dinner in 1861 the Rev. Leslie Stephen, another intellectual and leading light in the Club who had become a member at the same time as Tyndall, reflected his contempt for the value of science with respect to mountaineering. In his speech Stephen gave a mock account of an ascent of the then unclimbed Ober Gabelhorn and asked mischievously 'why those fanatics [scientists] have irrevocably associated Alpine travelling with science'.[41] Stephen would later read a paper at a Club meeting on 4 April 1865, which lampooned the scientists. It was published in the next *Alpine Journal* and recounted his ascent of the Rothorn in which he repeated his disregard for those who were seriously engaged in combining both the scientific and mountaineering aims of the club of which Tyndall was the publicly best known.[42]

Stephen had previously made fun in an article in the first volume of *The Alpine Journal*:

As it was we mounted with the loss of only one of the party. This was the thermometer which a benevolent but weak disposition had induced me to carry 'for scientific purposes'. To my inexpressible delight, it escaped from my hands, which were rather numbed by the cold, just as I took it out at the summit, and rattling merrily down the glacier slopes, disappeared from our sight. It may probably be found by a scientific gentleman who will drag the Œschinen See, immediately under the waterfalls in the south eastern corner, and I will make them a present of it for his trouble.[43]

Tyndall was sensitive to such taunting and shortly after wrote a letter of resignation to Whately.

When I accepted the vice presidentship of the Alpine Club I fully hoped to be able to attend your meetings and to fulfil to some extent at least the duties of my position. For a long time previous however I had entertained the idea that I ought to withdraw from the club, as I felt that I was a mere cumberer of the ground.

This idea has become stronger than ever within the last few days. I am and shall be oppressed with work and hence it is utterly impossible for me to attend your meetings or to do anything which could practicably promote the interests of your body. I therefore with regret ask you to accept my resignation . . . My brain at present is rushed almost to its bearing limits: Do not ask me therefore to correspond further on this matter.[44]

Despite Tyndall's request for no further correspondence on the matter Whately replied on 17 December 1861 informing him he had not the authority to accept his resignation but he would lay his letter before the committee at their next meeting, while expressing his personal regret for 'this most unpleasant duty'. On 27 January he reported to the committee that Tyndall had withdrawn from the Club.

When Forbes died on 31 December 1868, Adams-Reilly was one of the three biographers who shared the task of describing the various aspects of his life and work as a scientist, educator and pioneer alpine traveller. Reilly wrote three chapters dedicated to his hero's work as an alpine explorer, describing him adoringly 'as the father of Alpine adventure'. The last chapter of the book, entitled 'Forbes' contributions to our knowledge of glaciers', stresses in the opening paragraph the great care taken (by Forbes) to credit everyone who, to his knowledge, had previously published on the subject. It charges writers (such as Tyndall) who had accused Forbes of depreciating or suppressing the claims of others with 'not taking the trouble to read carefully what they criticised'. It then claims that 'the work of Rendu was so mixed up with error that it does not appear likely that in his hands it could have led to anything definite; for Rendu holds and enunciates, sometimes in the same sentence, facts, and errors utterly incompatible with them.'[45]

A letter of congratulation to Forbes from Rendu, dated 17 August 1844, is attached as evidence of Rendu's endorsement of Forbes' research, which proved the prelate's theory. The crux of this argument in favour of Forbes' integrity seems to be that Forbes' claimed Rendu offered four or five theories without indicating his preference – and that Forbes proved one of these theories to be correct. In Appendix A of the book is a paper by Forbes (dated 1860) in reply to Tyndall's remarks (in *Glaciers of the Alps*) about Forbes and his use of Rendu's theories. In Appendix B another paper by Forbes ('Remarks on the first discovery of the real structure of glacier ice'[46]) is also reprinted in answer to Forbes' critics. Tyndall felt obliged to respond to the reopening of the controversy with a bitter pamphlet entitled *Principal Forbes and his Biographers*, published in London in 1873. It is clear that Tyndall's criticism of Forbes' work was deeply resented by the latter's many friends and colleagues.

Time, in this case, did heal the old sores. Tyndall (like Forbes before him) was unanimously elected an honorary member of the Alpine Club in 1887.

Tyndall began the season of 1861 with a traverse from Meiringen of the Urbachthal and the Gauli Glacier from the Haslital to the Grimsel Pass. He was accompanied on this excursion by W. E. Forster, who had recently been elected MP for Bradford and was later Chief Secretary for Ireland (1880–1882). The expedition was led by Bennen supporting Tyndall, followed by a guide named Wenger, engaged by Forster whom Tyndall refers to as 'the statesman'. During this route they had to climb up over a deep bergschrund and ascend an exposed slope above that was steeper 'than a cathedral roof', whilst below them was 'a chasm into which it would be certain death to fall'. Bennen led, striking his ice axe above his head and pulling himself above the deep chasm of ice where he anchored himself to bring Tyndall up behind him. Tyndall remarked:

> I am speedily at his side, and we both tighten the rope as our friend Forster advances. With perfect courage and a faultless head, he has but one disadvantage, and that is an excess of weight of at least two stone. In his first attempt the snow-ledge breaks, and he falls back; but two men are now at the rope, the tension of which, aided by his own activity, prevents him from sinking far. By a second effort he clears the difficulty, is followed by his guide, and all four of us reach the slope above the chasm.[47]

They passed a few days at the Eggishorn and Bel Alp from where Tyndall, with Bennen and Wenger, moved to Randa to attempt the previously unclimbed Weisshorn.

From the Grimsel Hotel Tyndall strolled up the Sidelhorn one afternoon and stood on its broken summit observing the panorama on the opposite side of the Rhone valley. He wrote later of 'the Mischabel with its crowd of snowy cones . . . [and] the stupendous cone of the Weisshorn which slopes to meet the inclines of the Mischabel and in the wedge of space carved out between the two the Matterhorn lifts it terrible head'.[48] He was looking at his next theatre of operations, the field that would define him as a mountaineer. He next moved to the Hotel Jungfrau on the slopes of the Eggishorn and in the evening walked to its summit alone, from which he observed the mountains of the Oberland that feed the great Aletsch Glacier and the Valais connecting beyond to Italy and France.

He next set out to Bel Alp to stay at its new hotel in company with Bennen and Hirst. They met a group of people looking down into a crevasse and stopped lest a person had fallen in between its icy jaws. They found an unfortunate cow firmly jammed between the frozen sides and groaning piteously. Bennen took over and soon ice splinters began to fly. With ropes round the animal's horns and between its back legs, the cow was slowly extricated by the party 'like mariners heaving an anchor', all hands pulling and gaining a little each time, until the beast's forelegs gripped the ice edge and it was panting and trembling on the surface.

On 15 August Tyndall set out to climb the Sparrenhorn, which was two hours walk from Bel Alp; he found the scene strikingly beautiful. 'Nowhere have I seen more perfect repose, nowhere more tender curves or finer structural lines', he said regarding the grandeur of the Dom, the Cervin and the Weisshorn. Next day he descended Bel Alp for Brig and, taking a carriage to Visp, he walked with a porter to the village of Randa in the Mattertal. He had sent Bennen ahead to make preparations for what would be his greatest mountaineering achievement to date.

On 18 August 1861 Tyndall, with guides Bennen and Wenger, left the hotel at Randa. Bennen, at Tyndall's behest, had gone in advance to reconnoitre one of the last unclimbed 4,000m peaks of the Alps and entertained hopes of success. Wenger (who had guided Forster on the Strahleck) had impressed Tyndall, so he asked Bennen to hire him for the climb. Tyndall was feeling unwell and suffered from intense thirst. At a chalet two hours out he drank from a pail of fresh milk, which seemed to have miraculous effects on the scientist. 'It seemed to lubricate every atom of my body, and to exhilarate with its fragrance my brain.'

They reached their bivouac site, which was a ledge of rock jutting from the mountainside to form an overhanging roof. Tyndall's bed was made softer when Wenger removed the stones and considerably loosened the dry clay by stirring it with his axe. From his bed, lying on his left side, he commanded a view of the whole range of Monte Rosa, from the Mischabel to the Breithorn. Bennen had chosen the east ridge or *grat* as the route, because it was the most accessible of the three arêtes that intersect the three great faces of the colossal natural pyramid. When he skirted the mountain before supper with Bennen, his hopes sank as he began to comprehend the size and scale of the undertaking. The scientist, using the precise language of his profession, tells us that for supper Wenger produced a cheese section that he melted in the flames of their pine fire, and which 'fizzed and blistered and turned viscous' before being consumed with relish by them all. From his bed he witnessed the sunset:

Which had been unspeakably grand, steeping the zenith in violet, and flooding the base of the heavens with crimson light . . . After sunset the purple of the east changed to a deep neutral tint, and against the faded red which spread above it the sun-forsaken mountains laid their cold and ghastly heads. The ruddy colour vanished more and more; the stars strengthened in lustre, until finally the moon and they held undisputed possession of the sky.

They quit their bivouac at 3.30 a.m. and, seeing that there were no clouds in the sky, he 'disburdened' himself of his strong shooting jacket on the edge of the first snowfield. The sunbeams and his own exertion would keep him warm, he declared. Unroped, they first crossed snow, then cut their way through a piece of entangled glacier to reach and cross a bergschrund, which led up a frozen snow couloir to reach the bottom of the eastern arête of the great mountain. Crossing a snow saddle, they commenced rock-climbing cautiously up rock towers formed out of huge blocks and loose chips. 'The work was heavy from the first, the bending, twisting, reaching, and drawing up calling upon all the muscles of the frame.' After two hours of steady progress they looked back to observe two figures on the glacier, one carrying an axe, the other a knapsack and alpenstock. They realised that they might be challenged for 'the honour of the enterprise' by some of Randa's best climbers who had unsuccessfully asked Bennen to include them in the party. Tyndall wrote: 'On this point, however, our uneasiness was small.'

Resuming their gymnastics, the rocky staircase led them to a flat summit of a tower, separated from a similar tower by a deep gap. Bennen, with rope tied around his waist, was lowered and descended till he reached a ledge to which he fixed himself; Tyndall and Wenger followed one at a time. From there they reached the far tower from which they continued along the ridge behind it. The ridge was a mere cornice of snow, becoming narrower until it was a knife edge of fine-grained, moist powder. Bennen tested the snow by squeezing it with his foot and, to Tyndall's astonishment, 'the space he had to stand on did not exceed a hand-breadth'; then he began to cross it. Tyndall followed him 'exactly as a boy walking along a horizontal pole with toes turned outwards. Right and left the precipices were

Whymper's Weisshorn etching from Tyndall's *Glaciers of the Alps*

appalling. When they reached the opposite rock, Bennen was smiling toward Tyndall. He knew he had done a daring thing, though not a presumptuous one.

The rocks on the ridge they now passed were so loose that great caution was required to avoid starting rockfalls. It was hot and they halted at intervals where melted snow provided veins of liquid. A bottle of champagne, poured sparingly into their goblets over a little snow, provided Tyndall and Wenger with many refreshing draughts. Bennen feared his eyes, and would not touch champagne. Tyndall reflected: 'There is scarcely a position possible to a human being which, at one time or another during the day, I was not forced to assume. The fingers, wrist, and forearm were my main reliance, and as a mechanical instrument the human hand appears to me this day to be a miracle of constructive art.' Five hours after setting out they saw the summit over another minor summit, which gave it an elusive proximity. 'You have now good hopes' remarked Tyndall. Bennen replied, 'I do not allow myself to entertain the idea of failure.'

After three more hours on the East Grat (as the ridge is now locally known) using the same level of physical effort, they reached another false summit from where Bennen fixed his weary eye on the distant summit. Tyndall wrote: 'Bennen laid his face upon his axe for a moment; a kind of sickly despair was in his eye as he turned to me remarking, "Lieber herr, die Spitze ist noch weit oben."' Tyndall told his guide he must not persist on his account. Bennen said he was weary, but was quite sure of himself. He asked for food, and took a gulp of wine which mightily refreshed him. Looking at the mountain with a firmer eye he defiantly exclaimed, 'Herr! Wir müssen ihn haben!', and his voice, as he spoke, 'rang like steel within my heart.' Tyndall, on reflection, equated Bennen's fighting quality 'to fighting for duty even after they had ceased to be animated by hope.'

Continuing as before, another top now fronted them and they had no idea at what distance the summit lay behind that top. They scaled that height and above them, but clearly within reach, the silver pyramid projected itself against the blue sky. Tyndall was repeatedly assured by his companions that this was surely the highest point. He feared 'that it might take rank with the illusions which had so often beset our ascent' and he shrank 'from the consequent moral shock'. A huge prism of granite ended the arête and from it a knife-edge of pure white snow ran up to a little point. They passed along the edge, reached that point, and 'instantly swept with our eyes the whole range of the horizon. We stood upon the crown of the redoubtable Weisshorn.'

Bennen shook his arm in the air and shouted as a Valaisian, while Wenger raised the shriller yell of the Oberland. They looked downwards along the ridge and far below, perched on one of the crags, they could discern the two Randa men. Again and again the roar of triumph was sent down to them. They were not far along the ridge and turned back soon after to bring word of the success of the Tyndall party. When the two men arrived in the village, nobody in Randa would believe them that the Weisshorn had been scaled and it took the 'energy of their conviction' for their story to be believed by the most sceptical before Tyndall arrived.

The ascent had taken ten hours from their bivouac to the summit. Tyndall dispensed with his usual practice of making scientific observation. 'There was something incongruous, if not profane, in allowing the scientific faculty to interfere where silent worship seemed the reasonable service.' Bennen's red pocket handkerchief tied to the handle of one of their axes provided a visible sign of their success. It was seen from the Riffelberg Hotel and was still visible, to Bennen's extreme delight, three days later.

The descent to Randa took ten and a half hours to complete, during which time they had to take great care while back-climbing over loose rock and down steep icy couloirs. Tyndall had a basin of broth and a piece of mutton 'boiled probably for the fifth time' and a footbath before going to bed where six hours of sound sleep chased away all consciousness of fatigue. The scientist 'was astonished on the morrow to find the loose atoms of my body knitted so firmly by so brief a rest.'

The last great unclimbed peak of the Alps was now the Matterhorn and Tyndall and Bennen set their sights on its conquest. Alas, they were not the only ones.

The story of the Matterhorn's ascent spans a seven-year period of intense effort and John Tyndall was one of main players in the dramatic saga. His climbing of the Weisshorn (4,506m) with Bennen in 1861 left the Matterhorn as the main focus of their attention. To ambitious mountaineers the Matterhorn represented the last significant Alpine peak left to be climbed. Edward Whymper was another Alpine Club member who had serious ambitions to be the first to its summit. He was only twenty-two years old in 1861 when he made the first British ascent of Mont Pelvoux (4,103m) in the Dauphiné range. An artist and engraver by profession, his introduction to the Alps the previous year had arisen from a commission to illustrate Alpine scenes for publication. These skills were employed to good effect to illustrate Tyndall's first mountaineering publication, *Glaciers of the Alps*. Like Tyndall he was a bold climber with a practical streak. However, there were good reasons why the picturesque Matterhorn was still unclimbed. All the ridges of the great rock pyramid are steep and from the valley floor look very formidable, both from the Italian and Swiss sides; at that time local guides, particularly those on the Swiss side, were totally convinced of the mountain's impregnability.

Tyndall was among the first to explore the mountain seriously in 1860 when he and his faithful Oberland guide, Johan Bennen, were invited to join forces with an English climber, Vaughan Hawkins, to attempt the mountain from the Italian side. Hawkins and Bennen had inspected the Matterhorn in 1859 and had formed the opinion that the southwest ridge would lead to the summit.[52] At Breuil on the Italian side they inquired for a man to carry their sacks. Jean-Jacques Carrel was pointed out to them as the best mountaineer in the whole Val Tournenche valley. He was an experienced chamois hunter who had made several attempts on the Matterhorn between 1858 and 1859 in the company of several other locals,

J. J. Bennen of Laak

including a cleric named Abbé Gorret and his own nephew, Jean-Antoine Carrel. Jean-Antoine was a recently discharged soldier who had fought in the Second Italian War of Independence. These local attempts had concentrated on the southwest ridge, passing the Col Tournenche to reach the Tête du Lion, where they stopped at a steep chimney at 12,500 feet (3,810m). Despite that setback the younger Carrel still harboured an ambition to make the first ascent from the Italian side with an Italian party. He was convinced that the Swiss side was impregnable and secretly hoped that he would be the one to lead a successful Italian effort on Monte Cervino (the Italian name for the mountain) from the Italian side. Bennen and Hawkins had examined the Matterhorn the previous year from all sides. Bennen was convinced it was possible to reach the summit from the Italian side. Meanwhile three brothers from Liverpool, Alfred, Charles and Sandbach Parker, had made an unsuccessful guideless attempt from Zermatt that took them 11,000 feet (3,350m) up the formidable east face.

On 3 August 1860 Tyndall and Hawkins, with Bennen and Jean-Jacques Carrel as guides, reached the Col du Lion by climbing rocks that abutted against the Couloir du Lion on the mountain's south side. They climbed with difficulty to about 300 feet (91m) above the Col to reach the foot of the Great Tower (12,992 feet/3,960m). A height of about 13,050 feet (3,980m) was reached by Bennen and Tyndall before they turned back when daylight ran out.

The Parkers returned the following July (1861), again without guides. They climbed 200 feet (61m) higher, again on the east face from Zermatt. On 28 August Edward Whymper made his first impact on the scene when he arrived at Breuil. He had previously been in the area in 1860 and was fascinated by the Matterhorn and Weisshorn, both of which he hoped to climb. Since the Weisshorn had fallen to Tyndall on 18 August, he was anxious to get to grips with the majestic and picturesque Matterhorn. At Breuil he learned that Tyndall and Bennen had been there a day or two before 'without doing anything'.[53] It seems that Tyndall had sent Bennen to reconnoitre and to find some ledge or cranny where three men might spend a night and increase the possibility of reaching the summit in a day. However, Bennen's report shocked him:

> Herr, I have examined the mountain carefully, and find it more difficult and dangerous than I had imagined. There is no place upon it where we could pass the night. We might do so on yonder Col upon the snow, but there we should be almost frozen to death and totally unfit for the work the next day. On the rocks there is no ledge or cranny which could give us proper harbourage; and starting from Breuil it is certainly impossible to reach the summit in a single day. [54]

Tyndall was entirely taken aback by this report: 'I felt like a man whose grip had given way, and who was dropping through the air.' Bennen was evidently dead against any attempt upon the mountain, but Tyndall remarked, ' . . . we can, at all events, reach the lower of the two summits.' Bennen's reply to this proposal lays bare the guide's own motivation: 'even that is difficult, but when you have reached it, what then? The peak has neither name nor fame.' Later, Tyndall reflected on the conversation between them: 'Bennen made his report with his eyes open. He knew me well, and I think mutual trust has rarely been more strongly developed between guide and traveller than between him and me. I knew I only had but to give the word and he would face the mountain with me next day, but it would have been inexcusable in me to deal thus with him.'

Whymper was also having guide problems. He found Jean-Antoine Carrel back home from further service in the army, but Carrel wanted to wait for a friend to accompany them. The delay did not suit Whymper who immediately found himself another guide. But when he tried to procure the services of a second guide, all refused; indeed, one man wanted to be paid 200 francs, whether the expedition proved successful or not. This Whymper considered a prohibitive amount. He climbed to the Col du Lion with a single guide, where they slept wrapped in a new tent he had purchased 'which had looked very pretty when set up in London'. However, when pitched on the mountain 'it exhibited so marked a desire to go to the top of the Dent Blanche that we thought it prudent to take it down and sit upon it'.[55] The next day he arrived at the Cheminée and when the guide was unable to make progress Whymper got higher unassisted, but his guide would not follow. Whymper called him a coward and told him to go back to Breuil and mention he had left his 'Monsieur' on the mountain. When the man turned to go, Whymper asked him to come back to help him down safely, so he was obliged to give up at the Chimney (12,000 foot/3,650m).

Carrel, in the meantime, had taken his uncle Jean-Jacques with him and, climbing in clear view of Whymper, had reached a point named Crête du Coq at 13,230 feet (4,032.5m). He marked his high point (which was 180 feet/55m higher than Tyndall's highest point) with his initials, a cross and the date. Carrel, asserting his own right and desire to climb the mountain, had made his independence of the 'Monsieur' clear. Whymper was later told that Jean-Jacques Carrel had dropped one of his shoes and descended the mountain with a piece of cord and a handkerchief wrapped around his naked foot.

Whymper, acutely aware that a successful ascent of the Matterhorn would require a night to be spent high on the mountain, turned his attention to tents. He devised a ridge tent that would combine portability with lightness and stability and have capacity for four people.[56] Its base measured 6 square feet (0.56m²), and it was made from four ash poles, each 6½ feet (1.9m) long, with the ends pointed and shod with metal. The poles were drilled at the top to take a ¼ inch (6mm) diameter bolt; a cord tied to the right length was to be used to provide the ridge support. A single piece of calico 6 feet (1.83m) wide was thrown over the cord; the calico had sufficient length to allow 2 feet (0.61m) on each side to be tucked in under the floor. A Mackintosh plaid measuring 9 square feet (0.84²) provided the floor covering, and was large enough for the surplus material to continue up the sides to prevent draughts. One end of the tent was then permanently closed by a triangular piece of calico that was sewn onto the calico already in position. The other end provided the entrance, which was two triangular flaps that overlapped each other and could be fastened up by pieces of tape when the campers were inside. The tent was further secured by passing the end of a climbing rope over the poles and under the ridge, then fixing this to rocks for stability. The tent was identical in all essential points to the one developed by the Dundalk man, Sir Leopold McClintock, during his Arctic exploration work. It seems that Whymper had also constructed a smaller and lighter version of his tent for Professor Tyndall after the same pattern, substituting canes for the ash poles. This tent was lower and narrower and weighed less than 7 lb (3 kg).[57]

In January 1862 T. S. Kennedy of Leeds, one of the founders of the Alpine Club, attempted a winter ascent of the Matterhorn, climbing the east face from Zermatt to reach 11,000 feet (3,350m): 'till a gust fiercer than usual forced us to shelter for a time behind a rock. Immediately it was tacitly understood that our expedition must now end.'[58] Whymper arrived at Breuil in July that year with Mr Reginald Macdonald and two Swiss guides. However, cold and wind repulsed this early season attempt at 12,000 feet (3,650m). Jean-Antoine Carrel was in Breuil when Whymper came down and agreed to accompany him with another Italian guide named Pession and a hunchback porter name Luc Meynet. The Swiss guides were quickly dismissed and Whymper and Macdonald returned with the local guides on 9 July. They bivouacked above the Cheminée. They had to turn back before they reached Carrel's high point due to Pession's insistence on returning.

Whymper then hastened to Zermatt and inspected the Hörnli route, which he judged to be impractical. The want of guides at Zermatt drove him back to the Italian side to seek Carrel and Meynet but, to his frustration, both were engaged and unavailable. As a consequence Whymper decided to climb back up to where he had left his tent, which was buried in the snow. Next morning he continued his ascent, climbing the Cheminée to the base of the Great Tower. At one stage he soloed up a gully 'with minute ledges and steep walls . . . ledges dwindling away and at last ceasing . . . finding myself, with arms and legs divergent, fixed as if crucified, pressing against the rock, and feeling each rise and fall of my chest as I breathed . . . screwing my head round to look for hold, and not seeing any, and . . . jumping sideways on to the other side.' He reflected on 'the enchantment of such experiences', which 'arose from the calls made on his faculties, in their demands on his strength, and in overcoming the impediments which they opposed to his skill.[59]

Attaining a height of 13,500 feet (4,100m), he stopped at a remarkable piece of snow known as 'Cravate' and returned to his tent well satisfied with his progress, only regretting he had no companion to continue the climb to the summit. However, he left his ice axe behind in the tent when he set out to descend towards Breuil later in the evening. He was to regret his imprudence when he slipped and fell while passing over some iced-over rocks. He fell nearly 200 feet (61m), striking his head four or five times, with blood spurting out from more than 20 cuts. The most serious bleeding in his head he stopped by covering the wound with a big lump of snow just before he fainted. The sun had already set when he regained consciousness and, taking great care, he descended the last 5,000 feet (1,500m) to Breuil. The locals rubbed hot wine mixed with salt into his wounds.

It was a week before he set out again for the Matterhorn. This time Carrel agreed to accompany him with César Carrel (Jean-Jacques' son) and the porter Luc Maynet. They had succeeded in passing the Great Tower when bad weather overtook them, forcing them to descend. Whymper wanted to go again the next day but Carrel was nowhere to be found, so he went up with just the porter Luc Meynet whom Whymper had come to rely on and to trust. They passed Whymper's highest point but, overcome by the difficulty of surmounting steep and unstable rock, they returned. It was Whymper's fifth attempt that year. He decided to return to Breuil to have a light ladder made to 'overcome some of the steepest parts'.

When he arrived at the inn he found, to his surprise, that John Tyndall and the guides Bennen and Anton Walter were already there. To add to Whymper's understandable frustration, the Irishman had already engaged Jean-Antoine Carrel

Whymper's tent

Whymper's fall from his book *Scrambles in the Alps*

and César Carrel as porters. Tyndall had a ladder already prepared and the group were collecting provisions to start next morning. Whymper was astonished at the disloyalty of the Carrels and the change in Bennen's attitude to climbing the Matterhorn; he suddenly found himself guideless. Different accounts of what transpired next between Tyndall and Whymper were later related by each man. It is clear from both accounts that Whymper put his tent and the material in it at Tyndall's disposal. In the first edition of *Hours of Exercise in the Alps* (1871) Tyndall simply records: 'At night Mr Whymper returned from the Matterhorn, having left his tent upon the rocks. In the frankest spirit, he placed it at my disposal, and thus relieved me from the necessity of carrying up my own.'[60] However in the second edition, which was issued later in 1871, he elaborated regarding this exchange with an 'additional note':

It certainly would have enhanced the pleasure of my excursion if Mr Whymper could have accompanied me. I admired his courage and devotion. He had manifestly set his heart upon the Matterhorn, and it was my earnest desire that he should not be disappointed. I consulted with Bennen who had heard many accounts – probably exaggerated ones – of Mr Whymper's rashness. He shook his head, but finally agreed that Mr Whymper should be invited 'provided he proved reasonable'. I thereupon asked Mr Whymper to join us. His reply was, 'If I go up the Matterhorn I must lead the way'. Considering my own experience at the time as compared with his; considering, still more, the renown and power of my guide, I thought the response the reverse of reasonable, and so went on my way alone.

Tyndall, then aged forty-one, was a well-respected mountaineer and scientist in his full powers. His guide was of proven ability and had his full trust. Whymper, on the other hand, must have appeared to Tyndall as an impetuous young man; he was just twenty-two years old, with only a couple of years of alpine experience and a reputation for impetuosity, as evidenced by his recent fall and injuries.

Whymper's account of the exchange in *Scrambles amongst the Alps* differs significantly from Tyndall's:

An hour or so after he had accepted my offer (Tent etc.) he came to me and said (in a way which I thought seemed to imply that the answer might not be in the affirmative), 'Mr Whymper, would you like to accompany us?' I replied warmly, 'Certainly I should; it is the very thing I should like,' or words to that effect. Dr Tyndall then went on to say, 'If you come with us you must place yourself under Bennen's guidance; you must obey his instructions; you must follow his lead, and so forth.' Now I was quite ready to place myself under Bennen; I should have done so as a matter of course had I accompanied the party. But being called to declare that I would implicitly obey his instructions whether they were right or wrong, I could hardly avoid saying, 'You will remember Dr Tyndall, that I have been much higher than Bennen, and have been eleven days on the mountain, whilst he has been on it only for a single day. You will not expect me to follow him if he is evidently wrong? It was sometime afterwards, half an hour or more before Dr Tyndall came to me and said, 'Well, after all, I think that you had better not accompany us.'[61]

Tyndall, having employed all the guides available, had left Whymper without options. It is clear he made no allowance for Whymper's youthful brashness when having deferred to Bennen, thus he made the harsh decision to exclude his youthful rival. Whymper, whose climbing plans were upended by the arrival of Tyndall, must have been very angry at Carrel's betrayal and was bound to be argumentative with Tyndall who was clearly holding all the cards. The older man's response to Whymper, a fellow member of the Alpine Club, would appear short of generosity.

Leaving the hotel at midday, Tyndall and Bennen made their way to Whymper's campsite. A huge rockfall greeted the party on their way to the foot of the Great Tower. Rocks split 'into fragments as it smote one of the rocky towers in front of them'.

Whymper had re-ascended the mountain to recover some necessities from his tent that he had left at the Tower, but he waited at his campsite to welcome 'the Professor' before descending. They arose at 2 a.m. to a star-filled sky. Carrel made the fire and made coffee. They started at 4 a.m. Bennen and Walters combined to climb a steep wall giving each other assistance with pushes and pulls:

Bennen was close behind aiding him with an arm, a knee, or a shoulder. Once upon a ledge he was able to give Bennen a hand. Thus we advanced, straining, bending and clinging to the rocks with a grasp like that of desperation, but with heads perfectly cool. We perched upon ledges in succession – each in the first place making his leader secure, and accepting his help afterwards. A last strong effort threw the body of Walters across the top of the wall; and he being safe, our success thus far ensured.[62]

They were back on the ridge again and were approaching the conical summit seen from Breuil, which is positioned on the end of a nearly horizontal ridge. Within their grasp was surely the highest point of the Matterhorn. 'We shall at all events win the lower summit,' remarked Tyndall to Bennen. 'That will not satisfy us,' was the reply. At that moment they felt sure that within an hour they would stand on the top. They planted a flag on the first summit and followed the sharp ridge that abutted against the final precipice 'while ghastly abysses fell on either side'. Finally they sat down, 'and inspected the place; no glasses were needed'; 'it was so near'. Three of the four men muttered almost simultaneously: 'it is impossible'.[63]

They moved to a point at the base of the precipice that looked hopeful. The ridge was split by a deep cleft, which separated it from the final precipice. Such a savage spot Tyndall had never seen. This cleft was subsequently named the Enjambée. He sat down:

> with the sickness of disappointed hope. The summit was within almost a stone's throw of us and the thought of retreat was bitter in the extreme. Bennen excitedly pointed out a track which he thought practicable. He spoke of danger, of difficulty, never of impossibility; but this was the ground taken by the other three men.[64]

Tyndall was in fact 700 feet (215m) short of the summit, though he clearly thought at the time that he was closer. It took Bennen half an hour to accept defeat. Tyndall wrote: 'What could he do? The other men had yielded utterly, and our occupation was clearly gone.' Whymper recounts Carrel's version of events when Bennen was stopped at the Enjambée: 'the Carrels would not act as guides after having been hired as porters.'[65] Tyndall (in his additional note to the second edition of *Hours of Exercise in the Alps*) wrote displaying his loyalty to his faithful guide Bennen: '. . . of the guides and porters, Bennen was the man who entertained a thought of going on, and both Walter and Carrel shrank from the danger of the last ascent.'[66] This statement would seem to ascribe cowardice or lack of willingness or ability to Carrel, when the Italian guide appears to have had an issue regarding his subordinate role as a porter to the Swiss guides Bennen and Walter. It is worth noting that Tyndall had already written in Carrel's logbook the following, seemingly conflicting, testimony:

> Jean-Antoine Carrel accompanied me up the Matterhorn on the 27th – 28th July 1862. He proved himself an extremely good man on this occasion. He is a very superior climber, and, I believe, an excellent guide. Many times during this ascent I had occasion to observe his skill and activity. He has served in two campaigns, has been at Novara and Solferino, and the discipline of a soldier's life renders him acquainted with many things which are useful to a mountaineer. I can express without reserve my entire satisfaction as regards Carrel's conduct through a very difficult day. Breuil 29th of July, 1862.[67]

Meanwhile, from the village of Breuil, Whymper had observed a flag flying on the top of the subsidiary peak on the Italian side that now carries Tyndall's name (Pic Tyndall). While descending, the party used part of the wooden ladder that Tyndall had manufactured to overcome difficulties at a place now named the Grande Corde. Whymper could not bring himself to leave Breuil 'until the result was heard', and he 'lingered about as a foolish lover hovers round the object of his affections, even after he has been contemptuously rejected.'[68] The sun had set when the men were observed coming over the pastures. 'There was no spring in their steps,' Whymper observed: 'they too were defeated.' 'The Carrels hid their heads and the others said, as men will do when they have been beaten, that the mountain was horrible, impossible, and so forth.' Tyndall told Whymper that 'they had arrived within a stone's throw of the summit', and admonished him to have nothing more to do with the mountain. He understood Tyndall to say he would not try again, as he was inclined to believe that the mountain was inaccessible. Tyndall left his ropes with the innkeeper to be placed at the disposal of any person who wished to ascend the mountain; this was more, Whymper thought, 'out of irony than for generosity'. No one tried again in 1862.

Whymper, in company with the Carrels and Luc Meynet, took up the challenge again in 1863; but they had only reached the Great Tower when they were overtaken by a violent snowstorm. Snowstorms the next day put paid to his sixth attempt. The Carrels told Whymper that Tyndall's defeat the previous year had occurred because Anton Walter did not give aid to Bennen when it was required, and that the Carrels 'would not act as guides after having been hired as porters'.[69]

Tyndall made his last climb with Bennen when the pair crossed the Oberaarjoch to the Eggishorn on 22 July 1863. The following February Bennen died with a client named Boissonnet when he was buried in an avalanche apparently started by his party on the Haut de Cry while attempting a winter ascent with three local guides and two travellers. In Tyndall's opinion: 'Bennen as a mountaineer had no superior, and he added to his strength, courage and skills the qualities of a natural gentleman.'[70] With reference

Whymper's picture of the cannonade from his book *Scrambles in the Alps*

to the fatal accident, he wrote: 'Bennen was well acquainted with winter snow; but no man of his temper, and in his position, would place himself in direct opposition to local guides, whose knowledge of the mountain must have been superior to his own.' It appears Bennen allowed himself to be overruled by local guides regarding the safety of the route chosen; it also seems that he made little attempt to arrest his own fall with his ice axe when the avalanche, started by one his party, pulled him down the slope.

At this time a young Italian scientist called Quentino Sella was planning the formation of an Italian Alpine Society, in company with Felice Giordano. Giordano had climbed Mont Blanc in 1862 from the Italian side via Mont Blanc du Tacul. This pair thought the first ascent of the Monte Cervino (Matterhorn) would bring honour to the new institution at its birth. Unbeknownst to Edward Whymper, they were planning an all-Italian ascent from Breuil using Jean-Antoine Carrel as their main guide. Whymper returned to Breuil in 1865. There followed another failed attempt by a different route, in company with the Chamonix guide Michel Croz, the Bernese guides Almer and Biener, and the ever reliable Luc Meynet. The climbing party was nearly swept away by an avalanche of stones. When Whymper requested another attempt via the Hörnli ridge, the guides refused. Almer asked Whymper, 'Why do you not attempt a mountain which can be ascended?'[71]

Unable to find a Swiss or French guide to accompany him, the persistent Whymper journeyed back to Breuil, where Giordano was busy making preparations for the Italian ascent. The unsuspecting Whymper immediately engaged Carrel for an attempt from the Swiss side. Bad weather prevented them going, but when out and about Whymper met Carrel with an Italian traveller carrying a great deal of baggage. Carrel told him he was engaged after the 11 July with 'a family of distinction'. At this point Whymper discovered that the 'family' was Giordano and that everything was now in place for an Italian attempt. At Breuil the next day he met Lord Francis Douglas who, at nineteen years of age, was a rising star of the Alpine Club. Douglas was briefed on the Carrel situation and he and his guides (Peter Taugwalder senior and junior) decided to accompany Whymper to Zermatt. There they were joined by the Chamonix guide Michel Croz who had been engaged for an attempt on the Matterhorn by the experienced climber Charles Hudson and his nineteen-year-old friend, Douglas Hadow, who was spending his first year in the Alps.

This little band of very mixed experience, thrown together and inspired by the vision of conquering the most feared unclimbed mountain in the Alps, set out from Zermatt with the two Taugwalders as porters at 5.35 a.m. on the clear morning of Thursday 13 July. They carried provisions for three days with them and followed the ridge connecting the Hörnli with the actual peak of the Matterhorn, reaching the foot of the mountain at 11.20 a.m. Ascending the northeastern face, they found a good position for the tent at 12,000 feet (3,650m) shortly after noon. Croz and young Peter Taugwalder went scouting ahead to save time route-finding in the morning. They reported joyfully on their return that what they had seen was good and asserted positively that had the party gone with them they could have climbed the mountain. They made tea and coffee; Whymper, Lord Francis Douglas and the Taugwalders sheltered in the tent, while the rest preferred to stay outside in their blanket bags.

They moved before daybreak on 14 July, leaving the youngest Taugwalder behind at the camp. By 10 a.m. they had reached 14,000 feet (4,300m) without difficulty and with little need for the rope. The last 500 feet (150m) proved much easier than expected. The angle was less than 40° and the rock was covered with snow, in some places glazed with ice. The climb nevertheless required great care; because of Hadow's lack of experience he alone required assistance. Suddenly the angle eased so much that Whymper and Croz detached themselves from the rope and ran to the summit. They arrived at 1.40 p.m., with the others ten minutes behind them. It had taken them ten hours, including a two-hour halt for rest and food. From the summit Whymper spotted Carrel's party still 1,312 feet (400m) below, and celebrated with great shouts of triumph and the hurling down of stones. Carrel, in despair, abandoned his climb.

Triumph would soon turn to tragedy when, during their descent, the inexperienced Hadow lost his footing. The ensuing turmoil was described in a letter written by Whymper to *The Times* on 8 August 1865:

> Sir, after the direct appeals which I have received from the President of the Alpine Club and from yourself to write an account of the accident on the Matterhorn, I feel it is impossible to remain silent any longer, and therefore forward you for publication a plain statement of the accident itself, and of events that preceded and followed it . . . As far as I know, at

Johan Joseph Bennen, 1824–1864

Johan Joseph Bennen of Laax in the upper Rhone Valley was born in 1824 'within the limits of the German tongue and living amidst the mountains and glaciers of the Oberland.'[49] He was a man with many simple heroic qualities, which made him ideally suited to lead others up previously unclimbed peaks. He combined boldness and prudence with an ease and power peculiar to himself, so he had a faculty of conceiving and planning his achievements; a way of concentrating his mind upon an idea with clearness and decision that Hawkins never observed in any other guide. He was Tyndall's favourite guide. He was unmarried and worked most of the year at his carpentry trade. His knowledge of the Oberland district was learned from hunting the chamois with his friend Bortis, who was also a fine mountaineer. He first worked as a guide attached to the Eggishorn Hotel. Tyndall said he was 'a remarkable-looking man, between thirty and forty years old, of middle stature, but very strongly built. His countenance was frank and firm, while a light of good nature at times twinkled in his eye.'[50] The hotel proprietor told Tyndall that if he 'were killed in Bennen's company there would be two lives lost, for that the guide would assuredly sacrifice himself to save his Herr'.[51] He came to prominence as a guide working with Hawkins and Tyndall in 1858.

The quality of his climbing record speaks for itself. He famously climbed the Finsteraarhorn and the old Weissthor with the Carlow man in 1858. He was with F. F. Tuckett and guides Victor Tairraz and Peter Bohren in the first ascent of the stately Aletschhorn. He also made the second ascent in the same year with other clients. He alone among the Swiss guides attempted to climb the Matterhorn with Hawkins in 1860. In 1861 he made the first ascent with Tyndall of the Weisshorn by its east ridge and was back on the Matterhorn with Hawkins and Tyndall in 1862. He also made the second ascent of the Grand Paradis. Bennen was in the party with Leslie Stephen, Tuckett and guides Melchior Anderegg and P. Perren for the first direct ascent of Mont Blanc from St Gervais via the Aiguille du Goûter, the Dôme, and the Bosses du Dromadaire. He and one of his clients were killed in an avalanche on the Haut de Cry in the Valais in February 1864, when he allowed three local guides to overrule his caution with respect to the danger presented by the snow conditions on a large couloir. His body was recovered and he was buried in Aerneu churchyard. His headstone was erected by his old friends and employers, Hawkins, Tuckett and Tyndall. A liberal collection was made in England for his dependants.

the moment of the accident no one was actually moving. I cannot speak with certainty, neither can the Taugwalders, because the leading men were partially hidden from our sight by an intervening mass of rock. Poor Croz had laid aside his axe, and in order to give Mr Hadow greater security was absolutely taking hold of his legs and putting his feet, one by one, into their proper positions. From the movements of their shoulders it is my belief that Croz, having done as I said, was in the act of turning round to go down a step or two himself; at this moment Mr Hadow slipped, fell on him, and knocked him over. I heard one startled exclamation from Croz, then saw him and Mr Hadow flying downwards; in another moment Hudson was dragged from his steps, and Lord F. Douglas immediately after him. All this was the work of a moment; but immediately we heard Croz's exclamation Taugwalder and myself planted ourselves as firmly as the rocks would permit; *the rope was tight between us, and the shock came on us both as one man.* We held; but the rope broke midway between Taugwalder and Lord Francis Douglas. For two or three seconds we saw our unfortunate companions sliding downwards on their backs, and spreading out their hands endeavouring to save themselves; they then disappeared one by one, and fell from precipice to precipice on to the Matterhorn glacier below, a distance of 4,000 feet in height. From the moment the rope broke it was impossible to help them.[72]

The italics in the letter are Whymper's. He was making the point that when a climbing rope is properly used it is a great safeguard, but that if any slackness is allowed in the rope between any two climbers the whole party is endangered from the momentum that may drag down one man after another.

Alfred Wills, the then President of the Alpine Club, responded to public criticism with a letter to *The Times* on August 11: he agreed that 'young and inexperienced climbers should neither go or be taken on expeditions of this kind' and he warned against 'the slackened rope – the best friend of the climber converted only too easily into his most insidious and dangerous foe.' His letter was reprinted in the *The Irish Times* on 15 August. Another letter announcing the setting up of a fund to build a church as a memorial to the English victims of the accident was published.[73] An interesting letter ('From our Special Correspondent') in Zermatt was published in the *The Irish Times* on 28 August declaring:

That this little Swiss village is crowded this year with English tourists 'to look upon the Matterhorn, the death place of our enthusiastic fellow-countrymen, and to stand by the spot in which the remains of Hudson and Hadow are placed . . . Awful as it seems to the naked eye looking upwards to the Matterhorn, will you believe it? There are young men who profess to be anxious to try the ascent. They go about among the guides and consult them, and offer large sums to tempt them to accompany them, but the series of accidents which has happened this year have made them prudent, and they are against the liberal offers.

THE SCIENTIFIC VOLUNTEER.

"If ever I have to choose . . . . I shall, without hesitation, shoulder my rifle with the Orangeman."—*See Professor Tyndall's Reply to Sir W. V. Harcourt.* "*Times,*" Feb. 13, 1890.

From *Punch*, February 22, 1890

Punch Cartoon in *Life and Work of John Tyndall* E. and C. H. Creasy. (National Library of Ireland)

The same letter tells us later:

> Indeed the Irish visitors are everywhere, and some of the most zealous climbers are Dublin
> men. The name of Charles Barrington, brother of the Lord Mayor of Dublin, is spoken
> of at the hotels as achieving wonders, which trained guides shrink from, and the great
> authority on Alpine climbing is Mr John Ball, son of the late Judge Ball, and formerly
> Under Secretary of the Colonies. Professor Tyndall has been here within the past few
> days, but has left for Geneva for a meeting of savants.

Tyndall returned to the Matterhorn in 1868 to make his third and last assault. His desire
was 'to finish forever my contest with the Matterhorn by making a pass over its summit
from Breuil to Zermatt'. He chose for his guides the Maquignaz brothers, Joseph and
Pierre, who had made the fourth ascents from Breuil on 12 to 14 September 1867, and
in their ascent had overcome the difficulties presented by the Enjambée. It was clear that his guides
shared his ambition to climb the Italian route and descend by Whymper's Swiss route, thereby
making the first traverse of the mountain from Italy to Switzerland. Although fearful of the Swiss
route they reasoned that if Whymper and the Taugwalders had managed to descend, they ought
to be able to do the same. On Sunday 26 July they set out early, but not before Joseph Maquiqnaz
had attended Mass at 2 a.m. The party comprised three porters and a mule in support of the two
guides and Tyndall. As he climbed the familiar ground above the Col du Lion, Tyndall reflected
that although he no longer felt the intense fear of the mountain's savage inaccessibility that his
previous attempts had left ('particularly at the places of virgin difficulty where ropes now hung'),
the intrinsic grandeur of the Matterhorn could not be effaced. They stopped for rest where he had
camped in 1862. Soon he was 'scaling the crags and rounding the bases of those wild and wonderful
rock towers, into which the weather of ages had hewn the southern ridge of the Matterhorn.' There
was, he fancied, nothing 'more fascinating to a man given by nature and habit to such things than
a climb alone among these crags and precipices. He need not be *theological*, but, if complete, the
grandeur of the place would certainly fill him with religious awe.'[74]

They stopped at the place called the Cravate (a horizontal ledge of snow which from a distance
resembles a white necktie) where a cabin had been built in 1867. They collected water and spent a
comfortable night in the cabin. Tyndall woke to the guides preparing breakfast; at 6 a.m. he and
the two guides left the hut. They followed Bennen's route to pass the conical peak (Pic Tyndall) to
reach the final precipice along the horizontal ridge that had stopped them before. Joseph Maquignaz
halted on one of the sharpest teeth of the ridge; he turned and smiled at Tyndall, saying, 'there is
no room for giddiness here, sir.' Tyndall considered the precipice before him and recalled their
previous reaction. This time, he thought, 'the precipice did not look as vertical . . . no real climber
with his strength unimpaired would pronounce it, without trial, insuperable. Fears of this rock-
wall, however, had been excited long before we reached it. . . . It was probably the addition of the
psychological element to the physical – the reluctance to encounter new dangers on a mountain
which had hitherto inspired a superstitious fear – that quelled further exertion.'[75]

His barometer told him he was still 700 feet (215m) short of the summit. More than just a
stone's throw! Descending the end of the ridge they crossed a narrow cleft and grappled with the

Jean Joseph Maquignaz

rocks on the other side; then they took an oblique line bearing to their right and rounded a difficult protuberance of rock. An iced-up rope left there by Maquignaz the previous September hung down over the last remaining cliff. Despite using this rope it took a great effort to pull up over the top of the vertical and ice-glazed rock. A few minutes more brought the scientist to the 'lightning smitten top'. 'Thus ended the long contest between me and the Matterhorn', recorded Tyndall. The fog which on reaching the summit provided a cold and clammy atmosphere soon passed over to reveal above them a blue heaven, and far below the sunny meadows of Zermatt:

The mountains were almost wholly unclouded, and such clouds as lingered amongst them only added to their magnificence. The Dent d'Érin, the Dent Blanche, the Gabelhorn, the Mischabel, the range of heights between it and the Monte Rosa, the Lyskamm and the Breithorn were all at hand, and clear; while the Weisshorn, noblest and most beautiful of all, shook out a banner towards the North, formed by the humid southern air as it grazed the crest of the mountain.[76]

It was eleven o'clock. He took 'an ounce of nutriment and a gulp of wine' as he gazed down on Zermatt. Half an hour later they left the roof-like slope that forms the summit, but the gradient soon became more formidable. Understandably, they descended slowly but carefully using a spare rope to double round the rocks that jutted out of the arête from time to time. A lot of time was consumed setting up these additional top ropes and then retrieving them from below. The hottest part of the day had passed and the melted snow that covered the smooth rock made the slopes treacherous. Unfamiliar with the Zermatt side, they descended too far to the right of the Hörnli ridge and found themselves trying to find a safe way down steep slabs and ledges in the dark. When at last they got off the rock they became entangled in the brambles and bush of the woods of the Zmutt, before eventually finding the path to Zermatt, which they reached between one and two o'clock in the morning.

Tyndall had made the seventh ascent of the Matterhorn and the first traverse of the mountain from Italy to Switzerland and had finally got the Matterhorn off his chest. It is interesting to note that on each of his three attempts he made considerable progress over the previous height attained and on his third attempt he made the first completed traverse.

On 29 February 1876, at the advanced age of fifty-five, John Tyndall married thirty-year-old Louisa Charlotte Hamilton; in this same year he built a chalet for them at Alp Lusgen, just above the Bel Alp hotel at 2,133.6m. In recognition of his scientific work on the glaciers, as well as his love for the Alps, the citizens of Naters in the Rhone Valley below granted him citizenship and made him a freeholder in their commune.[77] He never lost his conviction to speak out publicly on some of the most contentious issues of his day, from Home Rule for Ireland (which he remained vehemently against), to the Darwinian theory of evolution (which he espoused in the face of both the Pope's outrage and Irish popular opinion).

Author at Bel Alp Memorial to Tyndall. (Courtesy Con Collins)

Tyndall died in December 1893 at the age of eighty-three, due to an overdose of chloral hydrate, which he took nightly to treat his insomnia. The dose was accidentally administered by his wife, who mistook the bottle for the magnesia that he took every other morning. When they both realised her mistake he was quick to instruct her: ' let us do all we can. Tickle my throat. Get a stomach pump.' She sent a message to the doctor and gave him a dose of mustard as recommended in *Whittaker's Medicine*. He drank coffee and drifted in and out of consciousness. They worked to save him all day, but he died at 6.30 p.m.[78]

Louisa erected an impressive granite memorial to her beloved John on the hill above Bel Alp and their alpine hideaway. From this petit summit the deep valley of the Rhone falls away and opposite stands the majestic pyramid of the Weisshorn, perhaps Tyndall's finest monument of all.

The Tyndall house at Alp Lusgen

Jean-Antoine Carrel, 1829–1890

Jean-Antoine Carrel was born in the village of Avouil in Val Tournenche under the shadow of Il Cervino (the Matterhorn). He was a shepherd, hunter, farmer and stonemason who fought as a sergeant in the Second Italian War of Independence at San Martino (1859). He was a proud Italian who wished to climb Il Cervino for the glory of Italy. He did his early climbing with his uncle, Jean-Jacques Carrel, an experienced chamois hunter. Three days after Whymper's ascent of the Matterhorn, Carrel made the second ascent by the harder and more technical Italian Ridge with Jean Baptiste Bich. Despite their rivalry on the Matterhorn, he remained good friends with Whymper. From 1879 to 1880 he climbed eleven peaks (seven first ascents) in Ecuador including the highest peak Chimborazo with his brother Louis and Edward Whymper. He went back to farming for livelihood and reared twelve children. He guided part-time, climbing the Matterhorn fifty times with clients from many countries. In 1890 he died from exhaustion, having guided a young client and a porter down from the upper hut on the Matterhorn after two days of confinement in a storm; their descent took them twenty hours non-stop and Carrel dropped to the ground on arrival, dying shortly afterwards. He was sixty-one.

4

Anthony Adams-Reilly: Mapmaker of the High Alps

I do not know which to admire most, the fidelity of Mr Reilly's map, or the indefatigable industry by which the materials were accumulated from which it was constructed.

Edward Whymper, *Scrambles amongst the Alps*, 1871

IF JOHN BALL was the most travelled and prolific of the Irish pioneers and Tyndall technically the most capable, then Adams-Reilly was the most poetic and endearing activist during the golden age. His legacy is a number of first ascents in the company of some of the greatest climbers of the age and two accurate maps of the two most popular areas in the alpine chain. As a reward for his industry a number of topographical features in the Mont Blanc range including a peak, a couple of cols and a glacier were named in his honour by the French surveyors who wished to acknowledge his unselfish exchange of information with them. Aiguille Adams Reilly (3,506m) stands to the west of the Aiguille du Chardonnet and is also adjacent to Aiguille Forbes, which was named after his great friend and mentor, J. D. Forbes.[1]

Anthony Miles William Adams-Reilly was born on 11 February 1836 at Belmont House near Mullingar, County Westmeath; although there is little record of Reilly's life at Mullingar we know that his father died in 1848 when the young Reilly was twelve years old. He was sent to boarding school at Rugby College in Warwickshire in February 1850 and, despite the privilege that such an expensive classical education would bestow, it must have been a traumatic move for the fourteen-year-old boy. Indeed it was as a pupil of Rugby's drawing master, George Bernard (an early alpine traveller and later an Alpine Club member) that Reilly developed fine skills in drawing and sketching, shaping his particular achievement as an alpine pioneer. Family fortune

Anthony Adams-Reilly, 1836–1886

- Artist and alpine mapmaker born on 11 February 1836 at Belmont House, near Mullingar, County Westmeath

- Educated at Rugby and Oxford

- Inspired to visit the Alps when he read Forbes' *Travels through the Alps of Savoy*

- Climbed with many of the great pioneers, including Leslie Stephen, Edward Whymper, C. E. Mathews and the guides Melchior Anderegg and Michel Croz

- Ascended Mont Blanc by seven different routes

- Made first ascents of Mont Dolent, Aiguille de Trélatête and Aiguille d'Argentière with Croz and Whymper in July 1864

- Surveyed and drafted the first correct map of the chain of Mont Blanc and a map of the Monte Rosa district.

- He was a loyal friend and disciple of David James Forbes and when he died contributed the mountaineering chapters to the Scotsman's biography

Facing page: Portrait of Anthony Adams-Reilly. (Courtesy the Alpine Club)

permitted him to progress to Brasenose College, Oxford, in 1855 and when he visited the Alps in 1861 he signed himself as a member of the college's mountaineering club. It appears he left Oxford without graduating and, although he was a student of the Inner Temple in London from 1874, he was never called to the bar.

His interest in the Alps appears to have been aroused by J. D. Forbes' *Travels through the Alps of Savoy* and, prior to his 1861 trip, his first climbs as listed in his application for membership of the Alpine Club were the Col du Géant and the Strahlegg, which would have familiarised him with the Mont Blanc chain and the Oberland district in Switzerland. Adams-Reilly's alpine season of 1861 is well recorded, for it was quite a whirlwind of effort and achievement. He began by travelling to the Oberland where he climbed the Oberaarjock Pass and the Jungfrau, the highest peak of the range. *The Alpine Journal* records his brief notes of these ascents: 'From the Grimsel by the Oberaarjoch. Ascended the Jungfrau. Maximum of cold last winter as registered by minimum thermometer at cave at Faulberg -13 °.[2]

Belmont House, County Westmeath, birthplace and home of Anthony Adams-Reilly

Moving on to Zermatt, he made the second attempt on the east ridge of the Lyskamm and climbed the Lysjoch and Bettliner Pass with the renowned guide Melchior Anderegg and fellow traveller Leslie Stephen. Reilly then crossed the Théodule Pass and climbed the Monte Rosa, which he recorded in the *Führerbuch* of Johan Taugwald: 'Johan Taugwald accompanied me as guide over the Col de Lyskamm: the St Théodule and the summit of Monte Rosa. From the Col de Lyskamm, we made an attempt to ascend the Lyskamm, and reached a point about halfway up, when we were stopped by the state of the snow. I found him on all occasions an excellent and careful guide and with acquaintance of the whole range.'[3]

Reilly continued his season at Chamonix where he climbed Mont Blanc twice by two different routes: first via the Rocher Rouge and Dr Hamel's tragic 1820 route[4] with local guides including

Andre Balm; then a week later he climbed it again by the Aiguille du Goûter and the Bosses Ridge, with the great Swiss guide Melchior Anderegg and Englishman Sam Brandram.[5] Reilly compared the two routes in a long letter to the *The Times*, discussing not only the differences in the difficulties encountered in each ascent but noting the higher costs demanded by the Chamonix guides and emphasising the fact that it was better to have a shorter distance to the summit on day two, as one had to descend from the summit to Chamonix the same day by either route.[6] He clearly favoured the Aiguille du Goûter route over the Grands Mulets route for that reason and because of the better views enjoyed during the whole ascent.

During the 1861 season Reilly detailed his journey in a series of six pocket notebooks.[7] When climbing, he would stop and take meticulous notes that recorded topography, surveying data, barometer and temperature readings, and make wonderful pencil and crayon sketches of mountain scenery, bivouac sites and his mountain colleagues. The diaries, written up later and referring to the sketches in his notes, provide a fascinating insight into his thoughts, his relationship with his guides and porters (including Melchior Anderegg, Michel Croz, Michel Payot, Johan Taugwald and Henri Charlet) and with his fellow travellers (such Alpine Club luminaries as Leslie Stephen, Edward Whymper and A. W. Moore).

On Thursday 18 July 1861 Reilly set out from Aigle for a chalet at Stiehreck, from where he would cross the Unteraar Joch or Pass. The proprietor rejoiced in a large flock of goats and 'busily engaged himself in raking up a netful of hay as a bed for "der herr".' When he returned later from sketching on the Eismeer Glacier, he 'partook of the refreshment of a little rum, with a goat milked into it, which is a beverage in my opinion very hard to beat.'[8] They left before five the next morning. Reilly found the route steep and strenuous but was aided by the frozen prints of a party who had passed the other way two days previously. On reaching the Col he remarked, 'we here halted and attacked our provisions with great relish'. These provisions included bread, meat and cheese, coffee, four bottles of *vin ordinaire* for the guides, and a bottle of Volnay for Reilly who commented, 'I finished my solitary bottle of burgundy, and was very sorry I had not taken the landlord's advice and provided myself with another.' To start their descent towards the Grimsel Hospice[9] they had to back-climb, facing inwards to the slope: 'it is all but perpendicular, and when standing upright with my feet thrust into the snow, I could touch the slope which rose in front of me with my elbow'. On the facing page of his pocket diary he captures the moment with a sketch of three men descending a steep snow slope above a bergschrund.

He reached the hospice at 5 p.m., 'finding it as usual full of people – though I had been eating hard eggs all day, I was dreadfully hungry when I arrived, but I waited for the 7 o'clock table d'hôte to which I did ample justice.' Suffering from a sore ankle he treated it with arnica and a pair of Interlaken boots 'which behaved nobly'; all of which made his planned ascents of the Jungfrau and Monte Rosa look feasible. He paid off one guide, Peter Michel, and retained Peter Enabrette until he reached the Eggishorn. Next day he walked down the Rhone Glacier to Grimsel where he stopped at the hotel and made arrangements to climb the Oberaarjoch with Enabrette and local guide Johan Wasbel who knew the pass well. They were provided with 'plenty provisions and a proportionate quantity of liqueurs as well as ropes and all things fitting.' They left at 6 a.m. Reilly, who thought from his bearing the landlord was a villain, was agreeably surprised when he found the bill was the most moderate he had had in Switzerland and he was only charged a single franc for filling his flask with rum instead of the usual three.

The route took them over glaciers and moraine until they reached fresh snow that led to the

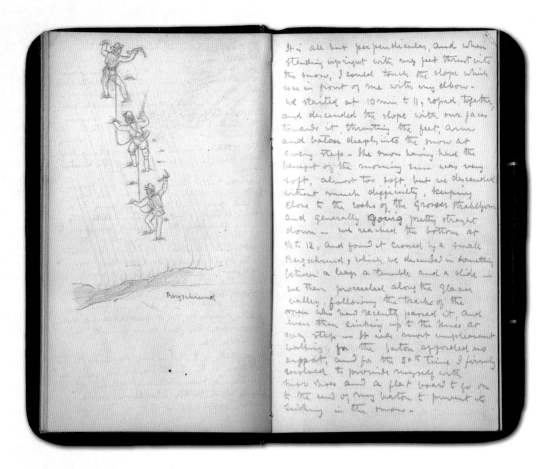

Above: An extract from one of Adams-Reilly's 1861 pocket diaries including a sketch of the party back-climbing to a bergshrund. (Courtesy the Alpine Club)

Viesch Glacier, rising in one rolling swell after another to the summit of the col. Wearing gaiters and spectacles they roped up for the final snow section, which Reilly found tiresome. He could not understand how the guides, though heavily leaden, managed to tread without sinking, while he sank up to his knees at almost every step. They 'called a halt in order to repair the immense destruction of tissue they had experienced just before the foot of the last slope to the pass at 10 a.m. Reilly liked to march on his stomach: 'I attacked the eggs with great violence, and floored 3 leaving 4 for future consumption.' Twenty minutes later they resumed and reached the summit of the col in another hour. The view 'which now burst upon us was past all description . . . range after range of peaks rose on all sides, extending in all directions, and presenting every imaginable combination of rock and snow'. The descent on the other side had them skirting the base of the Rothorn to climb down through broken seracs, winding in and out, climbing up and down, cutting steps to reach rocks at about 2 p. m. where they stopped at a spot with a snow patch 'to cool the wine and floor his remaining eggs'.[10]

The party reached the Eggishorn Hotel after thirteen hard hours on their feet. There they met the guide Ulrich Lauener whom Reilly described as 'nearly turned black' with a 'Scotch gentleman' who had come from Riffel. Reilly retired, having first 'dismissed both my guides as I found putting in a long day with a man whose language I could not speak was not a cheerful thing'. In conversation Reilly asked Lauener to put in a good word for him with his friend and fellow guide Peter Taugwald regarding Reilly's own future plans to ascent Monte Rosa. Reilly rested next day and on 23 July he climbed the Eggishorn, which was an hour and a half up from the hotel; here he spent eight hours on the summit sketching and describing the scene in his notebook.[11]

His next mission was to climb the Jungfrau (4,158m) and on Wednesday 24 July at 2.30 p.m. he set out for the sleeping place at Faulberg (3,242m) with two local guides, Dominic Bortis and Alexander Guntern, and a porter 'who carried a great faggot of wood and an immense bundle of straw tied up in the blankets, which gave him exactly the appearance of a great mushroom.'[12] As they approached Faulberg by the Fiescher Glacier, the crevasses became more frequent, in many places bridged by snow that was in an unsafe state. The porter carrying the straw cautiously attempted to cross one and fell through, but his immense bundle of straw was too big to fit into the crevasse and held him, his feet dangling down, until the remainder of the party came to his aid and pulled him out.

They soon found the cave where they would pass the night before their early morning ascent of the Jungfrau. As the guides lit a fire and prepared the bedding, Reilly stayed on the glacier to sketch before the light failed and was 'almost perished to death' when he made his way to the two caverns, one above the other, that were formed by a flat rock projecting from a spur of the Faulberg. In the larger upper cavern he found the guides and porter 'sitting around the fire in one corner like the three witches and superintending the concoction of coffee in a kind of a deep frying pan with four legs which was left in the cavern for visitors'. Reilly took a reading from a minimum thermometer erected by Alpine Club member Francis Tuckett to ascertain the coldest temperature in winter. The instrument had not been read since the previous October and so Reilly recorded a temperature of 13 ° below zero. The actual temperature that evening he recorded at 6 ° above zero. Reilly brewed some mulled burgundy in the frying pan to wash down the hearty supper they all enjoyed, and this he followed by a smoke on his pipe.

Occupying the lower cave alone, Reilly dressed for bed and put on every garment he possessed, one over the other: 'my night dress consisted 2 flannel shirts, my flannel blouse, waistcoat and light great coat overall, slippers and felt gaiters and two blankets; I was not the least cold all night though my bedroom had only two walls and a roof.' The night was clear and the moon shone brightly as he lay comfortable with cigar in mouth, looking at the white glacier which hung from the summit of the Faulberg. He reflected, 'Many people would have felt excited and sleepless; I felt at first more excited than comfortable, then more comfortable than excited, and then I didn't feel anymore, for I fell asleep.'

At 1 a.m. he was woken, and the party set off an hour later on a fine morning with the moon (surrounded by the largest and most vivid halo he had ever seen) shining with great brilliance. The group were unroped starting out, but when Guntern went in right up to his shoulders in the snow they roped up and as they made their way towards the base of the Rothorn Sattel, Reilly observed: 'It was now the dead hour of the night, that interval just before the pale dawn in which nature seems to die, and a silence and horror fall all around like a pall, presenting a perceptible difference between this and other periods of the night – this has been often observed, and it would appear not to exist only in the imagination, for it is invariably at this hour, that a dying man ceases to live.'

The first pale glimmer of dawn appeared above the summits of the Trugberg on their right at 3.30 a.m. and gradually dimmed the flickering of the stars. He wrote: 'the moon beams had rested on the right hand mountains pale and cold, but the dawn rose paler and colder still, and on looking from one range to the another, that the one which the moonlight fell appeared now to be bathed in a warm yellow glow, contrasting strongly with the other side, on which the first beams of morning rested, as pale and cold as the moonbeams had appeared before.' He remarked how the first rays of sun cast a crimson flush upon the summit of the Jungfrau. The final section was steep, through broken masses of large seracs that rose in confused heaps and were streaked with horizontal bands and fringed with icicles. Forced to cut steps in places, they had to scramble through large bergschrunds to reach the knife-edged ridge that led upwards to the last rocks. Despite its apparent nearness, it took three hours of step-cutting, because what looked to be a snow ridge proved to be ice.

'Chip, chip, chip, chip, right foot forward; chip, chip, chip, chip, left foot forward'; this movement repeated itself over and over; each step was two feet high. For the climbers following there was no turning around to look at the view, because 'independently of the disagreeable sensation produced by seeing every chip of ice descend about 12,000 feet (3,650m), and thinking that the very slightest slip off a step of ice which held little more than your toe would send you after them, the whole attention was necessary to clear out each step from the ice chips which filled it from above and plant the foot as firmly as possible, dividing the weight carefully between the foot, the left hand which rested in the step immediately above, and the baton which was struck into the ice with the right.' Reilly carried some prunes in his pocket and he wiled away the time by alternatively eating a prune and a chip of ice, which he choose carefully from those that came down in showers from Guntern. The sting in the tail was a final sharp arête, which Reilly moved up 'in a decidedly undignified and crablike manner, the toe of my boot overhanging the rounded plateau from which the Silberhörner rise, while the heel looked down on the glacier basin on the other side which lay an awful depth below – At length we reached the pointed mound of snow, forming the summit.'

Here the guide made a small platform of only 2 square feet (0.18 m²), from which Reilly took in the view whose beauty surpassed all description. It was 10 o'clock and there was no wind. Much to the disgust of Guntern, Reilly insisted on taking out his sketchpad and proceeded to sketch, choosing the Interlaken side where the view extended furthest in the warm sun. Indeed, Reilly observed more than one butterfly hovering over their heads and fluttering away in the direction of the Roththal where he speculated they would find no flowers. They drank their little bottle of champagne with great gusto and stayed there for twenty minutes. They could not detach a bottle left by a previous party, so left their own bottle on the summit with their names on a piece of paper inside.

Their route of descent was the same as the ascent, except faster, as the steps were already cut: 'it was not easy to let down the heel about 2 feet and plant it firmly in a little notch of ice – I know I made my way down with a deliberation which rather disgusted my guides', he wrote. He complained that the guides insisted on making a long halt at Faulberg, which they reached at 4 p.m. They lit a fire to make coffee and were 'evidently determined to finish everything eatable and drinkable before old Welly (the hotel proprietor) got hold of them'.

Reilly took a copy of the various thermometer readings to forward to Francis Tuckett, according to the directions contained in an Alpine Club journal article written by him. When Guntern signalled another stop within an hour of Grimsel, Reilly refused to stop. A huffed Guntern tried to out-walk Reilly the rest of the way. This amused Reilly, so the faster the guide went 'the faster I went, and he soon gave up the contest and laboured on in rather a despairing manner, declining all offers of refreshment at various chalets we passed.' The whole population turned out to meet them when they arrived and Reilly 'found himself rather a lion 'and had to undergo a severe cross examination. He immediately went to his room to dress and 'was soon occupied in worrying the petit diner.'[13]

In retrospect, Reilly acknowledged it was 'the hardest day's work he had ever done', yet he felt he had previously felt much more fatigue after doing infinitely less. He did not seem, from his diary entries, to have been the least bit grateful to his guides who had, after all, cut the steps and done the donkey work that took him to the summit of the Jungfrau. At lunchtime next day Guntern was still in bed in the basement of the hotel, snow-blind and tired from the previous day's exertions. Reilly set off for Visp with a porter 'carrying his traps' at about lunchtime, reaching the gateway to Zermatt via Brig in six and a quarter hours' solid walking. At the Hotel Soleil he battled with a room full of mosquitoes 'who attacked him viciously'; he slaughtered a great number and, 'though the survivors were many', he was too tired to be much disturbed. He woke with a swollen and inflamed ankle and decided to take a horse the remainder of the way to Zermatt in order to rest his ankle for a couple of days. His description of the picturesque sylvan countryside on the route to Zermatt on a rough white horse is charming. He recounts passing through pastures and woodland of birch and larch, and through the villages of Stalden, St Niklaus, Randa and Täsch overlooked by the mountains and crags of the Weisshorn, Dom and the distant peaks of the Mischabel, and of crossing bridges over white water torrents fed by massive glaciers. As he describes coming in sight of Zermatt, above which towered the then unclimbed Matterhorn, he displays his admiration for the climbing prowess of his countryman John Tyndall:

> His base (the Matterhorn) we saw, but he had veiled his head in clouds, and obstinately refused to look at us – It is quite wonderful the airs that some mountains give themselves when they think they are in alienable, but Tyndall is coming out, and has written for a guide, a 'fearless climber'. It is very possible that Mons le Mt Cervin may be more polite to strangers when he has the professor's flag stuck into his stupid old head.[14]

At Zermatt Reilly was unable to get entry to the favoured rendevous of wealthy English travellers at the Monte Rosa Hotel. It was bursting at the seams and so, disappointed, he had to settle for the inferior and 'very dear' Mont Cervin Hotel. The next day, Sunday 28 July, he attended a church service at his hotel. Surveying the other attendees Reilly remarked:

> one thin sour looking party, in ragged trousers, and an ancient shooting jacket, with a plaid wrapped around him – his legs were about the consistence of batons, and his body about twice as thick, while his unshaven face was in a state of peel, and his hands appeared cut to pieces by rocks – he spoke to me, and asked whether Kennedy had gone to the Æggishorn, as he heard I had just left it – We got into conversation and when I said I had no plans, he asked me to join him in an expedition he was going to make the next day, across the Col de Lyskamm to Gressonay, and then from that the ascent of the Lyskamm, whose summit had been frequently attempted, but never reached.

Reilly's first thought was to decline:

> but a new ascent, oh it must be done – I couldn't resist it, and so I said I would be
> delighted – We exchanged cards, and I found he was Stephen, the Stephen, one of the
> mighty lot who are never happy unless doing the impossible things without guides, and
> this of course made me more anxious to accompany him and see the 'lord of the glaciers'
> in the natural element.[15]

Leslie Stephen is best known as an author, magazine editor and literary critic, and first editor of the *Dictionary of National Biography*; he was later to become editor of *The Alpine Journal*. He married one of William Makepeace Thackeray's daughters (Harriet) and their daughter Virginia Woolf became the famous writer. Ten years after meeting Reilly he published *The Playground of Europe* and made the first ascent of Cima di Ball in the Dolomite range, which he named in honour of John Ball.

When Reilly met him, he was a fellow of Trinity College, Cambridge, and a Church of England priest. Stephen, although frail in appearance, was an accomplished athlete and a rowing coach at Cambridge. He had climbed the Col de Géant in 1857 and joined the Alpine Club a year later, climbing the Eigerjoch in 1859. Interestingly, it was during the 1861 season (when he met Reilly) that Stephen first climbed Mont Blanc and also made the first ascent of the Streckhorn with local guides Peter and Christian Michel and Christian Kaufmann. Stephen disavowed any credit or heroics in all his ascents 'except that of following better men than himself' and he wished 'that all men of the same class, in England and elsewhere, were as independent, well informed, and trustworthy as Swiss mountaineers'.[16]

Stephen introduced Reilly to Melchior Anderegg ('the best mountaineer in Europe', Reilly noted in his diary), who was to be Stephen's guide for the Lyskamm. Reilly resolved to have his own guide so the great guide went to find one with a little French and recruited Johann Zum Taugwald. Stephen and Reilly dined early at the Monte Rosa Hotel and then strolled together up the Riffelberg where they would sleep, 'passing the spot where the Görner Glacier and the Matterhorn rise beyond a foreground of ragged pines, every rock and tree of which seemed grouped by the hand of an artist'. Reilly was impressed with the reception Stephen received at the Riffel Hotel and enjoyed the glory it reflected on himself, particularly when a young man present came to Reilly and 'patted his back with great empowerment'.

They got started next morning at 2.10 a.m. He noted that 'Stephen took no kit whatever, for changes of temperature appear to have no effect on him, for he always keeps the everlasting old plaid around his shoulders in heat and in cold, and utterly eskews gloves and such effeminate things.' On a clear night they made their way up through the broken rocks of the Riffelberg and then followed a path to the glacier. After crossing the glacier, they worked their way up through rock and then followed a snow slope that led them to the foot of the Vincent Pyramide, on the right of which lay the Col they wished to pass. They attacked a large icefall that stretched across the valley forming a mass of seracs. They advanced slowly in soft snow, led confidently by Melchior who wound his way 'in and out, up and down while vast seracs rose all around them of a size and form perfectly astonishing'. Roped behind him, they climbed the sides of the seracs, 'skirting chasms of fearful depth', crossing the flat tops, until at last they came to a bay by an immense gulf that at first seemed impassable – an abyss about 40 feet (12m) wide and of unknown depth.

Melchior found a narrow bridge of ice and snow about 30 feet (9m) below, which was almost hidden from their view; he worked his way down and climbed two high steps that brought them back up to the same level. Reilly wrote:

> Melchior did not hesitate a moment – he cut steps down the steep ice, and we all got very well down to a kind of hollow between two seracs – we then planted ourselves as firmly as we could and held the rope which was attached to him – he disappeared around the corner and after a minute or two called out that he was alright, and had gained the bridge – we proceeded to follow him, one by one – It was a most peculiar place to go down for on rounding the projecting edge, we found that the wall of ice was not only perpendicular, but actually sloped inwards, so one had to descend by a wonderful succession of acrobatic performances with the feet in the steps, and the weight of the body thrown on the baton, which was held by him, as he stood on the narrow bridge below – Stephen, who is no bad judge said it was the most difficult place he had ever crossed, and that no other guide in Switzerland except Melchior would have attempted it.[17]

They reached the summit of the col that lay between the Monte Rosa and the Lyskamm at 9.15 a.m. and the party studied the face of the latter, deciding a ridge up a steeply inclined arête looked hopeful. However, when they got to top of the arête the ground ahead comprised a steep slope of loose rock over which a cornice of snow projected. Melchior said, 'they might do it, but that the chances of smashery were immeasurably great'. The debate was short and the 'nos' had it: 'Stephen said it would not do, and that one must draw a line somewhere, so we gave it up; he was terribly annoyed for it was the second time he was defeated; once by bad weather, and now by good.'[18]

Reilly slipped descending the steep ridge but was held on the rope by Taugwald. When they crossed the bergschrund they formed a line in a sitting position behind Melchior and slid down the last slope like lightening and stood again on the col. The party traversed and descended to the Bettliner Pass to the village of St Jean, where they found a hotel and were soon eating poached eggs with bread, butter and cheese and 'a very good vin du pays.' Next morning the party split, Stephen opting to cross the Schwarztor and Reilly opting for the St Théodule Pass, which would bring both parties back to the Riffel Hotel. Reilly chose to rest next day and asked Taugwald to come back the next evening for a try at Monte Rosa. Stephen and Melchior left later for Zermatt with plans to cross the Weisstor en route to the Eggishorn.

Reilly spent the day writing up his journal and finishing sketches and later, while dining, was pleasantly surprised to meet his old drawing teacher, Mr Bernard, from his schooldays at Rugby. They spent some time comparing sketches before Reilly retired to his double-bedded room, which he was enjoying having to himself. When the proprietor, Mademoiselle Seiler, came to him and asked as a great favour if he would let Mr Bernard have the other bed, he replied he would be delighted. His delight was short-lived, however, because Bernard promptly fell asleep and commenced snoring with a peculiar intonation. Reilly could not close his eyes and, as the hotel seemed to be one vast sounding board, he could hear exclamations – drowsy, remonstrative and even blasphemous – coming from the rooms around and above him.

On Thursday 1 August 1861 Reilly was called at 2 a.m. and set off with the guide Taugwald half an hour later to climb Monte Rosa, Switzerland's highest peak. Much of the route was the same as for the Lyskamm. At 7.20 they halted for a breakfast of hard-boiled eggs and cheese. His first egg dropped and took off down the slope, much to his annoyance; his second egg proved to be rotten so he 'sent it after the first', but after that he 'was more prosperous'. They reached the summit of Monte Rosa at 10.15 a.m. Reilly, delighted with his achievement, became frustrated when he tried to register his temperature observations (plus 15.5 °F) on the piece of paper provided by the Alpine Club, which he found rolled into a glass tube at the summit. He was at once serious and mocking in his remarks:

> as the Alpine Club paper had been filled long ago, and subsequent observers had recorded their observations on little bits of paper, which together formed a bundle a good deal too large for the tube; to add to the difficulty the top of the tube had been broken off, and the continual forcing in and out of the paper against the sharp edges of the broken glass, had given the Alpine Club register and the earlier record, the appearance of having been nibbled by legions of rats, much to the detriment of the valuable observations they once contained – I recorded mine on the back of Morshead's autograph, and having got them in at last, turned to contemplate the wonderful panorama around.[19]

Reilly returned to the Riffel Hotel and dined again with Bernard. Next day he walked to Zermatt and hired a horse for the journey to Visp. His eyes, burning with pain from snow blindness, had kept him wide awake most of the night. His next destination was Chamonix; on the way he stopped at Martigny where he repacked and sent some things back to his hotel in Geneva, then ordered a mule to bring him to Chamonix over the Forclaz Tête Noire the next afternoon. He slept better because his eyes were not hurting so much.[20]

In Chamonix Reilly lodged at the Hotel de Londres where, on arrival, he discovered a large party that had plans to ascend Mont Blanc the next day. Reilly agreed to join forces with them, but was naturally keen to find out exactly who they were. 'I thought at first they must be Americans, then from two names I saw in the livre des voyages, I was dreadfully afraid they were Irish, but I discovered afterwards that they came from North Wales and were connected with iron mines.' Reilly sent for the guide Venance Balmat, who lived at the quartier des Pèlerins and with whom he appears to have previously climbed, to request his services as his personal guide. Reilly was anxious to make his first ascent of Mont Blanc and wanted to be first to make the ascent under the provisions of the new tarif, which allotted three guides to one traveller, five guides to two travellers, with an additional guide for each additional traveller (the price per guide was also reduced from 100 to 70 francs per guide).

When they set out next morning about 9 a.m., the party consisted of three travellers, six guides and six porters for the climb, with three extra porters hired to carry food and drink as far as Pierre à l'Echelle; one of these carried a keg of vin ordinaire to be consumed at the point where they would move onto the ice. Reilly observed that someone appeared to have appointed Balmat (or he had appointed himself) to be chief guide of the party. They reached the point of departure onto ice at 1 p.m; Reilly critically commented, 'for some time before we reached it, it was evident to the most obtuse intellect that this was the recognised spot of luncheon, for egg shell, broken bottles and bones of poulets and gigots lay in positive heaps all round, rather doing away with the impression of grandeur and solitude to which the scene might otherwise to have given rise.' There 'the provisions were unpacked' and the guides set to work to gorge like wild animals and ate and drank and amused themselves exactly as if they were there entirely for their own amusement.' He also observed that his Welsh friends 'did ample justice to the provisions, and the small one, after a deal of vin ordinaire, brandy and beer, became rather disagreeably loquacious and at last fell asleep.'

In the afternoon the party ascended the Glaciers des Bossons towards the Grands Mulets rocks where a wooden refuge measuring 14 feet long by 7 feet wide (4.3m by 2.1m) had been built. It was equipped with a small but effective wood stove and a long, low table; in all nineteen people were looking for shelter in these cramped conditions. They spread themselves about in the evening sun, some inside the hut, some in the shelter of the rocks and some just lay out on the roof. Reilly spent some time sketching the beautiful sunset until it was quite dark. He then moved inside and found a space where he could lie on the floor. He borrowed some eau de cologne from one of the other travellers to overcome the atmosphere, which was very close inside the hut. He was awakened at 11 p.m. by a general move and, as it was impossible to avoid being walked over, he got ready like the rest and then got 'exceedingly cross' when he discovered someone had filled his heated tea bottle with sugar.

Outside Balmat and Reilly took up the lead position and, as the party formed, Reilly 'feared the condition of the other travellers'. The party roped-up, with a traveller between two guides, and they followed the old route zigzagging up snow slopes; Balmat used a lantern to light his way and those following had to find the steps in the dark. They reached the Petit Plateau at 2.30 a.m. and the level of the Grand Plateau an hour later. Reilly amused himself by observing, in a state of sarcastic indignation, the actions of the other travellers. Mr Barrow, who had shared his eau de cologne the evening before, looked like 'a venerable dancing bear', stamping his feet whenever he stopped as he had been instructed by his guide; the small man was doing 'petits verres of brandy' all the way from the Grands Mulets. The first glimmers of dawn were appearing when they reached the Rochers Rouges, beyond which they would follow the steep slope leading directly to the summit, the same route chose by the Russian climber Dr Hamel forty-one years previously. They had decided to use this in preference to the normal corridor route, because they would not need to cut steps, instead the lead climber could kick good steps in the frozen snow. However, the climbing was monotonous and tiring. At five o'clock the first rays of light struck the snowy summits to the right and produced the 'most wonderful chaos of mountain, mist and liquid light'.

As they rose they, could see people moving across the summit of the Dôme du Goûter, Reilly assumed they had come via the St Gervais route. He observed behind him that 'poor Mr Barrow was pounded and had to stop every five minutes', and the other pair of travellers were each being dragged by a pair of guides 'in a state of dogged despair, perfectly unconscious of anything that was taking place around them'. Shortly after 6 a.m. the bigger man gave up; two guides stayed with him while he rested, before they escorted him back in the direction of the Grands Mulets. Meanwhile, Reilly, determined to show his strength and being anxious to beat the St Gervais party to the summit, quickened his pace. He passed one of his guides and dragged Balmat, who was roped to him, along with him until they reached the Petits Mulets at 7 a.m., from where 'he could see the great chain of the Monte Rosa cloudless and clear, crowning the mass of peaks which stretched away almost from (his) feet.' There he untied the exhausted Balmat and, leaving him lying down on the snow, made the final ascent:

> I started alone to scale the final calotte, which stretched up above me white and rounded
> – I found it a very severe climb – for the ice was very hard, and having nothing to cut

steps with I was obliged to scramble up the best way I could, assisted here and there by the steps left by former parties, which I found in some spots – A sharp supporting wind of extraordinary keenness was sweeping round the sloping dome, but I felt none of the effects usually attributed to the rarefication of the air, except that I fancied I got blown rather sooner than I ought, though I was climbing very rapidly – I reached the dernier rochers at 7-20, and at last at ¼ to 8, stood on the summit of Mt Blanc – I gave one slow look around, and then made a rapid exploring expedition all over the top before sitting down to sketch.[21]

Reilly walked across the summit ridge from end to end and shouted down to the St Gervais party who were still toiling along the ridge between the Bosse and the summit. He rushed up to the little cross at the north end of the ridge, which was hung all over with thermometers and other instruments, noting that the 'minimum thermometer marked minus 21, but all the rest were in a hopeless state of bubbles.' He then set himself down to sketch the Monte Rosa chain before he was joined by the rest of the party. He had some food, champagne and a pipe while he took in the full panorama. The party stayed there an hour and a half before they descended – Reilly delayed and went to the northern end to meet the St Gervais party. Among them he met Mr Buxton of Trinity College, Cambridge, 'an imposing mountaineer, all over with sympemometers and other engines, and bearing an ice axe of appalling construction' and a Mr Robinson, 'who had been ill all day and was very much done up when he arrived.' He then bolted down behind the others and caught them a little below the Petits Mulets. They descended by the same route to the Grands Mulets in snow too soft to safely glissade and reached there at 11.20 a.m., a short time after the guns from Chamonix had announced their success.

Reilly was extremely satisfied with his season, having added Mont Blanc to his Monte Rosa and Jungfrau successes. He decided that once some mail he was expecting had arrived he would go home quietly. However, Robinson mentioned to him that Melchior Anderegg had arrived at Chamonix to meet an English client named Buxton, who was nowhere to be found. Reilly found the guide in a great state of indignation at his treatment. Reilly had a moment of inspiration. On 11 August 1861 he wrote:

'The sight of Melchior's brown face was evil for peace and quietness, and the weather was perfectly magnificent, and in short a brilliant idea struck me; suppose I was to ascend Mont Blanc by the Dome du Goûté, and thus be able to compare the two routes.'[22]

Anderegg agreed immediately. They would take one porter from Chamonix and sleep the next night on the Col de Voza. They learned that a Mr Brandram staying at another hotel had engaged two guides and two porters to make the same ascent. Next afternoon they had a 'hot walk' to Les Ouches, then up to the Col de Voza where they feasted on 'fraughans' of great size and quantity before Reilly had dinner at the Pavilion de Bellevue. Reilly had purchased some provisions: 'four large sausages for my private eating, and some prunes and chocolate'. When they set off at 6.30 next morning, Reilly was not feeling on top form and regretted eating so many bilberries for dessert the night before. The route to the hut required them to cross a couloir that was subject to regular stone fall. Reilly described it as follows: 'We came up to its edge, and as we did so we were received with a royal salute. A rumbling noise was heard above – it got louder and louder, and an immense rock appeared coming down the frozen surface of the couloir in gigantic bounds, followed by a tremendous family of smaller ones, bounding and rolling and whizzing past like cannon shots.'

They hoped that they would get across the couloir before the next rockfall. Anderegg stepped out and crossed the steep snow until he came to the watercourse in the centre:

> a simple glance showed him the only spot we could cross it, about 20 yards higher up, and we mounted directly towards it – two steps cut with the axe and we were across it, and as there was no snow on this side, he strode on, making first rate steps with one stroke of the axe, and in about two minutes we were sitting on a rock the other side smoking our pipes and watching the blundering hesitating proceedings of the others.

In his diary Reilly is not very complimentary regarding the Chamonix guides, whom he regarded as inferior to Melchior, clearly his ideal of what a guide should be. They climbed a rocky arête, which took them to the top of Aiguille du Goûter to the site of the wooden hut that stood on a narrow ridge. The hut had a sloping roof and measured just 8 x 12 feet (2.4m by 3.6m). It was constructed in a way that left many gaps for the cold wind to howl through and the floor was thick with ice. As the porters had brought no bundles of straw or blankets with them, it was clear a cold night was in prospect. So Reilly and Brandram set about hewing out large masses of ice that revealed 'a layer of rotten stew, bones and every kind of filth which made the place smell like 50 pigsties'. Warmed up by this action Reilly then sketched the Dôme in the setting sun and enjoyed a hearty dinner. They laid the floor with flattish rocks before retiring; Reilly was sorry that he had not brought more warm clothing.

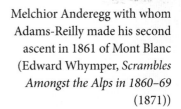

Melchior Anderegg with whom Adams-Reilly made his second ascent in 1861 of Mont Blanc (Edward Whymper, *Scrambles Amongst the Alps in 1860–69* (1871))

Next morning they breakfasted on a brew of hot wine before emerging at 4.15 a.m. Anderegg and Reilly went out in front, stopping to assist the others over a couple of crevasses up the slopes on the side of the Dôme, skirting seracs and crevasses to reach its summit at 5.35 a.m. They then made their way downwards toward the Bosses du Dromadaire that would lead them to the summit of Mont Blanc, which was just begining to light up with the morning sun. The snow on the ridge was firm and wide enough to cross without hesitation. They reached the top of the Bosses at 6.50 a.m. and spotted a party coming from the Grands Mulets while they were each drinking a mouthful of wine. Soon they were climbing the arête that led to the top of the 'collet' and followed a narrow ridge that took Reilly up to the summit of Mont Blanc for the second time. The large Grands Mulets party who had beaten them to it included a French artist, an English gentleman and several guides. The feasting started and 'the champagne as usual was delicious', but they were too hungry and thirsty to be particular. Reilly chose to descend via the Mer de la Côte this time, 'the celebrated slope of which Albert Smith had drawn such a fearsome picture' to find it 'merely a rounded bank of ice, lying at an angle of 46 °'; they went down the slope with perfect ease and soon found themselves standing on the surface of the Corridor. They descended to the Grands Mulets, glissading in the sitting position when the snow became too soft. He delighted in a quick descent through the Bossons Glacier, following the great Melchior through the labyrinth of seracs and noting that he never hesitated a moment and was never for an instant at fault: 'he went at a fast pace and it tasked my powers of head and foot to the very utmost to keep up with him'.

Back at the hotel Anderegg came to take his leave after dinner. Reilly wrote, 'We parted with regret, and I put my name in his book among the great ones of the ice: Kennedy Steven, et id genus – I was not the least fatigued, but I felt I had done a day's work, and was not sorry to get to bed.' Next evening he took his finished sketches to Sam Brandram; 'he was an AC, and he pressed me very much to belong to that august body, offering to do anything he could for me, and I agreed, giving him my address and achievements to submit to the secretary.'

Reilly was admitted to the Alpine Club on 4 March 1862, proposed by the Rev. Leslie Stephen and seconded by Sam Brandram, on the basis of these quality climbs plus the Col du Géant and Strahlegg, which confirms he had had an earlier visit or visits to the Alps.[23] He climbed Mont Blanc for the third time in 1862, this time by the St Gervais route with W. and C. Wigram. He then crossed the Col d'Argentière and was so much struck by the discrepancies between the existing maps and the appearance of the surrounding ranges that he resolved to make a serious attempt to ascertain their origin.[24]

The Alpine Club soon provided Reilly with access to and contact with many contemporaries who would influence and motivate his life's work. In 1863 Reilly met Forbes, whose work he greatly admired, particularly his accurate and detailed map of the Mer de Glace; they soon became great friends. Reilly took special interest in the chain of Mont Blanc and was upset that this most visited region of the Alps should be the most poorly mapped. He explained his frustration upon discovering that the French and Sardinian maps could not be reconciled where they overlapped with each other: 'I had failed not less signally in attempting to reconcile the Glacier d'Argentière, as laid down by the Sardinian engineers, with the same glacier as put down by the hands of nature.'[25] He was an excellent artist, and made panoramic drawings of different parts of the range with great facility and correctness. Forbes advised Reilly that 'no trustworthy results could be obtained without determining the real position of the doubtful peaks, by means of a theodolite'. He drew up for him a system of triangulation that would connect Forbes's own survey of the Mer de Glace with the Swiss cartes fédérales and fix the intermediate points with some certainty.[26]

The plan assumed the correctness of sheet xxii of Dufour's map of Switzerland, issued in 1861, which, however, only covered only one fifth of the range. With further advice from Forbes, Reilly took on the physical and technical challenge of reconciling the unsurveyed French side of the range with the finished work of the Swiss surveyors. Armed with a theodolite that featured a powerful telescope and a non-inverting eyepiece, plus a boiling-water apparatus and an aneroid barometer for measuring altitude, he set about a systematic survey of the chain. He started on 29 June 1863. He was supported by the Visp guide Albrecht and local strongman Henri Charlet, whom he hired to carry the theodolite (mounted on a frame 'suggestive of a very young five barred gate') and some long poles for marking the positions of his stations. First he found Forbes' original stations on the Trélaporte and Brévent and then set up his own first station on a little peak known as the Aiguille des Grand Montets, which rises above both the Nant Blanc and the Argentière Glaciers. He spent many hours there and before he left it he set up a great *homme de Pierre* (cairn or stone man, as they were popularly named at that time), to which was added a post that resembled a railway signal post. This was elegantly painted red and white by Albrecht. The next day the survey team set up the next station at Les Possettes, which overlooks the Tour Glacier.

This station provided the rationale for the first ascent of the Col de Triolet, which Reilly made with J. Birkbeck and G. C. Hodgkinson. Also in the company was Captain Jean Joseph Mieulet of the French surveying corps, with whom Reilly had become acquainted and had consulted regarding his surveying work on the chain of Mont Blanc. To get there he climbed up 'the steepest snow I ever crossed', at an angle of 55° and 60° in places, to reach the plateau of the col.[27] Over the next couple of days he set up four more stations on the ridge running northwest from Aiguille du Chardonnet to the village of Argentière, and then climbed the Col du Tour with Birkbeck and Hodgkinson to set up another on the ridge running northwest from Aiguille du Chardonnet.

Reilly discovered that the point referred to on the Swiss map as Pointe des Plines could be nothing other than the back of the Aiguille d'Argentière, although on that map these two points were located 1½ miles (2.41 km) apart. He submitted his findings to an international meeting tasked to reconstruct the map of the chain of Mont Blanc with representatives of French and Swiss cartographers on 16 July. They agreed the Swiss boundary line, which was then marked in the centre of the Tour Glacier, but actually ran along the arête of the Chardonnet to Mont Dolent to the east of the Argentière glacier.

The author on the summit of Mont Dolent in 2005. (Courtesy Con Collins)

He continued to establish another twenty stations from the Brévent and the Flegère, stretching out by the Col de Voza, Mont Joli, Mont Rosaletta, Col du Bonhomme, Col des Fours, Col de la Seigne, the Cremont and Mount Saxe, until they reached the Swiss border at Col Ferrex. From Orsières he explored the upper basin of the Saleinaz Glacier. At each point he took readings, recorded the data, and drew his own panoramic sketches. With only a meagre resource of time and money, he was confined to visiting each station once. Surveying completed, he then made his fourth ascent of Mont Blanc with J. Birkbeck on 7 August. He followed with an unsuccessful attempt on the unclimbed Aiguille Verte but was somewhat compensated in making the first passage of the Col du Chardonnet on 24 August; both routes were undertaken in the company of Sam Brandram.

During the winter of 1863 and spring of 1864 Reilly drafted a 1:80,000 scale map that could be used for direct comparison with the French manuscript. He determined 200 discrete points on his map using triangulation, each of which was located where his direct observations had placed them and without reference to any other map. He thought the future usefulness of this was of far more value than to construct a compilation of existing maps. So, with the exception of the details of villages and rivers (below the snow line) taken from the cartes fédérales and the details of the Valley of Chamonix, for which he used Forbes' records, he relied entirely his own data for the high-level mapping.

When he presented his draft map to the Alpine Club, it was resolved that it should be published. Before it went to the hands of the engraver, however, he undertook to revise the map thoroughly in the light of another series of expeditions to be attempted in the company of the young London-born alpinist Edward Whymper, then a rising star in the Club. Whymper later wrote:

> This extraordinary piece of work revealed Mr Reilly to me as a man of wonderful determination and perseverance. With very small hope that my proposal would be accepted, I invited him to take part in renewed attacks on the Matterhorn. He entered heartily into my plans and met me with a counter proposition – namely, that I should accompany him on some expeditions which he had projected in the chain of Mont Blanc. The un-written contract took this form: I will help you carry out your desires, and you shall assist me to carry out mine. I eagerly closed with an arrangement in which the advantages were upon my side.[28]

A letter from Whymper to Reilly on 18 January 1864 illustrates the extent to which Whymper (a professional engraver and perhaps the boldest and most ambitious climber of the era) supported Reilly in his work:

> The map is to be done by Kell; his estimate is for doing it on 10 stones, that being the number he considers necessary. I consider the number excessive, and think it ought to be done very well on 7, viz, 2 blues, 2 brown, black, red and green, but he ought to know his business. I have no doubt he will do it well. What you say about my editing is bosh; it is no great matter for one man to look over a map in progress for another and all the credit shall and will be yours.
>
> I dare say someone else will write to tell you that you can't return the map to Longman

(Mr) too soon, as there is really barely sufficient time left for it to be reproduced properly before next season. Don't delay doing this for your own sake. I am surprised to hear you say that you like the manner in which Bonney outlines are reproduced. Bonney usually sketches well, and the country is magnificent, so I think something better ought to have been done. I should be sorry to see your sketches come out poorly.

You haven't answered me about the height of the Col d'Argentière. Please do so . . . You are as usual full of excuses for not working. You must write an all MB [Mont Blanc] paper. I have plenty of notes written out for it *in extenio* since my return. It is not from any lack of material that I shall not, but simply because you are the proper man. So do it like a good fellow without anymore bother.

The grand scheme for a new map of the entire Alps is likely to fall to the ground. Keith Johnson requires 1500£ for producing the plates, and this frightens Longmans. There is a chance for you Mr Reilly Sir. You can do it like you have drawn your MB map, and you would stand a fair chance of being immortalised.

I have a great mind to come and see what you are doing. I don't believe it is anything more than loafing abroad with fishing rod and gun, and that you have gone out of the way only to avoid being bored by such as your devoted servant. I think I <u>must</u> have another go at the Matterhorn. I have got a most original idea of a route which I should like to try. Something totally different from any idea I have had before. I should however require Melchoir, Almer, Croz and two subordinates, and I fear this is likely to prove fatal to the outcome.

I am, Dear Reilly, Yours very faithfully

Edward Whymper[29]

Reilly wrote a paper on his surveying work as urged by Whymper. Entitled *A Rough Survey of the Chain of Mont Blanc*, he read it to the Alpine Club on 3 May 1864 and it was published in the first edition of *The Alpine Journal*.[30] In order to complete the promised map revisions Reilly needed additional data, which required visiting a number of unclimbed peaks. As a consequence he made the first ascents of the Mont Dolent, Aiguille de Trélatête and Aiguille de Argentière in

Above: Edward Whymper at twenty-two. His first ascents in the Mont Blanc range, the Dauphine range and on the Matterhorn made the young Englishman the most prolific and famous of all the golden age Alpine pioneers. (*Alpine Journal*)

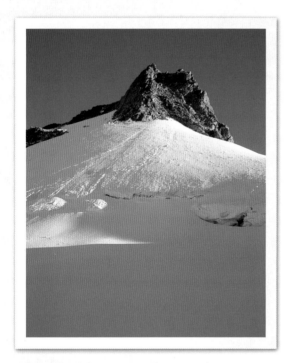

Approaching the summit of Mont Dolent by Reilly's route in 2005. (Author's photo)

the first half of July 1964. He engaged the guide François Couttet; Whymper was accompanied by the great Chamonix guide Michel Croz. They were joined by A. W. Moore (1841–1887), a civil servant and another English golden age pioneer who notably made the first ascent of Mont Blanc by the Brenva Glacier in 1865 (old Brenva Route). Moore was accompanied by the experienced Oberland guide Christian Almer.

Reilly 'found Whymper and Moore who had been doing everything in the Dauphiné' in Chamonix on 4 July.[31] The group first went to Chalets des Ognons (now known as Chalets des Lognon) on 5 July, from where they made an attempt on the Aiguille de Argentière the following morning from the Col du Chardonnet. However, at the Col the party (with blue lips and 'munching legs of poulets') were at the mercy of a furious wind that soon had them frozen and miserable. Moore and Almer went down to Orsières and the rest returned toward Chamonix. They stopped to look back at 8 a.m. and found the sky cloudless and observed they were out of the wind. They noticed another branch of the glacier rise far above the Col du Chardonnet close to the top of the Argentière. It looked a better route, so they about-turned and went at it with vigour. Croz cut 700 steps to climb the steep glacier and a gully that rose out of it so that they could reach the ridge, which they followed until they were within about 250 feet (75m) of the summit. However the ridge turned to shattered ice and soon they realised they were step-cutting through hollow, layered ice, while snow was spin-drifting over them. Whymper kicked hard and made a hole clear through his footing just at the same time as Reilly pushed one of his hands right through the roof. In the wind Couttet's hat was torn off and 'went on a tour of Switzerland'. The guides could find no firm footing. 'Suppose we go down,' suggested Whymper. 'Very willingly,' said Reilly. Despite their closeness to the top, the guides had no objection either, so they marched down again and crossed over to the Chapeau Glacier to spend that night at Montanvert.

After a late start next day, Reilly ascended to bivouac among the large stones at the top of the Couvercle with Whymper and the guides Michel Croz, Michel Payot and Henri Charlet of Chamonix. Their next objective was to reach the Col de Triolet. He describes lying awake, very cold, at their Couvercle bivouac site: 'feeling strongly inclined to brain Whymper with my boots', as Whymper 'snored in a provokingly comfortable manner.' At 5.30 a.m. next morning (8 July), led by Croz and Payot, they zigzagged their way over the upper slopes of the Glacier de Talèfre towards the foot of the Aiguille de Triolet, where they joined a secondary glacier that rose steeply from a corner to reach the Col. They ascended steep, frozen avalanche debris between the rock of Les Courtes and the glacier to reach the Col at 7.30 a.m, finding shelter from the wind among rocks on the southwest side where they unpacked their eatables. The descent was down steep ice spotted with projecting rocks, through which steps were cut from rock to rock to join a branch of the Glacier de Triolet. Their passage from there took them down névé slopes where they encountered more bergschrunds than Reilly had ever seen together in one place. Each one had to be crawled down, over, around, or jumped across, which 'made their lives a burden' on their way to Pré du Bar via the base of Mont Rouge and the snout of the glacier du Mont Dolent. It took eight and a half hours to reach the unoccupied chalets where they spent the night; they sent a porter to seek out milk and local produce.

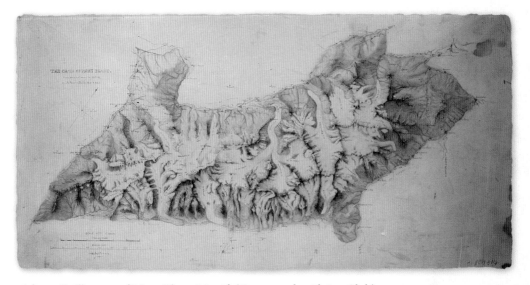

Adams-Reilly map of Mont Blanc Massif. (Courtesy the Alpine Club)

The ascent of the Mont Dolent the following day involved a little of everything: a grind over shaley banks, followed by a little walk over grass, then a tramp over a pleasant moraine path, and then a little zigzagging over the snow-covered glacier of Mont Dolent. A little bergschrund was followed by a little wall of snow, flanked by a little buttress to a ridge that led to a little summit at its highest point. He described the summit as 'a miniature Jungfrau, a toy summit – you could cover it with your hand'. His description of the sublime view from the summit of Mont Dolent, where the Swiss, Italian and French frontiers meet, makes one want to take off straight away and enjoy it for oneself: it has 'all the superiority of a picture grouped by the hand of a master, over the wild chaos of rock and snow which composes many mountain views . . . Passing from the chain itself to more distant mountain systems, the view itself is as extensive, and far more lovely than from Mont Blanc itself'. He observed the nearby Combin and Velan, the Oberland – the snowy Monte Rosa contrasted by the black rock of the Matterhorn and all the distant ranges of Swiss, French and Italian Alps. They descended by the same route to the Swiss Val Ferrex and continued in the cool of the afternoon to Courmayeur for food and night lodgings. It had been twelve hours of walking effort.

The Aiguille de Trélatête, the next station on Reilly's list, had many names and a topography that was only vaguely understood. No one knew which of its three peaks was highest and its

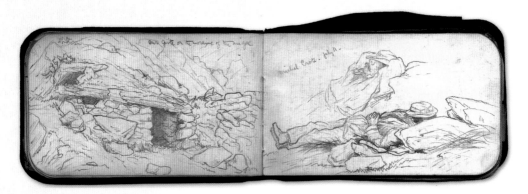

Adams-Reilly's sketches of Gite on the moraine of Miage (left) and Michel Croz, 11 July, in his 1864 diary. (Courtesy the Alpine Club)

accurate location and structure was a key to his finalising and verifying the accuracy of the map. They left Courmayeur in the afternoon (10 July) in a shower of rain to find a campsite on the misty Mont Suc for the ascent of the Aiguille de Trélatête. A porter was hired to carry a vast load of straw, which they deposited on the moraine of the Miage Glacier just above the Lac de Combal in a charming little hole that some solitary shepherd had excavated beneath a great slab of rock. Reilly enjoyed a 'delicious swim' in the Lac and recounted that the site was 'a little habitation, half hut, half rabbit-burrow, constructed by some ancient berger of luxurious habits.'

Because of rain and low cloud they slept in until noon next day, but then the weather improved and they set off at 4 p.m. On reaching the final plateau of Mont Suc below its snowy summit arête (9,700 feet/2,960m), they set up a makeshift tent. Reilly's diary of 1864 is a real revelation to the modern mountaineer. Many sketches were made to illustrate the position of the summit or station on which Reilly stood in relation to the neighbouring peaks. These pencil and blue marker drawings are incredibly accurate, sometimes of almost photographic quality, and each is labelled with numbers and letters; one drawing shows the climbers' track to a summit. However, the human dimension of the diary is equally fascinating, since Reilly has recorded the activities of Whymper and Croz, as well as his own thoughts and concerns. His sketch of the great Michel Croz, sleeping at their bivouac site on Mont Suc, illustrates the basic simplicity and boldness of the pioneering activity of the age. Whymper made etchings of several of the sketches for inclusion in his book, including the picture of the lean-to tent in which they spent the night.[32] He also included six pen-and-ink drawings, executed by himself, of Reilly reading a penny novel. Of that night on Mount Suc, overlooking the Glacier de Miage at about 9,500 feet (2,900m), Reilly wrote:

> Passed a large cave on the left but there was snow in it – sleeping place ¼ past 7 – After mounting plateau after plateau and finding no resting place our final choice was at the very top of Mt Suc, just below the snow arête & at the side overlooking Gl. de Miage – mounted a few feet higher to the top, and the view of Mt Blanc would have been magnificent but it was covered with manes of bruillard [*brouillard* or fog] – we were very high – looked clean over the S ridge of the Allee Blanche, to the bottom of the Ruitor – we were just opposite a peak of dark shale which must be enormously high, & commanded a splendid view – We made a tent of our two plaids sewn together, made a brew of hot wine & cloves, and after a curious repast of bread & butter, portable soup & cloves, I turned in, and slept exceedingly well.[33]

They left their bivouac at 4.45 a.m. and arrived upon the highest of the three summits of the Trélatête at 9.40 a.m., having previously passed over the lowest one. From here Reilly sketched the west face of Mont Blanc, which towered above the Aiguille de Miage, and at last understood the exact topography of the western side of the Mont Blanc chain. He wrote:

> For four years I had felt great interest in the geography of the chain; the year before I had mapped, more or less successfully, all but this spot, and this spot had always eluded my grasp. The praises, undeserved as they were, which my map had received were as gall and wormwood to me when I thought of the great slope which I had been obliged to leave blank, speckled over with unmeaning dots of rocks gathered from previous maps – for I had consulted them all without meeting with an intelligent representation of it . . . now from the top of the dead wall of rock which had so long closed my view, I saw those fine glaciers from top to bottom, pouring down their streams, nearly as large as the Bossons, from Mont Blanc, from the Bosse and from the Dome.

The tour finished on a high note on 15 July with the first ascent of Aiguille de Argentière (3,902m) by its west flank and northwest ridge. It was perhaps Reilly's finest first ascent on what is now a very popular and accessible mountain. The glacier that sweeps down the southwest flank of the mountain is named Mieulet, in honour of the French cartographer who helped Reilly with his work.

The map survey work completed, Whymper moved on to Zermatt where Reilly agreed to join him in a few days to make an attempt on the unclimbed Matterhorn by its Hörnli Ridge. While he waited for Reilly, Whymper amused himself describing and sketching the scene outside the Monte Rosa Hotel where Swiss, French and Italian guides and

Above: Adams-Reilly's sketch of Gite on Mt Suc in his 1864 diary. (Courtesy the Alpine Club)

the *messieurs* (mostly English gentlemen) mingled together in agreeable association. He wrote:

> Two dozen guides – good, bad and indifferent; French, Swiss and Italian – can be commonly seen sitting on the wall on the front of the Monte Rosa Hotel; waiting on their employers, and looking for employers; watching new arrivals, and speculating on the numbers of francs which may be extracted from their pockets. The *Messieurs* – sometimes strangely and wonderfully dressed – stand about in groups, or lean back in chairs, or lounge on the benches which are placed by the door. They wear extraordinary boots and still more remarkable head-dresses. Their peeled, blistered, and swollen faces are worth studying. Some, by the exercise of watchfulness and unremitting care, have been fortunate enough to acquire a fine Sienna complection. But most of them have not been so happy. They have been scorched on rocks, and roasted on glaciers. Their cheeks – first puffed, then cracked – have exuded a turpentine-like matter, which has coursed down their faces, and has dried in patches like the resin on the trunks of pines. They have removed it, and at the same time have pulled off large flakes of their skin. They have gone from bad to worse –their case has become hopeless – knives and scissors have been called into play; tenderly, and daintily, they have endeavoured to reduce their cheeks to one uniform hue. It is not to be done. But they have gone on, fascinated, and at last have brought their unhappy countenances to a state of helpless and complete ruin. Their lips are cracked; their cheeks are swollen; their eyes are blood-shot; their noses are peeled and undescribable.
>
> Such are the pleasures of the mountaineer! Scornfully and derisively the last comer compares the sight of his own flaccid face and dainty hands; unconscious that he too, perhaps, will be numbered with those he now ridicules.[34]

Reilly was to take a convoy of important stores with him to Zermatt, but first he wanted to explore the possibility of ascending Mont Blanc from the Glacier de Miage. For this route Reilly joined forces with J. Birkbeck and was guided by Michel Croz and porters Michel Clemence Payot 'the younger' and Marc Tairraz. They overnighted in a lodging at the village of Bionnaz on 4 August, where Reilly observed the children were especially remarkable 'as their countenances are generally decorated with a species of warpaint produced by their custom of living on little black cherries'. The party rose at 2.30 a.m. and, half awake, stumbled up the Col de Miage through glacial moraine before descending diagonally onto the surface of a large glacier that came down from the south side of the arête joining the Aiguille de Bionnassay and the Dôme du Goûter, gaining the top of this arête about its midpoint and following it to reach the Dôme.[35] He could not have avoided looking back over the full length of the Glacier de Trélatête to the summits of the Aiguille de Miage and Trélatête and admiring their unfolding beauty with the knowledge he had sorted out their complex topography. They followed the arête to the top of the Dôme, reaching there at 5 p.m., and decided to descend to Chamonix via the Grands Mulets. Resisting hospitable invitations to stay in the *cabane* at the Grands Mulets (where they arrived just as the sun was setting at 6.45 p.m.) they continued to descend through the Bossons Glacier, finally arriving in Chamonix at 10 p.m. Reilly had proved his new shorter route from Courmayeur to Chamonix was viable; he contended it was the highest and, in his mind, the most magnificent pass in the chain of Mont Blanc. It certainly rounded off an unbelievable fortnight of exploration in the Alps' premier range.

He then travelled to Zermatt to meet Whymper and assist him in his renewed attempts on the Matterhorn; on arrival he discovered that urgent business matters had obliged Whymper to return immediately to London. As a result Reilly missed his chance to make the first ascent of the Matterhorn. Whymper, as we have seen, would return the following year with Michael Croz and party.

The revisions being completed, the Alpine Club published Reilly's map of 'The Chain of Mont Blanc' with a scale of 1:80,000 that year.[36] Delighted with the map's success, Reilly began a new survey in the Monte Rosa district. He was helped again in this respect by Whymper's knowledge of the area and ability to identify competent local porters and guides to assist him in his work. Two wonderfully descriptive letters from Whymper to Reilly dated 22 April and 1 May 1865 illustrate this beautifully – as well as touching on Whymper's unquenched preoccupation with climbing the Matterhorn:

> As to guides; at Breuil there is no one except Luc Meynet who I have had frequently. He is a trifle old, very ugly, and in general appearances a scarecrow. Moreover he is slightly unclean but in temper he is perfect, and very plucky. He is as far as I know the sole man who has any inclination to be a guide at Breuil . . . The only man I know of in the Val Tournanche who is at all near first rate is Jean Antoine Carrel and he lives at V.T. he is as good a rockman as I have ever seen, very strong, and very easily riled. If you wanted a man for a new excursion in the V.T. he would do as well as Croz or any other man and I recommend you to take him, but his temper does not recommend him. He has another failing, he always quotes his relationship to the Chamonix Carrel at every halt, and endeavours on every opportunity to make you take a relative of his (another Carrel of V.T.) who is a hang dog looking fellow and is the man who went with Tyndall and Hawkins as related in Vueulin Tourists.
>
> There is yet another Carrel at or near V.T. named Caesar. He is young, ugly (well marked with small pox, I think) but is very strong, a good mountaineer, and good tempered. He showed up very well on the Matterhorn.
>
> There is another man I have had living at or near V.T. who as well as I remember, was named Walter or Walten; I should class him with Caesar Carrel perhaps not quite as good, not having as much experience.
>
> These are all the men . . . about whom I know anything, except one or two duffers, who would not be any use to you and I should say that of the lot, Luc Meynet or Caesar Carrel would answer your purpose best. They both speak French and the local patois; a very polyglot lingo, and you must have a man who does this, to be any use to you.
>
> I have planned something about the Matterhorn, but heavens knows if I shall carry it out for my business in Land perplexes me, and <u>may</u> prevent my going out. Should I go and be able to get out a decent lot of guides I should go at the Matterhorn again, and it will decidedly increase my pleasure if you come too.[37]

And again, on 1 May:

> My plans are doubtful, but if I go I shall try the Matterhorn in <u>June</u>, I wish with all my

heart you could be with me, do if you possibly can. Charlet I decide <u>not</u> to have in any case. I do not think men will rise to the general appeal for the map, it requires special application I think. I am very pleased you decided to do the M. Rosa business. I have an idea sketching around the S. myself, but abandoned that as you will do it.

My entering into competition with you is hopeless. My idea is, if business allows me to have a short and stiff mountaineering campaign and then about the beginning of July, to set to work at serious sketching which I have not had in the Alps since 1860. As I am entirely ruled by my business, it is impossible for me to fix anything, but I hope to do as I have indicated. I leave England about 8th of June. I am glad you think of reading an account of our M Blanc doings, the lot with your additional ones might be enough for a short paper. I don't believe you when say it is a lame and impotent account of them. If there is anything you want from my notebook about them, let me know by all means.[38]

Reilly described his 1864 expeditions in a paper he read to the Alpine Club on 6 June 1865 shortly before his visit to the Alps to work on his Swiss map. The paper, 'Some new ascents and passes in the chain of Mont Blanc', was published in *The Alpine Journal* in September of that year. Arriving in Breuil, he found a note from Whymper, dated 20 June; this was to be Whymper's last communication before the momentous events of the 14 July that bound his name to that of the Matterhorn forever:

I have directed the people here to let you have my properties just as I should have them myself. And I have told Luc Meynet who lives at the bottom of the hill that you will probably want him, at which he expressed delight. Should he want too much, cut him short & send for Caesar Carrel at Val Tournanche. I expect to be back here about the 10th of July, when I shall hope to meet you. I have had very bad luck as yet. Croz has become awfully bumptious not to say fractious.
Yours very faithfully, Edward Whymper[39]

The first ascent of the Matterhorn on 14 July of that fateful year and the fatal accident which overtook the summit party in descent left four of Whymper's companions dead, having fallen 4,000 feet (1,200m) to the glacier beneath. Whymper bore the brunt of criticism in the national press and was subject to the glare of publicity regarding the perceived folly and danger of mountaineering. It was while working on the Monte Rosa survey at Breuil on the Italian side that Reilly heard of the Matterhorn accident. Reilly immediately made his way to Zermatt to be of help and comfort to his friend.

The inquest that followed questioned the quality of the rope which had broken, finding that it was of inferior quality and had been improperly used. This led to criticism of Whymper and to an acrimonious debate questioning the rationale of alpinism itself. Whymper was at the centre of the storm. His *Scrambles amongst the Alps in the Years 1860–69*, which he illustrated himself, was published in 1871. It became one of the most popular mountaineering books ever written, because it included his own account of the Matterhorn accident. It also detailed the feats of his 1864 week with Reilly. Taken in the context of Whymper's overall mountaineering achievements the book helped to quell the media debate regarding alpinism.

After the Matterhorn accident Anthony Adams-Reilly took his Monte Rosa survey results back to London where he completed the map and presented it to the Alpine Club for publication. It was the map of choice for mountaineers for a quarter of a century, since it described the southern valleys of Switzerland's highest mountain so accuately. He climbed with C. E. Mathews (a founding member of the Alpine Club) in 1866, completing several new routes. Mathews, with whom he shared rooms, said of him: 'No mountaineer was ever better known in the valley of Chamonix; he had been seven times to the summit of Mont Blanc, and there were few of the guides and porters of the district who had not at some time or other been employed by him.'[40]

He did little climbing in the following years but was back in Chamonix in 1869 when he made his seventh and final ascent of Mont Blanc. While in Geneva he hurt his knee, which curtailed his ability to walk and climb. An example of Reilly's unselfishness and devotion to Forbes arose when, in 1873, the professor's son George was advised to travel abroad to recuperate from illness. The professor being unable to travel, Reilly volunteered and took George to Chamonix to see the glaciers that had played such a part in his father's work. While in Italy they climbed Mount Etna and Vesuvius. Mathews wrote touchingly of him:

> Reilly was unselfishness personified. I remember an occasion when he met an absolute stranger at a friend's house high up amongst the mountains. The stranger being taken ill was ordered home without a moment's delay. Reilly generously offered to accompany him, and took care of him as far as Geneva, but there [being] no improvement, accompanied him to Paris, then to Calais, and at last to Dover; and when he delivered the sick man to the care of his friends– and not till then – did he return to the Alps. Such an act of sterling kindness must be recorded, for how many mountaineers are there of whom such a tale could be told?[41]

Reilly loved life in London, being fond of the arts and theatre and attending meetings at the Alpine Club. He was popular but declined the presidency when it was offered to him, since he felt he did not have the gravitas for the role. He came back to Ireland to live at Delgany, County Wicklow, in 1881. Mathews came to visit him there three years later and found him poorly and needing sticks to come downstairs. He died a year later on 15 April, having suffered a stroke.

Mathews attended his funeral and wrote: 'Few of his friends will ever see the runic cross, carved with Swiss flowers, that mark his resting place above the waters of Lough Derg; but as long as men love the Alps, his work and his name will never be forgotten.'[42]

Detail of the Alpine flowers engraved on the headstone of Reilly's grave at Coolbawn Church of Ireland churchyard, County Tipperary. (Author's photo)

Reilly was ably assisted during his finest Alpine season in 1864 by Michel Croz from Chamonix. It is fitting that the contribution of Croz who, like Bennen, was destined to die in pursuit of his profession, be fully acknowledged and that his life story be included with the story of Reilly and his friend Edward Whymper.

Right: Michel Croz, the great Chamonix guide, who climbed during 1864 with Adams-Reilly and Whymper, and who died on descent following success on the Matterhorn in 1865. (Edward Whymper in *Scrambles Amongst the Alps in 1860–69* (1871))

Left: The gravestone of Michel Croz in Zermatt. (Author's photo)

Michel Croz, 1830–1865

Michel Auguste Croz lived at the village of Tour, in the valley of Chamonix where he was born in 1830.[43] He learned his trade in the Chamonix district and is first recorded in a party with William Mathews in an ascent of Mont Blanc in 1859. With Mathews he made the first ascent of Grande Casse, the highest mountain in southern Savoy, in 1860 and with Mathews and others made an attempt of the Pelvoux in the Dauphiné. He then went to Zermatt with Bonney and Hawkshaw where they climbed the Breithorn, Monte Rosa and the Lysjoch, crossed the Durand, Triftjoch and Adler Passes and later climbed the Strahlhorn. He usually worked as a sole guide or combined with his brother Jean-Baptiste. With J. J. Tuckett he made the second ascent of Pelvoux and crossed several new passes in the Dauphiné in 1862. He climbed Mont Pourri solo and the Pic Grivola with Mathews that same season. In 1863 the same party climbed the Grand Rousses in the Dauphiné.

In 1864 he was engaged by Whymper and A. W. Moore with Christian Almer of Grindelwald to make the first ascent of the Barre des Ecrins in the Dauphine. In July Croz accompanied Adams-Reilly and Whymper in a series of new expeditions from Chamonix, which included the Col de Triolet, Mont Dolent, Aiguille de Trélatête and Aiguille d'Argentière. With Reilly the following week he made the first passage of the Col du Dôme du Goûter from the chalets of Miage to the Grands Mulets. In 1865 Michel Croz was again with Whymper, who had also engaged Christian Almer and Franz Biener to climb the Grand Cornier and Dent Blanche. They subsequently crossed to Zermatt to make some attempts on the Matterhorn and thence to Courmayeur, from where they climbed the western summit of the Grandes Jorasses and then crossed the Col Dolent to Chamonix. Croz left Whymper to fulfil another engagement in Chamonix with the Rev. Charles Hudson and party, who were to make the second ascent of the Aiguille Verte. He then moved to Zermatt with Hudson where he met up with Whymper again and made the first ascent of the Matterhorn. Sadly Croz met his death in its descent.

Croz was considered to be first class on rock and the best ice-climber of his age, with an untiring ability when step-cutting. He had great physical powers, which facilitated cutting through a cornice or the crossing of difficult bergschrunds. His instinctive ability in route-finding, particularly in new ranges, was highly regarded. Whymper wrote that 'he was happiest where he was employing his powers to the utmost'. Of his climbing through a particularly difficult cornice, Whymper wrote: 'he acted rather than said, where snow lies fast, there man can go; where ice exists, a way may be cut, it is a question of power; I have the power; all you have to do is to follow me.'[44] The inscription on his gravestone in the churchyard at Zermatt carries the inscription 'bears honourable testimony to his rectitude, his courage and his devotion'.

5

Charles Barrington:
Eigerman

Not having money enough with me to try the Matterhorn, I went home.

Charles Barrington, letter to his brother published in *The Alpine Journal*, 1878

CHARLES BARRINGTON made just one visit to the Alps in his lifetime. He was then twenty-four years old and in the space of two days he climbed the Jungfrau, the highest peak in the Bernese Oberland, and made the first ascent of the Eiger. The Eiger (particularly the north face) is regarded to this day as perhaps the most notorious of all the Alpine peaks. His guides for both ascents were two very able Grindelwald guides, Christian Almer and Peter Bohren. Before he left Grindelwald for the Eiger ascent, Barrington and his guides had had to overcome the opposition of the guides' families, who thought the proposition foolhardy and likely to cost them their lives. The mountain had previously been attempted unsuccessfully by Sigmond Porges, an accomplished Viennese climber, who had made the first ascent of the neighbouring Mönch the previous year with Almer. Charles later told his brother that the Matterhorn had been in his sights after his success on the Eiger, but that lack of money had driven him home. One wonders if the first ascent of the Matterhorn would have waited another eight years if the undaunted young Wicklow man had brought more money with him to Grindelwald.

Because he never published a detailed account of the climb at the time, the identity of the successful climber who had engaged Almer and Bohren in 1857 was for a long time a mystery. His signature was erroneously ascribed to an Englishman, one 'Charles Harrington', unknown to anyone in the Alpine Club.[1] However, in the *Füherbucher* of Christian Almer, Barrington had faithfully recorded both ascents and, for good measure, he added his address, 'Fassaroe, Co. Wicklow', to his signature for his bold Eiger ascent.[2] Confirmation of his identity only came to

Charles Barrington, 1834–1901

- A Dublin merchant from a Quaker family, born at Fassaroe near Enniskerry, County Wicklow
- A sportsman with interests in steeplechasing, hunting, shooting and yachting
- As a part of his European grand tour itinerary Charles visited the Bernese Oberland and climbed the Jungfrau (4,158m), the highest peak in the range, on 9 August 1858, in company with the Grindelwald guides Christian Almer and Peter Bohren.
- Two days later he made the first ascent of the Eiger (3,970m), today perhaps the best known of all the peaks in the Alps, accompanied by the same two guides
- Despite his impressive debut, he never returned to Alps
- He was owner, trainer and jockey of *Sir Robert Peel*, the horse that won the first Irish Grand National at Fairyhouse Race Course on 4 April 1870. He used an alias to disguise his identity from those who would object to his involvement in horse racing
- He provided the prize for the winner of the first Irish hill-running event up the Sugar Loaf Mountain in County Wicklow

Facing page: portrait of Charles Barrington by Sir Thomas Jones. (From a photo by William Martin Lawrence, courtesy Ron Barrington)

light when, twenty-six years later, he wrote a letter to his younger half-brother, Richard, describing the circumstances of the first ascent, which was published in *The Alpine Journal* in 1878. His half-brother, Richard Manliffe Barrington, was a very accomplished botanist, mountaineer and a member of the Alpine Club who climbed the Eiger himself sixteen years later in the company of one of Charles' guides, Christian Almer.

The Barringtons were a philanthropic and wealthy Quaker family. The family fortune had been gradually amassed through a number of strategic business partnerships to form John Barrington & Sons, a well-known wholesale soap and candlemaking business in Dublin whose lemon-flavoured soap is mentioned in James Joyce's *Ulysses*. In 1836 Edward Barrington, Charles' father, rented 91 acres at Fassaroe ('red wilderness') near Bray, County Wicklow, on a 91-year lease and built a new house there for his family, planting 19,900 trees. The property lies in the vicinity of the Sugar Loaf Mountain and Bray Head on the fringes of the Wicklow Mountains. It was in this environment that his sons, Charles and Richard, were raised. Charles' mother and Edward's first wife was Sarah Leadbeater, granddaughter of Richard Shackleton of Ballitore, County Kildare; Sir Ernest Shackleton, the Antarctic explorer, was therefore a distant relation of the Eiger's first ascentionist.[3]

As Charles grew up, he moved easily into his role as city merchant in the family business, but he appears to have focused much of his life's passion on sports, including horse racing, hunting, shooting and yachting, and was generally regarded as 'the best of good fellows in club life'.[4] The letter that he wrote to his brother describing his ascent of the Eiger suggests he was an accomplished steeplechase jockey and trainer, which would account for his high level of boldness, fitness and agility:

> the facts are these: On Thursday, August 5th, 1858, I left Grindelwald at about 4 o'clock P.M. and walked up the glacier to a small hut, in which we spent the night. It was occupied by a goat-keeper. I was eaten up with fleas. Next morning we started with my two guides Almer and Bohren, and a French gentleman, and crossed the Strahlegg to the Grimsel, where we arrived on Friday evening the 6th.
>
> On the seventh I started with the same two guides, and walked to the Rhone Valley and up to the Eggischhorn Hotel. On Sunday the 8th I slept at the hotel, and in the evening started with Almer and Bohren, and two men to carry provisions. Had about 4 1/2 hours walk to the Faulberg, and slept in a small cave. Started early Monday, and got to the top of Jungfrau, and walked to Grindelwald, when I put up at the Bär Hof. Here I met some Alpine men whose footsteps I had tracked down the glacier. Talking about climbing, I said to them I did not think much of the work I had done, and was answered, 'Try the Eiger or the Matterhorn.' 'All right' I said. Slept with beefsteak on my face. In the evening of the next day , the 10th I made a bargain with the same guides for the Eiger, and walked up to the hotel on the Wengen Alp, stopping to play cards for an hour on the way, and found it quite full at 12 o'clock at night. Threw myself on a sofa, and started at 3.30 A.M. on August 11 for the Eiger. We took a flag from the hotel. When we came to the point where one descends into a small hollow I looked well with my glass over the face of the

Barrington's Western Flank route on the Eiger. (Les Swindin (ed.), *Bernese Oberland Selected Climbs* (2003))

Eiger next us, and made my mind up to try the rocks in front instead of going up the other side, which had been tried twice before unsuccessfully. Almer and Bohren said it was no use and declined to come the way I wished. 'All right' I said; 'you may stay I will try.' So off I went for about 300 or 400 yards over some smooth rocks to the part that was almost perpendicular. I then shouted and waved the flag for them to come on, and after five minutes they followed and came up to me. They said it was impossible; I said 'I will try.' So with a rope coiled over my shoulders, I scrambled up, sticking like a cat to the rocks, which cut my fingers, and at last got up say fifty to sixty feet. I then lowered the rope, and the guides followed with its assistance. We then had to mark our way up with chalk and small bits of stone, fearing we might not be able to find it on our return. We went up very close to the edge, looking down on Grindelwald, sometimes throwing over large stones to hear them crash down beneath the clouds. We got to the top the two guides kindly gave me the place of first man up – at 12 o'clock, stayed about ten minutes, fearing the weather, and came down in four hours, avoiding the very steep place, as looking down from above, we found out a *couloir*, down which we came, and just saved ourselves by a few seconds from an avalanche.

I was met at the bottom by about thirty visitors, and we went up to the hotel. They doubted if we had been on the top until the telescope disclosed a flag there. The hotel proprietor had a large gun fired off, and I seemed for the evening to be a 'lion'.

Thus ended my first and only visit to Switzerland. Not having money enough with me to try the Matterhorn I went home. Nothing could exceed the kindness of Almer and Bohren. I am sorry to hear the latter has passed away. Both were splendid mountaineers, and had I not been as fit as my old horse 'Sir Robert Peel' when I won the 'Irish Grand National' with him, I would not have seen half the course. I might add that when leaving Grindelwald for the Eiger I was surprised to see families of the guides in a state of distraction at their departure for the ascent, and two elderly ladies came out and abused me for taking them to risk their lives.

Your affectionate brother, Charles Barrington[5]

Richard forwarded the letter to be published in volume xi of *The Alpine Journal* with the attached note:

Sir – My brother has just sent me the following letter about the first ascent of the Eiger in 1858. As he never thought of publishing anything relating to it, no detailed account of his ascent has been kept. The facts may interest some readers of your journal, as the Eiger is such a well-known peak. The name of Harrington has been erroneously given in every notice of ascent I have seen. Perhaps you will excuse me sending you a copy of my brother's letter instead of a more elaborate and descriptive account.[6]

This account by Charles of his famous first ascent is further confirmed on pages 61 and 62 of Christian Almer's *Führerbücher* as follows:

Aug 11/58
Christian Almer has accompanied me as guide to the top of the Jungfrau from the Straggle. During the ascent he proved himself a first rate guide. Having a proper knowledge of the glaciers too much cannot be said of his strength and capabilities and to his unremitting care for my safety. It will always give me pleasure to recommend him to those wishing to make difficult excursions.
Grindelwald Chas Barrington[7]

And again:

Aug 13/58
Since writing the preceding page Christian Almer has been with me to the top of the Eigér and I must again report what I said was first rate that his qualities of a guide cannot be too highly spoken of.
Chas Barrington, Fassaroe Co. Wicklow

Although born into a well-off Quaker family, it appears Charles incurred the wrath of the Dublin Quaker community, since it was reported by 'an overseer' on 4 April 1860 to the Dublin monthly meeting of the Society of Friends that 'Charles Barrington had been married in a manner contrary to our rules. Thomas W. Fisher and Edward Alexander are appointed to visit him here-upon and report.'[8] Charles had become a member of the Church of England early in 1860 in order, it appears, to clear the path for his marriage to Louisa Grubb, daughter of Samuel Grubb a merchant from Clashleigh, Clogheen, whom he married on 22 March.[9] The official decision by the Friends is recorded later that year next to his name in the *Book of Disownments*: 'Disowned – married out of Society – married contrary to our rules and has been baptised in the Church of England.'[10] His marriage and his disownment by the Quakers did not affect his continued involvement in the family business, as his business address throughout his life was continuously listed as 202 Britain Street Great,[11] a city-centre shopping street whose name was changed, after the establishment of the Irish Free State in 1921, to its present name of Parnell Street.

We have seen that, in the letter to his brother Richard describing his exploits on the Eiger, Charles suggested he was more actively involved in horse racing than those of his entourage realised. His claim that he rode his horse Sir Robert Peel, the winner of the first Irish Grand National at Fairyhouse racecourse in 1870, is not supported in the newspaper reports of that event, however. *The Irish Times* on Tuesday 5 April 1870 reports that Sir Robert Peel, the winner of the inaugural Grand National event on Easter Monday 1870, won a prize of 147 sovereigns for its owner, a Mr L. Dunne. The name of the jockey is reported as Boylan. It seems that Charles Barrington was using an alias to disguise his identity and his passion for horse racing. Horse racing for prize money would not have been deemed acceptable behaviour for a Quaker and, at that time, would be equally unacceptable in his newly adopted Church of England. He may well have ridden incognito to save his family from further embarrassment. Whatever his reasons, the Irish Grand National soon became Ireland's most prestigious and valuable National Hunt race; it is run over 3 miles and 5 furlongs (5.83 km) on a right-handed circuit and has been run every Easter Monday since Charles Barrington's historic ride in 1870.

Charles was responsible for organising the first ever Irish hill-running race: it appears he saw a mountain race while visiting the English Lake District and decided to organise an event in Ireland.[12] He donated a gold watch to the winner of a race up and down the Sugar Loaf mountain, adjacent to the Barrington family home at Fassaroe. The race was won by the aptly named Tom Hill,[13] and the Charles Barrington Memorial Race is now an annual race in the calendar of the Irish Mountain Running Association, run in late December from the Glencormack Inn at Kilmacanogue to the top of Sugar Loaf.

Charles died on 20 April 1901 and was buried in Mount Jerome cemetery. Charles' sons, Manliffe and Cecil, were among the chief mourners and Mrs Charles Barrington is listed amongst those who sent wreaths.[14] There is no acknowledgment of his Eiger or steeplechasing achievements on his headstone, nor was there mention of these achievements in the reports of his funeral in either *The Irish Times* or the *Irish Independent*. However, a piece in *The Freeman's Journal* on 23 April 1901 records his sporting versatility: 'Mr Charles Barrington died at 18 Earlsford Terrace last Saturday. In every department of sporting life, Mr Charles Barrington was to the forefront at some time or other during his career. He had crack racers, he was a hard rider to hounds, a sure

Christian Almer, 1826–1898

Of all the pioneer alpine guides Christian Almer of Grindelwald had the longest and most splendid list of first ascents across the widest spread of Alpine districts. His early life was spent as a cheese maker in his native valley and he later worked as a shepherd. In the course of the Swiss Sonderbund War in 1847 he took part in the advance on Lucerne as a soldier in the 2nd Jäger company. His passion for chamois hunting had familiarised him with the upper reaches of his native mountains and gave him experience in travelling over snow and ice, which enabled him become a competent mountain guide. He was not an invited participant in the first passage of the Wetterhorn (now generally agreed to be the starting point of systematic mountaineering), but he and his brother-in-law, Ulrich Kaufmann (another chamois hunter), followed and overtook Alfred Wills' party, which was led by their neighbour, the Grindelwald guide Ulrich Lauener, in tandem with the reputable Auguste Balmat of Chamonix. When it was established that the two locals simply wished to take part in the ascent, rather than to race Wills' party to the top, they were roped into Wills' team. On the summit, Almer planted a fir tree that he had carried with him next to the iron pole brought by Lauener to mark Wills' achievement. Almer repeated the ascent in 1855 as an independent guide and in 1856 climbed the Jungfrau three times with clients.

His next first ascent was the Mönch with the Viennese climber Dr S. Porges, and in 1857 he completed the Grindelwald trio when he climbed the Eiger with Charles Barrington. In 1864 he spent ten days in the Dauphiné with Edward Whymper, where his list of first ascents included the Barre des Écrins, the Col des Aiguilles d'Arves, the Brèche de la Meije and the Col de la Pilatte; he later crossed Mont Blanc via the Goûter route with A. W. Moore. In 1865 he was with Moore's party again when they climbed the Grand Cornier, the Grandes Jorasses (west peak), the Col Dolent, the Aiguille Verte, the Col de Telèfre and made

Christian Almer. (Edward Whymper in *Scrambles Amongst the Alps in 1860–69* (1871))

an unsuccessful attempt on the Matterhorn one week before Whymper's ascent with the guide Michel Croz and party. During the same week as Whymper's fateful Matterhorn ascent, Almer climbed the Lauterbrunnen Breithorn and the north face of the Silberhorn with Messieurs Horby and Philpott. In 1870 he went back to the Dauphiné to climb the Ailefroide and the central peak of the Meije. He also made many first ascents in the eastern Alps with Tuckett in 1866.

Almer's climbing career came to an end when he was badly frostbitten while climbing the Jungfrau in January 1885; this led to all the toes of one foot being amputated. His two sons, Ulrich and Christian, followed their father in becoming reputable Grindelwald mountain guides.

Peter Bohren, 1822–1882

Peter Bohren was known as 'Peterli' when he was young because of his slight stature. When fully grown he stood not more than 5 feet tall, but was active, agile and courageous, proving that his diminutive size in no way reduced his strength and reliability in the mountains. Known locally as the *Gletscherwolf* ('glacier wolf'), since he was reputed to be first-rate and vigorous when cutting his way upwards through an ice slope, he had a reputation for being eagle-eyed and good-humoured, with an iron will and determination. His notable first ascents include the Eiger with Christian Almer and Charles Barrington in 1857, the Aletschhorn with F. F. Tuckett in 1859, the Lyskamm with H. B. George in 1861, and the Ebenfluh and Dreieckhorn with T. L. Murray Browne in 1868. He was in the party that made the first winter ascent of the Mönch in January 1874. He died on the job, carrying a knapsack on his back on the grass slopes of the Schreckhörner, in the company of his old friend and mentor Christian Almer, during an ascent with clients. He was sixty years of age. He is buried in the churchyard at Grindelwald.

Right: Peter Bohren, the Oberland guide nicknamed Gletscherwolf or 'Glacier Wolf'. (*The Alpine Journal*)

shot, an expert yachtsman, and the best of good fellows in club life.' This report was expanded in the next day's edition to include his great alpine feat:

> The remains of Mr Charles Barrington, senior member of the firm Barrington and Sons, Dublin, were laid to rest in Mount Jerome Cemetery yesterday. In our short notice of him yesterday we omitted mentioning a passage in his life singularly illustrative of his dash and determination. He visited Switzerland but once, in the fifties. He had then but attained manhood. At Grindelwald, then a remote valley, he went out for an excursion with a couple of guides. The Eiger, 13,000 feet high, attained his attention. The guides said all attempts to reach the summit had failed. 'Well then' said Mr Barrington, 'I am going up it.' The guides laughed and held back. He went ahead, they joined him, and all reached the summit in safety. At the hotel the next morning he was considerably chaffed at the joke they supposed him to be putting off on them having reached the summit. In the guide-books the honour of the first ascent is, of course, ascribed to 'an Englishman'.[15]

The grave of Charles Barrington, the first person to scale the Eiger, at Mount Jerome Cemetery, Dublin. (Author's photo)

6

Count Henry Russell: Wild Goose of the Pyrenees

We need not know the age of mountains, their weight, and the names of their plants and fossils, nor have broken any of our limbs on them, to speak of their beauties or their perils; and it is not in the Alpine Club I need fear to be contradicted, if I say boldly that there is no passion more innocent, more indisputable and more manly, than that of scaling peaks, even if science gains nothing by it, for in legitimate pleasures there is always wisdom; and, no ladies being present, I will not scruple to add, that of human passions those connected with peaks are often the strongest, although they last so long.

Henry Russell, 'On Mountains and on Mountaineering in General', 1871

Count Henry Russell, 1834–1909

- Born in Pau, at the foot of the French Pyrenees

- Part-educated at Clongowes Wood College, County Kildare

- His father and heirs received the title Count of Rome from Pius IX in 1862

- Made a remarkable six-month tour across America in 1857

- Made an extensive three-year tour of the rest of the world from 1858 to 1860, crossing Europe to Russia and visiting China, Japan, Indonesia, Australia, New Zealand and India

- During the remainder of his life he extensively explored and made many first ascents in the Pyrenees

- A member of the Alpine Club, he was also a founder of Société Ramond in the Pyrenees and of the Club Alpin Français

- He climbed the Vignemale thirty-three times, and was responsible for the construction of the first mountain hut on Mont Perdu and for excavating seven grottos on the Vignemale in which he often slept

- The account of his mountaineering exploits, *Souvenirs d'un Montagnard*, was first published at Pau in 1888

COUNT HENRY PATRICE MARIE RUSSELL was born in Pau on Valentine's Day 1834. The Russells (originally du Rozel) were of Norman descent, arriving in Ireland in the course of Strongbow's invasion. Despite their initially hostile settlement in Ulster, they intermarried with Catholic families and remained staunchly Catholic throughout Ireland's penal years in the face of royal inducements to convert to Protestantism. His mother was of Franco-Belgian aristocratic stock.

Henry's father and two uncles, William and Edward, all attended the newly founded Jesuit Clongowes Wood College in County Kildare; in the tradition of the Irish 'wild geese', the uncles would go on to fight as mercenaries in the Franco-Moorish war in Algeria.[1] William distinguished himself with the Croix de la Légion d'Honneur and a complimentary letter from the French Emperor Napoleon III. Henry's father, Thomas John Russell, Baron of Killough, was born in Swords, County Dublin, in 1801. His son Ferdinand, Henry's brother, wrote: 'My father left Ireland in the twenties of the last century for France, married very young, but soon became a widower. He re-married early in the thirties and lived happily to an advanced age in Pau. He had originally intended to spend a few months there at the time I was about to appear on the world's scene, but the charms of the place so captivated him, that, unmindful of the old country's claims, he settled down there for good.'[2]

Previous page: portrait of Count Henry Russell, a pioneering explorer of the Pyrennees (*Souvenirs d'un Montagnard, Tome 2* (1930))

At the age of six Henry (sometimes spelled Henri) is reputed to have made his first Pyrenean ascent, walking from Cauterets to the Lac de Gaube, where he had his first sight of the Vignemale (3,298m), a mountain with which he will be forever associated. In 1851, with his mother, Joséphine, a daughter of the Marquis de Flamarens of Gers, he walked from Luchon to Gavarnie over the Col de Cambiel; she was apparently a vigorous walker and is thought to have been a primary influence in nurturing his love of mountains. He was first educated at the College of Pons, near Saintes, and later at Pontlevoy where he studied until he was seventeen years old.

In 1851 the family moved back to Ireland temporarily and Henry and his brother Frank (then seventeen and fifteen respectively) followed in the family tradition and were sent to Clongowes Wood. (The family address in the school records is given as Ballygihen, Dalkey, and Pau, France.) The philosophy course that they followed grounded these sons of an Irish exile in Catholic doctrine; the accounts for their school fees make mention of charges for drawing materials as well as natural philosophy lectures.[3] Henry also loved music and dancing with a passion and became an accomplished violinist; he is reported as walking from Luchon to Bagnères-de-Bigorre, where he danced all night before walking back the following morning.

His boyhood ambition had been to join the French Navy, but because his father was legally a British subject he was ineligible and so he signed on with the French mechant navy instead. After various misadventures, including being officially bailed out of trouble in Peru by a well-connected relative, Henry found himself facing life as a gentleman of leisure who was not particularly well qualified for any profession. He decided to travel instead and was accompanied on his first trip by his Clongowes school friend, Francis Cruise. June 1857 saw them begin their tour in Canada with

Clongowes Wood College, County Kildare, in the early 1800s. (Courtesy Clongowes Wood College Archive)

Les Grottes Russell au Vignemale. (*Souvenirs d'un Montagnard, Tome 1* (1908))

a visit to the St Lawrence River, Quebec, Montreal, the Great Lakes and Niagara, before crossing the border to Detroit. Reaching Chicago, they moved on by rail to Dubuque, Iowa, and up the Mississippi to St Paul, then overland through trackless forest country to Lake Superior, returning by boat to Detroit, then on to New York, Philadelphia, Baltimore and Washington. They travelled to New Orleans down the Ohio and the Mississippi rivers via Pittsburgh and finally returned to New York by sea, via Havana, arriving back in France in November. The story of this remarkable non-stop tour of the New World was described by Henry in *Notes par Voies et Chemins à travers le Nouveau Monde*.[4]

Russell's first serious climbing season in the Pyrenees was during the summer of 1858, when he was twenty-four and climbed Pic Néouvielle. He followed this by making the first ascent of Ardidieu, before making three separate climbs of Mont Perdu. On the third Mont Perdu ascent he climbed alone (starting at midnight from Luz), was caught in a storm on descent, and spent a very bad night on the Brèche de Roland with neither food nor shelter.

Russell then set out to explore the rest of the world, leaving Paris in September 1858 to cross the breadth of Europe and Asiatic Russia, and reaching Peking within five months. He travelled by way of Japan, Hong Kong, Macao and Sumatra, arriving in Melbourne in January 1860. He then visited New Zealand, where he got lost in the bush for three days without food. His journey continued through Sydney, Ceylon and Calcutta to Darjeeling. He became sick with a fever he had picked up in Terai, a marshy afforested region of Nepal; this and political trouble seriously delayed him while he was within sight of the mighty peaks of the Himalaya, which he had planned to explore. His disappointment forced him to turn for Madras, and from there he marched across India from sea to sea on foot to reach Bombay. From Bombay he made his way to Constantinople and through Hungary to Trieste, and finally by sea to Marseilles. He was three years away on the third leg of what was, by any standard, a grand tour. He wrote an account of his journey entitled *Seize Mille Lieues à travers l'Asie et l'Océanie. Voyage Exécuté pendant Années 1851–1861*, which appeared in 1864.[5] The book is said to have inspired Jules Verne (who knew Russell) in writing *Around the World in Eighty Days*.

His desire to travel the globe had been satisfied it seems, for his principle interest during the rest of his life was to be the Pyrenees and, in particular, the second highest summit of the range, the Vignemale. When he arrived back in France this was the first mountain he set his sights on, climbing it in the company of Laurent Passet; shortly afterwards he made the first climber's passage of Col d'Astazou, reaching Mont Perdu by a new route. In 1862 he recorded an ascent of Pic de Ger and Le Canigou, followed in 1863 by an attempt on the rocky Pic du Midi d'Ossau; he was knocked down by wind on Col de Gourgy while climbing the Pic du Ger a second time. He climbed Perdiguero (alone) and Le Néthou (the highest peak in the range at 3,404m, situated on the Spanish side of the border where it is known as Aneto), and completed a half tour of Mont Maudit, from Hospice de Viella to Venasque.

Henry's father and his heirs received the title Count of Rome from Pius IX in 1862 in recompense for all the losses suffered by the Russells in their steadfast adherence to the Catholic faith and, as the Pope himself reportedly stated, 'on account of the family's great antiquity and renown'. More specifically, the title was to reward Henry's younger brother, Frank, who had commanded the Irish regiment in the Papal army in the war against the Piedmontese. As a result, Henry was entitled to call himself Comte Henri Russell and he always seems to have enjoyed and cultivated an aristocratic image.

It was about this time he made the acquaintance of Charles Packe (an English country squire) who, like Russell, was of independent means and who had made the exploration of the Pyrenees his life's main interest. Packe was a keen botanist, cartographer and geographer. He was educated at Eton and Oxford and although he was called to the bar in 1852, he never actually practised, preferring instead to roam the Pyrenean range, usually in company with his two big Pyrenean mountain dogs.[6] He pioneered exploration of the Ordesa Canyon and the massifs of Posets and Mont Maudit, finding and recording routes where only local shepherds and hunters had previously trod. These two men, one a romantic, jovial Franco-Irishman and the other a studious and articulate Englishman, met by accident at the Lac Bleu near Barèges. Their common love of the mountains initiated and sustained a long and fruitful friendship. Packe's book, *Guide to the Pyrenees: Especially Intended for the use of Mountaineers*, was published at about that time. Russell paid him the highest compliment when he called him the 'Tyndall of the Pyrenees', a reference to his all-round ability and industry as climber, botanist, map-maker and geologist.[7] The two men began a lifetime friendship and during the next ten years they were practically alone in making numerous ascents of the mountain range that today provides the natural border between Spain and France.

Russell was an enthusiastic musician and a skilful performer on the cello, but science did not appeal to him in any form, and he was frankly indifferent to such things as botany and geology. He told the Alpine Club that there was 'no passion more innocent, more indisputable and more manly, than that of scaling peaks, even if science gains nothing from it, for in legitimate pleasure there is always wisdom'.[8] Socially he was not only of charming manners, but also extremely witty and entertaining, his conversation sparkling with drollery and love of paradox, both expressed in language of admirable precision.[9] He had an endless supply of good stories and once described a mountain as 'Le Pic Péripatétique' because, as he pointed out, it travelled periodically from France into Spain and back again. His discussions about the treatment of poor Irish landowners by British statesmen were considered 'excruciatingly funny' by his obituary writer, Haskett Smith. 'It suggested a capering Irish bull sternly controlled by a lasso of French logic.'[10]

Russell was an unmistakable figure: very tall, with a military air and steeply sloping shoulders (like a champagne bottle, as he himself expressed it) that somehow increased the dignity of his appearance. In a local Pau publication he was caricatured as *le plus grand marcheur du monde: Sir Henri Russell Killow-Mètre*.[11] This was an acknowledgement of the Pyrenean custom of walking faster and longer with fewer stops than was normal in the Alps, and also of the fact that Henry was, for many years, recognised as the best amateur walker in the range, a title that was apparently well earned. He often walked for twelve hours and, like Adams-Reilly, he appears always to have had a ferocious appetite.

In 1867 he made his first and only visit to the Alps, climbing Mont Blanc with the guide J. Devouassoud via the Grands Mulets route.[12] He also climbed the Breithorn (4,148m) and the Col de l'Alphubel (3,802m) with the guide Johann Kronig. In 1864 Russell embarked on a seventeen-day zigzag tour from Pau through the Pyrenean range, making many first ascents including Pic Carlit, which he repeated three days later with Packe who he met up with many times on his walk. He again ascended Le Canigou and the Puigmal, then entered Andorra by Port de Soldeu for a brief stay and left by Port de Seigneur, ascending the Realp. This was followed by a series of first ascents when he climbed Pic des Hermittans, Pic de Luston and Cilindro de Marboré, before again climbing Balaitous, making this his third ascent of the peak.

In 1865, with Packe and two other local climbers, he founded the Société Ramond, which was purely a Pyrenean club. The club was named in honour of Ramond de Carbonnières, an early traveller and writer on the Pyrenees. In February 1869 he made the first winter ascent of the Vignemale. In May 1871 Henry read a paper to the Alpine Club entitled 'On mountains and on mountaineering in general'. He told the audience that 'Mont Blanc is, I fear, the highest peak I have ever climbed'. He prefaced his remarks about the Pyrenees by chiding the Alpine Club members for the lack of respect they seemed to have for his beloved hills, none of whose summits attained 12,000 feet (3,650m). He admitted that mere elevation has much to do with the attractiveness and prestige of mountains, but argued that no one could fix the height at which a peak was worthy of respect and deserving to be declared fascinating or perilous. He further claimed that such an approach would lead to the Alps being despised when compared with Tibet, since the altititudes of Alpine peaks are as nothing when compared; battles had been fought in Tibet at the same elevation as the summit of Mont Blanc.[13]

As for danger, he claimed the Pyrenees had plenty: 'let anyone who doubts it climb the frightful arêtes of the Balaitous, only 10,318 above the sea'. He said 'perhaps no one could ever paint or describe the calm and peculiar beauty of an autumn sunset on those Pyrenæan ranges. Certainly not I, except for the plains of Bengal, where face to face with the Sikhim Himalayas, and already surrounded by night, you can still see hundreds of snowy peaks, reddened with unearthly colours and shooting up six miles through the gloom and vacuum.'

He finished up his talk by recounting how he and a companion with two guides from Gavarnie were attacked at midnight while sleeping in a forestry cabin. His French companion was held down by seven bandits who held three blades to his breast and the muzzle of a gun in his face. He lost his purse, rings and watch and even his clothes. One of the guides, when discovered, was forced to bend his neck and feel the edge of an axe at the roots of his hair for several minutes before they released him. Henry had escaped by running madly downhill over loose stones before hiding stretched under a dark pine in the forest. When the editor of *The Alpine Journal* asked Russell for a description of the bandits' clothes in order to illustrate the story to accompany his paper, Russell sent the unsuspecting editor a photograph of himself dressed as the bandit, which he had worn for a fancy-dress ball.

He went on to attack those who did not recognise the dangers or who maintained that imprudence alone explained all accidents. He maintained: 'Danger is, no doubt, one of the charms of mountains, and in many cases their greatest attraction. It has a mesmeric effect. An easy peak is left alone, and deserves to be so. But that taken for granted, it is surely one thing to face peril, and another to deny its existence.' He took those in the Alpine Club to task for denying that the painful phenomenon known as 'mountain sickness' existed, or for discarding it as mere fatigue or exhaustion. He said that 'he could scarcely breathe on the summit of Mont Blanc and all including the guides were sick and they could barely walk more than thirty-four steps without stopping.'

Henry Russell demonstrates his lamb fleece sleeping bag. (*Souvenirs d'un Montagnard, Tome 1* (1908))

He made a telling point: 'Yet it was not fatigue, for we all ran down in two hours to the Grands Mulets in excellent spirits and health.' He also spoke in favour of climbing in the settled conditions of midwinter, when 'the sky is clear spotless and calm'. He reflected on his winter ascent of the Grand Vignemale, when the 'peak itself, which rises from the glacier like an island upon the sea, was free from snow, save a few specks here and there . . . As for beauty and majesty, nothing ever surpassed or equalled them in the finest days of July.'

In October 1872 he walked through the Basque country via Larrau, Ahusky, and Roncevaux to Bayonne; amongst his climbing companions was Belfast-born James Bryce who would later become the second Irish president of the Alpine Club and with whom he unsuccessfully attempted Port d'Oo. It was the third time that year he that he was stopped by wind and snow on the peak. *Biarritz and Basque Countries* was published a year later. He then made what is

Henry Russell in Gavarnie. (*Souvenirs d'un Montagnard, Tome 1* (1908))

thought to be the first ascent of Le Mail Barrat and the second ascent of Pico de Posets by the La Poule route.

In 1874 he made the first ascent of Gabietou and discovered the 'ice aiguilles' of its glacier. He helped found the Club Alpin Français (CAF) in the same year and contributed to the club's first *Annuaire* with a vigorous paper on climbing in the Pyrenees, in which he noted the absence of inns and huts and described his adoption of the sheepskin sleeping bag that permitted him time to stay and enjoy the mountains instead of his former climbing style, which he described as a series of long expeditions at express speed.[14] Two years later he opened a subscription for the construction of a mountain refuge on Mont Perdu, collecting (in partnership with Packe) from friends and through his personal written appeals to members of the Société Ramond and the CAF. They raised 1,250 francs and Russell was charged with managing the construction. He located a site for the hut and had it inaugurated with a large party in 1877. He was in the second party to climb the Soum de Ramon from the new hut, the first ascent having been made two hours before Russell's party reached the summit.

A prodigious walker, his list of recorded ascents over the next thirty years is quite staggering. It includes no fewer than thirty-three ascents of the Vignemale, thirty ascents of Pic du Midi and seven ascents to the summit of Mont Perdu. In 1881 Russell decided to construct a habitable grotto on the Col de Cerbillonas (3,200m) and in 1882, when it was completed, he made his eighth ascent of the Vignemale with F. E. L. Swan.[15] They spent three nights there. His argument in favour of excavating a cave had been simply that any other form of construction would detract from the appearance of the mountain. He called it Villa Russell. It was 3m long, 2.5m wide and 2m high, with an iron door fixed to the opening. He brought up the parish priest and some friends for the inauguration or baptism of the cave.

In 1883 he requested funds (2,000 francs) from Direction Central for a new refuge for Mont Perdu, which were granted on condition that it was built on French soil at La Brèche de Roland.[16] In 1884 he had Mass celebrated in the presence of thirty persons at the grotto site and the following year he organised the construction of several other grottos, including one for his guides (who had had to sleep outside as the first proved too small to accommodate all) and a third to accommodate women. In 1886 his friends pitched a large tent in front of Villa Russell, in which they banqueted for several days with music provided by invited musicians. He always received his guests with great refinement, offering them an incredible quantity of food, drink, wine and cigars. Hot wine was served at dusk by candlelight, after which they would walk to the summit (Pique Longue) to admire the sunset.

In 1888 Russell's account of his mountaineering exploits, *Souvenirs d'un Montagnard* (*Memories of a Mountain Dweller*) was published at Pau. The quality of his writing in French was much admired in alpine circles and considered to be of the very highest standard; the book is certainly considered a classic of mountain writing. Although he covers each peak in turn in topographical order, the work is a reflective testimony to his love of simply being among the mountains, rather than an account of peak-climbing conquests. He observes that many of the routes were previously only traversed here and there in the range by 'contrabandists'. Russell answers the oft-asked question 'What pleasure can there be in mountaineering?' with great conviction, while at the same time describing many of the first explorations of the Pyrenees.

He tells of his quest for the semi-savage life in a mountain environment and recounts tales of hundreds of nights bivouacking in the shelter of rocks and trees, in caves on cols or on summits, sometimes for eight to ten consecutive nights. He advocates the uniquely pleasurable sensations experienced when one is on the mountain alone and, indeed, suggests that this approach is the only school for acquiring the necessary self-confidence. He further suggests that the use of a rope in some situations only tends to increase the danger in proportion to an increased number of climbers in the party, suggesting that everybody should stand or fall in climbing on their own merits. Charles Packe, himself a regular soloist, when reviewing the great work of his friend, agreed with him that by far the larger portion of accidents in the mountains could be attributed to the folly or inexperience of those attempting them.[17]

In December 1888 he called on the prefecture of the department of Hautes-Pyrénées, requesting the lease of 200 hectares over 2,300m of the Vignemale for ninety-nine years. The request was, astonishingly, accepted for the symbolic consideration of one franc. As the height of the Vignemale was 3,298m, he had a 2m tower built on the summit to round it up to an even 3,300m. Since he found that in some years the level of the glacier covered the entrances to his caves, making them inaccessible, he built three new caves at a place he named Bellevue at the base of Glacier d'Ossoue at 2,400m. The site overlooked a splendid view of the Cirque de Gavarnie. He was now staying for a week to ten days at a time at the grotto sites and he recorded that 200 tourists, including fifteen ladies, had slept in his grottos up to that point. To savour fully the summit experience one night he asked his guides to dig a ditch as long as a tomb where he lay for a whole night in his sheepskin sleeping bag covered with stones up to his neck. His aim was to be 'part of the mountain' and he stuck it out with great stoicism till

4 a.m. when, covered with frost, he extracted himself, satisfied that he had 'felt the night and heard the silence.'[18]

In 1893, with the aid of dynamite, Henry's seventh grotto was built just 18m below the summit at 3,280m and named 'Paradis'; from there he made his twenty-third ascent of the Vignemale. As he became older he would spend more and more time in this cave. He climbed to the summit of the Vignemale for the last time on 8 August 1904; his final years were spent writing at Biarritz at the home of his brother Ferdinand. He was ill for much of the last year and died in Biarritz, aged seventy-five, on 5 February 1909; he is buried in the family mausoleum in the cemetery at Pau.

In Pau a plaque records the house where he lived on Rue Marca. There is also a street in the town named in his memory. His gourd, compass and copies of his books can be seen in the Musée Pyrenean in the Château fort de Lourdes, a fortified castle at Lourdes that dates back to Roman times. A peak formerly named Petit Néthou (small Aneto) was renamed Pic Russell in his honour at the suggestion of his old comrade Charles Packe; perhaps more fittingly, a mountain hut in the Ardiden range was named after the eccentric Irish Papal Count. A bronze statue in the Pyrenean village of Gavarnie replaced the one that was melted down by the Nazis. It depicts Henry Russell looking lovingly towards his beloved Vignemale, the mountain that he was once a part of, and declaring 'she will be my spouse.'[19]

Célestin Passet, 1845–1917

Henry Russell's favourite guide was Célestin Passet of Gavarnie.[20] His uncle Laurent took Russell on his first ascent of the Vignemale and his father, Hippolyte, accompanied him on his second ascent. Laurent's son, Henri, was Russell's guide for a February or first winter ascent of the peak. Henri became another very competent guide and was Charles Packe's main guide.

Célestin accompanied Russell on Mont Perdu and the Brèche de Roland in 1871 and again the following year with a new route on Perdu. He later climbed Gabietou with Russell and made the first winter ascent of Posets with Roger de Monts. Célestin famously climbed Couloir de Gaube, a long vertical fault on the northern cliff of the the Vignemale, in August 1889: he cut 1,300 steps with a Chamonix-made light ice axe borrowed from Henry Brulle. This ice-climbing route was not repeated for forty-four years. He and his cousin Henri also climbed in the Alps as guides with their regular clients. Whymper was so impressed by him that he offered to take him to Chimborazo in the Andes, but Celestin declined the offer choosing to stay with his mother and his farm. He died in 1917 and is buried in Gavarnie.

Whymper's sketch of Célestin Passet.

7

Robert Fowler:
Climbing Landlord

The Matterhorn: The fifth ascent of the Matterhorn this year has been made (the *Swiss Times* says) by Mr Fowler, an Irish gentleman, accompanied by the guides C. Knubel and J. Lochmatter of St Niklaus.

The Times, 22 September 1871

'A start in the dark' illustrates climbers and guides assembling pre-dawn outside a mountain hut for an Alpine summit ascent. The uncredited image was first published in Volume 2 of *The Alpine Journal* (1866).

Robert Fowler, 1824–1897

- Born Rathmoylan, County Meath
- Educated and graduated MA from Trinity College, Dublin, 1847
- Called to the bar in Dublin in 1850
- Visited Switzerland for twenty-five seasons from 1854
- In the 1865 season he climbed Mont Blanc, Finsteraarhorn, Weisshorn and the Dom, and made the third ascent of Aiguille Verte and the first ascent of the Aiguille du Chardonnet
- Joined the Alpine Club in December 1865
- Climbed the Matterhorn by the Hörnli Ridge in 1871 and made a Matterhorn traverse from Breuil to Zermatt in 1874
- His wife and eleven-year-old son died within a fortnight of each other in January/February 1879. Fowler resigned from the Alpine Club shortly afterwards

THE LAST OF SIX noteable Irishmen active during the golden era of alpinism was a County Meath landowner from a family well connected to the Protestant clergy and the political and legal establishment in Victorian Ireland. Robert Fowler of Rahinston, County Meath, was a very enterprising and accomplished mountaineer who climbed with many of the very best guides of the era, including Melchior Anderegg, Peter Knubel, J. M. Lochmatter and Michel Balmat. His diaries indicate he visited Switzerland every year for twenty-five years. He was a member of the Alpine Club from 1865 to 1887. His recorded climbs could easily be ranked simply as the classic best climbs of his era. The list is impressive: 1864, Monte Rosa; 1865, Mont Blanc, Aiguille Verte (the third ascent via a new route on the Grande Rocheuse), Aiguille du Chardonnet (first ascent), Finsteraarhorn, Weisshorn, Dom and an attempt on the Lyskamm; 1869, Weisshorn, Breithorn (first ascent from the north); 1871, Matterhorn, Dent Blanche (seventh ascent); and in 1874, traverse of the Matterhorn (from Breuil to Zermatt), Rothorn (from Zermatt returning by Moming Pass).[1] What is remarkable about Fowler is that his substantial alpine accomplishments are not recorded in any of his Irish obituaries. Alpinism appears to have been almost a secret pastime.

Robert Fowler was born on 15 March 1824, the son of Robert Fowler senior of Rahinston and Rathmoylan, Deputy Lieutenant and Justice of Peace in County Meath, and Jane Anne, daughter of John Crichton, granddaughter of the first Earl Erne.[2]

In keeping with the traditions of the Protestant ascendancy in Ireland, he was educated at Trinity College, Dublin, and called to the Irish bar in 1850, but it appears he rarely practised. He devoted his attention to commercial and civic pursuits, succeeding his father in managing the family estate at Rahinston in 1868.[3] Aside from his climbing, Robert was actively involved in the Meath Hunt and took an interest in the welfare and training of the children of residents of Trim workhouse.

His recorded alpine activity commenced in 1854 with ascents of a number of classic cols and passes, including the Col du Géant from Chamonix to Courmayeur, Triftlimmi and Nägelisgrätli, Gauli Pass and the Oberaarjoch. His account of his crossing of the Oberaarjoch, one of the great glacier passes, was published in the seventh edition of Murray's *Handbook for Travellers in Switzerland, Savoy and Piedmont* in 1856 (four of Fowler's 1854 routes were described in the same guide). His Oberaarjoch ascent was later reprinted in the *Alpine Journal*. He wrote:

On the morning of 27th Aug 1854, I set out from the Grimsel at 10 minutes before 3 o'clock with Melchior Anderegg of Grimsel and Arnold Kehrli as my guides, both of whom I strongly recommend. As far as the foot of the Unteraar glacier the route is the same as that of the Strahleck pass: here it turns along the edge of the Oberaar glacier on its right side, as far as some chalets, where we had to wait for 40 min., till the sun rising dispersed the mists which lay upon the glacier. At 6 o'clock we took to the ice; it is but little crevassed, and resembles much of the Unteraar glacier, but it rises with a much more rapid slope. Towards the summit of the pass the ice is covered with snow; we tied ourselves together with a rope, and some care was necessary to avoid the concealed crevasses. We reached the summit of the pass at 9 o'clock and soon commenced the descent, which at first is down snow slopes, then upon the glacier, over and among the enormous crevasses for nearly two hours. Having passed at the foot of the glacier which descends between the Rothorn and the Viescherhorner, we left the ice for a while, and descended by the foot of the latter mountain; afterwards we sometimes followed the glacier (which is always

The Aiguille du Chardonnet. (Author's photo)

much crevassed), sometimes its moraine of the mountain on its right, till at last, by a very steep descent Viesch was reached at 50 min past 3 p.m. Including stoppages of 1½ hours, this pass took 13 hours, of which 6 were in ice. R. F.[4]

The Grande Rocheuse on the Aiguille Verte. (Gaston Rébuffat, *100 Finest Routes*)

He was with Kehrli again when he made the first traveller's crossing of the Triftjock or Col de Zinal (3,539.9m), described in Ball's *Western Alps* as 'a mere notch in the ridge between the Gabelhorn and the Trifthorn a few feet in width, and so sharp that it is possible to sit astride with one leg on each side of the ridge. The view of Monte Rosa and the Saas Grat is of the grandest character.'[5] They also crossed the Lötschsattel descending to Fiesch. His inclusion in Murray's *Handbook* in 1856, indicates his prominence as a climber in the years prior to the establishment of the Alpine Club.[6]

In 1864 Fowler climbed Monte Rosa and the Alphubeljoch. He also stayed at the hotel in Eggishorn to make an attempt on the Finsteraarhorn with Antoine Ritz and Joseph Imhof.[7] The following year he climbed Mont Blanc and made the third ascent of the Aiguille Verte by a variation of Whymper's route, which involved the first ascent of Grande Rocheuse, then followed this by the first ascent of the prominent Aiguille du Chardonnet. He completed this wonderful season with ascents of the Finsteraarhorn, the Weisshorn and the Dom and, with J. M. Kronig, made an attempt on the Lyskamm. Fowler later wrote about his ascent of the Aiguille Verte and the Aiguille du Chardonnet in the *The Alpine Journal*.

It seems that on their way back to Chamonix on 16 September 1865, having ascended Mont Blanc with Michel Balmat, the guide suggested to Fowler that he ought to climb the Aiguille Verte next, and that he should engage Michel Ducroz and Balmat himself to make the ascent. Ducroz had accompanied Michel Croz with Messrs. Hudson, Kennedy and Hodgkinson on their ascent of the mountain in July. Fowler agreed and so it was arranged that they would start out that evening. They set out from Chamonix that afternoon, stopping on the way to eat at Montanvert.[8] They reached the Pierre à Béranger under the light of a lantern just after 9 p.m. Previous visitors had built a wall of stones inside an overhanging rock to form a cave and had left a bed of hay for sleeping and some firewood, with which they lit a roaring fire and mulled some wine. Leaving at 4.10 a.m., they crossed the Talèfre Glacier towards the Jardin and moved leftwards to the foot of the Aiguille Verte. To avoid the possibility of stone fall they climbed an arête leading to the top of a pointed aiguille between two couloirs that separate the Aiguille Verte from Les Droites.

When at the top of the rock ridge known as Les Rouges, they realised they should have crossed the wider of the two couloirs lower down. As a result they had to move to their right on rocks to gain the top of the smaller couloir.

In order to get onto the ridge coming down from the summit of the Verte, they had to descend steep rocks to an ice arête that was hard and blue. Ducroz, with the still uncoiled rope wrapped around his shoulders, cut steps on the northern edge of the arête, holding on with one toe over its edge, while his weight rested on the other foot. The cutting of steps proved so laborious, that he decided to go along *á cheval*. Fowler suggested roping up for the protection of the leader, but this should really have been done before Ducroz left the rocks in the first place. The guide, knowing the difficulty of roping up in such an exposed position halfway across the arête, made no response. With great courage Ducroz continued, soon to be followed (also *á cheval* and unroped) by Fowler and Balmat. Each used the spikes of their axes to drag themselves across the exposed, knife-edged ice. Fowler soon changed this 'for the extended position in which a sailor gets out along a spar, having my elbows knees and toes clinging to the arête, which was very narrow'.

Three small sketches used by Robert Fowler to demonstrate some techniques used during his ascents of the Verte and of the Chardonnet in his article in *The Alpine Journal*. (a) Note the right foot of the guide is holding him in balance as he cuts the next step.

They continued in this way until they had also crossed the great couloir and regained the ice slope, which led them up to the summit of the Aiguille Verte. At the top Fowler spotted 'two sticks with pieces of red ribbon left by poor Mr Hudson and his party in July'. He added a blue handkerchief that they had found on their way up to these poignant reminders of Hudson, Croz and the others, who had made the second ascent of the mountain by the Moine Ridge. It must have been a sobering reminder of his mortality to Fowler, since both Hudson and Croz had perished just a month earlier in the fatal accident on the descent of the Matterhorn – only a week after their Aiguille Verte ascent. He did not remain long on the summit. Whymper, who had made the first ascent in June with the guides Christian Almer and Franz Biener, had made use of both the couloirs that flanked the rock ridge used by Fowler's party. Fowler believed Whymper had climbed the lesser couloir on the right for some way, then crossed leftwards over to the greater one, climbing it until it turned to ice, at which stage he took to the rocks until just below the summit. This couloir is now known as the Whymper Couloir. In descent Fowler's party went down by these rocks until they reached the narrowest point of Whymper's Couloir. On two occasions they were forced to duck under cover to avoid stone fall, which made the crossing

(b) Fowler is between his two guides who are crossing a narrow ice ridge 'à cheval' style. He is pushing himself with his alpenstock, the metal point of which is planted into the hard ice.

(c) Fowler crosses an ice couloir between his two guides. The climbing rope and the two guides are stationary. He is fitted with a waist harness which secures a metal ring through which the climbing rope passes.

of the couloir very dangerous. Sheltered under a rock, Fowler watched anxiously while Ducroz cut roughly twenty steps across the couloir before he reached the safety of the central rock ridge. His companions hurried over to regain their route of ascent, which they followed safely back to Montanvert. Fowler recommended that those climbing the Aiguille in future might start earlier and follow his route of descent as a safer and shorter route, both to and from the summit. The route Fowler's party took is now known as the Grande Rocheuse Buttress.

While on the summit of the Aiguille Verte, looking north across the Glacier d'Argentière to the Aiguille du Chardonnet, Balmat again demonstrated his skill as a salesman and informed local guide by advising Fowler that this beautiful peak had not yet been ascended. So, with the same guides, Fowler set out at 3 a.m. on the morning of 20 September from the village of Argentière to climb the northeast bank of the Glacier d'Argentière, from where they followed a snow couloir in hopes of finding a way to the summit.[9] But, on reaching the col, they saw that the rocks of the arête leading upwards to the summit were too steep and smooth to be practicable. As a route to the glacier on the other side looked feasible, the guides tried to convince Fowler to give up his ascent to the summit and settle for the new pass. Fowler insisted on returning to a line on their right, which followed a black ice couloir. It was noon when they arrived back at the start of the couloir, where they ate before setting out again. This time they kept to the right of the black ice couloir as they ascended, to find another couloir hidden from their view below. This one led them to the arête between the top of the mountain and the col previously reached. From this point a climb of alternating rock and snow brought them to a sharp ridge, which ran to the apparent top. Fowler proposed they use the rope that Ducroz was carrying. After many efforts to untangle the rope, Ducroz threw it to the ground, took off his coat and danced on both, screaming out in a rage. Fowler and Balmat laughed heartily at his temper and, when he quietened down, helped him to undo the knots.

When they arrived at what they thought was the top, it was only to discover a peak considerably higher connected to their own summit by a sharp ridge of ice. Fowler claimed it was 'the sharpest ridge' he had ever seen. It ran across the top of the couloir that descends between the Chardonnet and the Aiguille d'Argentière. Rather than cross the ridge at its apex, they decided to use the rope to lower Balmat down to rocks that projected some 12 feet (3.6m) below them. From here he cut steps across the couloir. Ducroz and Balmat held the rope each side of the couloir as Fowler followed the rope running through a ring fixed to his belt. He observed that the slope was so steep he brushed his shoulder against the ice as he crossed. Ducroz did not follow, choosing to wait on the lower summit till their return. Balmat and Fowler reached the summit at 2 o'clock. The views were magnificent, with the Verte and Argentière so close at hand. Not having time to erect a proper stone man, they placed a bottle inside a circle of stones which they laid out on a large flat stone at the highest point. They returned by the same route, reaching the point where they had left their lantern just as it got dark. They arrived at Argentière at 9 p.m. and hired a carriage to take them to Chamonix. Reflecting on his achievement, Fowler thought it strange that a mountain as high as the Chardonnet (over 12,000 feet/3,650m) and so clearly visible from the Col de Balme should have been left untouched, and he also observed that the climbing was easier than that on the Verte and free of stone-fall danger.

Fowler joined the Alpine Club in December 1865, qualifying on the basis of his Alpine record. His name appears on five separate occasions in Peter Knubel's *Führerbuch* covering the period 1863 to 1872.[10] The first entry relates to an ascent of the Weisshorn on 10 September 1869; on 15 September Fowler records that the day before (14 September) they had been unsuccessful in their attempt to climb the Lyskamm due to the 'very high north wind which was blowing', reaching the col to the right of the Lysjoch; in the same same entry for 15 September he notes that Knubel was one of his guides when 'we made the first ascent of the Breithorn from the side of the Görner Glacier'. *The Alpine Journal* editor commented: 'the proposal emanated from G. Ruppen, the other guide. It is curious that Mr Fowler did not consider the expedition a difficult one.'[11]

On 7 September 1871 one of Knubel's sons, César, is recorded as one of his guides in his ascent of the Matterhorn. The other guide was his St Niklaus neighbour, the great Joseph Marie Lochmatter. This ascent was reported in *The Times*: 'The Matterhorn: The fifth ascent of the Matterhorn this year has been made (the *Swiss Times* says) by Mr Fowler, an Irish gentleman, accompanied by the guides C. Knubel and J. Lochmatter of St Niklaus.'[12] The ascent was the second Irish ascent of the superb peak; Knubel and Lochmatter had both had already made multiple ascents. A week later, on 13 September, Peter Knubel was again assisted by Joseph Marie Lochmatter in Fowler's ascent of the Dent Blanche. He was complimented by Fowler for showing 'much skill and activity on the steep and difficult rocks by which we ascended'.[13] The last entry is on 26 August 1874, when Fowler expresses the greatest satisfaction with Knubel following his ascent of the Rothorn from Zermatt, returning by the Moming Pass.

In 1871 Fowler was appointed Justice of Peace and High Sheriff for County Meath. He was a member of the Representative Body of the Church of Ireland from its inception, concerning himself with matters relating to financial administration, and was also treasurer to the Diocese of Meath, a post he held until his death. Further to this he was connected as an ex officio guardian with the Trim Union, and in that capacity was instrumental in introducing some useful improvements regarding the better management of the workhouse. He was clearly a progressive social thinker and took a leading role in having Trim Prison transformed into a building that could facilitate the industrial training of the workhouse children of County Meath.[14] His obituary records, 'He did this to remove the workhouse children from the associations and surroundings of a workhouse which must now considerably add to moral and physical welfare.'[15] In the seven years from when it was built until his death, he lived to see close to seventy of the inmates of the institution go out into the world to earn their own livelihoods.

On 25 January 1879 Fowler's wife, Mabel, died at the age of forty-six and within a fortnight of her death their youngest son, Francis, aged eleven, also died. His death certificate states that Francis died from heart disease (metral valve) and indicates his father's presence at his death.

These were understandably life-changing events for Fowler; his Swiss climbing diaries ended in that year and he also resigned from the Alpine Club. As a result no obituary ever appeared in *The Alpine Journal* for this great alpine pioneer.

In the same year that Fowler suffered his personal losses, Elizabeth, Empress of Austria (better known as 'Sisi') and wife of the Austrian Emperor, Franz Joseph, leased nearby Summerhill House as a hunting lodge. It appears that Sisi almost daily enjoyed hunting with the Ward Union and Royal Meath Fox Hounds Club and the Kildare Fox Hunt.[16] The Empress on one occasion presented a riding crop to the master of the Meath Hunt, who was Captain Robert Fowler of Rahinston House and the eldest son of the Irish alpinist. (The riding crop was found in the attic of Rahinston House in 2010 and sold at auction in London for €28,000.) The Empress returned again the following spring for another hunting season; however, the political situation and the disapproval of Queen Victoria put an end to her Irish 'gallop' and the Empress never returned. She was assassinated in Geneva in 1898, at the age of sixty, by an anarchist who stabbed her outside Hôtel Beau Rivage while she was waiting to board a steamer to Montreux.

On 23 October 1897, while on a hunting and fishing holiday at Ballynahinch, County Galway (a beautiful, mountainous place dominated by the moody Twelve Bens of Connemara), Robert died suddenly. He had maintained his Swiss diaries for twenty-five years and they were included in a list of papers for acquisition when the documents of the Fowler estate were surveyed by the National Library of Ireland in 1956. However, when the acquisition took place, the diaries were not included. The author hopes these documents will be found amongst family papers so that Robert Fowler's full story and personal perspective on his pioneering climbing can be more fully revealed. He is buried in the family vault at St Mary of the Angels, the Church of Ireland parish church in Rathmoylan. A memorial plaque in the church records Fowler, his wife and their young son's passing.

Statue of Elizabeth (Sisi), Empress of Austria and Hungary, at Lac Leman, Geneva, where she was assassinated. Sisi rode with the Meath Hunt in 1898, when Robert Fowler was Master of the Hounds.

Peter Knubel, 1833–1919

Peter Knubel of St Niklaus was one of the top guides in the Valais. In 1868 he was one of two guides to make the sixth ascent of the Matterhorn in the company of his neighbour Joseph Marie Lochmatter and a client, Rev. Julius Elliot Marshall; they climbed from the Swiss side after the terrible accident of 1865 that had killed four men, including the great Chamonix guide Michel Croz. For many years afterwards Knubel was considered Zermatt's Matterhorn expert, in the same way as Carrel and Maquignaz were considered the experts on the Italian side. He and his brother were the builders of the 'old' upper hut made famous by one of Edward Whymper's engravings. Like many guides he started out as a porter, taking on the role of guide at the age of thirty in 1863. Among his many clients were Robert Fowler and Baron Albert de Rothschild. With Fowler he made ascents of the Weisshorn and the first ascent of the Breithorn from the north by the Görner Glacier. He also climbed the Dent Blanche and Rothorn with him. He participated in 1868 in the first ascent of Mount Elbrus in the Caucasus with Horace Walker and Frederick Gardiner. In 1871, while descending the ridge of the Lyskamm, one of his party slipped and without a moment's hesitation Knubel threw himself over the other side of the precipice and remained suspended by the rope until his companions had regained their footholds.[17] Three of his four brothers (all guides) were killed with both their clients while traversing the same mountain in 1877. He had four sons, Solomon (who was swept away with an avalanche on the Wetterhorn in 1902), César, Rudolf and the famous Joseph, who was guide to Geoffrey Winthrop Young.

Peter Knubel (1833–1919) of St Niklaus who guided Robert Fowler to make early ascents of the Matterhorn and Dent Blanche (in *Pioneers of the Alps* Cunningham & Abney (1887))

8

Elizabeth Hawkins-Whitshed: 'Women Should Climb'

Stop her climbing mountains; she is scandalising all London and looks like a Red Indian.

Lady Bentinck regarding her grand-niece, 1879

Elizabeth Hawkins-Whitshed was a founding member of the Ladies' Alpine Club in 1907 and indisputably one of the foremost women of her era to pioneer alpine mountaineering. Her mountaineering achievements include a very impressive list of ascents of the major alpine peaks, and many first winter ascents in the Alps. She was notably a member of the first recorded unguided, all-female team to climb a major alpine peak. She also played an important role in the development and popularisation of winter sports such as ice-skating and tobogganing, as well as being the world's first mountain film-maker and the author of eighteen books on subjects as diverse

Elizabeth Hawkins-Whitshed, 1861–1934

- Born in London in 1861, daughter of the third Baronet of Killinacarrick, and brought up in Greystones, County Wicklow

- Married in 1879 at the age of eighteen to Colonel Fred Burnaby of the Royal Horse Guards, a seasoned soldier and adventurer

- Birth of their son Arthur St Vincent Burnaby in 1880 at Greystones

- Shortly afterwards, made her first visit to the Engadine, Switzerland, to recover her health

- Returned to the Alps in 1881 and 1882 when she climbed Mont Blanc twice, made the first winter crossing of Col du Tacul and first winter ascents of Aiguille des Grand Montets and Aiguille du Midi

- Her first book, *The High Alps in Winter*, was the first book on winter alpinism, published in 1883

- In 1884 she made the first ascent of Pointe Burnaby, Bishorn east summit (one of the last unclimbed 4,000m peaks in the Alps) with Joseph Imboden

- Captain Burnaby was killed in hand-to-hand combat at the Battle of Abu Klea in Sudan on 17 January 1885 while attempting to rescue General Gordon at Khartoum

- Married Dr J. F. Main (1854–1892), a professor of mechanics, in 1886

- Married Mr Aubrey Le Blond, an international art collector, in 1900

- Elected first president of the Ladies' Alpine Club (1907) and of the first British women's rock climbing club, the Pinnacle Club (1920)

- Became a very accomplished alpinist, climbing most of the classic routes, including many first winter ascents in the Alps; made many first ascents in Norway; made the first recorded all-woman traverse of Piz Palu with Evelyn McDonnell in 1900

- Winter sports pioneer and enthusiast, pioneer cycle tourist, expert mountain photographer and a pioneer mountain film-maker

Facing page: Portrait of Mrs Elizabeth Burnaby from her book *The High Alps in Winter* (1883).

as mountaineering, photography, her own family's history and guidebooks to Italian gardens and Spanish cities. Virtually unknown as Elizabeth Hawkins-Whitshed, she was commonly called by each of her three married surnames: first Mrs Fred Burnaby, then Mrs Main and lastly Mrs Aubrey Le Blond or Elizabeth Le Blond. She seems to have spent a lot of time apart from each of her husbands.

The only child of Sir Vincent Bentinck Hawkins-Whitshed, third Baronet of Killinacarrick, Lizzie (as she was always known) was brought up at Killinacarrick House, Greystones, County Wicklow. Her father died when Lizzie was only eleven years old, leaving her an extremely wealthy, well-connected ward of court whose cousin was the future Duke of Portland and whose family could trace their descent back to Catherine the Great of Russia. While in London for her first season she found herself attracted to a dashing cavalry officer who enjoyed celebrity status on account of the books he had penned about his travels in the Middle East and Asia Minor. By the end of that season she was engaged to be married to Frederick Gustavus Burnaby, a man who was twice her age. She wrote in her memoirs: 'that a man of the world, so much older than myself, whose adventurous travels, described in books that ran through edition after edition, should have taken a fancy to an inexperienced child such as, despite my 18 years, I certainly was, still fills me with surprise.'[1]

Killinacarrick House, Greystones, County Wicklow, the childhood home of Elizabeth Hawkins-Whitshed and where her son Arthur was born. (*Day In, Day Out* (1928))

This surprise seems a little disingenuous, for neither Lizzie's money nor her connections could have done a politically ambitious young officer any harm. 'Fred' spent a lot of time at the London Fencing Club, where he exercised to develop his already powerful physique. He specialised in weightlifting and could lift dumb-bells weighing 130 lb; after his death Lizzie would deny in her memoirs that he had once carried two ponies under his arms. But Burnaby was not merely a man of action; he had a real gift for languages and managed to find time (during lengthy periods of annual leave from the Royal Horse Guards) to act as foreign correspondent for *The Times* and the government's ambassador to the empire in Russia, Turkey and Asia Minor.

The wedding on 25 June 1879 at St Peter's Church, Cranley Gardens, was a splendid affair, attended by the exclusive group known as the 'the Prince of Wales' set'. Lizzie was given away by her cousin Arthur Bentinck (later Duke of Portland) and a guard of honour was formed by a troop of the Royal Horse Guards (The Blues). The guests then repaired to the Bailey Hotel, Gloucester Road, for a fork luncheon and an inspection of the considerable array of presents, which included a magnificent silver service presented by her Irish tenantry, a Benares smoking room service (received from His Royal Highness, the Prince of Wales), and a pearl necklace in its original morocco case that her great-grandfather Bentinck had given to his bride in 1791.[2] She remarked 'a greater change from the simple outdoor surroundings of my girlhood to what was known as "the Prince of Wales' set" could hardly have been imagined'. The guests included many friends of

Fred's: in addition to his military comrades, there were newspaper owners, journalists, and 'celebrities of every walk of life, not a few of whom live in memoirs and history'.[3]

The following year, after the birth of their first child and Fred's unsuccessful campaign for election as a Conservative member of parliament, Lizzie suffered a severe attack of an inherited lung disorder. She made the decision to go to Switzerland for her health and when she set out she was, in her own words, 'on the borders of consumption.' This was the start of her long association with the Alps, although her first impressions clearly

Elizabeth, aged eighteen, horse riding with Fred Burnaby. (*Day In, Day Out* (1928)).

did not inspire her to climb: 'When first I saw the Jungfrau from the valley of Interlaken it seemed to me nothing more than a far off vision of glittering snows on which none but the foot of folly could ever wish to tread. With all the intemperance of youth and inexperience, I denounced the wickedness of those who risked their lives "for nothing".'[4]

In 1881 she went to St Moritz (accompanied by Fred, baby Arthur and her maid) and also stayed in the Engadine for several months, her health gradually improving. One day she walked out from Pontresina, armed with a tall alpenstock, and went up to the Diavolezza Pass (2,575m) where she was struck by the beauty of the mountains and decided to take up mountaineering, to which she devoted the next twenty years of her life. Her early outings inspired her to go higher and explore the spectacular Mer de Glace glacier with three other girls and a couple of encouraging guides in Chamonix. Further walks brought her to Mauvais Pas and the Brévent, and she soon found herself at the Grands Mulets hut where she and her companion spent the night. In the morning she was confronted for the first time in her life with having to pull on and tie up her boots for herself, without the aid of a maid. Her high-heeled boots were by then reduced to pulp and the guides refused to take her to the summit in such unsuitable footwear. Before the summer was out Lizzie was properly equipped and attired and she climbed the great mountain twice, first from the Grands Mulets and the second time from the Italian side.

Her family were not pleased, however, and her grand-aunt Lady Bentinck wrote to her mother: 'Stop her climbing mountains; she is scandalising all London and looks like a Red Indian.'[5] Reflecting on this pressure Lizzie later wrote that 'I owe a supreme debt of gratitude to the mountains for knocking from me the shackles of conventionality, but I had to struggle hard for my freedom.'[6] Her mother clearly acted as a supportive buffer for her. It is nonetheless interesting to note that Lizzie held on to many of her class privileges; for instance, she would keep her personal maid by her in the mountains until the point at which the maid became more of a nuisance than a help. On one occasion her maid had to be physically carried by a mountain guide when their carriage became stuck in snow and icy conditions while attempting to cross the Stelvio Pass (2,757m) from Bormio in Italy to Meran in Austria.[7]

They had set out in a carriage with two German gentlemen and Lizzie's Chamonix guide, Edouard Cupelin, but they were forced by deep snow to leave the carriage halfway to the pass. They then hired a pair of reluctant Italian porters from the locality, and the maid (whose name

Lizzie never gives in the account) trudged along pluckily at the end of the procession, while Cupelin (with a heavy knapsack on his back) hovered about and encouraged everyone by turns. One Italian led the way for a short time, then halted and told Lizzie he was thinking of returning home. She replied in scornful tones that perhaps if she made the tracks he might manage to walk in them. He stood aside in order to let her pass. Meanwhile the other Italian engaged in a war of words with the guide. For an hour she ploughed on through powdery snow that often reached her waist. Then the Italian changed places for a little until they reached the stone pillar that marked the border between Italy and Austria. Snow was falling, a strong wind howled around them, and their view was impaired by a driving mist. After waiting a long time in the snow she observed a tall figure with a bundle on its back and two other individuals. She could not pick out her maid amongst them and was puzzled by her absence. She noticed as Cupelin approached that he sank nearly twice as deeply into the snow as she had done and that he appeared to be in an unaccountable state of intense heat and fatigue. When he came closer, she saw that fastened to his back with shawls was her maid, her face as white as the snow itself and in a state of unconsciousness.

Lizzie was horrified but Cupelin reassured her, saying she had fainted due to the effects of the thinner air and that now he was able to apply restoratives (brandy). It transpired that he had carried her without pause for an hour. They broke into a road-mender's hut, which had no furniture or straw, where they made themselves as comfortable as they could. The maid was put into the most comfortable corner on a couch made from their wraps. A fire was lit from some sticks found underneath the snow and later supplemented by wood from the stairs, which Cupelin used as a fuel store. Dinner was prepared (tinned soup, potted tongue, champagne and marsala) and Lizzie observed how one of the Germans made a speech lauding their courage and made the best of everything while the other contemplated his boots, pondering on the stock of rheumatism he was laying up. Lizzie used the rope for a pillow and a thin shawl as her only wrap; Cupelin stayed by the fire, which he kept going all night. One cannot but feel sorry for the unfortunate maid whose mistress chose winter mountaineering for her sport. Thereafter Lizzie left her maids behind when she went mountaineering. She explained the experience and some of her frustrations: 'One of the species had incessant hysteria whenever I returned late from an expedition' and 'another eloped with a courier'.[8]

Her self-realisation as a passionate climber came in the middle of September 1882. While at Courmayeur on the Italian side of Mont Blanc, she found herself with a vague desire 'to go up something' that became too strong to be resisted. She obtained the services of two porters and a guide to ascend the summit of the very formidable Grandes Jorasses. They set out at eight o'clock on a fine morning for the hut. On the second day no serious difficulties were encountered but, although the weather was uncertain and much step-cutting was needed, the summit (13,806 feet/4,208m) was safely reached at 11 a.m. The descent was made in 'hot haste', for it was important to reach the hut before darkness overtook the party. When darkness fell they were still en route and lit the only piece of candle they possessed, which served them to get across a dangerous glacier; when it went out they were left in total darkness while crossing a frail snow bridge over a large crevasse. 'Better make a night of it here than break our necks in a crevasse,' muttered the guides.[9]

They dug a snow hole and the consumptive invalid (who had in the recent past suffered long months of illness) used her knapsack as a pillow, covered herself with a shawl, and stoically made the best of the night. 'It was a dull time up there alone on the mountainside', she said, recounting the adventure later to a journalist. The guide and one porter set off in the black night to fetch some candles from the hut. The other porter served up supper. She dozed off, but was suddenly awakened by a distant cry. Jumping up, she dropped a flask onto the nose of the porter who was sleeping close to her and he woke up screaming, thinking he was being avalanched. Their companions returned from the hut supplied with candles to lead them safely to their *cabane* at 4.30 a.m. She was not deterred by the experience; on the contrary, she found herself becoming even more committed to the snow-clad mountains.

During the winter of 1882/1883, her health having being sufficiently restored, she began a series of excursions and ascents. These excursions also brought her fame, due to the fact that she found herself among a small number of climbers (male or female) who attempted or made winter ascents of major peaks. Such climbing would inevitably involve wading knee-deep in soft snow in both ascent and descent and climbing on rocks dusted with snow and glazed over with ice. On 20 December, with the guide Edouard Cupelin, she made the first crossing of the Col du Tacul (3,337m). Her objectives were threefold: she would be first to cross the pass, she would have discovered a new and shorter passage from the Glacier du Géant to the Glacier de Leschaux, and she would have found a new approach to the Aiguille du Tacul. In the days that followed she made the first winter ascents of Aiguille des Grandes Montets (3,225m) and Aiguille du Midi (3,842m) with Cupelin, who seemed to have a knack of identifying unclimbed peaks and passes for his rich clients. She foresaw the growth in winter sport when she speculated that francs would someday 'flow in January or February as they do in July and August'.[10]

From the early days of her climbing she took her own photographs and was advised by a local Chamonix photographer, Monsieur Tairraz, who gave her useful hints; it was in the company of one of the great pioneers of alpine photography, Vittorio Sella, that she attempted the first winter ascent of Monte Rosa in 1883. His picture of Mrs Burnaby illustrated the dustcover of her first book, *The High Alps in Winter; or, Mountaineering in Search of Health*, the first book of its kind to record winter mountaineering as a discrete discipline. Some 800 of her pictures have survived, including 420 paper prints and many others used in publications;[11] unfortunately, none of her negative plates have yet been found. To take quality photographs while mountaineering in winter she had not only to carry the weighty camera and plates, but to manage heavy and awkward tripods. Adjusting lenses with cold fingers and keeping her fellow climbers and guides from moving during long exposures in cold and windy conditions must have been very frustrating for all concerned. The quality of her output was high and she exhibited her pictures regularly, making her own slides to illustrate her mountaineering lectures. It is not surprising that her photographs won many competitions, including the 'royal medals' of the Royal Photographic Society of Bath in 1891, 1892, 1900 and 1901. The pictures were remarkable not just because of the exclusive nature of many of the shots, taken in places where few other expert photographers would dare to go, but also because she was a perfectionist in their development, which she was frequently forced to undertake in the total darkness of hotel rooms. Since she lived at a period when technological advances in photography were rapid and loved to keep abreast of the newest developments, she benefited particularly when the new cameras using high-speed focal plane shutters came on the market at the turn of the nineteenth century.

She began to prefer mountaineering in autumn rather than in summer. Her rationale, she later declared, was that she was:

a coward . . . and disliked tourists. It would terrify me into fits . . . to encounter a thunderstorm on a mountain peak and to have my ice axes singing and my hair standing straight on end. Ice axes emit a most curious hissing note when there is a thunderstorm, and this is a sound that always terrifies me. Now in autumn I avoid my two greatest aversions thunderstorms and tourists. I think tourists are the worst of the two evils, and I simply detest having to sleep in a hut designed for eight persons when it is crowded with perhaps twenty-four other climbers. In autumn there are seldom thunderstorms, and one almost invariably has the huts to oneself. Although in autumn the days are shorter, the air is fresher than in summer, and the snow is usually in first-rate condition for climbing; and so I prefer prowling about the Pennines Alps and the Oberland in September and October, than in August or July.[12]

In March 1883 Lizzie attempted the first winter ascent of the second highest peak in the Alps, Monte Rosa, in company with Vittorio Sella, who had made the first winter ascent of the Matterhorn the year before; the pair (with their respective guides) were turned back at 4,200m by a violent storm. She wore four pairs of woollen socks inside oversized leather boots and many layers of clothing underneath an oversized thick tweed jacket: undergarments of soft angora (including a silk and angora camisole), tweed knickers, two blouses of English flannel and a heavy Irish wool sweater. Under her thick tweed outer skirt Lizzie wore two more skirts of fine wool flannel. Two pairs of woollen mittens, a woollen helmet and a cashmere face scarf completed her ensemble on that aborted attempt of the great peak. Underneath all those layers she felt, understandably, 'tolerably warm'.[13] Nevertheless, the guide had to remove his outer mitts to grip his axe while step-cutting and soon was forced to stop because his hand was frozen. The thermometer had reached its lowest reading, minus 13 °F. In truth it was probably colder. The guide noticed Madame's nose was white with frostbite. He rubbed it hard with his icy mitten and when he stopped he said, 'Ah it's beautiful now.' 'Beautiful, what do you mean?' she asked. 'Yes it is now getting quite black,' he replied. Winter climbing clearly is not for the faint-hearted.

In May 1883 Lizzie guided a novice clergyman to the Col du Tour (3,281m), an event which she relished as she was sure it was the first time a woman had acted as guide to a man in the high Alps. She ascended her first unclimbed peak on 5 July when she climbed La Vierge (3,244m), a rock needle situated in the Glacier du Géant. This was also the year that *The High Alps in Winter* was published. Mrs Burnaby's writing style is of its time; it must be remembered that her climbing exploits shocked the Victorian society in which she lived and that her assertive and independent approach made inroads towards the acceptance of women in activities previously dominated by men. The book received a scathing review in *The Alpine Journal* from W. A. B. Coolidge who had climbed regularly with his aunt Meta Brevoort (1825–1876), a pioneer in her own right. He complained that it was 'a volume which is probably the flimsiest and most trivial that has ever been offered to the alpine public.'[14] It is clear that the book was intended for a wider readership and was not written for experienced alpinists. However, she does honestly share her own experience in successfully overcoming consumption and provides an insight into a rich young aristocrat's perspective on living in the Alps, her relationship with her guides, and her attitudes to other climbers and tourists. Coolidge's severe criticism possibly arose because she had stolen some of his late aunt's thunder: Meta Brevoort had herself made many first female ascents in the Alps, including the Weisshorn, Dent Blanche and Bietschhorn. Indeed, an article she wrote for *The*

Alpine Journal about her traverse of the Bietschhorn in 1870 was, in deference to Alpine Club prejudices, published under her nephew's name.[15]

In her second book, *High Life and Towers of Silence*, Lizzie describes the third ascent of the Dent du Géant ('giant's tooth') with guides Auguste and Edouard Cupelin and Michel Savioz.[16] The Géant (4,013m) was one of the most impressive and coveted of the 4,000m mountains in the Alps and was not climbed until 28 July 1882. The mountain has two summits 27m apart: Pointe Sella (4,009m) and Pointe Graham (4,013m), separated by a small col. The first ascent was controversial, because the Italian guide Joseph Maquignaz, with his son Baptiste and his nephew Daniel, spent four days placing iron stanchions and fixing ropes with metal nails to achieve the summit of Pointe Sella. The next day they brought their clients, Alessandro, Alfonso, Corradino and Gaudenzio Sella, to the point now named in their honour. The higher summit, Pointe Graham, was climbed three weeks later by Auguste Cupelin, brother of Lizzie's favourite guide, with Alphonse Payot and their client W. W. Graham. They used Maquignaz's ropes to reach Pointe Sella, from where they lowered themselves to the col between the two peaks in order to climb to the higher Pointe.

On 13 July 1883 Lizzie set out with the Cupelin brothers to make the third ascent; she describes the climb from the point at which they reached the foot of the impressive rock pyramid, having come from Montanvert via the Col du Géant:

The Caravan – Elizabeth takes a ten-minute halt for breakfast with her guide Edouard Cupelin and porters. (*The High Alps in Winter* (1883))

Before starting for the real scramble of the day, our ninety feet of rope was attached to us, in all its length, so that there was a considerable distance between each person. The party was arranged as follows; Auguste Cupelin led, his brother came next, I was third and Michel last. The climbing as far as Burgener's cairn is easy, but once there the whole aspect of the mountain changes. Directly above, some smooth slabs of rocks are placed at a considerable angle. They are smoothly polished, but are divided by a crack which runs down the centre of them. By the side of this crack, a rope has been fixed by means of a few iron nails, which have been placed wherever there is a crevice which will admit of their being driven in. Above these slabs the rock appears to rise in a sheer and unbroken wall, but as all the other sides of the peak actually overhang, it is up the face of this cliff that the traveller must go. Nor is it as bad as it looks. There are no

The Bishorn at dawn with the Burnaby Ridge in profile. (Author's photo)

loose stones save one, which has been called the rocking stone, and round which the rope passes in a loop. As the tension increases, the stone moves a little, which does not tend to steady the nerves of the climber, should he be unaware of the fact that the stone is too firmly jammed in to allow of its falling. The slabs were decidedly pleasant to ascend, as each person goes up directly above the other; this is always much less trying than traversing.

Above the slabs there is a ledge which must be followed for a little distance. Here there is a cord, which generally forms a handrail, but on this occasion it was buried in the fresh snow which was plastered up against it.

Next to challenge their skill was a short gully with an unpleasant amount of ice in it:

Emerging from this gully, the work becomes easier till some more slabs are reached. These have to be traversed, and I thought the few steps across them the most difficult of the whole climb, as there is hardly room for one or two nails in the side of one's boot, in the tiny ledges, and each step must be a long one. Then the rocking stone is reached, and soon afterwards some perpendicular gullies. A fixed rope hangs down the centre of them, and the ascent of this passage is very fatiguing for the arms, as almost all the whole weight of the body comes on them. It is a relief when a sort of shoulder, slightly projecting from the first peak is reached. Here there is a place large enough for several people to stand at ease before assaulting the last slope of the lower tooth. The flagstaff is not seen till one reaches this peak, but once there all the rest of the route is in full view.

The second peak is seen to be joined to the first by a sort of pass, consisting in a ridge which falls away with sheer cliffs to a depth of many thousands of feet on either side. To reach this little col, a descent of some forty feet or so must be made. The peculiarity of this *arête* which thus connects the two summits consists in a hump of rock perched on it which juts out on one side just where the ridge must be struck. This obstacle has to be passed round; it cannot owing to the peculiar formation of the ridge be climbed over. Consequently the traveller must clasp his arms round it and grasp what he can with his left hand, gradually worming himself in that direction. Meanwhile, the man above has a firm footing (what Cupelin described as 'solide comme un Boeuf!'), and could easily check a slip, and there is also good standing room on the ridge for the leading guide, so this awkward little passage is not really dangerous or even very difficult, though it is very uncomfortable. Once on the ridge the highest point is easily attained from there. We felt as if our platform floated in mid-air, amongst the spires and domes of the great mountains around, so completely did we seem to be separated from the earth below.

They enjoyed the view of the 'pointed Grivola and the Grand Paradis and the other peaks of the Grian Alps' for a short time before they felt a furious wind that signalled the rising cloud and before long they were descending in flurries of snow. It took two hours to descend and they were drenched to the skin by the time the hospitable doors of Montanvert opened to admit them. It important to note that Lizzie, although climbing in the Alps for only three seasons, regarded herself as able as any other climber, male or female, and that Cupelin, her guide, implicitly acknowledged this when he agreed to or advised on her climbing objectives.

The following year Lizzie made a notable first ascent of a 4,000m peak when she climbed the eastern summit of the Bishorn. This was a rare achievement in Alpine climbing history and in doing so she climbed one of the last of such peaks that remained unclimbed in the Alps; she named the peak Pointe Burnaby after Fred. On this ascent her companions were the Swiss guide Joseph Imboden and porter Peter Sarbach from

The author ascending the Burnaby Ridge in 2005. (Courtesy Con Collins)

Herbrigen in Mattertal. She had previously been denied a first ascent of a 'four-thousander' in 1883, when she was one of a party that attempted to make the first ascent of the Aiguille Blanche de Peuterey, then thought to be the last unclimbed 4,000m peak in the Alps (finally climbed in July 1885). Having being repulsed in 1883 by the sudden onset of a storm (with the Peuterey apparently in perfect condition), she was surprised to be confidentially told by Imboden that another 4,000m unclimbed peak existed. They christened the peak the Bieshorn (now spelled Bishorn), due to its proximity to the Bies Glacier, and on 6 August 1884 they set out unannounced to scale this unclimbed high virgin Alp, amazingly overlooked among the most popular and spectacular peaks of the Valais range. Their starting point was Herbrigen in the Mattertal valley. She tells us that Imboden 'led us up a beautiful little track from Herbrigen, winding steeply among the rocks and in three hours, bringing us to a collection of *chalets* high above the last trees.'[17] They continued their ascent until they reached a spot under an overhanging cliff at the foot of the Abberg Glacier, where they rested in sleeping bags until 2.30 a.m., when they rose for breakfast. At 3.45 a.m. they set out from there to the Brunegjoch, from where she tells us 'our peak rose white and glittering in the sun across the plateau of the Turtmann Glacier.'

After breakfast they photographed their peak and set out for the Bisjoch at 3.45 a.m., where the serious climbing began. Once on the Bisjoch they had a good view of the ridge to the right. It went up very steeply and was fringed with snow cornices, which hung over, sometimes on one side and sometimes on the other. When they discovered that the snow was powdery, they opted to traverse under the ridge and climb onto the ridge higher up on loose, 'rotten' rocks. An hour and a half of this sort of climbing brought them onto the ridge proper again. They knew its condition would determine if they could reach the summit:

> Imboden clambered onto the rock, and standing up, surveyed the ridge. Then turning to us, he remarked, 'it will go somehow, but I daresay you won't like the look of it.' A second or two more, and the other guide and I emerged onto the ridge, and saw what sort of work lay before us. We had a platform some three or four feet square to stand on, but from there the ridge quickly narrowed to a knife edge of hard snow, which after remaining level for a short distance, shot upwards in a narrow crest, from which a cornice of snow curled over, and glittering icicles hung and fell off, as they melted in the powerful rays of the sun. I confess that I by no means liked the look of it, and observed to Imboden that the ridge on the Weisshorn appeared less difficult. Imboden seemed amused by my remark, and informed me that there was no comparison between the two, and that a person who would not attempt to cross the ridge in front of us might feel quite happy on the *aréte* of the Weisshorn. I ascended the Weisshorn a few weeks later and most thoroughly agree with him on this point.

With such enlivening conversations our appetites were sharpened for luncheon. We left all the provisions, except one bottle of wine, at the beginning of the ridge, and the heat was so great that all wraps, even outer gloves, could safely be deposited there also. At 9.45 we began our long climb along the crest. The total absence of wind was greatly in our favour and enabled us to maintain our equilibrium along the first part of the ridge without difficulty. It is very impressive to look down from such an *aréte*, and it is rarely that one finds oneself quite on the crest of such a knife-edge, with one's feet well turned out, and one's axe almost useless from the absence of anything at the side to stick into.

The snow on the *aréte* was in perfect condition, firm without being too hard, and seldom requiring the use for the axe. We kept as much to the right as the extreme steepness of the slope rendered possible, for we were anxious to keep well off the cornice. Once we bore to the left, and tried to ascend by the rocks, but the footholds were so few and far between, and the detours, which the difficulty of the rocks rendered desirable, were so many,

Mrs Main with her snow shoes and the guide J. Gross during a winter attempt on Piz Morteratsh. (*True Tales of Mountain Adventure* (1904))

that we found it better to return to the snow. Every step had to be taken with care, and it was seldom prudent for more than one of us to move at a time. Thus more than two hours passed before we were within measurable distance of the summit.

'Measurable Distance' in climbing a new peak, is invariably a very short distance, as, until the last moment, it is seldom possible to know what unexpected obstacles may be met with. At last, however, we got off the snow, and began to climb the rocky point which formed the summit of the mountain. As Imboden placed his axe near the top, the stone on which he put it slipped away, and off went the axe, clattering down towards the Bies-glacier. A step or two more and the peak sunk to the rank of its surrounding brethren, and what I believe to be the last but one un-scaled mountain, over 13,000 feet high in the Alps, was conquered.

Not a sign of previous ascent could be discovered, so the peak was really ours. We built the regulation stone man, deposited our names in a bottle, and congratulated each other in no measured language. Then as we had a long descent before us and the clouds had begun to boil up from the valley, threatening a thunderstorm, we began our downward way. The descent of the ridge was easier than the ascent, owing to the good steps which we had made while mounting; but, for a short distance, the steepness of the slope rendered it advisable for us to go down face inwards.[18]

It is interesting to note that Imboden and Mrs Burnaby, having reached the east summit (now called Pointe Burnaby), climbed back down to the Bisjoch without climbing to the clearly higher main summit. It is even more intriguing that Imboden returned twelve days later on 18 August 1884 to make the first ascent of that separate higher summit. This time he was in the company of another paying climbing party, including Mr G. Barnes and Mr R. Chessyre-Walker with the porter J. Chanton. That Imboden deliberately deceived her is not clear, but it is hard to believe she would not have wanted to climb the other unclimbed and higher main summit if she had known it was there for the taking.

In her favour it is a matter of record that the ascent of the Bishorn's east summit was one of the very few Alpine first ascents in which a woman had a serious involvement. One suspects that Imboden was well compensated by two wealthy 'English' clients, each credited with a first ascent of 'the last 4,000 metre unclimbed Alp'.[19] Lizzie's pride in this achievement can be gleaned from her observation: 'I find in Ball's "Western Alps" the following notice of the Bieshorn (as we christened it), on page 308: "The ridge which circles round from peak 4161 [the Bieshorn]" . . . "did not seem practical at any point".'[20] She also remarked that since ascending the mountain she had met several climbers who told her they had resolved to make the first ascent. Soon after she made light of climbing the Weisshorn by Tyndall's east ridge with Imboden: 'I think next to ascending a new peak, there is no delight so great as making the acquaintance of one of the classic giants of the Alps. Every feature is already familiar from the descriptions of the pioneers of mountaineering, and there is a sensation of being thoroughly at home which is intensely pleasant.'[21] In the concluding chapter of *High Life and Towers of Silence* she wisely advised the climber 'on no account to unnecessarily handicap yourself by taking either guides or friends with you about whose climbing powers and endurance you feel any doubt.'[22]

Female climbers of the Victorian age had to overcome considerable social prejudice. Dress code forced them to wear skirts, often over trousers or breeches and the practice of camping and bivouacking overnight in remote locations in the company of local guides and male climbers to whom they were not related was considered very improper. It took someone with the confidence and considerable social standing of Elizabeth Burnaby to shake off and dismiss such conventions. A recent biography of Lizzie quotes a Swiss guide who described her as 'an ugly, skinny woman' to a 1936 meeting of the Swiss Alpine Club; the author of the biography adds that she was one of those 'Amazons whose boundless ambition may well have contributed seminally to the development of mountaineering.'[23]

Lizzie, like all women venturing into a male preserve, simply had to disregard such blatantly sexist remarks. Her obituary in the Alpine Club's journal was more appreciative of her personal attributes describing her as a 'slight but very strongly built' woman, whose 'chief characteristic was her extraordinary judgement which has never been surpassed in any mountaineer of the so called stronger sex'.[24] Cecily Williams, in her profile of female climbers, says, 'she was the personification of elegance and no doubt found a maid a necessity'.[25] Yet despite such inverted snobbery and prejudice Lizzie rose above it and discovered that mountaineering and its pursuit had liberated her socially. She also challenged her mountaineering peers (male and female) when she wrote: 'try mountaineering in winter, and you will not be disappointed.'[26]

It appears her husband Fred was by then abandoned to live alone in his London bachelor chambers at Charles Street and her son Arthur, who was delicate, was being minded by his grandmother. Fred is reported as commenting regretfully on his own pursuit of bodybuilding and how it affected his marriage: 'I don't know how to put it better but I'm sure I'm overdeveloped. I've seen little slips of fellows get the passionate love of fine women, while great athletes are never remarkable lovers.'[27] He spoke with bitterness and the reporter took it as a personal confession, for he had noticed the same truth, and everybody knew later that poor Burnaby's marriage was not happy.

Fred found his fulfilment in military matters and conquests; he died on active service at the Battle of Abu Klea in Sudan on 17 January 1885 in an abortive and controversial unofficial attempt to rescue General Gordon at Khartoum. Fred had bravely ridden out, sword in hand, to help some comrades who were left stranded when 12,000 Sudanese warriors charged their small band of 1,500 British soldiers. Lizzie, refusing to write anything negative about her husband, was always loyal to Fred's memory and evidently very proud of his honour, bravery, sense of duty to his comrades and his ultimate sacrifice. Her last words regarding Fred in her autobiography were, 'He died as he would have wished, facing the foe'. In a footnote she tells us that Gordon himself was killed nine days later on 26 January 1885.[28]

Lizzie had quickly evolved into very skilful climber and, in the opinion of E. L. Strutt, who climbed with her on a number of ascents in winter and summer, had only one female rival (Katherine Richardson) in her day.[29] Her chief characteristic was her extraordinary judgement and, in Strutt's opinion, 'Her staying powers were quite outstanding; she was slight but very strongly built with the finishing stride of the first class guide. She was certainly the first lady to make "man less" ascents and, if these did not rival the feats of a later generation, yet they were considered extraordinary – if slightly "improper" in the Victorian era. She was very reticent on all such, but I can recollect a traverse of Piz Palu, a first ascent of the season, her sole companion being, I think, Lady Evelyn McDonnell.'[30]

Lizzie also climbed with the eminent guides Émile Rey and Alexander Burgener, traversing the Matterhorn in the company of the latter. Her account of the traverse (in *High Life and Towers of Silence*) is testimony to the peak of endurance and fitness she had reached, and her sheer ability as an accomplished alpine climber. Interestingly, Burgener had also traversed the Matterhorn with Meta Brevoort who had made the fourth female ascent and the first female traverse of the beautiful but notorious peak. It is not surprising that he formed the opinion that females 'really can climb'.[31] Women like Lizzie, Katherine and Meta stepped outside the prescribed boundaries of hearth and home set for women in society and found personal and physical fulfilment in climbing for its own sake; in the process they matched the achievements of their male compatriots.

On the morning of 19 August 1883 Lizzie left Visp for Zermatt, walking as far as St Niklaus and taking transport from there. The weather was cloudless and after dinner she decided she would like to climb the Matterhorn next morning. Alexander Burgener was asked if he would go. He had crossed the Matterhorn that day with a client from a hut on the Swiss side and descended into Italy, returning by the Furggenjoch. Despite that huge effort Burgener decided to go with her at 11 p.m. She dressed herself for climbing and had supper. They set off to reach the hut at 3 a.m., where they stopped to make coffee. The climb to the summit was trying, owing to the intense heat of the sun beating straight onto their backs. Once on top, a cool breeze greeted them and they spent an hour of intense enjoyment looking at the magnificent view around them and the distant mountains free from a trace of cloud. Lizzie noted: 'the pointed Viso standing like a sentinel looking towards the plains of Lombardy. No words can convey more than the faintest idea of the charm of such a view seen on such a day.'[32]

They started to descend towards Breuil, encountering verglas (rocks glazed over with a thin film of ice) that made the climbing slow and treacherous until they reached a rope ladder. She described the view of two ropes descending in parallel across a slab and then disappearing below an edge down a steep, dark precipice:

> looking down one can see the pastures near Breuil. Below the rocks the two ropes form a ladder, which falls sheerly at first and then is held back in a loop by its lower end being attached to the nearest point at which there is standing room. Consequently, as soon as

A roped party traversing beneath Piz Bernina and Piz Roseg from Piz Palü.
(*Elizabeth Main (1861–1934) Alpinist, Photographer, Writer* (2003))

the traveller is fairly on the ladder, it begins to swing and the rungs not being directly below each other on account of its curved shape much strain comes on the arms while the feet grope for the next rung.

In keeping with the norms of the time, she used the word 'he' and 'his' when referring generically to climbers, for example, she continues: 'a glance should not be missed by the climber who is sure of his head, the sight is sensational in the extreme.'

Descending while passing over the snow-covered Tyndall arête, they were overtaken by darkness. Here they stopped on a ledge about 3 feet wide and 12 feet long (0.91m by 3.66m) to wait for the moon to rise, the guide and his porter taking the opportunity to sleep on the spot. Elizabeth describes the ascent of the moon thus:

I walked backwards and forwards along the ledge. Far away lay the plains of Lombardy covered with a slowly rising mist. Through the curling vapour rose the Viso and other Alpine towers of silence, with the first shimmer of moon on them. Higher she came, and the ice of the glacier began to glitter, and the black shadows to fall across the streams of light, and the slumbering valleys below to become visible and show to us at what a height we were above them.

Two hours later she awoke Alexander and they continued their descent, stopping again when the moon sank until the grey light of morning allowed them continue in the frozen conditions. When they reached the glacier it required step-cutting from its top to bottom and they suffered silently from parched and swollen throats and tongues as they zigzagged down the slope. She tells of the delight with which they 'filled their drinking cups when they reached a patch of rocks over which flowed a tiny stream'. It was 8 a.m. when they reached Breuil, where they had breakfast and hired a mule and a donkey, on which they rode to the glacier edge en route to the Col de Saint-Théodule. They walked from there to Zermatt, which they reached at 5.30 in the evening, thus ending a period of continual exertion that had lasted forty-two and a half hours. She reflected on their lack of sleep: 'out of this time, the guides had had two-hours sleep, while I walked about to keep myself warm, but Alexander had been at work the whole of the day on the evening of which he started with me; and I, on the other hand, had come on foot from Visp to St Nicholas that morning, so we all had taken quite as much exercise as was good for us, to say the least of it.'

A year after Fred's death, she married Mr John Frederick Main, a natural scientist and professor of mechanics at the Imperial College of Science in London. The *St Moritz Post* recorded the arrival, on 14 December 1886, of Dr and Mrs John F. Main and maid from England, with Master Burnaby and nurse at the Kulm Hotel. He does not appear to have travelled with her in subsequent regular visits there.

In a period of twenty years from 1882 to 1903 she made about 130 major tours, including climbing the Weisshorn in four hours (excluding halts), crossing the Zinalrothorn twice in the

A party approaches Piz Roseg and Piz Bernina from Piz Palü.
(*True Tales of Mountain Adventure* (1904))

same day, and climbing Piz Bernina direct from St Moritz in the record time of 4 hours 20 minutes from the Boval Hut. She made several first ascents in winter in the Bernina region and significantly made the first winter ascent of the western and main peak of Piz Palü on 20 February 1889 with the guide Martin Schocher. Her other major winter first ascents include Piz Sella, Piz Zugö and Monte Disgrazia.

In 1892 Dr Main died in Denver, Colorado; they appeared to have spent very little time together. It is clear Lizzie was usually at the Kulm Hotel in St Moritz during both the winter and summer, a favourite spot for rich English gentry, many of whom were there for health purposes and engaged in winter sports. She was busy organising events to support a charity, the St Moritz Aid Fund, which she had set up to enable those of smaller means to avail of the resort for health purposes. To this end she ran bazaars and sold her own photographs, which were highly valued. Among those who were present in the Engadine resort during 1894–1895 was the creator of Sherlock Holmes, Sir Arthur Conan Doyle; she once photographed him dressed as a Viking at a fancy-dress ball.[33]

Mrs Main, as she was best known in the hotel, was involved in the Cresta Run committee, which organised toboggan races with the rival English community who lived at nearby Davos. She was also involved in ice skating and insisted on taking the skating test devised for men by the St Moritz Skating Association; she passed it on her second attempt (becoming the first woman to pass) and went on to hold the Association's gold badge. She was a central figure among the wealthy English society who stayed there, organising picnics for aristocratic visitors and trips to La Scala opera house in Milan.

A roped party approaching the Agüzza saddle with Disgrazia in the background. (*Elizabeth Main (1861–1934) Alpinist, Photographer, Writer* (2003)). Elizabeth Main made the first winter ascent of Monte Disgrazia (3,678m) in February 1896, having first traversed Monte Sissone (3,330m).

Wherever she went, Lizzie photographed everything; astonishingly, she is credited with having taken the first short cine films in the Engadine in 1899 to illustrate the growing popularity of winter sports. During summer she took to the bicycle, touring the shores of Lake Como and once cycled to Rome.[34] For many years postcards made from her cycling photographs around Lake Como were for sale at Lenno. Her technique for controlling her downhill speed on long, steep hills was unorthodox; she tied branches with broad leaves behind her saddle so that they dragged behind the bike. In the years before her third marriage in 1900 she produced further publications under the name of Mrs Main, which featured her photographs: *My Home in the Alps* (1892), *Hints on Snow Photography* (1895) and a travelogue, *Cities and Sights of Spain* (1900).

Lizzie practised what she believed, seeing absolutely no reason why women should not climb mountains on equal terms with men. She wore breeches for climbing with a skirt over them, which was removed once she was out of sight of civilisation. A strong sense of independence, a love of adventure, physical bravery and a cool head were the hallmarks of her character. With her health restored, she was able to enjoy to the full the pleasures of mountaineering. In addition to making most of the classic ascents in the main Alpine centres and making some remarkable winter ascents in the company of first class guides, in 1898 Lizzie and Evelyn McDonnell were the first rope that season to traverse Piz Palü (3,901m) and probably constituted the first ever 'male-less' or all-women's rope party in the history of mountaineering. She did not write about it and 'it was hushed up and regarded as somewhat improper', because the two women judged that their success on a tough, early-season ascent might be more than the male-dominated climbing establishment could handle; they were also unsure how wider society might view two women 'alone' facing such dangers.[35]

Lizzie climbed summer after summer with Joseph Imboden and his son Roman, who acted as second guide and porter, and she was very thankful that due to their excellence her expeditions were always 'free from all disaster'. As Roman came of age and gained experience, he was increasingly engaged as a guide in his own right. However, on 10 September 1896, when he was acting as guide to his new client Max Güntner (a young professor who lived in Cologne) and in company with a second guide, Peter Ruppen, his party broke through a cornice and fell to their deaths while traversing the east ridge of the Lyskamm bordering Italy and Switzerland. Naturally Joseph was greatly distressed by his son's death. Tentative plans, it seems, had already been place for Roman to go to the Himalaya with Güntner on an Everest attempt. Lizzie commented on the tragedy:

> But in a moment all these brilliant hopes were shattered. By an act of carelessness, such as nothing but youth could account for, these two young men, together with a second guide, persisted in an ascent of the Lyskamm in misty weather and ventured too far out on the snow ridge. An exceptionally large cornice projected from it, and owing to the bad condition of the snow, it broke away while all three were passing along it, projecting them down the face of the precipice.[36]

She felt she could not ask Joseph to go on climbing in the Alps with their painful associations, so instead asked him to accompany her to Norway the following year, a country he had already visited; there they climbed many of the better-known mountains in the vicinity of Sognefjord, such as the Skagastølstind, Slogan, the Romsdalshorn, the Vengetind and Mjölnir. When she heard tales of mighty glaciers flowing right down to the sea and pinnacles of rock that had never known the foot of man shooting up thousands of feet through ice and snow, she felt sure that if

The guide Joseph Imboden and Mrs Elizabeth Le Blond in Zermatt, September 1896. (*True Tales of Mountain Adventure* (1904))

they travelled some 160 km beyond the Arctic Circle they should find a climber's playground well worth exploring. Cecil Slingsby, an English climber and friend of Lizzie's, had been there the season before and had made many first ascents of fine peaks. Slingsby, whom she met en route at Tromsø with an English party, was camping in the vicinity at Jaegervand, near Ullsfjord and both parties competed to make the first ascent of the conspicuous Kjostind, a race which Slingsby's party won.[37] Emil, Joseph's second son, accompanied them and Lizzie enjoyed the beauty of fjord scenery as much as the mountains in the southern districts. There was no accommodation and local access was made by rowing boat. This meant that her party of three – her two guides and herself – would have to climb from a camp by a lake or fjord and be dependent on their own resources for food. She tells us that the inhabitants were puzzled as to what had brought them there and their relationship with each other. The Imboden climbing relationship lasted fifteen years. A photograph of the interior of her tent illustrates a relatively high level of comfort: a single bed is covered with a quilted bedspread and pillow; alongside it stands a rough timber improvised bedside locker, on which sit her washbasin, hairbrushes and combs, and the floor is covered with a bedside carpet. It looks altogether cosy and must have given rise to a lot of luggage.[38]

They spent three summers in Norway from 1897 to 1899, during which time they made thirty-three ascents, mainly in the Lyngenfjord area, twenty-four of which were first ascents of unclimbed peaks, two were first-recorded ascents, a further two were second ascents by different routes, while the remaining three were second ascents. Imboden and Lizzie immortalised themselves by naming two peaks in their own honour, namely Elizabethtind and Imbodentind:

> Imboden when out shooting had noticed a rather sharply pointed mountain near the beginning of the Strupen valley, and had kept it in mind as a suitable peak to ascend when the higher and harder ones would be unsafe . . . we strolled over bilberry-clad slopes to the foot of a little glacier, at the head of which our mountain, with a hood and cape of fresh snow covering it to below the shoulders, coquettishly waved some delicate wreaths of mist between ourselves and her charming face.
>
>   We had seen from the beginning of the glacier a heap of stones at the bottom of the peak, and from this Imboden made sure that where the stones came down was a gully, and up that gully we could probably go. And go up it we did – somewhat hastily, it is true, to minimise the risk of our being swept down it by further stones. When near the ridge we entered the region of the new snow . . . did not bother us much, and the climbing was fairly easy, and by midday I was photographing on the summit, while Emil erected his

'Stopped by a crevasse': a photograph by Mrs Main from *True Tales of Mountain Adventure* (1904)

stone man. Our point of view was grand, and as the weather was now fine and warm, we were able to enjoy it to the full. I ventured to call the little peak the Elizabethtind, finding no neighbouring glacier or valley after which to name it.[39]

She recorded their activity in a new book published in 1908, *Mountaineering in the Land of the Midnight Sun*. Aubrey Le Blond, her future third husband, is mentioned once in the second chapter as accompanying her swimming during the 1898 visit and then vanishes from the narrative, turning up again in a later chapter in 1899. There she recalls that during three summers 'my husband and I, with our native maiden Hildur to cook for us had an excellent time camping by those northern fjords and lakes.'[40]

The book was published under her third and final married name and she added her new position to the title page of the book, 'President of the Lyceum Alpine Club'. This new club had been established in 1907 by a group of women as a section of the Lyceum Club;[41] in 1909 it became an independent organisation renamed the Ladies' Alpine Club. Mrs Le Blond was elected its first president, a post she stayed in until 1912. She wrote in the first annual report in 1913: 'a club like ours must grow and expand in a natural and healthy manner . . . It must be nourished by the unceasing interest and labour of our members and above all its high standards must be maintained, so that, as membership carries with it a guarantee of efficiency, it may ever be an honour to belong to it.'[42]

Mr Francis Bernard Aubrey Le Blond of Aldeburgh, Suffolk, was the son of a rich merchant and an enthusiastic collector of oriental antiques, particularly ceramics. After their marriage in 1900, they spent the winter of that year on the islands of Sicily, Sardinia and Corsica and cycling along the

Interior of Elizabeth's tent. (*Mountaineering in the Land of the Midnight Sun* (1908))

Riviera. Lizzie had stopped climbing but returned again with Aubrey to St Moritz in February 1903, staying at a private hotel. She wrote *True Tales of Mountain Adventure*, illustrated with her excellent black and white photography. However a year later she was back in the Kulm Hotel, alone, and back into her old ways, writing and photographing. At this time she wrote a novel, *The Story of an Alpine Winter*, whose plot unfolds in a grand hotel in her favourite Swiss resort. The story was inspired by her long experience of the rich English set living there. Coming from the daughter of an old establishment family, the novel is less than complimentary about the newly rich merchant classes who were filling the palatial hotels. She was old-fashioned and snobbish in her perception of the new order and its tastes. She also compiled *Adventures on the Roof of the World*, which comprised extracts from journals and books by leading climbers of the age. She provided twenty-eight photographs to illustrate Henry Inigo Triggs' book, *The Art of Garden Design in Italy* (1906), and wrote a biography of one of her ancestors, Charlotte Sophie, Countess Bentinck (1912). Using the unused photographs shot for Triggs' book and some new additions, she craftily produced her own book on Italian gardens in 1912, *The Old Gardens of Italy: How to Visit Them*. In 1913 she brought out a translation from French of the autobiography of Charlotte Amélie, Princess of Aldenburg (1652–1732), and supplied the photographs to produce *Winter Sports in Switzerland*, in collaboration with other pioneer St Moritz winter sport enthusiasts.

Lizzie also travelled widely with Aubrey to the Middle East, Asia, Manchuria and other parts of China, and visited Siberia and Russia before the revolution, seeing things there that would never be seen again. In Japan they procured, cheaply, a fine collection of Korean pottery plundered from illegal diggings.[43] Aubrey later presented part of this collection to the Victoria and Albert Museum in London. Lizzie arrived back to Flims in Switzerland to see her son, who was obliged for reasons of his health to live abroad. It was just before the outbreak of the Great War in 1914 and her return to London was almost held up by the war's first dramatic days. At home she found that her husband and his brother had both offered themselves for military service. Aubrey was given national work and his brother was offered a commission in the Rifle Brigade, however, a failed operation for appendicitis ended his life before he entered the war.

Lizzie tried to enlist with the Red Cross but was deemed too old at fifty-three. Around this time she read a newspaper account written by an English nurse about the lack of helpers in the French army's hospitals at Dieppe. Soon she was shaping a role for herself in l'Hôpital 37, stationed in the Metropole Hotel at Dieppe. Not part of the medical nursing staff, she spent hours coaxing suffering men to take their food and washed men who were unable to wash themselves; she was constantly moving wounded limbs into comfortable positions for the bedridden and writing letters home for them. In short, Lizzie did the tasks that the busy nursing staff had little time to do, such as organising entertainments and generally trying to relieve the monotony of the patients' lives. Returning to England two years later she was asked to take charge of the appeals department of the British Ambulance Committee, raising £1,200 per week for the service from early 1917 until the end of the war.

After the armistice Elizabeth was engaged by the War Office to give lectures to British troops stationed in France and England. She maintained her close links with France and had a special interest in maintaining the entente between the two countries. She did this on several fronts, including the organisation of the British Empire Fund towards the restoration of Reims Cathedral and the erection of a statue of Marshal Foch near Victoria Station in London. For this she was awarded the Légion d'honneur by the French government and was invited to Reims in May 1927 for the formal opening of the great nave of the cathedral.

Following advertisements in the *Manchester Guardian* in 1920, the Women's Rock Climbing Club was founded at a meeting chaired by Eleanor Winthrop Young at the Pen-y-Gwrid Hotel in Llanberis, North Wales, on 21 March 1921. The name was subsequently changed to the Pinnacle Club. Elizabeth Le Blond was no longer climbing, but was still the best known and respected female climber in Britain and, as a result, was invited to become the new club's first president. She visited America, travelling by train to California where her son Arthur had taken a bungalow, still in pursuit of good health. And she could not stop writing. Her autobiography, *Day In, Day Out*, was published in London in 1928. Then she co-wrote a romantic historical mystery (*The Dunkelgraf Mystery*, 1929), a tale of intrigue based on the European aristocracy that includes a daughter of Marie Antoinette as one of the characters. Three years later in 1932 she translated the letters of a French colonial administrator, Marshal Louis Hubert Gonzalve Lyautey, whom she had met in Morocco in 1918; they were published as *Intimate Letters from Tonkin and Madagascar*.

Remarkably, in 1932 when she was already seventy-one, she was elected again for a second term as president of the Ladies' Alpine Club on the written invitation of club members. She accepted the honour, saying it was 'one of the nicest things that has ever happened to me' upon being told that the invitation was at the suggestion of the younger members.[44] She was no token president, diligently attending club meetings, and it was no accident that she was regarded and honoured in this way by the young women as their elected leader. She had embodied the cause of female climbing and given it a high profile, not just with her first ascents and first winter ascents, but in her writings, photographs and public lectures. She had been one of a very small group of adventurous women who had paved the way for women of a later day, women who had calmly ignored the criticism that they were 'unwomanly' and had instead asserted themselves by the standards of excellence they achieved in their own climbing.

Her health began to fail in 1933 and, following an operation in 1934, she went to recover at the home of her sister at Llandrindod Wells, Radnorshire in Wales. Aubrey was there and her son, Arthur Burnaby, arrived with his American wife just in time to see her before she died on 27 July. He survived his mother by only a few years.

Skating on Lake Sils in Engadine. (*Elizabeth Main (1861–1934) Alpinist, Photographer, Writer* (2003)). Elizabeth Main was one of the first to photograph winter sports and the first person to make short cine films in 1899 to illustrate the growing popularity of winter sports

Left: Portrait of Mrs Elizabeth Le Blond. (*Ladies' Alpine Club Yearbook 1935*)

Edouard Cupelin, 1840–1906

Edouard Cupelin was born in the valley of Chamonix. He was nicknamed 'Canut' by his friends, *un canut* being the generic pseudonym in Savoy for a tall, powerful man who walks with a long stride. He started climbing as a guide to a Monsieur Bisson (a photographer whom he led to the summit of Mont Blanc) and he worked as a porter to Capt Mieulet, the French mapmaker, in his survey work. He is one of the few Chamonix guides who also climbed in the Oberland and Zermatt. He climbed Mont Blanc eighty-nine times in his career. He made more winter ascents than any other Chamonix guide of his time and climbed on the first winter ascents of Aiguille du Midi, the Col des Grand Montets, Col du Chardonnet, Fenêtre de Salina, Col d'Argentière and the first passage of the Col du Tacul with Mrs Elizabeth Burnaby.

He was forced into retirement as a result of an accident while climbing the Aiguille Verte in 1884. He was pulled off the steps he was cutting when a falling boulder struck his rope. He arrested his fall, but he severely injured his right knee in the fall. He took a lease on the Cabane Pierre Pointe where he became popular among the patrons.[45]

Edouard Cupelin, Mrs Elizabeth Burnaby's guide on the Bishorn ascent. (*High Life and Towers of Silence* (1886))

9

William Spotswood Green:
a Passion for Mountains and Fishes

I hold that the essence of all true sport consists of the pleasurable feelings experienced when natural difficulties, whatever they may be are overcome by skill.

Rev. William Spotswood Green, *The High Alps of New Zealand*, 1883

WILLIAM SPOTSWOOD GREEN from Youghal, County Cork, was a focused mountaineer who made a significant impact outside of the Alps in three previously unexplored mountaineering arenas: Lofoten Islands, Norway, the New Zealand Alps and the Selkirk range of the Canadian Rockies. The last two were short, successful and well-publicised climbing expeditions in the late nineteenth century: one to explore and climb Mount Cook in the Southern Alps of New Zealand in 1882 and the other in 1888 to explore and map the Selkirk range in Canada, during which he summited Mount Bonney, an impressive peak in the Rogers Pass area. Either of these exploits alone would merit his inclusion in any history of Victorian mountaineering pioneers. Interestingly, on each occasion he published a scientific paper followed by a popular book for the public. His mountaineering achievements have been discarded and categorised as among the lesser known and bizarre, reflecting his false image as an eccentric Irish clergyman who turned to mountaineering and science to relieve the boredom of his life as a country rector.

A broader Irish perspective of William Spotswood Green would credit him as the dynamic first Chief Inspector of Fisheries who made a very substantial contribution to the economic development of the Irish southern and western seaboards, through the establishment of a practical fisheries research capability, the construction of many new fishing piers and the instigation of practical initiatives to organise the equipping of small Irish fishing vessels with internal combustion engines. His initiatives led to a marked improvement in the welfare of Ireland's coastal population, an achievement that was shamefully neglected by the first government of a newly independent Ireland. His undoubted skills as an experienced and accomplished alpinist, combined with his practical expertise as a sailor, fisherman, shooter and hunter, gave him an extraordinary capacity for self-reliance and competence in wild and difficult terrain and waters. These skills, added to his abilities as a historian, artist, mapmaker and an informed observer of natural science, gave him a natural calling for writing in the tradition of Ball and Tyndall.

Rev. William Spotswood Green, 1847–1919

- Born in Youghal, County Cork
- Ordained Church of Ireland (Anglican) priest
- First ascent of a summit (Higravstinden) by a mountaineer in the Lofoten Islands, Norway
- First ascent of Mount Cook in the Southern Alps of New Zealand
- Organised the first Irish dredging expedition to investigate the fauna of the 100-fathom line on the southwest coast of Ireland
- Exploration and mapping of the Selkirk range in Canadian Rockies, including the first ascent of Mount Bonney
- Appointed first Irish Chief Inspector of Fisheries

Facing page: portrait of William Spotswood Green. (*Among the Selkirk Glaciers* (1998))

William Green was born in Youghal, County Cork, on 10 September 1847. When he was twelve, he was sent to a boarding school in the Dublin suburb of Rathmines, which was owned by the Rev. Charles W. Benson, an enthusiastic naturalist who encouraged all his students to study wildlife. Green's first written observations on natural history date from that period. A paper (dated 1860) was pasted later into one of his adult diaries; it indicates that he collected and identified seashells at Youghal in 1860 when he was barely a teenager.[1] In it he described the substrates and numbers of each species he had collected, evidence that at this early age he was an active amateur biologist. Family members recorded that William spent every possible hour of his youth sailing and fishing along the south coast of Ireland. We are told his house was so close to the sea that its dining room was occasionally flooded at high water.[2]

Green's first diary is entitled 'Diary of My Aquarium', and recorded his observations on the animals in three tanks located in various parts of his home. He was influenced by popular publications relating to collecting fauna and the pastime of keeping aquaria. He demonstrated his talent as an artist by producing colour illustrations of some of the species in his collection. It appears he owned a microscope and in November 1866 he conducted dredging operations in Youghal Bay and made a record. His diary records that his mother actively helped him in his shore collecting activities. He was interested in wild birds and tried unsuccessfully to rear young nightjars but apparently did better with stock doves.[3] He writes of visits he made to the habitats of Bull and Booterstown in 1866 and 1868 to collect specimens and water for the aquarium. His companions on these trips included members of the Ball family who were close friends and eminent members of the scientific community in Dublin.

On 1 July 1867 he entered Trinity College, aged nineteen. His academic career was undistinguished in the sense that he received no special awards or honours and the college records include many blank spaces opposite his name where one would have expected to find exam results or details of attendance at lectures.[4] On 9 February 1869 Green went for a week-long cruise with some college friends in a trawler belonging to a Mr Good. Setting out from Ringsend, they trawled from the Kish to Greystones, netting plaice, ray and sole until they were forced to 'put in at Kingstown in bad weather'.[5] Greens' first foray to the Alps took place in the same year as the trawler cruise. While not a successful experience, it nevertheless whetted an interest and opened up a new world for him. As he explains:

> In 1869 a friend induced me to join him in a six weeks trip to Switzerland, and so relinquish the cruise about which I had built castles in the air during the long evenings of university study. My friend was unfortunately taken ill at Grindelwald, so I had to go alone, and after being driven back from the Alphubel Joch by a blinding snow-storm, and thwarted in my intended ascent of Monte Rosa by my guides burning the soles off the only pair of boots I possessed on the stove at the Riffelberg, I returned home feeling that a whole new world had opened out before me. All the next winter my mind was full of plans of ascents possible and impossible; and when summer came round it found me on the glaciers with two companions whose interests I had awakened in Alpine expeditions.[6]

Green's courses during the Hilary (post-Christmas) term of 1870 included experimental physics, logic and mathematical physics. This indicates that his degree was in science rather than in the arts, although Dublin University awarded the degree of BA for both at that time. In 1870 he returned again to the Swiss Alps in company with J. S. Lyle and kept a brief journal.[7] His account tells us that he started on Monday 18 July on the Bristol steamer *Iverna* from Passage East in County Waterford. They encountered 'some difficulties at Bristol with Lyle's passport on account of the Franco-Prussian war', and continued by train to London where they went to the Royal Opera at Covent Garden to see the comic opera *L'Étoile du Nord*, leaving the show early due to the heat. They proceeded to Paris and made visits to the Louvre and to Notre Dame before moving on to Geneva. They kept a common purse of £20 10s and Green made an Alpine belt (rope waist harness) for Lyle. From Geneva they crossed Lake Leman by steamer to Le Bouveret at the upper end of the lake and made their way to Martigny. Next day they hired mules for the Col de Balme to the Forclaz Pass and down to Chamonix. At Chamonix they stayed at Hotel Mont Blanc, paying just 7 francs for the week.

The following day they set out to climb the Brévent, which overlooks Chamonix like a sentinel. They left at 11.30 a.m., arriving at the summit in thunder and rain, and were back in the hotel at 6 p.m. They then visited glacier caves and engaged a guide, Alexander Burgener, to cross the Col d'Herens on 4 August. Green's cousin Harry Swanzy had joined them by then. On Sunday Green records that a service was held in the Mont Cervin hotel and that he received communion. They then walked up to Riffel with Peter Knubel of St Niklaus and two other guides whom they had engaged for an ascent of Monte Rosa. That same morning they heard of an accident involving Mrs Geo. Marke and the guide O. Gay on Mont Blanc. This did not put them off their own ascent, which he records simply: 'Climbed Monte Rosa in soft conditions, starting at 3.10 and on summit at 12 o'clock. Arrived back at Riffel at 5.45.' He further notes they were out for fourteen and a half hours.

An attempt on the Strahlhorn from the Adler Pass on 11 August was abandoned due to wind and cloud. He writes that they were lost in heavy snow on descent before making their way to the Matmuk Inn. They made their way from there to Bel Alp, from where they walked up the Sparrenhorn on 15 August. They walked from Bel Alp to the Eggishorn and 'had a very pleasant bathe in a little lake on the way' and 'engaged two guides for the ascent of the Finsteraarhorn for 50 franc each.'

They set off next afternoon for Faulberg from where they would start their ascent. His brief journal notes record: 'Starting at 1.30 feeling unwell at Aletsch Glacier. Sick at Grünhorns Lake. Reached ridge at 7.30, summit at 9.30 (am). Back at 8pm at Faulberg (18½ hrs).' He also notes 'one of the guides on the way back down drank too much and got quite drunk.' Near the bottom he slipped and was stopped by the rope and Lyle (who held him on the axe), but cut his finger very deeply on stone embedded in the ice. After the Finsteraarhorn they took a car to the Rhone Glacier Hotel where, on Sunday 21 August, 'H. Swanzy read service'. From there they walked to the Grimsel Pass and on to Meiringen, where Green bought wood carvings. The next day they walked to Grindelwald; from here he made his way home three days later, taking the train from Berne to Paris and encountering many soldiers in good spirits.

As he passed through London he took time out to view Turner's pictures at Royal Academy before taking the train to Bristol and arriving in Cork on 31 August aboard the *Juno*. It is clear from this journal that Green was purely interested in climbing for its own sake, as there is no mention of scientific observations or experiments. He had crossed or climbed a number of Switzerland's notable passes: the Col d'Herens, the Adler Pass and the Grimsel Pass, and had reached the summits of two 4,000m peaks, the Finsteraarhorn and Monte Rosa. He had also climbed with two of the most famous and capable alpine guides, Alexander Burgener and Peter Knubel. He had sampled the weather and atmosphere of the classic climbing centres of Chamonix, Zermatt, Bel Alp and Grindelwald. And he had overseen an excellent introduction to alpinism for his two companions.

In June 1871 Green graduated and left Dublin that evening to explore alone the snow-covered rocky peaks of Lofoten Islands off the west coast of Norway, which are inside the Arctic Circle. Whilst these peaks are no more than 1,210m high, the snowline even in summer is as low as 244m because of the latitude. Green was one of the first mountaineers to explore what has since become a very popular area for mountaineering. He planned his itinerary, availing of scheduled transport, to reach a mountainous area that he knew was largely unexplored. He would repeat this strategy in his later explorations in New Zealand and Canada.

In his concise Norwegian diary Green tells us: 'June 28 Arrived Dublin at 4.30 a.m. Not particularly well. At one o'clock Hand and I went into the hall and had our degrees of A.B. conferred. I then went out and got my hair cut and made sundry preparations for my journey and started in company with Hand by the Holyhead boat at 7 o'clock.'[8]

He travelled to Hull by train, where he took a berth on the *Tassa* to Trondheim at a cost of 7 guineas, provisions included. Coming out of port he observed the fine trawlers of about 70 tons and a great number of Dutch-looking barges, windmills and houses. They sailed up the east coast of Scotland. Looking out of the porthole on 2 July, he saw they were steaming along Molde Fjord. 'The water was like glass the land not far off. The lower slopes covered with a dark clothing of pines then came a band of white fleecy clouds, and then above towered up the black peaks seamed with snow.' They stopped at Molde to drop off passengers and then steamed back into the open sea to enter Trondheim Fjord and, in a glorious sunset, arrived in port at midnight.

On 4 July he boarded the *Jupiter* to bring him to Stokmarknes in the Lofoten Islands. Green seems to have enjoyed a very convivial time on board, playing games with the other passengers, such as 'buckets' (which appears to have involved throwing basket rings into a bucket from a distance and running races in laps round the deck). His romantic nature is also reflected in his tale of an encounter with a wedding party (including the bridegroom's dog) on their way to or from their wedding ceremony in the midst of an Arctic Circle landscape of bare rock and still water dotted with little flocks of eider duck.

He arrived at Stokmarknes on 7 July and reluctantly left the ship with its pleasant party on board, but was encouraged by the fine day and the grand crags in view. On arrival ashore in a small boat, he hired a *carjole* (horse and trap) driven by a small boy who brought him and his luggage to Melbo where he stayed in the lodgings of Fra Colvine for four days. He sketched the house and the sulky mountains, which were covered with a veil of clouds. After dinner he strolled along the foot of cliffs and then climbed to the top where he noted an eagle wheeling about its eyrie, and heard its young screaming loudly. Miss Colvine, who could speak some English, played the piano 'with great taste' before he retired to bed. He hired two men and a boat for the next day for the sum of 6 marks, so that he could go where he liked. When the clouds rolled back he wrote: 'It was so lovely, I don't think I ever felt a more intense pleasure. The sea was like glass dotted here and there with sea fowl of various descriptions then the long line of snow-capped peaks softening

A view of the distant summit of Higravstinden (1,146m), the highest peak in the island of Austvågøya in the Lofoten archipelago, Norway, as seen from the summit of Trollfjordtinden. W. S. Green made the first ascent of a lower summit to the left. (Courtesy Harry Connolly)

from rugged purple crags to emerald green slopes as they approached the sea.'

Green set his sights on a peak that appears to have been Higravstinden (1,158m), the highest in Ost Vaagen and the Lofoten Islands, and which lies at the head of the Stover Fjord. His boatmen were very pleasant fellows; they pulled the oars while he lay luxuriously in the stern steering and jabbering away in bad Norse and asking questions, mainly about the seabirds. He waxed lyrical in his diary regarding the pristine quality of the Nordic hills: 'Nothing can surpass the beauty of this Fjord, it beats the Bay of Uri hollow.[9] The Aiguille du Verte is tame compared with these snow scarred pinnacles, and the Emerald Isle itself must blush at the greenness of its shores.'

He left the boatmen at twelve o'clock, jumping ashore. They agreed to await his return and pick him up at whatever place he chose to descend to. He carried an alpenstock in his hand, his paintbox, some potted beef, biscuits, figs and a small flask of brandy in his pockets, with his sketchbook slung in a strap around his neck. He took off across boulder-strewn terrain covered with fern, alder bushes and wild flowers; this gradually became steeper, giving way first to rock and then to a snow slope, which led to the col that was his object. The ascent took an hour and a half and he took the precaution of marking his way with pieces of white paper, lest he had any difficulty finding his way on his return. He found the view from the col 'glorious'; after sketching it, he picked up the route to the mountain top through steep, hard snow, some of which he had to cut steps through. A long slope through a gorge was topped by a cornice he classified as 'a fearful precipice'; here he turned to the right of the rocks, flushing out a Ptarmigan in the process. To his delight he found himself on the edge of a wide, snow-covered plateau from the opposite side of which rose up the true peak. He sketched the attractive peak again from his vantage point and was relieved by the flat walking on hard snow he now enjoyed. Steeper climbing led to the dome,

View of Trollfjordtinden (1,045m) from Higravstinden. (Author's photo)

which was iced and required step-cutting to reach the easy slope to the summit. It was 4.30 p.m. He surmised that it must be more than 4,000 feet (1,219m) high, as he had lost no time and walked at a fair pace. 'The view was magnificent; I have yet to see the Alpine view that surpasses it. The mountain chain of the mainland was in view I should say for 100 miles, then the Westfjorde studded with islands. The whole chain of the Lofoten Islands and islets [are] the crowd of the most fantastic peaks that I ever beheld.'

He lay down to eat some beef, biscuit and figs and built a cairn with what stones he could collect, then made a sketch of the view of Vest Fjord. He reflected: 'Only one drop of bitterness was in my cup and that was the presence of a neighbouring crag that evidently overtopped my own. It was too far off to try, it also it looked quite inaccessible, at least I should be sorry to try it by myself.'

It is thought that the summit climbed by Green was Norge or North Higravstinden,[10] one of the Higravstinden's several summits, its highest point being the highest in the islands. Green's climb was the first recorded ascent in the range by a mountaineer. He descended by a different route, glissading in ten minutes what had taken an hour to climb, and passing through some difficult moraine to reach 'a beautiful little lake in which the peaks were mirrored to their summits'. From there he scrambled through a wood to reach the Fjord beach, then worked his way round the foreshore, often getting wet while scrambling over the base of the mountain. At one point he took off his clothes to swim. To raise the attention of the boatmen he yelled and made attempts at yodelling. He was in the boat at 6.30 p.m., feeling comfortably tired and wet, to a change of boots, socks and trousers. By 8.30 p.m. he was back in Melbo, in time for a good dinner followed by coffee and bed. He spent the next three days fishing, sketching and bird-watching: he caught two dozen trout (including one very large one which gave him 'great play'), as well as observing a pair of white-headed eagles and the breeding place of the common local bird called a *heste*, which he likened to a puffin. He listed all the shells he identified and took eggs of a *heste* and a small gull as specimens.

On 11 July he left Melbo for Stokmarknes to meet the steamer expected at midnight, which took him back to Trondheim. During the remainder of Green's Norwegian holiday he travelled towards Christiana (now Oslo), hiring local guides and (depending on the terrain to be travelled) using a combination of rowing boats, ferries, hired horses and ponies and sometimes traps, carts or carriages to carry his portmanteau, rucksack and provisions. He took a guide on one occasion to cross the Jostedals Glacier from the village of Gredding to Jostedal on the Sognefjord. On the day of his arrival in Gredding, everybody in the village and surrounding valleys appeared to be drunk and merry because a local festival was in full swing. A young guide named Torg Anton took his brother to assist him with carrying Green's portmanteau and on the way they caught a horse that was grazing to carry the heavy luggage until they reached steep rocks at the side of the glacier. As they crossed the ice-covered pass, Green reflected that: 'it was with difficulty that I could think myself anywhere than in the Alps'. They wound up 'among the blue crevasses' and a little after 1 p.m. came to a stop under a 'bold snow-covered mountain'. Green was thrilled, while eating lunch, to see five reindeer come into view. They crossed the 2,083m pass where he observed Lodalskåpa, a fine peak, and immense tracts of undulating snowfields as far as the eye could see. They descended by Stykke Bolt Brae and arrived at 5 p.m. at a *saeter* (dairy), from where they got milk and from which he hired packhorses to bring him 7 miles (11.3 km) down the valley to Faaberg. He paid off his young guides, commenting in his diary: 'They are both fine fellows if they do not ruin themselves with aquavite.' During the last few days of his journey through Norway he travelled 165.5 (English) miles (266.3 km) in a hired *carjole*, arriving at Gjøvic on the Mjosen Lake, where he and his *carjole* boarded a ferry that brought him to Eidsvoll and from there to Christiana where he commenced his journey home.

In 1872 William was ordained a deacon of the Church of Ireland and the following year he was ordained to priesthood and travelled extensively in France, Italy, Austria and Germany. In 1874 an element of settled life was introduced on his appointment as curate of Kenmare. A sketchbook records an 'oceanographical cruise' in the yacht *Prima Donna* in the same year. While a curate at Kenmare in 1875 he married his cousin Belinda Beatty Butler, whose father owned the valuable salmon and trout fishery on the Cummeragh River nearby at Waterville.[11] Their son, Charles, would later follow in his father's footsteps as an inspector of Irish Fisheries.

From January to March 1877 Green temporarily abandoned his parish, his wife and his infant children for another journey, this time to explore the Orinoco Delta and the West Indies. The outward voyage from Southampton to St Thomas (3,187 miles/5,129 km) aboard *Tasmania* took fourteen days.[12] He transferred to the steamer *Eider*, which was cruising to Port of Spain, Trinidad, and stopped on the way at St Kitts, Antigua, Basse Terre in Guadeloupe, Roseau on Dominica, Martinique, St Lucia, Barbados, and St Vincent. While in Trinidad, near San Fernando, he visited two active volcanos, one of which erupted the next day, throwing mud to a height of 60 to 70 feet (18 to 21m). He was taken to see a couple of opium dens there, where he observed: 'four or five wretches in different stages of insensibility, smoking opium'. Later, travelling up the Orinoco, one of the vessels he used was employed to collect gold from the mines operating there at the time. In all his travels he describes in detail the flora, fauna, local people, their habits, food and events. When he returned home, the Green family moved to Carrigaline, County Cork, following his appointment there as curate (he would subsequently become rector). One more holiday appears in the diaries (a second visit to the Swiss Alps), and then his life as an explorer and scientific observer took a more serious turn.

The modern climbing guide to Aoraki/Mount Cook, published by the New Zealand Alpine Club, explains that in the late 1880s the Mount Cook region, as it was known then, became the hub of climbing in New Zealand and has remained so ever since. In the early 1860s Julius von Haast, a German scientist, explored, surveyed and mapped most of the eastern approaches in the region. He was followed by others, including gold miners and surveyors such as Sealy, Broderick and Douglas.[13] During the 1870s, however, the lure of the unclimbed Mount Cook provided an attraction that the itchy-footed Green could not resist:

> Meanwhile wishing to see for myself the grand scenes of nature in quite another form I wandered off to the tropical forests of the New World, but unfortunately there contracted fever and ague that I could not shake off, till once more, in 1879, I returned to the Alps, where the crisp bracing air of the glaciers gave me the relief which I sought. With renewed health came back the old Alpine longings in all their former strength. I thought of trying some of the peaks of the Andes, taking those between the Argentine Republic, and Chile, as Mr Whymper was exhaustively exploring the mysteries of the more northern part of the chain.[14]

During the British Association Jubilee meeting at York in 1881, Green met 'a gentleman lately returned from New Zealand' who gave him an account of his travels and showed him some photographs of the peaks of the Southern Alps, including Mount Cook, which convinced him that the conquest of this unclimbed peak was 'well worth the trouble of a long journey. So I made up my mind that now was the very time for this expedition to the antipodes'.[15]

He explored the library of the Royal Geographical Society (RGS) and found a book on the geology of Canterbury and Westland: the work of Haast. He procured a copy and realised the seriousness of the mountaineering exploration he was undertaking and the fact that he needed to bring additional mountaineering expertise with him. He contacted the Swiss hotel owner Emil Boss, of Hotel de l'Ours in Grindelwald (also a keen mountaineer), and asked him to induce one of the Oberland guides to accompany Green to New Zealand. Boss consulted the experienced guide Ulrich Kaufmann, who was willing and ready to go, and Boss also volunteered himself to accompany them. Green had his team and immediately set about organising what he called 'his outfit'. The outfit consisted of three tents, one of which was 7 by 7 foot (0.65 by 0.65m, approximately) and made of strong cotton 'duck' (canvas); he says it had seen some service but that he had from time to time altered it, so that 'it was now all that could be desired'.[16] The tent had two upright poles, from which two hammocks were slung, leaving room for one or two cork mattresses on the floor. A ridge pole kept the two poles apart. The tent also had a snow valance, on which stones could be put in places where pegs could not be driven. He borrowed a similar tent from a friend and constructed a third. This tent was made of calico steeped in linseed oil, 'on the plan of Mr Whymper's Macintosh Alpine tent'. It had a sewn-in groundsheet and a door at only one end; the support poles were contained within hems or sleeves (so that the tent would stand without guy ropes once the poles were inserted), and it was held down by rocks or snow placed on external extensions known as 'valances'. The tent measured 7 foot long by 6 foot wide (2.13m by 2.13m) and weighed 13 lb (6 kg). As it could not take hammocks, Green had three sleeping bags made out of felt, which he explained was particularly light when dry. To this a Macintosh groundsheet was added and a lighter sheet of oiled calico, blankets, and an opossum rug. It was all packed into oiled and painted canvas bags of a size suitable for attaching to pack saddles. A large water canteen, a little spirit lamp and 'a saucepan cuisine made for mountain expeditions' completed the camping gear. He does not discuss his climbing clothes or gear except to say:

> Besides my old ice-axe which had been my companion on many a mountain peak, I got a second in case of one being lost. An Alpine Club rope of sixty-feet and a slighter rope of equal length were packed with the tent ropes, but held sacred for purely mountaineering purposes. A new aneroid barometer graduated down to fifteen inches, and other instruments made by Negretti and Zambra, with books, drawing materials, and ordinary personal gear, completed my outfit.[17]

Green's rationale and explanation for abandoning his parish and family responsibilities to go climbing are not deliberated in his book, except to express the difficulties that would-be explorers experience due to the timing of southern hemisphere seasons:

> The difficulty of arranging for the proper carrying on of the ordinary business of life has deterred many of our most enthusiastic mountaineers from attempting those interesting fields for exploration which are to be found in every quarter of the globe. This difficulty is greatly increased by the fact that mountain regions, like Arctic regions, can only be approached in their own particular seasons, and these seasons often coincide with the busiest time of the year.[18]

He justified his engagement in important pioneering exploration by using something like the maxim 'if you want something done give it to a busy man', and wrote:

> If the Alpine Club was recruited from the idler ranks of society this difficulty would not exist; but it is a fact worthy of notice, and one of which our members should be proud, that our best climbers are to be found amongst men who are most diligent in business and most active in taking their share in the work of life. I at length succeeded in making an arrangement, which would enable me to be absent from home for six months. It was a short time for such a long journey, but if all went well I calculated on having at least two months in the New Zealand Mountains.[19]

The difficulties of a pastor abandoning his parish at Christmas time did not deter Green from his goal. Robert Lloyd Praeger, a prominent Irish botanist of the period, jibed at exactly how Green managed to use his concern for his own health to justify an extended period of 'sick leave' to the Antipodes: 'Never robust, he was advised not to spend the winter of 1881–82 in Ireland, and when he discovered that Mount Cook, the highest of the New Zealand Alps, had never been climbed and that its ascent was considered impracticable, he naturally went out and climbed it.[20] Later, another who also knew Green's character would say of him, 'The only ecclesiastical post he really would have liked would have been that of chaplain on board a pirate ship.'[21]

This expedition seems to mark a transition in Green's climbing status and motivation; he moved from climbing purely for its own sake to become Green the mountaineer, scientific observer, mapmaker and explorer. His strategy was rewarded when he received a £30 grant from the Royal Irish Academy (RIA). He also managed to elicit (from the New Zealand Minister for Railways) free passes on the country's railways for himself and his guides during their stay in the colony.

He left Plymouth on 12 November 1881 on the steamer *Garonne* bound for Melbourne. Smallpox broke out on the ship, which caused Green a serious delay at the Cape and three weeks' quarantine at Melbourne. As a result he did not arrive in Port Chalmers, on the South Island of New Zealand, until 5 February. Ulrich Kaufmann and Emil Boss, who had departed a day later than Green, were forced to wait patiently for him there. He visited Dunedin by train and then steamed on the *Te Anau* with his companions to Port Lyttelton. Arriving in Christchurch by train, he declared: 'I thought that were I free to choose my home in the world, notwithstanding the misfortunes which attended such a choice in the days gone by, I would select the "city of the plains".'[22]

In Christchurch he met Dr Haast, the great authority on the topography of the Southern Alps. They perused his photographs and maps of the area and discussed the feasibility of potential routes to reach the summit of Mount Cook. Haast thought that their only chance would be by ascending the Tasman Glacier. The Rev. Green expressed amazement at the amount of tea drunk in New Zealand. 'It was most satisfactory to find that practically tea may take the place of and supplement to a great extent alcoholic drinks; so different from my last colonial experience, in the West Indies, where the gin cocktail destroys more lives than the yellow fever which has given such a bad name to our lovely possessions in the tropical seas.'

They went by train to Timaru next morning where they picked up some provisions: 25 lb flour, 12 lb oatmeal and 16 lb biscuit formed the bulk of their stores. They proposed to take a sack of baker's bread from the last place it could be procured; for a change of diet a dozen tins of sardines, some rice, cheese and a few luxuries were bought. For beverages they purchased 5 lb tea, some chocolate and cream ready-mixed, and filled their flasks with brandy and whisky as a standby in case of need. Green had already stored in his luggage a few pots of extract of meat, and a 7 lb tin of mutton.

They were assured that they could procure fresh mutton or lamb right up until the snows of Mount Cook, so they took little tinned meat. At Albury Green hired a wagon, three horses and a driver and managed to procure one pack saddle; after loading the wagon they covered it with a single oilcloth to keep it dry. The plan was to abandon the wagon when it could go no further and transfer the goods to the horses. The horses would return with the driver and, at an agreed date and place, come back to take them out again. They were soon moving and enjoyed a view of the great snowy range and its ice-seamed peaks, which Green said contrasted strikingly with the brown, flattened downs over which they travelled until they came to the bed of the Tasman River. At Fairie Creek they bought bread from the last baker they were told they would pass. They headed west to Two Thumbs Mountain and turned southward up an incline to Burke's Pass to follow the headwaters of Opihi River. Green noted that this portion of Canterbury, including all the lands drained by the headwaters of the Waitaiki, is called after a certain freebooter named Mackenzie, a sort of Robin Hood in the short history of New Zealand who engaged in sheep stealing.

An artistically finished suspension bridge supported by concrete piers came into sight, affording them a passage over the Tekapo, after which they halted at a comfortable hotel situated on the farther shore. A neat bed was allotted to each of the party and the sitting room commanded a pretty view of the lake. The landlord was an Irishman; he told them of the difficulties that he had encountered in grubbing boulders out of the ground to make a garden but said that he had been well repaid for his efforts because a goodly supply of vegetables was always ready for his guests.

The next day they crossed the highest ridge of the downs over which they were travelling and at last they overlooked the broad valley of the Tasman Glacier. It lay several hundred feet below them, its wide waste of gravel laced by innumerable streams, and bounded by the parallel ranges of grand alpine heights, with Mount Cook towering over all, blocking the vista to the right with its pyramid of rock and ice, and forming one of the grandest scenes of the southern hemisphere. On drawing closer to his objective, Green reflected that all of their troubles seemed to be atoned for in that one instant: the 12,000-mile journey, the quarantine and all the other trying circumstances involved in their long absence from home.

They spent the night in the sheep station at Birch Hill, having travelled until darkness fell, with the help of a local guide. When the shepherd in charge arrived, a young Scotsman named George Sutherland, he promised to kill a sheep and to come after them with it in the morning. At the first streaks of dawn they were on their way, turning their backs on the last human habitation; despite some raindrops and a few wreaths of golden mist that wound around the mountain peaks as they glowed in the brightness of the sun, it was evidently clearing into a glorious day. They would soon be alone with those grand, snowy peaks. Contemplating the peaks, the Reverend thought: 'The secret of their attractiveness lay no doubt in their spotless purity and the blush of the sunrise seemed at this hour to intensify their power and called forth admiration.' He reflected that the few Maoris who migrated to the South Island called Mount Cook 'the heaven piercer' or 'heaven world', according to the translation of the word 'Aorangi'. He had been told that before the advent of man these lovely virgin peaks had rendered up their beauty as a tribute to their Creator, and to him alone.[23]

The shepherd Sutherland helped them transport their loads across the Hooker River by horse when the wagon could go no further. When they crossed the first branch of the Hooker, the horsemen swam the packhorses over, but the rest waded across in the cold glacier water. In order to restore circulation to their extremities they ran across the flat shingle, the stones being as hot as the waters had been cold, to reach the next branch of the river, which proved to be the main channel. This stream had to be crossed by all on horseback, and the loads on the packhorses to be halved. It took Sutherland more than two hours to deliver them all safely to the other side; finally he recrossed the river for about the twentieth time to make his return to Birch Hill, leaving them all grateful for his expert help. They camped underneath the great southern spur of Mount Cook and many pretty marsh flowers peeped through the tussock grass and clumps of 'wild Irishman' (also called *matagouri*, a thorny bush found only in New Zealand) became more frequent as they drew near to the steep hillsides. The mountainside had recently been destroyed by fire and Green admired splendid clumps of New Zealand flax (*Phormium tenax*) in the unburnt patches.

The weather was bad for the first couple of days, but Green used the time to familiarise himself with this complex world of snow and ice. The Tasman Glacier ran up towards a range of splendid peaks. On catching his first close view of the upper reaches of Mount Cook he wrote:

> No words at my command can express our feelings when we stood for the first time in the midst of that glorious panorama . . . the present scene so completely asserted its own grandeur that we all felt compelled to confess in that instant that it surpassed anything we had ever seen. My old idea was that from the summit of Col d'Erin in Switzerland on a cloudless day was the most charming Alpine scene I had ever beheld. Now I felt rather bewildered on the subject, and can only conclude that comparisons of such ineffable glories are worse than useless.[24]

Their first two attempts to reach the summit were made by the south ridge and then from the east via the Hochstetter Glacier, starting out from a camp at the edge of the Great Tasman Glacier; on both routes they were beaten back by the chaos and dangers of the hazardous glaciers, stone fall, couloirs and seracs. However, during their explorations they did discover that above the Hochstetter was a plateau of ice, which they thought might provide safe access to the summit. Before making their final attempt and in order to be nearer and to shorten their summit days, they moved their camp higher and adjacent to the Ball Glacier, which descends from the south ridge of Mount Cook to the Tasman Glacier. Green named this important glacier in honour of his fellow countryman, botanist and first president of the Alpine Club, John Ball, whom Green acknowledged as 'one of the founders of Alpine exploration'.

While crossing the Ball Glacier, Green, ever the practical scientist, attempted to establish its depth at an open crevasse. He played out the full length of the 300 foot (91.4m) ball of cord he had brought for the purpose, and then extended its length further by tying in his climbing rope, which added 60 feet (18m) to his measuring capacity. When still he could not reach its bottom, he resorted to dropping large stones and timing their fall. The mean time, calculated over a number of observations made with his watch, gave him five seconds before the first crash was heard, followed by a series of crashes that lasted as long again. He concluded that the crevasse must be at least 500 feet (150m) deep and further remarked that even when the sounds ceased the glacier floor might not have been reached. At 6,500 feet (2,000m) among the tiny alpine plants he found some unfamiliar forms present, one of which turned out to be a species of the genus *Haastia* that was new to science. Hooker identified it later and labelled it *Haastia greenii* on his return. Green also observed that in these Alps at 7,000 feet (2,150m) above sea level, nature assumed an aspect that was characteristic of 10,000 feet (3,000m) in the European Alps.

Moving to a higher camp involved a good deal of ferrying, including transporting sufficient dry firewood for cooking. Since they were forced to reduce the provisions they carried, the guides (who knew, as Green coyly remarks, that the heaviest share of the 'swagging' would fall to them) cut out the bones from the mutton and half-boiled the flesh to ensure its keeping. Green carried 35 lb of gear, including his personal waterproof cape, plaid, camera, gun, ammunition, and a tin of methylated spirits; the guide Kaufmann took three times that load (a hundredweight, or 112 lb), and Boss took the remainder. They ferried between the two camps over two days, at times in heavy rain (including a gale accompanied by a deluge at midnight), until they had transferred all they needed to the upper camp. They spent the following day route-finding and reached a height of 8,000 feet (2,500m) on the right bank of the Hochstetter Glacier. Realising that this route was steep and dangerous, they managed to locate a longer but more viable route from the other side of this formidable glacier by climbing to a higher viewpoint to observe the terrain. They arrived back to their tents after thirteen hours of strenuous effort and decided to give their bodies the benefit of a full rest day with a good feed before their final push, which they realised would involve a bivouac.

It is difficult to believe that any modern mountaineer would be as self-sufficient and creative in survival technique. To build themselves up they indulged in bread-making, mixing soda and tartic acid with flour and water; meanwhile they lit a big fire of deadwood on a boulder. When the boulder was very hot, they divided the dough into tiny loaves and set these on the top of the boulder, covering them with a flat stone upon which the remainder of the fire was placed. After 45 minutes they had fine bread. One loaf, left in 'the oven' while they ate dinner, they found to be 'harder than the boulder' when they came back for it. They had a multi-course meal of parrot (*kea*) and duck soup (which they had shot), followed by a fish course of sardines with sheep's tongue, and a main course of boiled duck and bacon. They finished the banquet with rice, marmalade, cheese and ice for dessert. Despite their feast, they regretted not having had a sheep at their disposal as they 'retired early to their tent full of hopes for the morrow'.

At dawn on 1 March they left camp in a dense fog to cross the glacier. As the morning wore on Green enthused: 'it was rent asunder by bright shafts of sunshine which made the icefall shine resplendent while at intervals hoarse rumbles among seracs told [us] it was waking up to its daily life'.[25] It took two hours to reach the far side of the Hochstetter Glacier. Close to the foot of an icefall they followed each other down over loose boulders at first and then uphill to the lower part of what Green named the 'Mount Tasman Spur'.

At first the climbing was easy and they made great strides as the wind carried away the clouds and they felt the heat of the sun. Soon they met vertical rock that compelled them to leave the ridge and climb its face. When they were able to resume the arête, it was loose and rotten, provoking them into using their rope because in places the consequence of a slip would have been a 'rapid descent to the ice-fall'. They found that on some parts of the ridge the rocks were split by frost and were piled in the most extraordinary confusion. At midday they scrambled, parched, onto one great slab and found a little hollow that contained about two pints of water; obviously they selected the spot for their midday halt.

They took in the grand vista below, and Green took a photograph looking southwards and another of the summit of Mount Cook, which was standing out clear against the blue sky. Three more hours of scrambling brought them to an elevation of 7,000 feet (2,150m), to the upper termination of the rocks. From a saddle of ice visible above them, steep slopes curved upwards to the highest ridge, which rose higher and higher in the direction of Mount Haidinger and presented a series of jagged, rocky teeth, alternating with bosses of heavy glacier ice. Over these icy domes lay their route, but as they could see no prospect of a bivouac ledge on which to spend the night they determined that under an overhanging rock they must make their nest. It was 5 p.m.; they melted water and boiled a 'Liebig' (beef concentrate cube) for supper. The scene over which their view extended had taken on the purple tints of evening. One of the peaks of the Malta Bruin chain was particularly striking, and every now and again either Kaufmann or Boss would give expression to their admiration of its bold outline, thrusting like a pyramid of rock from the glaciers that clung to its flanks. Referring to the Matterhorn, Green suggests 'this Malta Bruin may well claim its brotherhood'.[26]

They then smoothed out a place to sleep by turning over any sharp stones and covering the ground with the oilskin; two of them rolled in the possum rug and Kaufmann had the sleeping bag. They woke at 4 a.m. and made tea while they waited for the light; at six o'clock it was clear enough to move. Green says: 'Great banks of clouds had settled in the valley; out of which the mountain peaks rose like islands, clear cut against one of those pea-green skies so peculiar to New Zealand. Other fleecy masses had sailed aloft to the summits of the higher range, and we tried to think that our virgin peak was putting on her bridal veil.'[27]

A few minutes out from their bivouac they started up a snow slope, crossed a bergschrund, and struck up a direct line for the crest of the ridge; when they finally gained the flattened summit a most splendid prospect opened up before them, as they were overlooking a massive plateau to their left (the top of the Hochstetter icefall), and before them lay the great peak of Mount Cook and the cliffs of Mount Tasman. But first there was a wide, flat field of ice to be crossed, 6 miles long by 2 miles wide (9.66 km by 3.21 km), and scarred with narrow, deep crevasses that (thankfully) crossed the field in parallel lines. A glacier between Mount Cook and Mount Tasman absorbed their interest, for it provided the key to the summit; Green christened it the Linda Glacier, after his wife Belinda. 'It was much crevassed and broken, but its upper portion wound round the couloir between the rocky ribs of Mount Cook and promised a practicable route, by which we might reach the upper part of the arête.'[28]

They had two main choices, a rock-stepped arête on their left or the crevassed glacier; as they advanced, the rocks looked worse and Kaufmann took off up the glacier without another thought. At ten o'clock they had breakfast at a level place just before they entered a steep maze of crevasses; from there they took a sharp turn right towards the base of the final peak. When close to the arête that connects Mount Cook to Mount Tasman, they were elated at their success and indulged in the most sanguine hopes for the rest of the climb. The wind had, however, changed ominously to the northeast, and thin filmy clouds began to form in the higher peaks, while along the northern horizon dark cumuli were piling themselves up beyond the distant ridges.

During their short halt the clouds on the top of Mount Tasman increased and, to their dismay, wreaths of mist began to form around Mount Cook. There was no time to lose. They calculated the summit could not be more than 3,000 feet (900m) above them, but it was certain to be a stiff climb. So they discarded the camera, the food and the flask to lighten their load for a summit bid. The crevasses then took on a different character: they widened and extended the full width of the glacier, causing the group to make many long detours. Green recalls that the snow was in that most unpleasant of all conditions: 'having a crust just strong enough to bear their weight until they prepared to make a step, and then letting one through over knee deep.'[29]

Kaufmann led throughout, despite many offers from Boss and Green to relieve him of the step-breaking duty. Three hours' plodding brought them to the head of the glacier. They crossed a bergschrund using a snow bridge only to encounter hard ice above it, which had to be cut with the ice-axe pick. On leaving the Linda Glacier they ascended a steep slope and crossed a ridge to the foot of a couloir that led upwards between two rocky ribs, nearly parallel with the main northern ridge. On this slope the steps had to be cut very deeply and the greatest caution had to be observed, as all that lay below them was what Green called 'a profound abyss'.[30] They followed up through the couloir that lay at an angle of 45°, getting steeper near the top, and when an avalanche of ice blocks and splinters showered from the mists above they clung to the rocks on the side of the gully. Just before the couloir exit they caught a fleeting view of the western sea over the Mount Tasman arête, and then they entered the clouds and found themselves enveloped in dense, driving mists.

Matters had taken a serious turn. It was 3 p.m.; the rocky ridge they were climbing ran out. Ahead of them lay an ice slope that stretched right to the blue wall of a great bergschrund, curving around the summit of the mountain in the mist. They tried to climb out directly overhead but this led to a series of loose seracs; so, retracing their steps, they held a short council of war. The rocks on the opposite side of the couloir extended upwards, and might 'go'. Should they risk finding their way through the ice ramparts ahead, from which the avalanche had come, or cross the dangerous couloir to reach the rocks? This was the challenging question that Green put to his men. 'My men asked me did I see the danger. I said of course I did, and feared we must turn back. This would have been a sore disappointment to me, and, as I saw by their faces, an equally great one to them, I asked them were they ready to chance it? They replied that on leaving home they expected to meet some danger; here it was, and they were ready, but I must give the word. "We will top the peak if we go on," said Boss; "to turn now is to give it up altogether." The 24,000 miles of travelling also rose in our minds as a strong argument against retreat; and as the sun had gone in, which lessened our risk, and no avalanche had gone down for some time, I said "Forwards".' Cutting steps across the dangerous couloir, Kaufmann picked a traverse line towards a large avalanche block that afforded shelter from any further avalanche at the midpoint. He cut with all his might, and no time was lost in following him across to the rocks and scrambling through the notch at the other side. The rocks above, which they climbed to reach the ice slope beyond, proved to be 'the nastiest bit of climbing in the whole ascent'. It was 4 p.m. and a partial clearance of the mist showed them the top of the slope before it rounded off to the summit – and the last rock of the main northern arête. Kaufmann thought it would take an hour to cut up the slope. They asked Green if he was prepared to spend the night on the peak. Green replied 'yes!' Soon Kaufmann was sending the ice flying about their ears at every blow of his axe. At this point a rapid thaw set in and, as they broke through the thin crust of frozen snow that lay on the ice, water spurted out, filling the steps that Kaufmann was cutting and soaking their clothes wherever their knees and arms came into contact with the wet slope. The slope was now washed with a continual stream of disintegrated ice, some large pieces striking and hurting their mitten-clad hands.

At 5.30 p.m. they reached the highest rocks, from which an easy slope led up to an icicled bergschrund that started at the cornice of the arête and ran around the cap of the summit, from left to right; Boss remarked, 'If we had taken to the Mount Tasman arête that would have cut us off'. The wind struck now, for the first time, with all its fury; they had to shout in order to hear each other. And, athough they 'had ocular demonstration that it was not actually freezing, the blast seemed bitterly cold'.

They moved to the left to avoid the highest part of the bergschrund above them and, surmounting the cornice without any difficulty, at 6 p.m. stepped onto the topmost crest of Aorangi.[31]

Mount Cook was now practically climbed. They advanced rapidly along the cornice, which rose at an angle of about 20° towards its highest point, now and then cutting a step for greater security, but in most cases trusting to the grip gained by the nails in their boots. Sometimes a blast would hit them with such ferocity as to compel them to crouch low and drive in their axes firmly, to prevent their being blown off into space.

The mists vanished, giving a clear view of the summit, to be quickly replaced by inky black clouds almost obliterating Kaufmann from Green's sight, though the Swiss guide was only 8 yards

(7.3m) distant. From the moment they gained the arête, anxiety about beginning the descent was foremost in their minds. Green wrote, 'as should darkness overtake us on the summit of the mountain, our chances of ever returning to the haunts of men would be but slight'. The wind was unsettling and fear of it blowing any harder was a real worry to them. There was no chance of a view:

> We were hundreds of feet above any rocks, so that we could build no cairn, or leave any record of our ascent. We were all agreed that we were fairly on the summit of the peak, and that we ought to commence our descent. Ten minutes more and the last bit of snow would be under the sole of my boot when there came a sudden gap in the cornice. A bergschrund broke through it. There was no open crevasse, but a step down off the cornice of five or six feet, a flat and then a step up of eight feet. To go round it to where Kaufmann pointed with his axe would have been easy enough, as the summit of the mountain was now completely flat. But when little more than an hour of daylight remained, we dared not risk the loss of twenty minutes, for what seemed a mere matter of detail.[32]

Green continues:

> So pulling out my aneroid, I took down the reading of 19.05 in my notebook, scribbled a sketch of the ridge, and, shouting the word retreat, we commenced the descent. Owing to an unfortunate accident having happened to my thermometer I was unable to take the exact temperature; that it was above freezing point was however evident, as the ice was wet, and our clothes, which had been soaked coming up the last slope were still soft. In similar situations in Switzerland I have often had my clothes and beard frozen hard; but now, though our fingers were benumbed and painful, I believe the temperature was not lower than 35°, and it may have been as high as 40°.
>
> The slope beyond the gap where we turned was about thirty feet higher, and this would make my measurement, when compared with the simultaneous observation at sea level, coincide almost exactly with the trigon metrical height of Mount Cook – 12,349ft.

Green the scientist attached a footnote to his report:

> The barometrical reading for the position of Mount Cook, at sea-level on the afternoon of March 2nd was 30'02"; temp 65°. These observations were kindly furnished to me by Dr Hector, F.R.S., from the office of the Meteorological Department, on my sending him the observations I had taken on the mountain. Taking the temperature at the summit at 35 °, which is the lowest possible, owing to the thaw visibly going on, the result worked by Baily's tables is 12,317 ft. A higher summit temperature would increase the figure.

When they returned to the highest point of the rocks over which they already had passed, they could find no material with which to build a cairn, however, they cleaned out a small crevice in the yellow sandstone rocks, into which they deposited Green's handkerchief and Kaufmann's tin matchbox. These relics were intended to provide evidence of their ascent to the summit plateau. In their naivety they believed their goal achieved. The height of Mount Cook in 2007 was measured

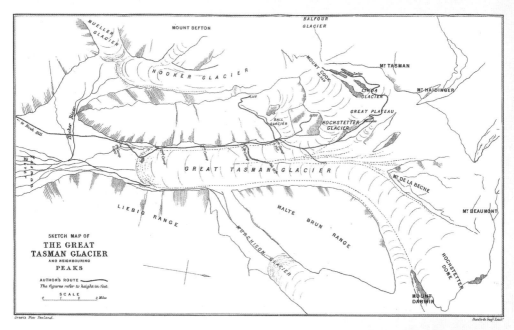

Map of the Great Tasman Glacier. (W. S. Green, *The High Alps of New Zealand* (1883))

at 12,316 or 3,754 m, in other words only one foot lower than Green's barometric calculation based on an estimate of summit temperature.[33]

Getting down the mountain turned out to be a real epic of endurance; it is doubtful if turning back a few minutes before the summit made any real difference, as there was already no chance that they might descend to safe ground before darkness overtook them. Green provides a graphic account of their dramatic descent. They began to retrace their steps to the point at which they had first struck the arête, facing inwards towards the ice and descending backwards to improve their grip, with Kaufmann urging Green to step downward faster all the while. Green observed that the steps Kaufmann had cut on the way up seemed very far apart now that they were using them to descend, and that he had difficulty in finding the next step below and keeping a secure grip at the same time.

Finally, in the dim twilight, they reached the brink of the steep arête. Green and Kaufmann gave Boss assistance in lowering him down with the rope, and Kaufmann gave Green a top rope. Kaufmann had no top rope when his turn came, so Boss stood up and helped him down, while Green jammed himself into the only crevice available. Boss cut steps down to the rocks on the side of the couloir that they had earlier ascended and crossed; sometimes they had only rocks frozen into the ice for handholds. In the dark they at last found a suitable bivouac ledge for the night and, squeezing the moisture from their socks and gaitors, were preparing for a night perched in the narrow space; suddenly a huge ice-block fell from above and landed less than a metre away from where they stood.

They did not wait for a second icefall. In the faint moonlight they took again to the ice slope, descending slowly to the lowest part of the rock ridge and turning left into its shelter; here, out of the prevailing wind, they found standing room on a safer snow-filled ledge. They scraped the snow off a 2-foot (60 cm) wide, outward-sloping ledge, which forced them to hold on with their hands

Mount Cook (3,754m), seen here from the Hooker Valley, is the highest mountain in the Southern Alps of New Zealand. The Rev. William Spotswood Green reached the summit plateau in 1882. (Jörg Hempel)

to feel secure. They were over 10,000 feet (3,000m) above sea level and 5,000 feet (1,500m) above the snowline. They stood in the same positions on the ledge all night; Boss and Green enjoyed one good handhold to secure them, but Kaufmann, who was more exposed, had no handhold at all, and between them they had no belay to secure their position for the night. Their discomfort was added to by the rapid thaw going on around them; they stood listening to the roar of avalanches all night long and not a quarter of an hour elapsed without a distant rumble, or a thundering roar that caused the rock on which they stood to vibrate. Green produced a box of Brand's meat lozenges, which he had kept for a case of absolute necessity, serving one out three times during the night. They were consoled by the thaw and the rain, knowing it would spare them the frostbite that would have resulted had there been clear skies. However, the thaw gave them cause to worry regarding the bergschrunds of the Linda Glacier, which they would have to cross come morning. Would the snow bridges survive or would they be impassable?

They stamped one foot at a time and slapped their legs to keep life in them; they refrained from looking at their watches until they thought four hours had passed, only to discover it was just midnight. The storm howled above them and the avalanches continued to roar and the cold rain hissed unceasingly, all the sounds blending into one monotonous hum in their ears. Each had great trouble staying awake, so they devoted their energies keeping one another alert. They forced conversation on each other by discussing politics, telling stories and singing; and although Boss regretted that their tobacco was a thousand feet beneath them, he and Kaufmann were happy to at least have had their pipes to suck upon and, by the sheer force of their imagination, they enjoyed several good smokes. They poked one another if they suspected one of them was drifting into sleep and then the accused would come to life and demonstrate alertness by vigorously stamping each foot again. At 4 a.m. it was still so dark that they had difficulty reading the watch, but at 4.30 came the first glimmering dawn of the third day of March.

The light came slowly, since the rain clouds hung in heavy masses on the ice slope. At 5.30 they moved when they perceived a little glow of heat from the rising sun and resumed their cautious backwards descent down the ice steps, their hands slowly warming as they gripped the ice axes. Kaufmann's hands were blistered from the long spell of ice-cutting on the ascent. Soon they reached the feared bergschrunds of the Linda Glacier. The snow bridge was badly washed away, but still provided a possible route across the crevasse. Boss buried himself in the snow and gave Green, who belayed Kaufmann, a tight rope; the guide crept on all fours across the rotten bridge to reach the far side. There he secured an anchor, which made safe their passage across 'the fathomless chasm'.

That great source of anxiety removed, they followed their tracks of the previous day until these were obliterated by the debris of a huge avalanche that had fallen from one of the hanging glaciers of the Tasman arête. They congratulated themselves for having stayed where they stood for the night and speculated that if they had started their descent an hour earlier the previous evening they would have been swept in its path. At 8.30 they reached the knapsack in which they had left their provisions and and enjoyed the pleasure of cold duck and twenty-day-old bread and their first sit down in the twenty-two hours since they had left the same spot. The halt was short; they continued downwards, observing the debris of an avalanche that they estimated covered an area of 200 acres and now conveniently filled a crevasse that they had had to make a detour around the day before.

Soon they were on the Grand Plateau looking down on the Hochstetter Glacier and the weather was clearing. Then they were wading, waist deep, in the glacier's soft, floury covering of snow over steep ice; they knew that this was very susceptible to avalanche, so they found a safer line of descent that brought them down to where they had left their rugs. The ridge seemed to Green to get longer and longer as they descended and, as it would not do to be benighted again, they took off the rope after thirty-six hours of continuous use and reached the Tasman Glacier at 6 p.m. They scrambled over the moraine at 4 miles (6.4 km) an hour to reach their camp at 7.30 p.m; finally, their 62-hour-long expedition was over. After a supper of porridge and soup 'within a half hour they were ensconced in a state of blissful, dreamless unconsciousness'.[34]

Their return journey from the Tasman was supported by Sutherland and his horses and a bigger cart transported them back to Albury, where a row developed with the owner regarding the charges being levied on Green. 'After trying to settle amicably my account with the owner of the wagon and team, and as he tried to "lay it on" very hard I gave him my address, and told him to sue me for the amount as soon as he found it convenient.' He sent a brief telegram from there to Haast at Christchurch, which clearly indicates that Green and his companions were satisfied that they had reached the summit: 'Reached summit at six-twenty March second on third attempt will see you Monday W S Green.'[35]

Whether Green was entitled to make such a claim is a subject for debate to this day. By his own admission one plain fact is clear: he did not reach the actual highest point on the mountain. Having pushed out the boat so far, it must have been a source of deep regret that they had not finished the job conclusively. They took the train to Timaru and, while staying at the hotel there, related their experiences to the press. The papers the following Sunday overflowed with the ascent of Mount Cook, right down to a detailed description of the nails in Green's boots.

Dr Haast was in Auckland when Green arrived at Christchurch; he stayed at his house for four days, during which he was entertained at a public dinner given in their honour by the Christchurch Athletic Club at Coke's Hotel. In reply to toasts, Green impressed on his audience the importance of founding a New Zealand alpine club and to devoting club subscriptions to the building of huts in the Southern Alps. One day while out walking, he was served with a summons from the owner of the wagon. The summons was pinned to the bill (which Green noted had increased from what was first asked). Green immediately offered to pay half of the amount billed, through an intermediary whom he had befriended at Timaru. His offer was accepted and the matter was settled. He left Christchurch on St Patrick's Day and was seen off by members of the Athletic Club. He noted that Ireland was represented in that town by Armagh and Tuam Streets and remarked, ' The homes of Irish farmers were often conspicuous amongst the others by mud wall and thatched roofs, exactly similar to the homes of their fathers, only they looked cleaner and the whitewash and neatness of the surroundings were pleasant to see.[36] Regarding young men emigrating to make their fortunes in the colonies, he speculated, 'if a man can't or won't do anything in the old country he can't do much in the new',[37] and in respect of climbing with or without guides, he says, 'Inexperienced amateurs are a source of danger to any party, and should only be taken where the difficulties are well known, and not serious.'[38]

On their way home they made an attempt on Mount Earnshaw from the head of Lake Wakatipu but, with little time at their disposal, they were stopped by heavy snowfall. Green bemoaned the time he had lost in quarantine and, in reference to their local guide, demonstrated his Christian upbringing when he observed, 'A man must not be judged at his worst.'[39] They sailed home on the *John Elder* via the Suez Canal, stopping at Port Said and the Bay of Naples where he parted company with Boss and Kaufmann, of whom he said he 'could not find better companions for any journey in the world.'[40] Green later wrote admiringly about Kaufmann in relation to the final slopes of their climb up Mount Cook:

> Kaufmann hewed away at the hard ice for five hours without a pause. I should be afraid to say how many steps he cut in that time, for I did not attempt to count them. It was not until the next morning when we were leaving the narrow ledge – on which we had to stand out nine-hours of a cold, stormy night – that he showed me the palms of his hands red with great blisters, and merely did so then as a kind of apology for not being able to wield his ice-axe as effectively as he would wish.[41]

When Green arrived home he lost little time in preparing a paper on his exploration, which demonstrates his ability as a scientific observer since it covers the geological, geographical, atmospheric, metrological, glacial, botanical and zoological aspects of his trip. A series of letters

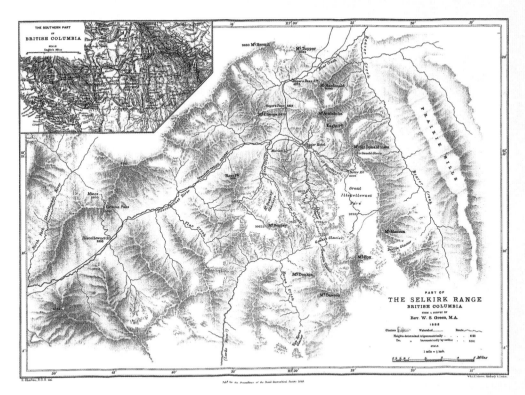

A map drawn from a survey of part of the Selkirks in 1888 by W. S. Green.
(*Among the Selkirk Glaciers* (1890))

written by Green to Julius von Haast illustrates Green's rigour and determination to get the topography right.[42] In his first letter, dated 11 July 1882, he tells Haast that Dr Hooker has confirmed that the plant Green found at 6,500 feet (2,000m) on the southern spur of Mount Cook is a new species of the genus *Haastia*. He also tells Haast that the first account of his Mount Cook climb would appear in *The Alpine Journal* for August and that it would be mainly illustrated by Haast's map, which Green obtained from the RGS. The account would be continued in two further editions, accompanied by a large-scale map of Mount Cook made by Green himself. He also informs Haast that he has taken the liberty of naming one of the glaciers after John Ball.

A letter dated 31 October 1882 was accompanied by a small bit of the 'little Haastia', of which (he tells Haast) Hooker has said, 'it is a beautiful little thing'; he continues, 'and I hope other climbers may be fortunate in finding it in blossom . . . above the glacier which I named after my wife . . . I feel much pleased at your wishing to have my name on some of the peaks. What greater honour could a climber desire!' In another letter from Carrigaline to Dr Haast, dated 21 February 1883 (which accompanied the last of his papers in *The Alpine Journal* and the sketch map published by the RIA), he tells Haast that the Alpine Club had decided to ask Haast to accept an honorary membership of the club.

His next letter on 29 May 1883 acknowledges Haast's letter announcing Dr von Lendenfeld's ascent of the Hochstetter dome with his wife who, Green says, 'must be a lady of wonderful pluck.' In a letter of 12 June 1883 he says, 'It is very good of Von Lindenfeld to call a peak after me. I hope it is some peak I had the pleasure of seeing. And so long as he does not call it 'Mt Greenhorn' I shall be very proud of the honour.' (Mount Green (2,838m) is a beautiful pyramid of snow in the Aoraki/Mount Cook National Park and is accessible from the Mount Cook village. It was first climbed in 1909.) A postscript to this letter informs Haast that Mr Graham has started for Kanchenjunga, that his Zermatt guide has had to go home, and that Boss and Kaufmann are on their way to join Graham at Darjeeling.

His letter to Haast on 14 May 1884 expresses gladness that Haast liked Green's 'little book'. Green was also happy to tell Haast that (following Green's efforts) Haast has been awarded a gold medal by the RGS, which also conferred honorary membership on the New Zealand pioneer. In a letter of 30 September 1884 he tells Haast that this season is the first he has managed to spend in Switzerland since the New Zealand trip. He recounts his stay at Boss' hotel in Grindelwald and reports: 'He [Boss] is now a Major in the federal army and Kaufmann was also there. We went over the Mönch Joch to the great Aletsch glacier and to the top of the Jungfrau being my first trip of the sort since I was on Mount Cook, the comparison was interesting. Though the Jungfrau is a thousand feet higher Mt Cook is essentially a more difficult ascent. The scenery of the Aletsch is not at all unlike the Tasman but having paths in the lower slopes makes a vast difference.' He would later write to Haast with the news that 'poor Emil Boss has had to be lodged in a lunatic asylum he has been going on in a mad way for some time but lately got so bad that his brothers had to send him into confinement.'

A letter dated 26 October 1885 replies to Haast's letter regarding the doctor's intention to visit London to see the Colonial Exhibition. He expresses the hope that Haast may be able to 'pay me a visit and see a little of Ireland – Mrs Green would hope to make acquaintance of you and your good lady and your little daughter. There is no fear of your being boycotted!'[43] He also revealed his new passion to Haast:

> I had charge of a Dredging Expedition during the past months off the west coast of Ireland; we did not work deeper than 150 fathoms. We got a good many new Framinan fish and a sea anemone which forms a new genus and a lot of new things which specialists have not yet worked out. The steamer was paid for by R.I. Academy. And we look forward to another trip next year. I am to lecture on N. Zealand in Belfast in February next and have been painting some new lantern slides for it. I had an audience of 1,300 at Birmingham for the same lecture.

His new passion was to change his life and occupation. Green, because of his practical and topical knowledge of marine biology and his expressed enthusiasm for dredging operations, was entrusted to find and hire a suitable vessel by the RIA's newly formed fishery committee. He hired the *Lord Bandon*, a steam-powered paddle-driven tug, and the team spent a week in August 1885 investigating the fauna of the 100-fathom line off the southwest coast of Ireland. In the following year the fishery committee chartered the *Lord Bandon* for a second cruise. From a zoological point of view this expedition was a great success, for many remarkable forms of animal life, including quantities of the white coral *Lophelia prolifera*, were discovered.

In addition to the RIA activity, in 1887 he was asked by the Royal Dublin Society to collect and report on the views and opinions of the local population as to how the fishing industry in the south and southwest of the country could best be promoted. Green, the friendly clergyman who knew much about boating and fishing and who loved to converse with local fishermen, was an inspired choice. He focused his enquiries and research on three ports (Youghal, Baltimore and Kinsale) and divided it into three sections: supply, demand and means of development. He found there was enough capacity to meet demand and the most urgent need he reported was to improve marketing and transport of the catch. He was impressed with the success of Baltimore fishery school and stressed the need for proper training of young men entering the fishing industry, urging government financial assistance to aid fishermen in increasing their efficiency.

In the last letter of the Haast collection, dated 30 September 1886, Green reveals to Haast the findings regarding the composition of the pieces of rock brought back from the top of Mount Cook. He also boasts to Haast that his most recent New Zealand lecture was to the London Institution.[44] He appears to have revelled in his new-found fame as a mountain explorer and lecturer, so much so that this activity obviously inspired his next expedition to climb in the Selkirk Range of Canada. It is clear from his letters that he loved to lecture and was always trying to improve the scope and quality of his presentations.

His companion this time was another Corkman, his cousin and alpine partner, the Rev. Henry Swanzy, who was six years older than Green and shared his interest in pure science. Swanzy was a member of the British Association for the Advancement of Science (BAAS) and attended a novel first meeting of the Association held in Canada in 1884; he was involved (in company with the accomplished Irish climber and naturalist Richard M. Barrington) in a post-conference excursion offered by the Canadian Pacific Railway (CPR) to see the proposed link to the existing west coast line through the Rocky Mountains. The conference party travelled by train to Laggan and went on foot to Lake Louise, accompanied by a guide. To round off their Canadian experience, Barrington and Swanzy decided to walk from Lake Louise along the planned route, passing the location of the modern town of Golden, crossing over by the Rogers Pass to the Shuswap Lakes, walking down to the Kamloops, and rejoining the existing railway that took them to the Pacific Coast. The Barrington and Swanzy journey was a tough 170-mile trek through forests and lakes supported by pack mules, which took them seventeen days to complete. Regarding his cousin Henry Swanzy as a travelling companion, Green observed with his usual wit: 'We had travelled together in Switzerland and had attained to the great stage of perfection that of being able to squabble with impunity.'[45]

In 1888 the cousins made up what was perhaps the first solely Irish expedition team to explore and map any new mountain range outside of Europe. Remarkably, both men were from the same extended family and were both ordained ministers with wide interests in travel and scientific observation, and both were members of diverse scientific societies. Neither, it seems, let their ministry take priority over an opportunity to explore and lecture afterwards. In an introduction to a reprint of Green's book on the Selkirks,[46] R. W. Sandford (a vice president of the Alpine Club of Canada), reflects that when one went abroad during the Victorian era the serious traveller was expected to do something constructive for the Empire. The most prestigious thing the visitor could do to exemplify the drive and energy characteristic of his nationality abroad was to explore and map areas not known to locals. To Green, it must also have seemed as if he was upholding the standards of Ball, Tyndall and Adams-Reilly during the golden age of alpinism.

Lake Louise and Mount Lefoy.
(*Among the Selkirk Glaciers* (1890))

Green and Swanzy set off from Cobh on 28 June 1888 in the *City of Rome*, arriving in New York on 6 July. Green, using all his charm and skill, had negotiated a free rail pass from the president of Canadian Pacific Railways and a return ticket for the price of a single journey from the Anchor Line Steamship Company for his Atlantic crossing. They steamed on to Montreal and then proceeded to Ottawa, where Green had the good fortune to meet Major Deville, the Surveyor General of Canada, and was therefore able to trace the 2:1 (inches to miles) manuscript map for the railway line through the Selkirks. He was assured he could trust it as far as the railway detail was concerned. From Ottawa they set out on the four-day train journey to reach the Selkirks where they put up at the Glacier House, a hotel built to a Swiss chalet plan; this would prove to be a good base because passing rail traffic stopped for refreshment at the hotel.

His description of the approach to the Rocky Mountains for the benefit of the RGS is vivid:

> For 900 miles west of Winnipeg stretch the great plains; their rolling billowy downs clothed for the most part in the yellow prairie grass, and often gay with flowers. Near Calgary the purple snow tipped rampart comes into view to the westward, and as we penetrate through the foot hills, where prairie flats and mountain ruggedness seem for a few miles to be struggling for the mastery, we come suddenly on great bare cliffs with strata tilted at high angles in huge slabs, and at once recognise the singular appropriateness of the name 'Rocky' as applied to this mountain range *par excellence*.[47]

That Green's writing was by now well developed is evident as we read his descriptions of life in the Canada at that era, including the conditions of the Indians, the vastness of the Canadian interior and the deliberate decimation of the herds of bison. He considered the gear they carried somewhat extensive: 'Besides our ordinary luggage we took with us three tents, blankets etc.; three photographic cameras (two half plate, and one a Stirn's patent detective); three ice axes, rifles, rope, and the set of surveying instruments kindly lent by your Society.' They set out first to fix the neighbouring peaks and the Illecillewaet Glacier and its snowfields with the aid of a packhorse. However, they were seriously hampered by a lack of help to carry their camping and surveying equipment and supplies. On one occasion in dense, tangled forest Green and Swanzy made 1½ miles (2.41 km) in seven hours. At one stage a volunteer came forward who expressed a desire to join them and accepted their terms, but when he heard that both men were parsons he 'chucked it up' in disgust.

The first days of exploration revealed to Green and Swanzy the difficulty of penetrating the complex and densely afforested landscape. They started by climbing a ridge between the Illecillewaet (pronounced 'illy-silly-wat') and Asulkan Glaciers to make their first survey readings and establish a datum line with the railway line and structures. Green's wit comes to the fore in his telling of nature's fight with the railway infrastructure and of the near tragic end to Swanzy:

> The cascade which forms such a feature in the view from Glacier House is no small source of difficulty to the railway people, as it objects to being controlled in any way. A bridge has been built for it to go under, but in the true spirit of freedom it uses the bridge only occasionally, and just then was with much hilarity dashing right down on the railway and knocking away all foundation from the track. By balancing ourselves carefully on the rails we crossed it without much difficulty; and H. lay down with his chest on the rail to regale himself with a drink. Suddenly to my horror, a freight train, coming down the gradient, swept round the curve. Men stood on the roof of every car screwing down the brakes. The whistle was evidently blowing but the cascade drowned all other sound. I shouted to H. 'Here's the train.' He took no notice! There was no time to speak twice; but at the very last instant he perceived the danger and rolled himself aside just as the train roared past. After this we were careful not to lie down with our heads on the main track again.[48]

This was followed by a bad experience with a packhorse (*cayeuse*) as they went to survey and climb Mount Sir Donald. All went well for a mile and, as the horse was going along as 'quietly as a cow' and the evening was warm, Green saw no harm in hitching his knapsack on the pack, along with Swanzy's heavy rifle; in this way they happily walked through a meadow and then up the bank of a glacier. The path was getting steep and Green thought to himself 'the pack needed bracing'. Later he wrote: 'However, some idea of a similar nature must have crossed the mind of the cayeuse, for without the slightest warning he took a fit of buck-jumping, tumbling down, rolled over and over down the slope, and when our goods were thoroughly mashed up and scattered to the winds, he got on his legs and shook himself with apparent satisfaction.'[49] Green picked up the little ivory scale from the sextant (which had been smashed to bits in a bush) and the shivers of glass from the thermometer (which he recalled had been carefully tested at Kew). He was afraid to look at his photographic plates as he reflected what fools they had been to be taken in by the deceitful calm of the *cayeuse*. Retelling the misadventures of the two Irish parsons became part of the folklore of the Canadian railway workers for years afterwards.[50]

Undeterred by the difficulties of their work, they continued their attempt on Sir Donald (one of their main mountaineering objectives), but when they reached the top of a rock pinnacle 10,000 feet (3,000m) high they found themselves separated from the last great crag of Sir Donald by a notch 200 feet (61m) deep. At its bottom a narrow arête joined the cliff below them with the face of the final peak. Green observed that the cliffs rising on the opposite side were so steep that not a speck of snow clung to them. Neither had they the 200 feet (61m) of rope he thought they would need to descend from their steep perch and gain access to 'as inaccessible a piece of rock as any climber could wish to see'.[51] There were some cracks and ledges that might, one day, be used by someone else but 'the quest was not for me' he reflected.

They did, however, make the first ascent of Mount Bonney, which Green later calculated was 10,622 feet (3,238m) high and reached the summit of Mount Abbott at 8,087 feet (2,465m). He named the former after Thomas John Bonney, a fellow of the RGS, president of the Alpine Club from 1881 to 1884, and Professor of Geology at both Cambridge and University College, London. A small lake on the approach to Mount Abbott he named Marion Lake after one of his own daughters.

They decided to establish a camp from which they might access Mount Bonney, and set out to supply it with four bags of equipment and provisions, starting out from a high trestle bridge at Loop Valley and going upstream parallel to Loop Creek. Each man carried a pack, which he set down before returning for the other and moving on again, thus always going over the same ground twice. To carry a pack continuously on their backs proved impractical when they were continually skirting obstacles such as fallen trees, great heaps of boulders that had crashed from cliffs above, or dense alder scrub. They resorted at times to tumbling the bags down slopes and pulling them up behind them over fallen trees and boulders. After four hours of this strenuous work they stopped for lunch. When they resumed, they met with an area of fallen cedars brought down by avalanches. The snow surface provided good footing, but huge fallen tree trunks were serious obstacles; the forest beyond was so dense that there was no place to camp, so they retraced to a boulder-strewn area they had previously rejected as a campsite. They levelled the site with flat stones cushioned with spruce tips, on which they pitched the tent and arranged a few stones adjacent for a fireplace. They soon had the frying pan sputtering with bacon and a kettle steaming on their cedarwood fire to the music of the torrent and the fragrance of the pine forest. A downdraught from the glacier made the air icy cool as they turned into their sleeping bags.

After breakfasting hastily, they set out for a glacial col above them at 4 a.m. next morning, leaving their campsite intact. Their arduous path led up from the river bed through densely forested slopes to reach the crevasses of the Lily Glacier before finally arriving at the Ross Pass about midday. They set up their plane table and took bearings on some new points, as well as points that they had observed from previous stations. They were determined to climb Mount Bonney for the view it would afford them in their survey and to compensate for their failure on Sir Donald, and were resolved to overcome whatever physical or technical difficulties presented themselves; but reaching the summit of Mount Bonney from their camp with their surveying gear was going to be a massive effort, involving more than 6,000 feet (1,850m) of ascent.

On descent it started to rain and they soon were soaked to the skin from close contact with the dripping undergrowth of alder and rhododendron. They enjoyed a little compensation, however, when they found an abundance of blueberry bushes laden with rich fruit. They were twelve hours out when they finally reached the tent; the fire to cook their bacon and dry their clothes was soon burning brightly, since they had wisely left dry tinder and firewood inside their tent. They declared the next day a rest day; Swanzy went back to where he had cached some provisions and his heavy plate camera in the forest below the campsite, while Green wrote up his notes on the geology, flora and fauna and reviewed his survey data. He shot a hare and a marmot and had them stewing in a pot when his cousin returned (they had included a twelve-shot repeating Winchester rifle and a doubled-barrelled shotgun in their expedition kit).

The following day they rose at 3.30 a.m., lit the fire, made a cup of tea and were off. Green carried the plane table and provisions and Swanzy took the camera and rope as they climbed again to the Ross Pass where they planned to descend in a southeasterly direction to gain a ridge running up to Mount Bonney. The route from the col took them through a strip of forestry, then a boulder field, more tangled forest and into a ravine; at this point they were climbing through tall trees and then struggled for more than an hour through a patch of alder scrub. Here, unfortunately unarmed, they became aware of the presence of a bear. A glacier stream led them under tree-clad cliffs that towered above them and were pierced with caves and a waterfall at their base. They were four hours out and had gained just 1,600 feet (488m) as they followed moraine under the cliffs looking for a place to attack the peak. When the moraine ran out they were forced onto the glacier itself, which was icy at first and required step-cutting, but then became softer; by zigzagging up its centre they could kick their toes into the surface and make quicker progress. A bergschrund facilitated them in reaching rocks and avoiding a cornice and, by 10.30 a.m., they stood on the higher col. An arête on the left towards Mount Bonney was wide and free from snow, so they resumed their ascent over a series of knobs, the next one of which was always blocking their view ahead as they progressed blindly upwards. They carefully followed a treacherous ridge of snow-covered loose shale, until they came out on top of a curved peak. A furious shower of hail accompanied by a strong wind greeted them. However, it passed over quickly and they could finally see the highest crest of the peak looming up ahead, with a massive cornice overhanging the vertical cliffs that edged it.

They reached the summit at 3.10 p.m.; the barometer indicated a height of 10,600 feet (3,231m), which was more than 6,000 feet (1,850) above their camp. They quickly put up their plane table and took a series of observations and then Swanzy set up his camera to photograph views in every direction. Swanzy and Green (who no doubt remembered the summit plateau of Mount Cook) confirmed their ascent to those who would follow by building a small cairn of 'the most beautiful fine grained, white quartzite, speckled with a few spots of oxide of iron or manganese.'[52]

At 4 p.m. they commenced their descent, trying to take a more direct line down than in ascent; to do this they had first to drop down a short, steep crag that led to a snow slope and finally the glacier. At one place Swanzy buried himself as deeply as possible in the snow on a steep slope and slowly fed out the rope to Green who faced inwards to the rocks as he went over an edge onto another snow slope, where he buried the shaft of the axe to its head. He had just stepped gently onto a rock in the middle of snow-covered slabs when the rock and the snow beneath it slid under his weight and slowly the whole snow slope cracked across, rushing with a swishing noise downwards in one huge avalanche. Swanzy held Green tightly as the debris crashed noisily beneath and hauled him back to safety. They retraced their steps and decided to take the 'same road that they had come up'.

To descend the steep upper rock slopes, they were force to push off tons of loose slate and shale at each step. At the steepest points, where both the rock and snow were so treacherous that their axes were of no use, they first lowered the axes down on one end of the rope and then hung the remainder of the rope over a rock spike using a 'bowline hitch'. One at a time they scrambled down, using the rope for 50 feet (15m), then recovering the rope by giving it 'a smart chuck'. They repeated this operation until they reached more secure ground where they ate a few biscuits and tinned beef before reaching the summit of the col at 6.30 p.m. A 'beautiful sunset glow flushed the Rockies with bright carmine while the nearer peaks glowed with deep crimson', wrote Green later. Night was close, so they ran and glissaded down the glacier until crevasses forced them onto the safety of the moraine. 'Running and leaping from boulder to boulder, wading streams and taking a straight line through everything', brought them with bruised shins to the edge of the forest at twilight. They followed the stream downwards to reach a pole they had fixed that marked their exit from the forest, high above the campsite. They stumbled in the dark, feeling for fallen logs and fending off branches from their eyes. In despair they thought of sitting the night out on a log, but Green's zoological wit shone through as he joked: 'we hoped that we might not tread, by accident, on the tail of a grizzly, but took comfort at the thought of their deficiency in such appendages'. Steering by the sound of the river, they at last came to the boulder field; at 11 p.m. they were once more 'round a blazing fire sipping chocolate and picking the bones of a marmot.'

They made two more surveying expeditions, one to Beaver Creek and the other to a valley beyond Asulkan Valley (which was named by Green in the language of the native Shushwap Indians for the wild goats that abounded). Despite the lack of help in their physically onerous task, the two clergymen (using four existing railway survey baselines) conducted their survey in the difficult terrain, sketched and photographed panoramas from various vantage points, and used twenty-two plane-table stations to take temperature and barometric readings, as well as bearings with a prismatic compass. From this data Green constructed the map that accompanied his RGS paper; however, due to the broken sextant borrowed from the RGS, he was unable to calculate the elevations of those points he had failed to reach. He named Mount Fox and Mount Donkin after two fellow members of the Alpine Club who were killed with their Swiss guides while climbing in the Caucusus when Green was in the Selkirks. The ever-astute Green did not forget his Canadian hosts, naming Perley Rock after the manager of Glacier House, Mount Deville for the Surveyor-General of Canada, and Mount Macoun after the botanist John Macoun of the Geological Survey of Canada.

Following their survey of the Rogers Pass area, Green and Swanzy travelled west to the Rockies. Green was particularly impressed with the beauty of the Lake Louise area and wrote of the grandeur of Mount Lefoy and the avalanches that constantly fell down the glacier and were observable from the lake. His advice that this area was probably the most interesting spot on the railway line was followed up immediately by the railway owners who quickly developed a hotel there.[53] The small chalet that opened on the shores of the lake in 1890 grew to become Chateau Lake Louise. Today Lake Louise is the most popular tourism attraction in the Canadian Rockies. While in America Green had also visited a number of American fishing ports and a US Fisheries Commission research facility, reporting that the Americans were engaged in tracking the movement of fish stocks and disseminating the information they gathered to interested parties. On his return to Ireland Green advocated the same information-gathering process and recommended that, to this end, an institution similar to that of the US Fish Commission be established. His next cruise was funded by the British Museum, which wanted specimens for public display. Green organised and supervised trawls down to 1,000 fathoms off the Cork coast, chartering the *Flying Fox* from the Clyde Shipping Company. The weather was perfect and reports on the many specimens obtained included a species new to Irish waters: an egg capsule of *Chimaera monstrosa* ('rabbit' or 'rat' fish).

The year 1890 was life-changing for the Green family. Firstly, following the death of one of the existing three inspectors of fisheries the previous year, Green was appointed to replace him; he retired as rector at Carrigaline and moved his family to the Dublin suburb of Rathmines. He was to remain in this job for twenty-four years, during which time he devoted all his energies to the development of fishing in Ireland. Secondly, government and Royal Dublin Society funding enabled the financing of two further research trawls led by Green: the first from Cobh to Killybegs in 1890 aboard the *Fingal*; the second in 1891 aboard the fishing vessel, *Harlequin*, along the southwest and west coasts of Ireland, stopping at ports en route including the Aran Islands. These two cruises added much to the existing knowledge of the marine biology of the Irish coastline and Green's reports supplied valuable information regarding fishing grounds, bait, possible developments, boats, harbours and ancillary works, fishing gear and particularly the people who fished. It was felt that the findings would be of great value to the government in dealing with the problems to be solved in the impoverished and so-called 'congested' districts of the western seaboard. When the Congested Districts Board was established in 1891, Green was appointed to the Board and was therefore responsible for the building of the many small fishing piers still in use today along the west and southwest coast.

In April 1900 the duties of the Inspectors of Irish Fisheries were transferred to the Department of Agriculture and Technical Instruction for Ireland, and Green was appointed Chief Inspector in September.[54] In 1901 the Department took part in the Glasgow International Exhibition and an official handbook dealing with Ireland's economic resources was published. Green contributed two sections on the history of Ireland's fishing industry, with special mention of the development of inland commercial salmon fisheries at the time. He was elected to membership of the RIA on 11 November 1895, along with Francis Elrington Ball, the renowned historian of County Dublin.

His last coastal expedition was a voyage aboard the Congested District Board's vessel the *Granuaile* to make a scientific exploration of Rockall in 1896. Rockall is a small, pointed islet in the north Atlantic off Ireland's northwest coast. The team of distinguished Irish naturalists who sailed included Robert Lloyd Praeger, John A. Harvie-Brown and Richard Manliffe Barrington, who presented the expedition for funding to the RIA. Green's son, Charles, was also amongst the crew. Due to bad weather the expedition fell very short of its objectives, failing to land on Rockall after two separate attempts out of Killybegs. However, they came close enough for Green to paint several beautiful watercolours and for his son to photograph Rockall.

Green was acutely aware of the benefits that the internal combustion engine would bring to the fishing industry. As Chief Inspector he used his position to organise the building and equipping of Ireland's first motorised fishing vessel at Tyrell & Sons boatyard, Arklow, County Wicklow. The 48-foot (14.6m) *Ovoca*, with many features for the comfort of the crew, proved a great success.[55] In 1907, when the replacement of the existing fishery research vessel was due, Green and his son Charles (also a department official) were responsible for the general design and specification for a fast new fishery protection and research vessel, built by the Liffey Dockyard Company.[56] The 47m-long *Helga* (with a 1,000 horsepower engine) was, when commissioned, regarded as one finest research vessels of her time. However, Irish native pride in the vessel suffered when it was used by the military to bombard Liberty Hall during the 1916 rebellion.

Green was made a Companion of Bath in 1907 by King Edward VII. He was a fellow of the Royal Geographical Society and was conferred with the rare distinction of honorary membership of the Royal Dublin Society. He was therefore honoured by membership of both the RIA and RDS for his practical ability in applied and academic science.

But Green's huge imagination could not be constrained by pure science. Whilst travelling the Irish coast, he always kept an ear to the ground in the hope of recording seafaring traditions and legends and was particularly interested in locating the wrecks of the Spanish Armada. In 1895 he made use of his maritime and historical knowledge and (using the pseudonym Petrel Fulmar) wove a novel about the life of the sixteenth-century Irish warrior queen, Grania Waile.[57] It is a story of seas, galleys, wreckers and the French and Spanish fishermen who fished off the west coast of Ireland, and it was illustrated with Green's own, very distinctive, watercolours. At Green's retirement breakfast in 1914 Mr T. P. Gill, Secretary of the Department of Agriculture, commented on his 'broad human sympathy, tempered and regulated by a fine Irish sense of humour', affirming that 'Mr Green is personally acquainted with every fisherman along the west coast and on our rivers and lakes, and in every fisherman's cottage his name is a household word.'[58]

After his retirement William Green left Dublin to live at West Cove, County Kerry, where he died on 22 April 1919. He is buried at Sneem, close to the sea in County Kerry; his grave is just inside the gate of the church whose bell tower is remarkably and aptly crowned by a salmon for a weather vane, in place of the usual cock.

The grave of William Spotswood Green in the churchyard of the Church of the Transfiguration, Sneem, County Kerry, where he is buried with his wife, Belinda. (Author's photo)

Ulrich Kaufmann, 1840–1917

Ulrich Kaufmann of Grindelwald was a tall, graceful and very handsome man, an excellent step-cutter and rock climber.[59] He had no history of first ascents in the Alps, although he was a highly respected guide in the Grindelwald range; his main claim to fame was his ascent of Mount Cook with William Spotswood Green and his hotelier friend Emil Boss, when he became the first European guide to visit the New Zealand Alps. However, the fame that arose from his performance on Mount Cook (and Green's recommendation), led to WilliamWoodman Graham extending an invitation to Kaufmann and Emil Boss to replace a sick Josef Imboden on Graham's expedition to the Garhwal Himalaya. There they made an attempt on Dunagiri 23, but were turned back by bad weather short of the summit. They climbed another peak marked A21 (6,863m) on their rough map, then moved to Sikkim,where they made an ascent of Kabru (7,412m) from the east, reaching its lower summit; unfortunately steep ice in the final section denied them the summit. Their ascents were later disputed by Survey of India. Kaufmann had a reputation as a 'strongman' (as demonstrated in New Zealand), yet he was a very reserved man, a gentle giant who was amiable and unselfish. Once, when out with a client on a descent from the Eiger during a hailstorm, he ran up a snow slope to cover his client's head with his arms in order to protect him against a sudden shower of rocks loosened by a rushing stream of hail spindrift. Luckily for both guide and client the rocks showered past, missing them narrowly. He always saw his main duty as the protection of his client. He died of pneumonia, aged seventy-seven, on 25 March 1917.

Ulrich Kaufmann from Grindelwald.
(Cunningham & Abney, *Pioneers of the Alps* (1887))

10

R. M. Barrington, Hart, Cullinan, Joly, Carson, Scriven, Parnell & Bryce: Wealth, Education and Discipline

There are ample opportunities [in Ireland] for acquiring the art of mountain craft, the instinct which enables the pedestrian to guide himself alone from crest to crest, from ridge to ridge, with least labour. He will learn how to plan out his course from the base of cliff or gully, marking each foot and hand grip with calm attention; and knowing when to cease to attempt impossibilities, he will learn to trust in himself and acquire that most necessary of all climber's acquirements a philosophie, contemplative calm in the presence of danger or difficult dilemmas.

H. C. Hart, in Haskett Smith & Hart, *Climbing in the British Isles*, 1895

RICHARD MANLIFFE BARRINGTON, Henry Chichester Hart, Frederick FitzJames Cullinan, Charles Jasper Joly, Thomas Henry Carson, George Scriven, Henry Tudor Parnell and James Bryce and were all active Irish climbers in the the Alps during the late nineteenth century. Botany took Barrington and Hart into the Irish mountains and to many of Ireland's remote islands and, in Hart's case, north to explore the frozen Arctic. Cullinan was an Irish civil servant at a volatile period of Irish history, while Joly was an accomplished mathematician, a Trinity professor and the Astronomer Royal at Dublin's Dunsink Observatory. Carson was a distinguished scholar at Trinity, and became a barrister practising in London and writing successful legal textbooks. He was a rare second generation alpinist, his father having crossed the Théodule Pass in 1845 and the Weisstor in 1850. Scriven, a physician who practised in Dublin, was not only an Irish international rugby player but the team captain and the first president of the Irish Rugby Football Union (IRFU) in the same period as he was climbing in the Alps in the company of the celebrated Sir Martin Conway. The young Carson climbed with the notable C. C. Tucker and Douglas Freshfield, both celebrated members of the Alpine Club. Bryce was a historian, jurist, academic, politician and (for a very brief period) Chief Secretary for Ireland. He became the second Irish president of the Alpine Club and, significantly, he was the first politician to attempt to introduce legislation for access to Scottish hills. All bar Parnell, an absentee landlord and brother of the most famous Irish politician of the age, were members of the Alpine Club. Parnell, with a decent qualification list, was refused membership when he applied to join the exclusive Club – one suspects his brother's politics caused his blackballing. All of these men were university educated, most of them at Trinity College, Dublin.

Richard Manliffe Barrington (1849–1915): nature's gentleman

Honesta Quam Splendida (Honesty is better than splendour)

Barrington Family Motto

Charles and Richard Manliffe Barrington were half-brothers, both sons of Edward Barrington of Fassaroe, County Wicklow. Charles' mother was Sarah (née Leadbeater), his father's first wife.[1] Richard, the only son of Huldah (née Strangman), Edward's second wife, was born on 22 May 1849. Richard's early education was conducted largely at home as he was a delicate child; he had a keen interest in natural science and a diary he kept from January to March 1864 reveals an industrious fourteen-year-old boy, enthused with strong self-motivation and a kind nature.[2] His diary also reveals his interest in reading and there appears to have been an extensive library of books at

Facing page: Bivouac Ledge on the Dom. George Scriven (second from right) with Sir Martin Conway (second from left) and Franz Andermatten (far right). (*The Alpine Journal*)

Richard Manliffe Barrington sitting in the porch at his home, Fassaroe House, Enniskerry, County Wicklow. (Courtesy Ron Barrington)

Fassaroe. His earliest published note (*Zoologist*, 1866),[3] concerned the food of the wood pigeon, and from that time until his death he was busy with zoological and, to a lesser extent, botanical fieldwork. His elder half-brother, Edward, gave him books on natural history and made a point of reading them himself so he could be 'a more intelligent helper'.[4]

Richard entered Trinity College, Dublin in 1866, graduating BA (Hons) in experimental and natural science in 1870 and LL.B in 1874. When in college he became acquainted with Alexander Goodman More of the Dublin Natural History Museum who was a strong influence on the younger Barrington. Barrington spent many weeks every summer on the islands, mountains and lakes in the south and west of Ireland, recording and gathering notes on plants and birds. He was one of a small group of enterprising young botanists, which included another Trinity-educated mountaineer Henry Chichester Hart, who helped More in the preparation of the second edition of *Cybele Hibernica*, published in 1872. Robert Lloyd Praeger, who knew both well, commented: 'Yet except for their strong interest in natural history, their indomitable energy and zeal, and the advantages which accrued from belonging to old "landed gentry" they had little in common. Barrington was an ideal companion, full of enterprise, originality, humour and a never failing friendliness: Hart was somewhat dictatorial, impatient, difficult to handle.'[5] Barrington's reports on the flora of Lough Ree, Lough Erne, Ben Bulben, Tory Island and the Blasket Islands off the west Kerry coast were variously published in the *Journal of Botany*, the *Irish Naturalist* and the *Proceedings of Royal Irish Academy*. He is quoted as an authority for new localities of plants in the 'Recent Editions' supplement to the 1872 edition of *Cybele Hibernica*. The pair of budding naturalists would become a strong climbing team in the Alps later.

In 1872, when he was twenty-three, his diary outlines a family visit to London and the southwest of England.[6] He travelled to London with his father and his sister Letitia, by steamer and train via Kingsbridge and Holyhead. They stayed at 48 West Abbey Road with relations. It is very clear that the visit was well planned in advance, for it catered for all his diverse interests. Amongst other things, he managed to take in the English Derby at Epsom and made visits to the London Exhibition. At London Zoo he 'saw Rhinoceros and sea lions of Falklands Island (two varieties)'; at Kew Gardens he visited its herbarium. He visited Madame Tussaud's Wax Museum, the British Museum, London Bridge and St Paul's and completed a tour of the House of Commons. He took in four separate lectures at the Royal Institution on different days, including one by John Tyndall and a speaker named Tyler 'on the development of belief and custom among lower races of men'. During the second week the family went to the Isle of Wight by train and steamer and stopped in the Esplanade Hotel. There he went walking and collecting plants. They travelled home slowly via Holyhead, stopping at Plymouth, Bristol and Chepstow en route.

In early August that same year his diary records a summer hillwalking holiday in Killarney, when he travelled with a relation, Mr Edward Shackleton, who is frequently mentioned in his diary.[7] On Friday 1 August Richard and Shackleton went by train to Mallow where they were met by a pair of horses and rode down into Killarney. Next morning they took a boat from Muckross up the rapids to the upper lake, from where they walked to the Gap of Dunloe. They returned in the evening the same way. He noted the 'scenery superb'. Next day Barrington 'set out at 10.00 from the hotel with a Kerryman [local guide] and pony . . . got to the base of the Carrantuohill Mountain at 1.30 and were on the summit at 3.40. Got milk and potatoes after coming down, home at Muckross at 11 pm called at Victoria Hotel on way home. Had view from top.'

On Sunday Barrington 'set out for the top of Mangerton with another young gent. Very misty on top but the view from Punchbowl was good. Walked round it after coming down and went to Torc Waterfall by self. Afterwards back to Muckross.' On Monday he travelled with Shackleton by car to Glencar and on to Breen's Hotel at Lough Caragh. There they 'found the hotel full of Cambridge men and walked then across hills to Caragh Lake'. He 'went down to Killorglin and stopped the night there. Lough Caragh was a beautiful spot. Got Ericaceous.' Next morning they left Killorglin; 'It is a dirty town and bad hotel', he noted. They then walked to Crosmane Point about 8 miles (13 km) away and took a boat across; afterwards, it was on to Anascaul and Dingle, about 20 miles (32 km) or so. He noted the former 'a small village . . . two miles from coast', and commented 'mountains all along the coast to Dingle but much nearer cold water than I expected'. In Dingle they stayed at Petrie's Hotel and took a car to Ballybrack to walk up Brandon Mountain; Barrington says, 'walked up to very near the summit, it was foggy and misty. ES did not want to go the whole way up – coming down we went a little astray due to fog.' Next day they took a car from Dingle to beyond Ventry from where they walked up Eagle Mountain and saw Sybil Head in the distance. They bathed at Ventry and walked back to Dingle along the coast. The following morning they travelled to Killarney via Tralee on the mail car, changing horses twice. On Saturday 11 August they took the train home from Killarney to Dublin. Shackleton stayed at the Shelbourne Hotel, while Barrington took the train to Bray and home to Fassaroe.

In April 1874 he describes one of many hikes he must have made from the family home at

Fassaroe, this time in the company of a friend called Letterdale.[8] They walked up to Lough Bray, where they bathed and then carried on up the cliffs to the top of Kippure and down to Coronation Plantation; from here they headed home by a bridge crossing the Liffey between Lough Bray and the Sally Gap, then down straight over the hill into Glencree Valley and back to Fassaroe. It took them ten and a half hours.

The following month his diary tells us that after reading an article about Iceland in *Cornhill* magazine he went straight to the RDS library where he read more on Iceland, and then on to Trinity College library to read even more. Perhaps he was already planning his 1881 expedition. After a trip to London in May (during which he visited the Alpine Club), he was back in Killarney for a June visit with a family group of eight, and climbed Purple Mountain from the Gap of Dunloe, as well as Mangerton for the second time. He tells us: 'Got off pony at Punch Bowl and walked to the top by self and then down the gully of a torrent into the Horses Glen, which is magnificent. Got some plants [in] three lake glen. Met Pony again near foot of Mangerton and rode home to Victoria Hotel.'[9] He went fishing at Glencar (and had one 'glorious rise' of a salmon), then climbed Carrantuohill from there with a local guide, ascending by Lough Acoose and coming back down into the Black Valley, before crossing over the ridge into the Hags Glen and back to Killarney.

Although he was called to the bar in 1875, he preferred farming and was engaged professionally as a purchasing inspector for the Land Commission. On the death of his father in 1877, he became more closely involved in the daily management of the family farm: under his direction the farm accounts books were meticulously maintained and show that over a ten-year period a profit was made every year. In 1888 he acquired the holding under Lord Ashbourne's Purchase of Land (Ireland) Act, agreeing to make the repayments over twenty and a half years: he paid the Land Commissioners £200 a year,[10] with interest of £132 per year and rent of £62 for an additional 32 acres, making a total payment of £394 per annum. He operated the 'four years' course' (a schedule of crop rotation pioneered in Norfolk) and in 1890 grew barley, oats, wheat, potatoes, mangolds, turnips and grass; in addition there were cattle (including dairy cows whose milk the farm sold direct to the people of Bray), sheep and pigs. Labourers on the farm earned the right to a cottage and 12 shillings per week, the normal wage for the area, although usually without the house. Richard's land steward, John Kenny, worked for him for thirty-three years and was recommended by Barrington for his exceptional neatness and accuracy in keeping the accounts, also for trustworthiness and care during that long period.

On 28 November 1874 Richard delivered a lecture to the Dublin Friends' Institute, which was based on his 'reading of John Tyndall on Heat'. It is clear from his diaries that his scientific interests were now very broad and included native mammals, agriculture and meteorology, as well as Irish science and economics. He was already contributing to a variety of journals and was a member of the Royal Irish Academy (RIA) and several societies, notably the Royal Dublin Society, the Royal Zoological Society of Ireland, the Statistical and Social Inquiry Society, the Dublin Friends' Institute, and the Irish Society for the Protection of Birds.[11] He was also one of the founders of the Dublin Naturalists' Field Club and an original member of the Climber's Club (an English hillwalking and climbing club) – certainly the only member of the latter with an Irish address. Known in Dublin society for his personal charm and kindly sense of humour, he was (as we have

R. M. Barrington camping at Skomar Island, Wales. (Courtesy Ron Barrington)

seen) a firm personal friend of many of the most noted naturalists of his day, including Robert Lloyd Praeger and William Spotswood Green.

Richard commenced his alpine mountaineering career in 1876 by repeating his half-brother Charles' feat and making his own ascent of the Eiger. He climbed the route with one of the two guides who had accompanied his brother, the great Grindelwald guide Christian Almer. Peter Bohren, he discovered, had passed away. Concerned to put the record straight regarding the identity of the Eiger's first ascentionist, he asked Charles to write an account of his own ascent; he then forwarded Charles' letter, as we have seen in Chapter 5, to the Alpine Club.

Meanwhile he visited and wrote reports on the plants and fauna of the western islands of Ireland and Scotland: Tory Island (1879), Blasket Islands (1881), St Kilda (1883), North Rona (1886), the shores of Lough Erne (1884) and the Ben Bulben range in County Sligo (1885).[12] On these occasions he always arrived at the height of the breeding season, living in each location for a week or more in the company of fellow zoologists and botanists. He also visited Iceland in 1881, when he walked extensively across the extraordinary landscape of glaciers, waterfalls, volcanos and geysers and climbed Mount Hekla.

In 1882 he made a spectacular return to the Alps where he completed a ten-day tour de force, starting out from Schwarzegg Hut on 25 July: he climbed the Schreckhorn and returned to Grindelwald on 26 July; to Gleckstein Hut on 27 July; Lauteraarjoch to Grimsel Pass on 28 July; Oberaarjoch to Rothloch on 29 July; climbed Finsteraarhorn and went down to the Concordia Hut on 30 July; to the Eggishorn and back to Concordia on 31 July; climbed Jungfrau and back

North Rona in the Outer Hebrides, visited in 1886 by R. M. Barrington.
(Courtesy Ron Barrington)

to Eggishorn on 1 August; Visp to Zermatt on 3 August; and finally climbed the Matterhorn on 5 August. This itinerary, which is typical of Barrington's preparation and planning, demonstrates his fitness and ability as a climber and long-distance walker. It all added up to 84,500 feet (25,756m) of ascent in ten days and perhaps by including the Matterhorn it was his way of trumping his half-brother Charles.

Ornithology had become Richard's other great interest and in 1882 he began correspondence with Irish lighthouse keepers on the migration of birds, a passion that culminated in the publication of his report, *The Migration of Birds as Observed at Irish Lighthouses and Lightships*, in 1900. The report included many new records for Ireland and the specimens sent to him by the keepers were either preserved by himself at his private museum at Fassaroe or passed to the national museum in Dublin. This fascinating collection may be seen today free of charge in the Natural History Museum in Dublin.

In 1883 he visited Hirta, the largest island of the St Kilda archipelago and one of the most remote of the Outer Hebrides, which lies about 50 miles (80.5 km) west of the Sound of Harris and 100 miles (161 km) west of the Scottish mainland. He later wrote an article for the Alpine Club's journal about the men of that island, whose people subsisted largely on seabirds and their eggs.[13] He relates that Stack-na-Biorrach (the 'pointed stack') is a sea stack lying off the island's shore and that it was said that 'the man who cannot climb it, never gets a wife in St Kilda'. Given the island's diet, it was not unreasonable to suppose that a girl of St Kilda (having regard to her future welfare) might find a way to test a potential lover's suitability, and the test arrived at was evidently to climb Stack-na-Biorrach. Barrington contended there was no part of the world where the practical advantage of being a skilled cragsman was so well recognised and where the chief topic of conversation was climbing and birds. He comments that 'a certain rivalry between myself and an elder brother who first ascended the Eiger induced me to visit St Kilda in 1883 as I wished to test the ability of the natives as cragsmen, to compare them with Swiss guides, and to study the fauna and flora of this remote island, of which little is known.' The islands were sadly abandoned in 1930s, having been continuously populated since prehistoric times.

Richard went to the island with his nephew and, not knowing Gaelic, he brought an interpreter from Glasgow. The man proved useless, since he was afraid to go within 10 metres of any cliff and could not understand the Hirta dialect, but he acted as caretaker of Richard's old Crimean tent, which they pitched on the only flat spot on the island near the landing place. None of the natives could speak English, so it took Barrington two weeks to persuade them to take him out to Stack-na-Biorrach. When they finally agreed, he was not allowed to wear his climbing boots on the expedition and they did not want to use his modern climbing ropes, preferring to use the three ropes that were handed down to each man, from father to son, over the generations. These ropes were constructed with a horsehair core covered by a cowhide outer sheath. The boat was rowed by a crew of eight, with Barrington and his nephew as passengers. When they arrived underneath the stack an hour after pushing off, there was a great Atlantic swell. A man named Donald McDonald mounted the bow of the boat with a horsehair rope tied round his waist; on the rise of the swell he jumped on to a small ledge of slimy seaweed below the high-water mark and secured himself. He then proceeded upwards by sticking his fingers and toes into small, wind-worn cavities on the western face of the stack. At the height of about 30 feet (9m) he turned to the east, moving out onto a small, narrow ledge that could not have more than 2 to 3 inches (5 to 8cm) wide, and reached a projecting knob of about 2 square feet (0.18m²). He hauled up a second rope and tied it around the knob, at which point Barrington was signalled by another man in the boat, Donal McQueen, to follow. Despite its vertical steepness he was able to ascend the wall using his feet and the rope, hand-over-hand style, so that finally he was standing beside McDonald on the knob. However, looking down, he saw to his horror that Donal McQueen had started up the rope behind him; soon all three of them stood on the small projection, unroped, above the crashing sea.

Barrington clung to the face of the cliff while McQueen immediately tied a rope around his own waist and moved upwards to a sloping ledge that was wet with sea spray and angled steeply upwards. Arriving on the ledge, he reached above himself and grasped yet another overhanging, narrow, horizontal ledge about 4 inches (10cm) wide that sloped outwards; then, with his feet dangling in mid-air, he hand-traversed the 15-foot (4.6m) long ledge, one hand patiently alternating with the other. McDonald fed out the rope; it was clear to Barrington that if McQueen fell, both he and McDonald would tumble to the sea. McQueen's traverse brought him to a better stance and he was now about 70 feet (21m) above the sea. The rope was tied around Barrington's waist, with one end being taken in by McQueen above and McDonald feeding out the remainder. His feet also dangled when he reached the traverse and, midway across, he lost his grip due to the slipperiness caused by guillemot droppings. However, a massive jerk from above at that moment on the horsehair rope raised him by a foot, during which he spotted a good hold and, grasping it with one hand, was soon standing on the ledge beside McQueen. McDonald quickly joined him.

The rock above was also overhanging and Barrington was curious to see what would follow. A lasso was made and, after a number of failed attempts, it was thrown over a projection 14 feet

(4m) overhead. After several vigorous pulls they were satisfied it was secure and McQueen hoisted himself above the overhangs to the point at which the stack began to lean back. The final section of the climb was, Barrington asserted, 'not more difficult than many first-class Clubmen could contend with'. Once at the top, the seabirds were captured using long fishing rods to which horsehair nooses were fitted. Barrington, who had already achieved success at this skill on a more accessible cliff, was delighted to be greeted back in the boat with cries of 'Saulia', which was interpreted to him to signify he was a great climber like a famous St Kildean of that name.

He went back to St Kilda briefly in 1896 when returning from an expedition with Spotswood Green to Rockall, which lay 170 miles (274 km) further west into the Atlantic. He met Donal McDonald, who then looked very poorly. He could not find Donald McQueen or get any news of him, and so he feared he was dead, as it was in the tradition of the islanders not to speak about the dead.

In 1884 Barrington and the Rev H. Swanzy were two of a group of 150 members of the British Association (BA) who attended the BA Annual Meeting held at Winnipeg in Manitoba, Canada. They sailed aboard the *Empress of Ireland*, a steamer owned by the Canadian Pacific Railway Company. Their Canadian hosts provided an opportunity for visiting members to travel by steamer across Lake Superior and onwards by train to the foothills of the Rocky Mountains, using the (still under construction) Canadian Pacific Railway. Swanzy and Barrington proposed to strike off on their own at the end of the line (which then extended to the Selkirks) and to cross the mountains on foot with packhorses heading for the Pacific Ocean. Barrington kept a journal during the excursion and Swanzy wrote a newspaper account. In Swanzy's words:

> after leaving Kicking Horse Pass on Friday 12th of September Mr Barrington and I managed to get down along with our baggage on a construction train – having carried our traps across the break caused by the fall of rocks near the tunnel – some fifteen miles down the valley as far as the Ottertail River. Here we invested in a couple of small horses or caruses, to carry our baggage; and met with a young engineer Mr William Morris who was returning over the Selkirk Mountains and knew the track, so we joined company. We loaded ourselves with the baggage and with a supply of provisions sufficient to last some days, in fact until we reached the first crossing of the Columbia River, where we got a fresh supply. We passed the Ottertail River to the Kicking Horse Valley, where one of our horses buck jumped twice, throwing his pack off, and of course, in the muddiest part of the road. The same horse afterwards fell over a bank some sixty feet high, and rolled over and over until he fell into the river at the foot; but strangely enough without being much the worse, the pack probably protecting him. He tried the same trick again, but this was once too often for his leg was so badly cut that we were obliged to leave him behind; the worse was that we were afraid that we could not take his pack on with us, and should not have been able to do so but for the kindness of Mr Allan Rodgers, who came up at the time, and by dividing out among his horses our pack we managed to carry it on to the second crossing of the Columbia River.
>
> We found some parts of the pack trail very bad indeed, the horses frequently rolling over with their packs in the deep bogs. Another party who followed us lost one of their horses, as it fell and broke its back. We were obliged to do all our own baking, cooking and packing, and at first we were awkward at it, but by degrees we improved and even

invented a new way of baking; the old way was to put the bread, or rather bannock, in the frying pan, and then leave it to roast afterwards, but we generally were too hungry to wait patiently the necessary time, and so we laid the cake in the pan, put a tin plate over it and covered it with the hot ashes. We shot a good many partridges, fool-hens [spruce grouse], grebes, ducks etc., but got no heavy shooting as we saw no bear or caribou on the track, and our time was too limited to allow us to look for them.

On leaving the first crossing of the Colombia River we went up the Beaver River and camped on the summit of the Selkirks where the view of the Syndicate Peak and other snow covered mountains was very grand. Then we went down the Illecillewaet River, which we were obliged to cross twice. We had to walk each day through mud and water, which was often knee deep; the ruts were often three feet deep, while the tree stumps were left standing. Across the trail the fallen trees were thick, and over these we had to climb while the horses jumped over in a wonderfully agile way. The views of the mountains were very grand all along the road and the snow-capped peaks looked very beautiful. We crossed the Columbia River for a second time in a boat, the horses swimming behind and beyond this there was a good road. We were kindly entertained by Mr and Mrs Wright. We reached the Eagle River and found a pass beyond, and a landing on the Shuswap Lake, which we reached just two weeks from the time we left the Ottertail River. On the Shuswap Lake, we found a good

A photograph taken by R. M. Barrington in Canada in 1884 of a Blackfoot chief named Kopeassesuean. (Courtesy Ron Barrington)

The grave of R. M. Barrington at the Barrington family's private graveyard at Glen Druid, Cabinteely, County Dublin. (Author's photo)

steamer; on her we went up for a day to the Salmon River and had a beautiful sail. Next day we came down to Kamloops, on the Thomson River and there took a stage for about 80 miles to Spencer's Bridge, where we struck the eastern end of western part of the Canadian Pacific Railway. Here we took a ticket as far as Yale, where we met the manager of that division of the line, who gave us a pass to Port Moody. Thence we came by steamer to New Westminster and Victoria, where we spent a day coming on to Portland, Oregan. Here the Northern Pacific Railways when they learned that we were members of the British Association kindly gave us tickets for New York at half-rate, and we arrived in New York via Chicago on Sunday the 12th at 7am and once more reached Montreal this morning, very much pleased with our excursion, and delighted with the kindness of everyone that we met.[14]

Barrington's handwritten journal gave a more detailed account of their daily adventures and described more misery:

Sat 27th Sept. 1884 – It continued to rain all night. This morning everything wet only for old wooden bedstead or box we broke up we would be very wet. This morning our blankets wet – put on wet trousers, wet stockings and wet boots – feet have been continuously wet since we started. Had ponies up last night – this morning one of the ponies missing – nervous lest we might be reduced to one. Found him however a small distance up track. Started at 10 am – made good way and reached Shuswap Lake at 4.45 pm by my watch . . . Shot a grouse today good road (except a few miry spots) this days march. The day was in the main dry –only a shower. Some pretty scenery – forests fire must have raged with violence here – trees reduced to poles. Undergrowth poplar and grey lime – pretty – very pleased to get here safe our troubles are now I hope over – Swanzy's hands sore as well as mine. Drunken man on road. Indian male female and child came to store in evening in a canoe. Campfires round lake look well tonight. Weather calm as usual – Swanzy took a row in canoe.[15]

His black and white photographs of this expedition include many fine shots of Native American camps; there is also some indication of his agricultural and economic expertise.

Barrington did not apply for Alpine Club membership until 21 February 1886 when he was proposed by the Rev. W. S. Green and seconded by Dr Scriven. His application was made on the basis of his short but impressive Alpine climbing career and wider exploration experience; like his proposer and friend Green, he did not include any reference to his very significant scientific achievement. He had clearly delayed his application until his climbing achievements would be sufficient to support it. His membership was passed on 11 March 1886.

In late August 1889 he accompanied Hart from Grindelwald to Zermatt from where, with Christian Almer and three other guides, they crossed the Triftjoch to Monulet and came back the following day over the Col de Moming.[16] Hart wrote: 'owing to unfavourable weather we were thwarted in several intentions.'[17] They did, however, ascend the Weisshorn from the Hohlicht Hut and the Dent Blanche from Stockje. Hart remarked: 'Christian Almer is 63 years old and he is a marvellous man for his years. He has the speed and strength of any of his juniors and an amount of fearless confidence which few of them possess. Also he is always cheery and full of enjoyment. It is a real pleasure to climb in his company. On the above expedition my friend Mr Richard M. Barrington was with me and as other guides Caesar Knubel, Irdolen Kuplier and Johan Andermatten.'[18] Hart signed himself Henry Chichester Hart (AC).

In 1892 Barrington and Hart set out on an expedition to the Sperrin Mountains in County Tyrone in search of a specimen of the long-lost cloudberry, *Rubus chamaemorus*, to prove the accuracy of their mentor More's judgement that the original record of the plant's existence was correct. The climbing partners triumphantly found the plant and agreed to keep its exact location a secret, lest they precipitate its demise. Several years later Barrington received an official appointment from the Irish Land Commission and must have found that he was left with little spare time; certainly there are no further records of mountaineering expeditions.

His wife, Lena, whom he married in 1897, proved a great support to him in assisting with his publications and it was she who suggested that he open the rare Irish bird museum at Fassaroe. After his retirement from the Land Commission he had a most enjoyable season successfully recording all the rarest Irish breeding birds, as well as finding a new colony of Sandwich terns. He died while driving his motor car home from Dublin on 15 September 1915 in the company of his young son. He had the great presence of mind to pull up and stop the car without showing any sign of suffering before he expired. In his will Richard left Fassaroe House and its lands to his wife until his son reached the age of twenty-one.[19] His natural history collection was left to the Science and Arts Museum, Kildare Street, Dublin, together with £100 for cataloguing the same. He requested that he 'be buried at Glendruid . . . and that if any burial service is held – it should be in accordance with usages of the Society of Friends to which religious body – I should be glad if my children belonged.'

Henry Chichester Hart (1847–1908): 'hard man' Hart

Hart ascended the Weisshorn (14,800 feet) and Dent Blanche (14,300 feet) in Switzerland. The days were fine and five or six other parties were climbing the same peaks independently. Hart proposed to give them all one hour's start, and, not withstanding these tremendous odds, the Irishmen on each occasion reached the summit first.

Richard Barrington, who accompanied Hart in 1889

HENRY HART was one of the most noted Irish naturalists of the nineteenth century. In his lifetime he distinguished himself in three spheres of activity: physical, scientific and literary. He climbed in the Alps with Richard Barrington, was an early pioneer of mountaineering in the Isle of Skye and is perhaps best known in Ireland for his successful completion of the Hart Walk with Sir Frederick Cullinan on 20 June 1886. This 75-mile (121 km) walk (a mix of road and hillwalking) was done to settle a wager of 50 guineas with Richard Barrington. The wager required Hart to walk from the tram terminus at Terenure in Dublin to the summit of Lugnaquilla, Wicklow's highest mountain, and back within twenty-four hours. The route followed the military road to the Sally Gap and Laragh to Drumgoff, and from there ascended open hills to the summit of Lugnaquilla at 3,009 feet (917m). The return route was mostly a hill walk via the Wicklow Gap, Tonlegee, Mullaghcleevaun to Ballysmutton Bridge and back by road to Terenure. Hart and Cullinan completed the walk in 23 hours 50 minutes.[20] The route has provided a challenge to generations of hillwalkers and hill-runners to this day.[21] Regarding the walk Barrington wrote: 'He [Hart] was accompanied by Frederick Cullinan (now Sir Frederick Cullinan, CB), also a member of the Alpine Club, who equalled Hart in endurance, if not speed.'[22] One wonders what time Hart might have achieved, had he done the walk solo?

Henry Chichester Hart was born 29 July 1847 in Raheny, a north-side suburb of Dublin city, the son of Sir Andrew Searle Hart (Professor of Mathematics and Vice-Provost of Trinity College, Dublin) and Frances MacDougall, whose father was a Dublin QC. The family roots were in Donegal and he was educated at Portora Royal School, Enniskillen, and at Trinity College, Dublin, where he qualified with a BA Moderatorship in experimental and natural science in 1869, one year ahead of Barrington. During his college years he was a noted athlete, handsome and tall (6 feet 1 inch), a powerful swimmer and champion walker for the college.[23] When he was seventeen years old, he and his brother George began to scour the mountains of Donegal each summer for wild flowers. The two brothers (using the key in Bentham's *British Flora* to make out the names of those gathered) identified each one. He came into prominence as a botanist alongside fellow mountaineer R. M. Barrington when under the guidance of A. G. More, and contributed to the 1898 edition of *Cybele Hibernica*. His early published works include *Flora of Donegal* (1898) and *Scripture Natural History; the Animals Mentioned in the Bible* (1888).

Hart was conscious of his athletic superiority and the majority of his walking companions could not keep up with him; as a result he carried out most of his botanical expeditions alone. Barrington, who had a common interest in the study of nature, developed a strategy when accompanying him.[24] This was to make sure that he always suggested the ascent of some difficult gully or awkward traverse along the ledge of a nasty precipice; the resulting experience made the expedition equally enjoyable for both of these able climbers. 'Always look for Alpines in Ireland high up on the north-east face of the precipice', was Hart's advice to botanists.[25] Barrington contended that no naturalist was ever likely to approach Hart in the amount of ground covered in a single day and that some plants found by Hart were unlikely to be verified by ordinary explorers because of their inaccessibility on cliff faces. His botanical work was referenced almost exclusively for information on the northwest of Ireland by Robert Lloyd Praeger in his *Irish Topographical Botany* (1901). Henry was also interested in studying climate, in support of which he maintained meteorological equipment at his Donegal residence at Carrablagh, Croaghross near Letterkenny.[26]

In 1875 he served as naturalist in the Arctic expedition under Sir George Nares on board HMS *Discovery*. The two-ship expedition left England 29 May 1875, stopping at Disko Island and at Upernavik before entering Kennedy Channel to reach the north side of Lady Franklin's Bay. Nares went further north with HMS *Alert*, but Hart's furthest north was 86° 50´. Hart was not involved in any of the expedition's exploratory sledge journeys, as he was clearly required to focus his efforts on his scientific activities. However, it is interesting to note the comments of the naturalist aboard HMS *Alert*, Colonel Fielding, who wrote: 'Physically, he was I think the finest man I ever knew.'[27] Hart collected flowering plants and ferns at various points, from Disko Island onward, but his most important work was done in the northeast part of Grinnell Land between 80° and 81° 50´. Three other Irishmen were on the expedition, including surgeons Richard William Coppinger and Thomas Colan, as well as Hart's

Henry Chichester Hart, naturalist, mountaineer and literary editor. (*The Irish Naturalist Vol XVII*)

shipmate on *Discovery*, Able Seaman James Hand from Bray, who perished from the effects of scurvy after the return of his sledging party from an exploration of the northwest coastline of Greenland. Hand was buried at Polaris Bay, two degrees inside the Arctic Circle.

On its way home the expedition stopped at Valentia Island on 27 November 1876. The botanical notes of the expedition were edited by Sir Joseph D. Hooker, director of Kew, who himself had been to Antarctica with James Clark Ross and Francis Crozier on HMS *Erebus* and *Terror* (1845 to 1849). Hooker was astonished by the extent of the species obtained on the Nares expedition and identified a new species of fungus from Hart's collection, which was named in his honour (*Urnula hartii*). The expedition's scientific observations and collections produced geological, astronomical and botanical data for forty published reports and articles.

Hart was also invited to participate in an expedition to examine the geological structure of the Jordan Valley and Western Palestine. The expedition set out to undertake a scientific examination of the Arava Valley from the Gulf of Aqaba through the Sinai Peninsula to the Dead Sea. The expedition sponsors, the Palestine Exploration Fund, wished to scientifically record and map all the places named in the Bible. Hart was selected for this largely Irish-manned scientific expedition by its leader, Professor Edward Hull FRS who was both the Director of the Geological Survey of Ireland and Professor of Geology at Trinity College, Dublin. The party included Hull's own son and the County Kerry born Captain Horatio Herbert Kitchener of the Royal Engineers (who later became Lord Kitchener), as well as Sergeant Major James Armstrong, also of the Royal Engineers. During the expedition Hart, who was aided by the Royal Irish Academy, travelled overland to Venice from where he sailed to Egypt. In Egypt he managed to give his Arab guides the slip and climbed the Great Pyramid of Giza alone.[28]

Travelling through Sinai, Hart ascended Jebel Zebir (2,247.3m), which has a fine viewpoint at 1,186m; four days later he climbed Jebel Musa (Mount Sinai, 2,285m) and continued on the same day to Jebel Katarina (Mount Catherine, 2,602m), the highest point on the peninsula. They were now travelling through the very heart of the desert of the Exodus, and Hart and Kitchener ascended Jebel el Aradah (979m) on 25 November. The party reached Akaba (now Aqaba) on 29 November, from where they set out north for Wadi el Arabah to ascend Mount Hor (1,341m, approximately) from their campsite near Petra. They then reached Ghor el Safi on the Dead Sea on 17 December, where they stayed for ten days waiting for fresh horses. Hart discovered the ruins of Khurbet Lebrusch. Hart and Reginald Lawrence, the meteorologist of the party, ascended the ridge of Jebel Usdum (Mount Sodom), which previous explorers had considered inaccessible.[29] The party arrived at Beersheba, Gaza, on 1 January 1884, where they spent five days in quarantine before they travelled via Jaffa to Jerusalem. Kitchener had left them the day before to return to duty. They continued on to visit Jericho and the Jordan Valley; a heavy fall of snow stopped further work in Northern Palestine. Hart and Lawrence crossed Lebanon and Herman to Damascus, visiting Baalbek. Letters and reports by Hull, Hart and Kitchener were produced for the Palestine Fund; Hart's narrative and scientific report was entitled *Some Account of the Fauna and Flora of Sinai, Petra, and Wadi Arabahi*.

Hart not only walked and climbed in Ireland; he visited the Isle of Skye in 1887, where he traversed the Inaccessible Pinnacle on top of Sgùrr Dearg, made the first ascent of Sgurr Mhic Choinnich and ascended Sgùrr Alasdair in a single day.[30] *The Alpine Journal* recorded: 'botany did not seem to detain Mr J. C. Hart of Dublin, who with Mackenzie, has since crossed the pinnacle on Sgurr Dearg, passed over this nameless peak, descending by the difficult drop, and Sgurr Alister in one day, found amongst other alpine plants "Arabis Alpina" for the first time in the British Isles. He confirms our opinion that Alister is the highest mountain in Skye. His barometer gave 3,260 feet as its height.'[31] Hart's ascent of the Inaccessible Pinnacle was the third; at a later date Norman Collie would report in an article in *The Alpine Journal* that his own ascent of the Inaccessible Pinnacle was the fourth, 'only Pilkerton, Stocker and Hart having been up before us.'[32]

Hart's irregular occupation (he later became Professor of Law at Trinity College) left him

The Inaccessible Pinnacle (986m), Sgùrr Dearg, Isle of Skye. Henry Hart traversed the exposed pinnacle, making its third ascent in 1887. (Courtesy Paddy O'Brien)

the flexibility to pursue his studies without the hampering ties of business or official routine. He displayed considerable literary ability and in later life was an editor for the Arden edition of William Shakespeare's plays. He also began collecting non-standard words current in Donegal English, and his work was later used by Michael Traynor in his 1953 publication, *The English Dialect of Donegal*. His application for membership of the Alpine Club was passed at a meeting on 17 May 1889 and his election was confirmed on 4 June.[33] His address was given as Carrablagh, Croaghross, Letterkenny, County Donegal and his occupation listed as 'Justice of Peace and Fellow of Linnean Society'. Remarkably, for a climber of such ability and experience, his qualifications for membership were purely scientific. On his application he wrote: 'Scientific; a number of publications on Alpine Botany.' His proposer was John Ball and his seconder was F. J. Cullinan, indicating the growing network of Irish alpinists with scientific and botanical interests.

Hart was, however, soon to be active in the Alps. Barrington later wrote: 'In 1889, in company with the writer, Hart ascended the Weisshorn (14,800 feet) and Dent Blanche (14,300 feet) in Switzerland.'[34] Their guide was the great Christian Almer. Hart filled out the *Führerbuch*.[35] The days were fine and five or six other parties were climbing the same peaks independently. Hart proposed to give them all one hour's start and, not withstanding these tremendous odds, the Irishmen on each occasion reached the summit first.

Hart wrote the Irish chapters for Haskett Smith's climbing handbook, *Climbing in the British Isles* in 1895.[36] The first volume covered England, the second Wales and Ireland, and a third was to cover Scotland but was dropped when Haskett Smith was informed that the Scottish Mountaineering

Glenalla House and Gardens, Rathmullan, County Donegal, the home
of Henry Chichester Hart. (Author's photo)

Club was planning its own guidebook. The second volume of this 200-page, pocket-sized guidebook (illustrated with many maps and sketches of notable features) included Fair Head, the One Man's Pass at Slieve League, Achill Head, the Cliffs of Moher and maps of Connemara and Mayo, the Mourne mountains, County Kerry and Killarney District. In the introduction Hart wrote: 'The climbing described in the following pages was chiefly undertaken with the object, or excuse, of botanical discovery. All the mountain experiences, except where the contrary is stated represents the personal – usually the solitary – experience of the writer.' It is clear from his narrative that Hart was accustomed to climbing solo up steep ground, gullies and cliffs in search of botanical and wildlife specimens. He comments:

> There are ample opportunities [in Ireland] for acquiring the art of mountain craft, the instinct which enables the pedestrian to guide himself alone from crest to crest, from ridge to ridge, with least labour. He will learn to how to plan out his course from the base of cliff or gully, marking each foot and hand grip with calm attention; and knowing when to cease to attempt impossibilities, he will learn to trust in himself and acquire that most necessary of all climber's acquirements a philosophie, contemplative calm in the presence of danger or difficult dilemmas.[37]

In the section on County Donegal Hart recalls the local practice of cliff-climbing at Horn Head to retrieve bird's eggs. He particularly remembers his own climb from a boat to retrieve a green cormorant's eggs from a nest at the entrance to a notable cave called the Gap of Doonmore; the last part of the cliff was overhanging but the rock was reliable, with one to one and a half ledges. The proprietor of the Doonmore estate told him a story about the son of one of his men called John Stewart. Apparently the youth was about seventeen years old when he went looking for eggs in the cliffs 'and fell about 500 feet to a shingly beach, rolling the first part of the way down a steep grassy bank for about 100 feet, and then a sheer drop of 150 feet to another grassy bank where a holly bush grows. When picked up (of course quite dead) he had a holly branch in his hand.'[38] He describes a walk from Bundoran to Sligo as: 'Full of interest to a mountaineer and the descent into the valley north of Sligo from King's mountain is one that will never be effaced from his memory. It is not easy to find the passages leading down. The valley is a vast amphitheatre almost enclosed by cliffs, sheer and including talus, about 1,000 ft. high.'[39] In relation to Killarney, he warns would-be visitors about the so-called 'guides' they might encounter:

> Guides swarm here. None of these have the slightest knowledge of climbing, and should one be engaged the first deviation from the easiest ascent, or departure into gully or ravine, will put a conclusion to his services. A wiry bragging, long legged shepherd undertook to accompany the writer by any ascent he selected from the Hag's Glen to Carrantuohill, to be paid 5 shillings at the summit. At the foot of the first gully, with many heart felt remonstrations and gesticulations, he disappeared, not even thinking it worthwhile to make an easier ascent.[40]

Hart went on to suggest at this point in his guide the necessity of having an ordnance survey map and a good compass, and recommended bringing an aneroid barometer to help in mist to identify a lake or peak.

It is interesting to note that in the pages for Wicklow he lists a number of 'one day' walks, which can be undertaken from Dublin city. These include a walk from Bray over Bray Head, Little Sugar Loaf, Big Sugar Loaf, Djouce Mountain, Kippure, and Lough Bray to Terenure (about 11 hours). He also provides his timetable for the 75-mile (121 km) 'Hart Walk', which he describes simply: 'Terenure: Lough Bray (3 hours); Laragh (7½ hours); Glenmalure; Drumgough Hotel (9 hours 5 minutes – 1½ hours' rest); Lugnaquilla (3,039ft. 12¾ hours); Tonlegee Summit 16¼ hours; Mullaghclevaun Summit (17 hours 40 minutes); Ballysmutton farm (19 hours 40 minutes – 35 minutes rest); Ballinascorney Gap; Terenure (23 hours 50 minutes; 75 miles).'[41] In Hart's obituary Barrington warned readers of Haskett Smith's guide to treat the times given by Hart in the Irish section with caution, noting 'some walks and climbs in this country mentioned therein, in a light and airy fashion, would be quite impossible for an ordinary man to accomplish in the times given.'[42] Hart was a hard man and indifferent to weather; he treated rain, wind and mist, even in the mountains, with disdain.

The Wicklow section also includes the Powerscourt Waterfall, which Hart describes as presenting an 'Arctic appearance'. He also mentions a recent account of it that was sent to an Irish paper in February 1895: 'The climb was effected by a friend of the writer's (a member of the Alpine Club) and another with ropes and ice axes. The cliff was covered with snow and ice. The same party ascended Djouce (2,384ft.), which lies above the waterfall, during a blizzard at a temperature of 18 ° Fahrenheit, upon the same day.'[43] The 'friend' referred to was likely to have been Richard Barrington. It is interesting to read how Praeger, who knew both men well, compared them:

> Yet except for their strong interest in natural history, their indomitable energy and zeal, and the advantages which accrued from belonging to old 'landed gentry' they had little in common. Barrington was an ideal companion, full of enterprise, originality, humour and a never failing friendliness: Hart was somewhat dictatorial, impatient, difficult to

handle. I have always rejoiced in the story Barrington tells of a rainy day spent with Hart, when neither of them would give way. I venture to tell it again in Barrington's words: 'By appointment he [Hart] turned up at Fassaroe one dreadful day to botanise on the cliffs around Powerscourt Waterfall, and to hear, if possible, the Wood Wren. Well knowing that if the expedition failed, the incident would for years be a theme for ridicule, a few slices of bread were hastily wrapped up, and we started in torrents of rain, absolute silence being observed regarding the atmospheric conditions. Both wet to the skin "in no time" Hart deliberately kept walking among the shrubs, briars and long grass by the river's edge, so as to discourage his companion. To prove utter indifference to moisture, the writer, walked into the river and sat down on a submerged stone and began to eat lunch. Hart, with the utmost nonchalance, and without saying a word, did likewise. Saturation soon complete all rivalry ceased and friendship prevailed for the remainder of the day.' Barrington was a 'friend to the world'. I knew him for twenty years and rejoiced in his acquaintance.[44]

Hart was elected fellow of the Royal Geographical Society in 1891; he was also a fellow of Linnean Society and a member of the Royal Irish Academy and the Royal Dublin Society. He served as Justice of the Peace for County Donegal and was High Sheriff in 1895. He married Edith Susan Anne Donnelly in 1887 (when he was already forty); however, the marriage seems to have run into difficulties because on 18 June 1897 his wife successfully petitioned the Probate Court, Dublin, seeking a divorce on the grounds of his misconduct and cruelty.[45] Hart made no appearance in court. Evidence was presented that the couple had lived happily together 'but he [Hart] developed intemperate habits and became a confirmed drunkard which rendered it impossible for her to live with him'. Evidence was presented that Hart was guilty of misconduct with three named women (two of them married), one with an address in Dublin, another with an address in Armagh and another who lived in London and Brighton. Letters to and from Hart to two of these women were read out in court. Evidence was given that when Hart was served with the petition for divorce he had been living in the Metropole Hotel, Brighton, with one of the named women for three months. Records show that he resigned from the Alpine Club in 1897.

In his later years his literary scholarship engrossed his attention. He edited *Othello*, *Love's Labour's Lost*, *Measure for Measure* and *The Merry Wives of Windsor* for the Arden edition of Shakespeare. He married Mary Cheshire in 1907, following Edith's death in 1901. His garden at Carrablagh was a source of delight to him and he loved to show people the rarities within it personally. He died at his beautiful residence on the shores of Lough Swilly on 7 August 1908 at the age of sixty-one. He was buried at Glenalla, in a spot chosen by himself, amidst the wild glens and valleys where he had spent the happiest days of his life.

F. J. Cullinan (1845–1913): 'Monsieur Coolinan'

As he crossed the couloir lower down, a great stone falling from the summit rocks whizzed past 'Monsieur Coolinan' with great velocity, just at the same moment Lanier shouted his name. They watched as it bounded in great leaps to the snow below.

Frederick Cullinan, 'The Aiguille de Talèfre', *The Alpine Journal*, 1882

FREDERICK CULLINAN was a friend and climbing partner of both Richard Barrington and Henry Hart, famously accompanying Hart on the 75-mile (121 km) walk that he undertook as a wager with Barrington: from Terenure over the summit of Lugnaquilla and back to Terenure within twenty-four hours. He was also an accomplished alpine climber, who made many notable first ascents in the Mont Blanc range.

He was born in Ennis, County Clare, in 1845, son of Dr Patrick Maxwell Cullinan of Harmony House, Ennis, and was educated at Ennis College and Trinity College, Dublin. He joined the civil service as a clerk in the Office of the Chief Secretary of Ireland in 1864 and in 1878 was appointed Clerk in charge of the Irish Office in London, a branch of the Chief Secretary's Office kept open during the Parliamentary session, and at other times for the convenience of the Irish Chief Secretary.[46] He was thus a senior civil servant in London at the time of the bitter struggle between Charles Stewart Parnell's Land League and the British administration.

Cullinan started climbing in the early 1870s. In 1876 he climbed the Diablons in the Turtmantal valley, Col Durand between Zinal and Zermatt, Ober Gabelhorn, Weisshorn and Furggenjoch with A. H. Simson. He also climbed the Strahlhorn and Triftjoch with the guide Peter Knubel. With these ascents he was elected a member of the Alpine Club in February 1877.[47] Frederick's older brother, Maxwell Cormac Cullinan (1843–1884), an academic, was also an alpine climber and member of the Alpine Club, with an impressive list of ascents, including the Adler Pass and Strahlhorn, Schwarzberg Weisstor, and the Rothorn (all with A. H. Simson), as well as the Matterhorn with Peter Knubel.[48] In 1877 Frederick himself would make the ascent of the Matterhorn. His five-year posting to London in 1878 enabled him to attend Alpine Club meetings and marks a period of increased alpine activity, during which he made a number of noteworthy ascents. He climbed principally in the Zermatt, Chamonix and Oberland districts. Gerald Fitzgerald, an alpine climbing companion, said of him: 'He was naturally of a very retiring disposition, but to those who knew him intimately he had many great attractions: he was a good climber fast, light and safe, and always most even tempered, unselfish and agreeable companion.'[49] His first major ascent after the Matterhorn came in September 1878 when, in company with Gerald Fitzgerald and with Peter Knubel and Joseph Moser as guides, he ascended the Täschhorn by the arête leading from the Domjoch to the summit.[50] Starting from the usual sleeping place for the Täschhorn (about three hours above Randa), they reached the Domjoch in six hours and twenty minutes, including a halt for daylight of three quarters of an hour. He also climbed the Biesjoch.

Cullinan's life in London, out of reach of mountains and working long hours in an office, was not the best preparation for alpinism. Recognising this, his solution was 'pedestrianism over hills and hollows'.[51] Once a week, 'be the weather what it may', he managed to put in 'his five-and-

Sir Frederick FitzJames Cullinan, Irish civil servant and mountaineer (Cullinan Family Genealology Web Project)

twenty or thirty miles on foot through beautiful scenery and fresh air, leaving town in the morning and returning the same evening'. Combined with moderate daily exercise he found that: 'I arrive at the foot of my mountain with a fair prospect of reaching its summit without undue physical exhaustion.'

On 18 August 1880 Cullinan, Fitzgerald and J. Baumann, with their guides Moser, Lanier and Rey, climbed the Aiguille du Midi. On descent Lanier picked out a line of ascent (on the southwest flank) that would lead them to the summit of the 'virgin' Aiguille de Telèfre. They waited a few days at Montanvert for some bad weather to pass and finally left at 2.15 a.m on 28 August by lantern-light. They ascended the Glacier de Leschaux and, with Lanier leading the way, turned their backs on the Pic du Tacul and crossed the glacier diagonally towards rocks and grass to reach the Glacier de Pierre Joseph. From the base of the rocky face of the Aiguille de Telèfre, they made their way up by zigzagging across two very high-angled couloirs descending downwards slightly from the last rocks before the summit; Lanier, still in the lead, had to cut steps because the rocks proved unsound and rotten and it was difficult to avoid kicking stones down on the skulls of those below. Then he moved leftwards and gained a higher and sounder rock ridge, on which he made safer and speedier progress. This 'friendly' ridge led them to the top, though cautious climbing was still the order of the day. They climbed up to a steep crown of rock, which appeared to be the highest summit of the aiguille; but on gaining it, they found that there was still another summit to the north, manifestly a few feet higher.

It took them twenty more minutes to reach the highest point in warm, calm conditions where they gorged themselves on the tinned delicacies that Cullinan and Baumann had brought from London. This they preferred over the 'hard stringy meat, hard boiled eggs and superannuated chicken' which the guides usually fished out of their knapsacks.[52] They also thought the hitherto virgin peak deserving of one of the three tinned plum puddings they had had among their food stock, and Baumann in particular stowed away enough to have killed most people at Christmas. From their lofty picnic site they admired for an hour and a half the striking and magnificent precipices of the Grandes Jorasses before descending by their route of ascent. They stayed close together to reduce the dangers of knocking stones on one another. Nevertheless, as he crossed the couloir lower down, a great stone falling from the summit rocks whizzed past 'Monsieur Coolinan' with incredible velocity at the very moment that Lanier, with Gallic accent, shouted his name in warning. They watched as it bounded in great leaps to the snow below. They quickly moved on to reach the safe ground without further incident. The modern Alpine Club guidebook advises that the southwest flank is possibly the quickest from the French side but warns that the rock is quite dangerous, with atrocious rock quality and the ever-present threat of stone fall.[53]

Cullinan and Joseph Moser continued to climb with Baumann and Émile Rey that season, making the second ascent of the Aiguille du Dru eleven days later and the second ascent of Dent d'Herens from Tiefenmattenjoch on 8 September. *The Alpine Journal* recorded both these ascents:

> The party having slept somewhat higher up than did Mr Dent's party on the occasion of the first ascent [of the Aiguille du Dru], started at 4.15 am on the morning of the 29th (August). They reached the summit at 9.15 am and remained there till 10.20. The sleeping place was regained at 3.40 pm and after resting there for an hour the party returned to Chamonix, the hotel Couttet being reached at 8.30 pm. The entire time occupied by the expedition from the sleeping place to the summit and thence down to Chamonix, was therefore sixteen hours and a quarter; bearing out Mr Dent's assertion that it could be done in sixteen to eighteen hours. Both guides behaved admirably, but especial credit is due to Rey, who took the lead throughout the day, and who on this occasion, as well as on other occasions this season while with the same party, displayed the qualities of a first-rate guide. The number of the 'Alpine Journal' containing Mr Dent's account of the first ascent was carried by the party, and was referenced to several times and found very useful in more than one doubtful spot as indicating the right way up. The Alpine ropes left by Mr Dent's party were found in good preservation and quite trustworthy; but the ladder is a rickety old structure indeed, and, though still in place, is very much weather worn and is no longer safe. They found evidence left by Dent on the summit. The weather throughout the expedition was perfect.[54]

The journal also reported that:

> On September 8, Messrs J. Baumann and F. J. Cullinan, with Guides Émile Rey of Courmayeur and Joseph Moser of Täsch effected the ascent of the mountain [the Dent d'Herens] by the arête leading straight to the summit from the top of the Tiefenmatten Joch. The party left Stockje at 3 am reached the summit of the pass at 5 am and the summit of the mountain at 8.40. They left the summit at 9 am; and returned by the ordinary route, regaining Stockje at 12 o'clock noon.

The party expressed surprise that the ascent by this arête had not been more often repeated and noted their progress was slow due to a violent southerly wind to which they were so exposed, however they recommended the route as the rock was good.

When Cullinan was transferred back to Dublin Castle in 1883, it was to a city reeling with the aftershock of the Phoenix Park murders. The five men convicted of the murders were hung at Kilmainham Jail in the course of that summer and the city was in political turmoil. His relocation curtailed his attendance at the Alpine Club meetings; and, although he went to the Alps as often as he could, the length of the parliamentary sessions often prevented him from going out before

September. His next recorded routes are not till 1885, when he climbed the Eiger with W. E. Davidson on 13 August, Strahlegg and Gross Lauteraarhorn with Davidson and Gerald Fitzgerald, Lauteraarjoch and Gspaltenhorn with Fitzgerald, Gross Fiescherhorn with Davidson and Fitzgerald, and attempted the Jungfraujoch with Davidson. There is no record of him climbing in the Alps after this date. He seconded the successful application of Henry Hart to join the Alpine Club in May 1889. Hart was proposed by John Ball.

However, he must have been exercising himself on Irish hills, because on 20 June 1886 he accompanied Henry Hart to win his wager with Richard Barrrington when the pair walked the 75 miles (121 km) to Lugnaquilla and back. In 1892 he married Elizabeth, daughter of Sir William B. Kaye, who was for many years Assistant Under-Secretary and then Under-Secretary for Ireland. During his time at Dublin Castle, Sir Frederick Cullinan was largely occupied with the arduous work of the Chief Secretary's department and had close professional relationships with several Lord Lieutenants and Chief Secretaries; his role demanded supreme diplomatic skills during this period when the struggle for Home Rule was becoming increasingly bitter. In January 1892 he had a narrow escape from death. In response to a bell summoning him to the Chief Secretary's office, he left his own apartment and had only gone a few yards when an explosion occurred, completely shattering the room in which he had been writing. It appears that some repairs had been carried out in the Chief Secretary's wing of the Castle, and that the presence of the workmen had been utilised by republicans as an opportunity to plant a bomb.

In 1902 Sir Frederick Cullinan was appointed chairman of a committee to enquire into the question of the 'employment of children during school age, especially in street trading' in the large centres of population in Ireland, and to report upon possible alterations in the law and other steps that might be desirable. The committee made many recommendations regarding the licensing of street trading and measures to improve school attendance, as well as emphasising the desirability of providing day 'industrial schools' in Dublin, Cork and Belfast for children, and the creation of a juvenile court to hear the cases of children brought up for breaches of the by-laws and other offences.[55]

Frederick attended the first dinner of members of the Alpine Club resident in Ireland, which was held at the University Club, Dublin, on 26 January 1906. In honour of the occasion the members of the Club had invited their fellow 'Alpinists' to meet the Right Hon James Bryce, ex-president of the Alpine Club and former Chief Secretary for Ireland. The following are recorded in the *Journal* as assembling to welcome Bryce to Ireland: H. de Fellenberg Montgomery[56] (senior member) in the chair; Sir F. J. Cullinan, CB, Hon. G Fitzgerald, Rev. W.S. Green, H.Warren, G.Scriven, R. M. Barrington, Rev P. S. Whelan, H. Synnott,[57] W. J. Kirkpatrick and G. B. Tunstall Moore.[58]

Cullinan retired on attaining the age of sixty-five in 1911. He was created CB (Companion of the most honourable order of Bath) in 1894, Knight Bachelor in 1897 and KCB (Knight Companion of the most honourable order of Bath) on his retirement. He died on 27 December 1913. At the time of his death he lived at 55 Fitzwilliam Square, Dublin. His old Alpine Club mate, Fitzgerald, reported: 'His end came somewhat suddenly; he had just finished building in North Wales a house where he hoped to spend parts of the years of his retirement, surrounded by his family, among the Welsh mountains he loved so well.'[59]

Charles Jasper Joly (1864–1906): Astronomer Royal

He was a true mountain lover and an active climber with a real knowledge of mountain craft. Gifted with a keen sense of humour and an imperturbable temper, as well as great physical endurance, Joly was an ideal companion on a mountain; and those of us who formed a small guideless party at Arrolla in 1896 will never forget the skills and judgement with which he led us in some difficult and anxious situations.

George Scriven, Obituary for Charles Jasper Joly, 1906

CHARLES JASPER Joly was a mathematician, astronomer and a competent rock climber and alpinist.[60] He was born at St Catherine's rectory, Tullamore, County Offaly (then King's County) on 27 June 1864. He was the eldest of the five children of John Swift Joly, rector, and Elizabeth Joly (née Slator), and second cousin to John Joly, a geologist and physicist who was the eminent Professor of Geology at Trinity College, Dublin from 1887 to 1933 (and who was himself a keen traveller, especially to the Alps).[61] Charles' father was involved with William Spotswood Green and D. J. Cunningham in the development of a scheme of marine research in order to improve Irish fisheries; in 1901 he became a commissioner of Irish Lights.[62]

Charles was first educated at Portarlington and then attended the Grammar School, Galway, for four years where he earned a reputation and won many prizes for his mathematical ability. He entered Trinity College, Dublin in 1882 on a mathematics scholarship and graduated with first place in the subject in 1886, with experimental physics as his second subject. He then moved to Berlin to work in Herman von Helmholtz's laboratory to follow his interest in experimental physics, but he was back in Ireland within the year following the death of his father. In the seven years that followed he attempted to win a competition for students studying both classics and mathematics, whose prize was a fellowship at Trinity College. His persistence in this regard was to be rewarded in 1894; meanwhile he worked as a tutor and published (at a request of the Trinity College board) a number of mathematical papers based on the study of the application of quaternions, also editing the works of Irish mathematician and astronomer William Rowan Hamilton, who had first described them.

His alpine climbing exploits appear to have started in Switzerland in 1892 when he climbed the Weissmies and crossed the Alphubeljoch. He continued there in 1893, when his routes included the Cols du Mount Rouge and de Seilon, Aiguille de la Za, Tour de Collon, Mount Collon, Dent Blanche, Col de Grande Cornier and Lo Besso. In 1894 he visited the French Dauphiné range first, and his list of routes includes ascents of the Grande Aiguille de la Bérarde, Pic Coolidge, Le Plaret and Pic du Tacul, and traverses of the Pointe du Vallon des Étages and Barre des Écrins (ninety-fourth ascent). In Chamonix he completed a traverse of the Grand Charmoz and in Switzerland he made another Irish ascent of the Eiger. These routes provided the basis for his successful application to join the Alpine Club in spring of 1895. His proposers were fellow Trinity College climbers George Scriven and William Spotswood Green and his candidature was passed by the committee on 19 February ; he was duly elected by members on 5 March 1895.[63]

Charles Jasper Joly, astronomer and mathematician. (Wilson, *Album of Spain*, Royal Irish Academy series 15)

In the year of his election he went to the Italian Dolomites, where he climbed Cimon della Palla, Pala di San Martino, Campanile, Cima di Val di Roda, Cima di Ball, Cima di Canali, Saas Maor and Cima della Madonna.[64] George Scriven remembered Joly as 'a singularly gentle, simple minded and lovable man . . . He was especially fond of rock climbing and among the Dolomites of San Martino and Cortina he spent some of his happiest mountain holidays.'[65]

He married Jessie Sophia, daughter of Robert Warren Meade of Dublin on 20 March 1897; they had three daughters. In the year of his marriage, upon the resignation of Arthur Rambaut, Charles was appointed by the Board of Trinity College to the joint position of Andrew's Professor of Astronomy and the Astronomer Royal for Ireland at Dunsink Observatory. His observational work at Dunsink was published in the ninth part of *Astronomical Observations and Researches made at Dunsink*.[66] He graduated with a doctorate in science in 1901. In 1902 he edited a new edition of Preston's *Theory of Light* and brought out the *Manual of Quaternions* for Hamilton's centenary in 1905. In 1904 his scientific labours were further recognised by the Royal Society, which conferred on him its Fellowship. In Dublin he was active in scientific life in his membership of the Royal Irish Academy, to which he was elected a member in 1895, becoming its secretary from 1902 to 1906. He was a trustee to the National Library of Ireland and a council member of the Royal Dublin Society.

Joly's principal contribution to astronomy was an expedition to Spain in 1900 to study a total eclipse of the sun, during which he secured some remarkable photographs of the corona – the immense streamers spreading out from the sun and visible only during the short periods that the sun's disc is hidden by the moon.[67] The results were published in the *Transactions of the Royal Irish Academy*.[68] At Dunsink he supervised observational work that concentrated mainly on providing accurate star positions for stars that are only faintly visible in the band of stars over which the planets and minor planets pass; this was for what was known as the 'zodiacal catalogue', a work commenced by his predecessor. The first mechanical calculating machine at Dunsink was acquired in his time.

In 1905 Joly took part in the British Association visit to South Africa. Shortly after his return from this trip he and his daughter contracted typhoid. It is thought this was due to polluted water from the well at Dunsink.[69] He died of pleurisy that followed on from the typhoid on 4 January 1906, aged forty-one years; his daughter Jessie, who had contracted the fever before her father, survived.[70] He is buried at Mount Jerome Cemetery, Harold's Cross, on the south side of Dublin.

Away from his professional life, Joly had cultivated an extensive knowledge of literature (especially Italian literature) but climbing was his passion and he spent every holiday in the Alps. Despite a delicate appearance, it seems that he possessed endurance, courage and a keen sense of humour. In his obituary tribute, Scriven concluded: 'Of an extremely modest and retiring nature, Charles Joly was not perhaps known to a wide circle in the Alpine Club, but by his friends, both within and outside the climbing fraternity, his loss will be deeply felt and sincerely mourned.'

Thomas Henry Carson (1843–1917): 'legal eagle'

I sometimes think we do not sufficiently realise the solid happiness which the love of mountains and the exhilaration born of mountaineering bring into the life of the professional man, 'halving the sorrows and doubling the joys' of everyone who has once become devoted to them.

'In Memoriam for T. H. Carson', C. Comyns Tucker[71]

Thomas Henry Carson was born on 24 November in 1843. He was the son of Rev. Joseph Carson DD, Vice-Provost of Trinity College, Dublin, who was himself an early traveller in the Alps, having crossed the Théodule Pass in 1845 and the Weisstor Pass in 1850. His mother, Harriet, was the daughter of William Pitt Blunden of Wellington, Kilkenny. He was educated at Marlborough College Wiltshire, under the tutelage of Dr George Granville Bradley, during what was considered to be that English public school's most brilliant period. Among his fellow pupils there was Charles Comyns Tucker, one of the great English alpine pioneers, who went on to make many important first ascents in the Italian Dolomites and in the Caucasus, often climbing with Douglas Freshfield who later became a distinguished editor of *The Alpine Journal*.

Young Thomas Carson's first acquaintance with the Alps came in 1863 under the auspices of Marlborough's inspirational head teacher, Bradley. The school group (which included Tucker, also on his first Alpine season) started at Leukerbad in Switzerland, from where they crossed the Gemmi Pass, followed by an ascent of the Torrenthorn and excursions from Chamonix to the Jardin at Montanvert and to the Grands Mulets. They then completed a low-level circuit around Mont Blanc from Chamonix to Courmayeur, crossing mainly low passes. The educational tour closed with the crossing of the Little St Bernard Pass and a disquisition on 'Hannibal's Pass', the conclusions of which may not be agreed upon by modern historians.[72]

Carson returned to Dublin to complete his education at Trinity College, Dublin, where he simply excelled; he was elected a Scholar in 1863, which was followed by the Wray prize for Metaphysics in 1865; he graduated with a BA in 1866, achieving gold medals in both classics, and ethics and logic. Carson repeatedly returned to the Alps during the following ten to twelve years; Tucker was in his company, either alone or with others, for six of those seasons. In 1864 they climbed the Strahleck and Monte Rosa and crossed the Weisstor and the Col de Valpelline. The following year Tucker and he climbed the Dent de Morcles and, while crossing the Zocca Pass without the aid of guides or a rope, they experienced a few anxious moments. Tucker, told the story in Carson's obituary:

> In the earlier years of our wanderings we doubtless, like others before and since, exposed ourselves pretty freely to the risks run by imperfectly trained amateurs when not under the supervision of a professional guide. I recall one such experience which may serve as a specimen. Arriving alone on the summit of Zocca (usually I believe, a simple passage enough) we found the glacier on the N. Side cut off, along its whole width, from the lowers slopes by a formidable bergschrund – nowhere, so far as we could see, choked or spanned by any sufficient bridge of ice or snow. The obstacle was a sufficiently serious one for a couple of comparative 'tiros' but it was, after severe searching of the heart, negotiated . . . by a wild leap onto the lower lip of the chasm. The drop I calculated at from 12 to 14 feet, and I remember that we went very quietly for the rest of the afternoon.

They finished the season by completing a tour of Bernina, including the first passage of the Fuorcla Cambrena (Cambrena Sattel), the second passage of the Passo di Gambre, the Fellaria and the Roseg Glaciers. They also crossed the Sella Pass.

In 1867 Carson was in the company of Douglas Freshfield, a friend of Tucker's, who he accompanied during many other seasons. Freshfield had been born into a wealthy household, had a passion for mountains and classical civilisation.[73] He was the son of the solicitor to the Bank of England, educated at Eton and Oxford, and his family usually spent their holidays in the Alps. He climbed Mont Blanc while still a schoolboy and during the 1860s and 1870s made about twenty first ascents, mainly in the Dolomites. With Carson they all but completed an ascent of the Dent Blanche under difficult weather conditions. They made the

Thomas Harry Carson.
(*The Alpine Journal*)

first ascent of the Tour du Grand St Pierre, the first passage of the Col du Grand Etret and the first ascent of La Tour Ronde and its pass. Within the next six days they crossed Col de Miage, Col Ferret, Col d'Argentière, the Buet and Col de Tanneverge, Lysjoch with direct descent to Alagna, Mischabeljoch and Weisstor.

In 1869 Carson was called to the bar in London. While he completed his legal studies in the chambers of Mr Justice Joseph Chitty, he came to prominence for his great learning and courage as an advocate against the heaviest odds and with a singular intellectual honesty that procured for him the respect and confidence of every judge before whom he practised.[74] He contributed many papers to legal literature, notably the *Real Property Statutes* of Shelford, for many years the accepted book of reference for property conveyancing, which appeared in many successive editions. He was appointed King's Counsel in 1901 and was elected a bencher of Lincoln's Inn six years later. Carson married twice: his first marriage in 1876, when he was thirty-three, was to Mary Sophia, a sister of his friend and schoolmate Charles Tucker; his second marriage took place in 1887 to Mary Louise Emma, daughter of Albert Bernouilli Barlow.

Carson was with Freshfield and his favourite guide, François Joseph Devouassoud, again in 1869 when they ascended Uri Rotstock, the Streckhorn, Monte Rosa, and Ruitor. He was back the following season with Tucker when they climbed Monte Cristello and Monte Antelao, again with the guide Devouassoud. Their tour was interrupted by the outbreak of the Franco-Prussian War. Tucker and Carson were next in the Alps together in 1872 to climb the Grossglockner, Grossvenediger and Marmolata and then made the first ascent of the Kassel Kogel, which is the second peak of the Rosengartenspitze. Tucker had no record of Carson climbing in 1866, 1868, 1871 or 1873.

However, in 1874 he was back with Devouassoud and Tucker when they ascended the Galenstock and Basodine, and then made the first ascent of Monte Gleno in the Bergamese Alps, before moving on to climb Monte del Castello and make the first ascent of Federer Kogel, later known as the main peak of Rosengartenspitze. Devouassoud regarded this route as one of the most difficult rock climbs he had ever accomplished.[75] Tucker explained Carson's approach to alpinism:

> He was one of those climbers who assiduously and successfully explored the Alpine chain from Monte Viso to the Gross Glockner. It was at a time when mountaineering was still regarded as a legitimate form of travel from place to place when a mountain tour was a real perambulation over wide spaces and not merely the prolonged study of a limited locality, still less the scaling for its own sake of the 'overhangs' of some particular formidable summit, when, in a word, passes predominated over peaks as daily food. Notwithstanding this, a fair share of peaks fell to Carson during these years. He was an untiring and indefatigable pedestrian, a sound climber, with an infinite capacity for taking pains, eminently safe on rock or ice, and at either end of the rope, neither can I at this moment recall, during all the years I climbed with him, a single serious slip on his part – a record of steadiness which could be matched I imagine, by few of our most accomplished gymnasts. To his perseverance and thoroughness in dealing with loose rocks (at times a trial to the patience of less careful companions), discreet witness is borne in the account of the descent of Monte Gleno in Freshfield's 'Italian Alps'. It was characteristic of Carson's temperament, both as a climber and a lawyer, to leave no doubtful points unexamined.[76]

Freshfield, a friend of Tennyson's, wrote about the many new routes he had made in the Brenta Dolomites with both Carson and Tucker. He elaborated on the descent of Mount Gleno in the Bergamasque Alps and remarked on Carson's character thus:

> Had it not been for the course of action pursued by one of my companions we might perhaps have gone down in shorter time. Having some old grudge, as what Alpine clubman has not, against a loose stone, he had this year constituted himself the foe of the race, and the chief adjutant of time in his attack on the mountains. Did an unlucky rock show the smallest tendency to looseness, down it went. Resistance was useless, for my friend's perseverance and patience are proverbial; the rock might retain roots which would have held it for a century, but an ice-axe will serve also as a crowbar, and sooner or later down it went.[77]

For how many years Carson returned to the Alps we cannot be sure, however, in the only written piece he ever contributed to *The Alpine Journal* (a tribute in 1917 to his late guide François Devouassoud), he tells us in his own words that in 1883 François had accompanied H. A. Beachcroft and himself in Piedmont during a month of wonderful weather, during which they were fortunate to make an ascent of Monte Viso and the Ciamarella under the most perfect conditions. He recounted delightful memories of climbs they made in the Pralognan district of Savoy and among the high peaks of Val Maggia, and told of a particular night they were benighted in the Primiero Dolomites on a shelf of rock high up in the wild Val Pravitale. He warmly remembered 'the sight of Francois tending the small fire which we had succeeded in lighting at our bivouac, while a brilliant moon lit up the huge boulders round us and the lofty cliffs which shut up the valley.'[78] Remarkably, his own obituary appears in the same edition of the *Journal*, warmly written by Tucker his schoolmate, climbing partner and brother-in-law.

Carson's professional life was always busy; in later years he became a member of the governing council of Marlborough and also took an active interest in running of a school mission at Tottenham.[79] But he continued to visit mountains for relief and recreation, sometimes accompanied by his son who was serving in the army at the time of his father's death in 1917. Tucker observed in his obituary, 'I sometimes think we do not sufficiently realise the solid happiness which love of mountains and the exhilaration born of mountaineering bring into life of the professional man halving the sorrows and doubling the joys of everyone who has become devoted to them. The love of – nay the passion for – the mountains belonged to Carson always and in full measure, and the inner light which it brought into his life never became dimmed, and remained with him to the end.'

George Scriven (1856–1931): green jersey and ice axe

Still at the height of his playing career he was not only elected president of the union, but was also appointed captain of the Irish team for the season. As the union committee still picked the team on a system of ballot, Scriven had the unique distinction of being president of the union, captain of the Irish team and chairman of the selectors in the same season.

Edmund Van Esbeck, *One Hundred Years of Irish Rugby*

GEORGE SCRIVEN was a wonderful rock climber and alpinist who divided his loyalty for rock and ice with the exertions of the scrum and excitement of playing rugby for Leinster and Ireland. He was born in Dublin on 9 November 1856. The name Scriven is English, of Norman origin, and derived from *escriven* or writer; it is found in Dublin in the late seventeen century, but is mainly associated with County Cork.[80] His father was William Barclay Broome Scriven, a physician from Hampton Hall, Balbriggan in North County Dublin and his mother, Sarah, was a daughter of Henry Hamilton of Tullylish, County Down.

George, a prominent Freemason,[81] was educated at Repton School in Derbyshire and at Trinity College, Dublin, where he was president of the University Rugby Club from 1897 until 1920.[82] He graduated with a BA in 1879 and qualified in midwifery at the Rotunda Lying-in Hospital, Dublin, then as Bachelor of Medicine in 1880. He further qualified as Bachelor of Surgery in 1881 and Doctor of Medicine in 1884. Scriven spent some time as a surgeon in the London Homeopathic Hospital before establishing a practice as a physician in Dublin. His wide range and depth of scientific interests are demonstrated by his election as a fellow of the Royal Geographical Society and his membership of the Council of the Royal Zoological Society of Ireland and the Royal Dublin Society. He spent many seasons climbing in the Alps particularly in the Dolomites, with climbs recorded from 1877 to 1895.

Scriven clearly also had an abiding interest in the emerging sport of rugby football when he made his application to join the Alpine Club in 1878. He played rugby at club level for Trinity College and Lansdowne Rugby Club, where he was captain during the 1878–79 season. On 1 November 1879, as a representative of Dublin University Club, he was elected to the board of the Irish Rugby Football Union at its inaugural meeting. He had already played at interprovincial level for the winning Leinster team in its very first fixture with its (now) arch rival, Munster, at College Green on 26 March 1877.

Remarkably, that was also his first season in the Alps, where he climbed with Martin Conway, who was to become one of the most widely travelled climbers of the period. Scriven played seven times for Leinster against Ulster and Munster,[83] and was also honoured with eight international caps for Ireland in the seasons 1879 to 1883, when he played in matches against both England and Scotland. Edmund Van Esbeck writes of his appointment as president of the IRFU on 20 January 1883: 'Still at the height of his playing career he was not only elected president of the union, but was also appointed captain of the Irish team for the season. As the union committee still picked the team on a system of ballot, Scriven had the unique distinction of being president of the union, captain of the Irish team and chairman of the selectors in the same season.'[84]

Incredibly, Scriven exceeded that achievement while still captain of Ireland; he was asked to referee the international match between England and Scotland at Blackheath in 1884. The match ended in a disagreement regarding the interpretation of the rules, which led to a disputed try for England. As a result of the row that followed Scotland did not meet England in the 1884–5 season. To resolve such future rule disputes the IRFU, with Scriven as its president, proposed the establishment of an international board, which formally came into being on 6 February 1886 at a conference in Dublin.[85] It was during this, his second presidency, that the design for the crest on the Irish team jerseys was changed to the iconic shamrock pattern that Irish teams have worn since. On the negative side, the record also shows that Scriven was never on a winning team, as Ireland lost all of the matches in which he played. Despite this, he was twice elected president of the Irish Rugby Football Union.

His climbing record was much more successful. His first routes are recorded on his Alpine Club proposal form.[86] His address (given as 3 St Stephens Green, Dublin) was the Dublin Homeopathic Hospital where he was a resident. He was proposed by W. M. Conway, a major figure in British climbing, and seconded by W. Penhall both of whom he had climbed with in the previous two years. His qualification list commences with the Monte Rosa where he combined both the Nordend and Höchste Spitze (now Doufourspitze) summits with Penhall. He climbed most of that season with Martin Conway, ascending a fine combination of peaks and passes: Rimpfischhorn, Zinal Rothorn, Matterhorn, Strahlhorn, Brunegghorn, Flujoch, Brünig Joch, Biesjoch, Old Weissthor and the Triftjoch. He was elected to the Club on 19 December 1878. Conway later wrote of that 1877 season:'. . . accompanied my old school fellow George Scriven, the best climbing companion man ever had, I made my way to Zermatt for the season of 1877, and was destined to here spend five out of the six following seasons.'[87] In 1881 he was back climbing with Conway and a Miss Parker, in company with the guides Franz and Adolp Andermatten; together they made an ascent of the Ober Gablehorn (3,910m).

George Scriven.
(Courtesy Rugby History Society Website)

In 1888 he climbed in the Dolomites with H. H.West, ascending Cima della Rosetta, Cima di Vezzana, Cima di Ball, Monte Colbricon, Pala di San Martino, the Tognazza and Monte Pavione, as well as making the third ascent of both Saas Maor and Cima della Madonna, which they climbed in the same day. In 1889 he read a paper to the Alpine Club to promote climbing in the Dolomites of San Martino di Castrozza, in which he explains how the name 'Dolomite' came to be conferred on the South Tyrol range, which abounds with magnesian limestone identified by the French geologist Marquis de Dolonieu.[88] He described Cima di Ball ('named after our countryman whose guide-books have done so much to open up unfrequented districts' and whose first ascent 'was made by Mr Leslie Stephen quite alone'): 'The rocks of the Cima di Ball are like most of the rocks in this district, very firm, and afford excellent hand and foot hold, by reason of the numberless little cavities which permeate the dolomite.'

He described his ascent of Pala di San Martino with West and Michele Bettega, the only guide in the valley. He had been surprised to find that their mountain guide was also the polite person (resembling 'a stage brigand') who had carried their luggage into the hotel. It transpired that Bettega was the hotel's equivalent of 'boy about the place' and, when needs must, also the carpenter or mason; on Sunday he officiated as churchwarden at the little chapel. Leaving at 5.15 a.m. they had made their way through steep slopes of alder shrub and loose rocks to cross torrents, more steep rocks and grass, arriving at the snowline before 8 a.m. Soon steps had to be cut to reach the point at which the rock of the north face of the Pala di San Martino came into view. Bettega put on his local roughly made crampons (*ferri*) and trudged to the foot of the rocks, while Scriven and West bemoaned the absence of cut steps as they scrambled up behind him; they left behind two axes at that point, bringing just one with them.

At the highest point of the snow Bettega gathered all the rope and swarmed up steep ice-glazed rocks to disappear above their heads. Next came the cry 'Sicuro' and down came the end of the rope. West tied on and soon joined the guide above; he untied and down came the rope for Scriven. Arriving at the top, he found them both in a hole in the face of a cliff just large enough for two men 'sitting with a crouched attitude'. The hole 'afforded an excellent anchorage between the two most difficult bits on the mountain.' Bettega gave instructions to his clients before he headed around the face of rock on a very narrow ledge. Soon he shouted 'Sicuro' again, and Scriven then wedged himself into the hole and took a tight hold of the rope. West, unattached now, used the rope held tight between Scriven and the guide as a handrail to traverse the face of the cliff to where the guide was seemingly secure. Scriven followed on the other end of the rope. 'There is not much to recommend this mode of progression, except that time is saved by not reroping the party before this point', he declared. Thankfully, they then all re-roped and followed the route across the face, crossing a deep, ice-filled gully. They were now able to make more distinctly upward progress, and soon the rocks became less steep and yielded more convenient ledges and steps, which they could quickly scramble up to reach a snow arête. After two and a half hours of good rock work, they reached the summit. Through the mist they caught glimpses of Cima di Canali before returning the way they had come.

In a practical contribution to mountain medicine, Scriven also read a paper to the Club entitled 'Prevention of snow burning and blistering', and produced a short article for the *Alpine Journal* urging the use of lanolin ointment as a protective ointment before going out on snow-covered mountains.[89]

In 1889, again with H. H. West, he climbed Rosengartenspitze, Grohmannspitze, Marmolata, Cima di Canali and Fradusta, Sasso di Mur, made the second ascent of the northwest slope of Cimon della Pala, Pala di San Marino, Adamello, Presanella, Cima Tosa, Brenta Alta, Cima di Brenta, Brenta Bassa, Torre di Brenta and Monte Gazza. An account of their second ascent of Cimon della Pala (3,185m) in July of that year was related in *The Alpine Journal*.[90] It appears the first ascent of this route had been made a few days earlier by Dr Ludwig Darmstädter's party, and that Scriven, West and a Mr A. C. O'Sullivan, with the guides M. Bettega and G. Zecchini of Primiero, attempted to follow Darmstädter's instructions. They left San Martino at 2.15 a.m. but strayed badly off route and had an epic ascent up the east face over steep, rotten, eroding rock, to reach the summit at 9.15 a.m. Trying to descend by Darmstädter's route, they had an equally torrid time climbing down a 120-foot (37m) high steep wall. The climbers were lowered, one at a time, with each descent taking seven minutes; Bettega, who followed last, was forced to remove his boots to negotiate safely the last 10m without slipping.

In 1891 and 1893 they were again in the Dolomites with routes on the Geislerspitze, Croda da Lago, Antelao, Tofana and Cima di Focobon, where he made a second ascent with a route variation. Scriven returned in 1895 with Mr and Mrs P. S. Whelan to climb again in the South Tyrol, ascending Campanile, Cima di Val di Roda, Cima di Ball, Cimon della Pala, Saas Maor, Cima della Madonna and Cima di Canali. Whelan appears to have been an Irish clergyman and a member of the Alpine Club, as he attended a dinner for Irish Alpine Club members in 1906 in Dublin.

On 15 December 1900 George Scriven married Violet Fetherston and, for a time, the family lived in London while he worked in the Homeopathic Hospital. Hampton Hall, their home, was sold in 1928 and became the venue in the same year for the Irish Hitler Youth summer camps. George died on 18 December 1931 at Brown Gables, Lower Bourne, Farnham, Surrey.

Henry Tudor Parnell (1850–1915): enigmatic absentee landlord

A younger brother of Mr Parnell, who bears a close resemblance to his illustrious relative, and who also, I believe, lives in Brighton, is a strong conservative; and has his troubles with his tenants.

T. P. O'Connor, *Charles Stewart Parnell: A Memory*

HENRY TUDOR PARNELL, the youngest brother of Charles Stewart Parnell, the foremost Irish political leader of the late nineteenth century, spent many seasons climbing in the Alps and reached such a level of competence that he engaged in winter alpinism and applied for membership of the Alpine Club. He appears not to have shared his brother's political views or the ambitious goal of Charles' Land League to reduce the power of landlords to treat their tenants unfairly and to evict them in times of hardship. In fact Henry was himself an absentee landlord who sharply managed his own estates in Carlow and Kilkenny through an agent, something which often caused electoral trouble for his prominently reforming brother. Membership of the Alpine Club, which he sought unsuccessfully in 1878, would have brought him into social contact with W. E. Forster, Chief Secretary for Ireland, an esteemed member of the Alpine Club and a close personal friend of John Ball. Forster was, for a time, one of his brother's main political adversaries.

Henry was one of the eleven children of John Henry Parnell and Delia Tudor Parnell who lived at Avondale House and estate at Rathdrum, County Wicklow. His father, like his father before him, was a well-respected and improving landlord among the Protestant Anglo-Irish ascendency. Henry himself was born in Paris in 1850 where his American mother (who never fully integrated into the Protestant Wicklow ascendency society) would later reside most of the year, away from her husband.

When their father died suddenly in 1859, Charles (then about thirteen years old) was left the Wicklow estate at Avondale, John (the eldest living son) was left the family-managed estate at Collure in County Armagh, and Henry (then aged eight) was left property at Clonmore in County Carlow, which his father appears to have acquired shortly before his death in order to provide an inheritance for his youngest son.[91] The extent of the Clonmore estate according to the 1911 Ordnance Survey map was about 22 square miles or 13,000 acres.[92] Since all three estates were highly encumbered, the three boys (who were wards of court pending their coming of ages) appear to have begun life rather deeply in debt.

Avondale was rented to a railway engineer and the family moved first to a house named Khyber Pass at Dalkey (about 8 miles from Dublin) for a year or so, where the older boys swam at the gentlemen's bathing place on the West Pier at Kingstown (Dún Laoghaire). The family thereafter seemed to be always on the move. They moved to Kingstown and later to 14 Upper Temple Street, Dublin, where the children had tutors and the older ones went to various schools and colleges. It appears none of boys attended Eton, where both their father and grandfather had previously been pupils. It seems instead that their education consisted of an unstructured mixture of private tuition, small private schools, Parisian tutors and pre-university crammers.

Henry was a teenager in 1867 when he attended the celebration of the coming of age of his brother Charles Stewart Parnell at Avondale. The main event was a three-day cricket match featuring the Wicklow eleven against the Dublin officers' garrison team. The match was organised by Charles, and Arthur Dickenson (Charles' future brother-in-law) was reported to have described it as 'a scene of fun and flirtation which surpassed description and which was probably never before been equalled on the old haunts of Avondale. In every shady nook and corner were to be seen an isolated couple engaged in the pleasant pastime of love-making'.[93] By the second day the partying had clearly affected the concentration of the cricketers because the players openly 'preferred to dally in the woods with the ladies of the party'. Charles (up until then still a ward of court) now took charge of the affairs of his inheritance – Avondale House and estate.

There appears to have been a close bond between the older Parnell children (Emily, John, Charles, Fanny and Anna) that did not extend to the younger ones (Sophia, Theodosia, or the youngest son, Henry). Indeed Henry is a something of a mystery figure, rarely mentioned in any of his brothers' and sisters' memoirs. R. F. Foster observes: 'They all married young, were more self-effacing and conventional and all except Sophia chose to live outside Ireland.'[94]

Charles Stewart Parnell, although a Protestant landlord, was elected MP for Meath in April 1875 on a platform of land reform and home rule for Ireland and soon became the political leader of the Irish Party. He formed an alliance with Michael Davitt leader of the Land League in order to reform the Land Acts based on the League's demands regarding the three Fs – fixity of tenure, fair rent and free sale. However, Henry's own behaviour as a landlord and his absenteeism from Ireland suggests he was not aligned with or sensitive to his brother's views. Some members of the Parnell family led quite isolated lives and met infrequently and there is much evidence of the independence of each in their political views.

Regarding Henry, his sister Emily claimed that by 1874 he was married and turned to housekeeping and superintending babies, which he varied by mountain climbing.[95] A contemporary account by T. P. O'Connor MP asserts 'that a younger brother of Mr Parnell, who bears a close resemblance to his illustrious relative, and who also, I believe, lives in Brighton, is a strong conservative; and has his troubles with his tenants.'[96] Another source claimed Henry was educated to the bar and was 'owner of landed property in the county Kilkenny. He mostly lives in England.'[97]

Henry, when he came of age, did not take long to sell off much of the Clonmore estate lands. He had his land affairs settled by 1875, the same year he was admitted to the bar at Lincoln's Inn. He never practised as a barrister although he gave it as his profession on legal documents, including his application to join the Alpine Club. His brother John wrote in his memoirs that Henry 'went through Cambridge, but was too nervous to pass his examination for a degree. He was a barrister who did not practice.'[98]

With the proceeds from his Clonmore estate sales, he bought a 600-hundred acre farm in County Kilkenny, while retaining 300 acres in Clonmore. He used the assets of these lands to raise money in 1884 and 1891, putting part of the Kilkenny estate in the trusteeship of his mother-in-law and his brother-in-law, the solicitor Alfred McDermott, as security for £6,000, which was advanced to him when he married. As an absentee landlord he seems to have managed his lands through a middleman or agent. The harsh reputation that he gained as a result certainly tarnished his brother's credibility, both in the Dublin election of 1875 when the Conservatives circulated a broadsheet advertising 'Mr Parnell's many disputes with his tenants at Tombay' (a townland in the Clonmore estate), and in an anonymous letter to the *Irish Times* in 1880, which accused Parnell of being party to the Clonmore land speculations. In 1885 a correspondent of Michael Davitt's complained that Parnell was not condemned as roundly as other landlords, and added 'I have heard it said that his brother is as bad a landlord as any other.'[99]

Family records indicate he spent much of his time travelling because of his delicate health.[100] However, nowhere in any previous history of the Parnell family is there a mention of his serious mountaineering or Alpine activity. Yet on 5 May 1878 he was proposed for membership of the exclusive Alpine Club with quite a respectable qualifying list of ascents, including Piz Bernina and Piz Palü in the Bernina Alps, the Jungfrau in the Bernese Oberland, and Monte Rosa, Breithorn, Weisstor and the Alphubal in the Pennine range.[101] The wide range of peaks in different districts suggests he had spent a number of seasons in the Alps.

Henry may also have been the 'Mr Purnell' who is recorded as one of the early clients of the great Saas Fee mountain guide, Alexander Burgener. An *Alpine Journal* article in 1951 reported that, because Alexander lost his first *Führerbuch*, Martin Conway wrote a testimonial in the front of the highly rated guide's second book, which listed (from Burgener's memory) all of his principal routes and clients.[102] For ascents of the Aiguille Impériale, Aiguille Rouge and the Aiguille Floria by a new route during the 1876 season he names among his clients a 'Mr Purnell'. T. S. Blakeney, the author of the Alpine Club article, suggests that the unknown Mr Purnell may have been the Mr Parnell who was known to have frequented the Alps during that period.

The Alpine Journal does, however, confirm Henry's identity when the Rev. Cecil E. B. Watson, in August 1878, reported the presence of a brother of the Irish member Charles Steward Parnell on Piz Bernina as follows:

On February 4 the ascent of Piz Bernina was successfully made and I am told the first ascent in winter, I send a brief record of the facts. Mr H Parnell, brother of the Irish member, was author of the expedition, and took as guides A Colani and Christian Grass, son of the older guide of that name. As Hans Grass was away, I secured the services of Old Christian Grass and Valentine Kessler; and Hans, son of old Christian Grass, and V Kessler, who had been engaged as porters to the Boval Hut, went at the request of the guides with us, on a separate rope, only stopping short of the arête.

Starting at 1.55 am from the hut, we ascended the W side of the great Morteratsch ice-fall, and emerged from it about 8am. Mr Parnell, who had had a cold on him for some time, was unfortunately here overtaken with sickness, and was obliged to abandon all idea of the arête. This I reached with my guides about 11.15 am and after ½ hr. halt, we gained the summit at 3.20 pm.

Returning by the Bellavista route, and profiting by the steps of Mr Parnell's guides, who had decided to go back that way, we reached the plateau about 5.30 pm, just when it was beginning to get dusk; and keeping along Mr Parnell's tracks, which young Christian Grass with praiseworthy forethought chipped in the spots where the snow frozen, we reached Festung about 10 pm. Mr Parnell it seems had had considerable difficulty in getting down the first part of the Festung in the dark, for his lantern was broken and there was no moon, and we found him waiting there behind a low wall his guides had built, thinking it safer to wait for day light. Old Christian, however after the side of the second lantern had been made good with paper, pioneered a way with two porters and then we started down, to make a long story short, returned by Isola Pers, eventually reached the Boval hut at 4.45 am on February 5th.[103]

Henry's application to join the Alpine Club was proposed by G. O. Spenser and seconded by C. M. Handfield-Jones. He gave his address and profession as H. T. Parnell, 43 Fitzwilliam Square, Dublin – Barrister. Although his membership was passed by those attending the meeting on 5 May 1878, his proposal was rejected at the following meeting on 4 June. This was not unusual, as the members of the Alpine Club quite often turned down applications to its ranks. A number of high profile and competent mountaineers were turned down for membership around that time, including W. M. Baker, who was rejected in 1878 and had a fine alpine record, and W. W. Graham in 1882, who had made the first ascent of the Aiguille du Géant and whose lists of climbs was a distinguished one. Graham would later achieve fame in the Himalaya; his Alpine Club application had been rejected by a large majority due to personal animosity.

The specific reason why Henry Tudor Parnell, brother of Charles Stewart, was turned down by the board of the Club is not recorded. However, it is easy to imagine that the brother of a politician campaigning for reform of the Land Acts might not be welcome among the ranks of the Club members of that time, since most were wealthy representatives of the landowning classes. Henry's attendance at Cambridge and his legal profession should, however, have acted in his favour, as many members of the Club were barristers and Oxford and Cambridge graduates. The same members also rejected the great Alfred Mummery on his first application to join (because he was a 'mere' tanning merchant), and twenty years later they would blackball Captain Valentine Ryan of Tipperary, who had ascended more new routes than any Irishman before or since. As we will see in a later chapter, Valentine was rejected because it was reported that he was rude to some Club members in a mountain hut.

It is hard to imagine the same members, steeped in the English establishment, admitting the

The only known picture of Henry Tudor Parnell, taken the day after Charles was interred: (l–r) their sister Emily Dickenson, Henry (centre) and one of Charles' nieces, Alfreda or Delia McDermott. (UCC Multitext Project in Irish History)

brother of Charles Stewart Parnell, an advocate for the dissolution of the Union between Ireland and the rest of Britain and a politician publically perceived to be closely associated with land agitation extremists. This would have been particularly so in 1878 when Charles, as leader of the Home Rule Party at Westminster, was successfully orchestrating obstructionist tactics in the House of Commons that made the passing of laws and the operation of parliament tedious and unworkable. His strategy of speaking endlessly and making spurious amendments on minor sections of every bill under consideration clearly enraged the privileged classes who largely supported either the Liberals or the Conservatives in Parliament. The membership of the Alpine Club would almost to a man have opposed anyone linked to such 'enemies of civilisation'.[104]

Henry Parnell married Penelope Jane Luby on 21 October 1882; the wedding was not mentioned in the Dublin papers, although the bride's father (who had died in 1870) had been a well-known Fellow of Trinity College, Dublin. The service probably took place in London; Penelope's address, as well as her mother's, was given as Grosvenor Hotel, Buckingham Palace Road. Penelope was a cousin of a well-known Fenian named T. C. Luby, although there is no evidence that Penelope herself had Fenian sympathies. The couple had three children. Little is known about Henry's final years, except that the family lived on the south coast of England. When Charles Stewart was looking to rent a discreet retreat in Eastbourne the early 1880s, he discovered to his surprise that Henry was living in the same town.[105] In 1884 Henry was living at Folkstone and in 1891 at Ramsgate.

He is largely absent from the public and private memoirs of his famous brother's life; he did, however, turn up to defend his brother's good name in 1905, when his sister Emily (Dickenson) claimed in her memoirs that Charles (while at Cambridge) had seduced a local farmer's daughter and abandoned her.[106] Henry went to some trouble to discredit his sister's story when her book appeared. He wrote to the master of Magdalene College receiving corroboration that no such incident had ever been heard of, and wrote to the newspapers denying that there was any veracity in the tale.

His last recorded mention in the many accounts of his family's story occurred when he was observed standing in the crowd at Dublin's City Hall during the lying in state of Parnell's body on 11 October 1891; Katherine Tynan recounted afterwards that she had been 'shocked to come face to face with Mr Henry Parnell who bore a striking resemblance to his brother'.[107] Henry's shadowy appearance as the public filed past, paying their respects to his idolised brother's coffin, is consistent with his largely unrecorded and very private life. A photograph taken at Charles' grave on the day after his burial at Dublin's Glasnevin Cemetery provides the only image of Henry found by the author. He is pictured in a family group with his sister, Mrs Emily Dickenson, and a niece 'Delia' or Alfreda McDermott. Henry died on 24 November 1915, at the age of 64.[108]

Rt. Hon. Viscount James Bryce (1838–1922): Biblical mountain explorer

He took his peaks as they came – they were like fences in a day's hunting.

Douglas Freshfield, Obituary for James Bryce, *Alpine Journal*, 1922

FOLLOWING IN THE FOOTSTEPS of John Ball, another Irishman, James Bryce, became president of the Alpine Club in 1899; in many respects he was an extraordinarily capable man. He was energetic and multi-skilled as a jurist, historian, politician and diplomat, and served for a short time as Chief Secretary for Ireland in 1906. He was not a dedicated alpinist, rather he was a much-travelled man who liked to walk and climb when motivated by historical or geological enquiry. Significantly, he was the first politician to attempt to introduce mountain access legislation for Scotland as early as 1894.

Born in Arthur Street, Belfast, on 10 May 1838, Bryce was descended from frugal Scottish stock that valued independent thinking, determination and a good education. James' father had a life-long interest in natural history and the results of his research into the fossils of the Lisa, greensand, and chalk beds of Antrim were published in the *Philosophical Magazine* from 1831 onwards. His major papers included investigations and descriptions of the Giant's Causeway and studies on the Jurassic rocks of the islands of Skye and Raasay. He received an honorary LLD from Glasgow University in 1858 in recognition of his pioneering work in urging the reform of the constitution of Scottish universities and for campaigning to make the Scottish education system independent of London. At the age of seventy he was killed instantly by stone fall while examining a granite outcrop at the Pass of Inverfarigaig on the shores of Loch Ness; it is presumed he disturbed loose rock searching for fossils or rock specimens, precipitating the rockfall.

The young James spent his first eight years in Ireland at his grandfather's Whiteabbey residence on the shores of Belfast Lough, after which he followed his father to Glasgow on his appointment as rector of the High School there. From his earliest years young James was encouraged to take an interest in geography, botany and geology, which was discussed on every country walk and ramble as well as at home. His mother was well read and was a powerful conversationalist who possessed a clear and forceful mind, combined with fun, liveliness and quick gifts of repartee. James took a delight in swimming, fishing, walking and climbing and shared in his parents' absorption in Celtic traditions. At the age of eleven Bryce, starting from Cushendall, climbed Trostan (550m) in County Antrim.[109] He described the event as the birth and growth of his lifelong 'passion for mountain climbing and exploring every new region where one happened to be', a natural consequence of the way in which he had been encouraged in geological and botanical interests from childhood.[110] He spent a year studying under his uncle, Dr Ruben John Bryce, at Belfast before entering the University of Glasgow in 1854. With a degree from Glasgow he gained a scholarship to Trinity College, Oxford, where he was very successful, taking the best first in the *literae humaniores* ('Greats') and first class in law and history in 1861. He also contributed at that time to a *Flora of the Island of Arran*, published by his father in 1859. He was active in many intellectual groups, including the Old Mortality Society which adopted advanced democratic radicalism, secularism and the cause of Italian unity. Indeed, he was close to volunteering to join Garibaldi in 1860, but decided to stay to complete his degree and compete for a fellowship at Oriel to which he was elected in 1862. At Oriel he won the Gaisford Prize for Greek prose and met Alfred Tennyson. He associated with a group who were mostly of Scottish or northern English origin and were considered enlightened radicals. He was remembered best at Oriel for his well-balanced skills, organisational ability and for his good humour, rather than any extraordinary work or originality of mind.

He journeyed to Switzerland and Germany in 1862 and spent a semester at Heidelberg University with visits to Salzburg, Venice and Munich. His close friend Albert Venn Dicey said of him: 'He stirs us all up, rushes around like a shepherd's dog, collects his friends, makes us meet, leads us into plans and adventures and keeps everything going.'[111] His history, *Holy Roman Empire*, was published in 1864 and this gave him a reputation as a historian. Bryce moved to London and studied for the bar at Lincoln's Inn, being called in 1867 and serving on the northern circuit for a few years. He was called back to Oxford as Regius Professor of Civil Law (1870–1893) and Professor of Jurisprudence at Owen's College, Manchester (1870–1875). He loved Italy and its history and visited Florence, Rome, Naples and Monte Casino.

During this period Bryce used the steamers and the railway system to gain access to the Alps, climbing the classics in Switzerland and Italy including the Streckhorn, Monte Rosa, Monte Pelmo and Marmolata. In 1866 Bryce persuaded another intellectual, Leslie Stephen (who, unlike Bryce, had no aptitude for travel apart from walking and climbing), to go with him to the Carpathians.[112] They climbed Csalhó in Romania. Stephen recorded their adventures in the first edition of his book, *The Playground of Europe,* where the range was condemned as only a loftier and wilder Jura.

Bryce's interest in the Icelandic sagas inspired an expedition across Iceland in 1872 with his Oxford university friends Aeneas Mackay and Sir Courtney Ilbert. He warned would-be travellers: 'In Switzerland and most mountain countries the difficulty is getting to the top of your peak. In Iceland it is to get to its bottom.'[113] The great mountains, he

Viscount James Bryce in 1902. (Charles Beresford/National Portrait Gallery, London)

explained, are very scattered and required long, tedious journeys. He wrote of the lack of roads and the necessity that every requisite for life be carried on horseback, including the horse fodder, because the area of high peaks on the island is like a desert – uninhabited, grassless, and waterless among the lava fields that surround the hills. They journeyed from the east coast at Seyðisfjörður; by Mývatn Lake to Akureyri on the north coast, across the central plateau just east of Langjökull to Hvítárvatn (White Lake) and by the geysers to Reykjavik. He commented: 'we managed to ascend several mountains, (including Mount Hekla 4,892 ft.) and found some interesting plants on their slopes and enjoyed some noble views from their summits. But as we encountered no more perils or obstacles in these ascents than one may find on Ben Nevis or the hills of Skye, I have not the face to write a description of any one of them.'[114]

He visited the Pyrenees in 1873 when he climbed Maladetta, Vignemale, Pic de Néthou and Canigou. While there he met and climbed with Count Henry Russell, with whom he made an unsuccessful attempt on Port d'Oo in bad winds. In 1876 he became the first European to climb Mount Ararat in Turkey, to which he travelled with Mackay. The route took them through St Petersburg and Moscow to 'Ninji' and from there by river steamboat down the Volga, past the towers and domes of Kazan to Saratov, where they took the railway that brought them through the dry, dusty, plains and beech forests of the steppe to the foot of the Caucasus, the line stopping at Vladikavkas, a trading centre and military fortress. 'An icy pinnacle soaring up into the air 14,000 feet above us seemed no further off than Pilatus looks from Luzern. It was Kazbek, the mountain where Prometheus hung in chains. Hither nymphs came to console him; over this desert to the north I wandered, driven by the gadfly of Hera.'[115]

From here they travelled by road to the southern capital of Tiflis (now Tbilisi), sharing a vehicle with two Russian ladies across the Dariel Pass, then descending by a series of long zigzags through open green pastures that were in stark contrast to the steppe. He noted that the populations in three of the towns they passed through seemed quite distinct: one Russian, one German and one Oriental. From there they set out for Yerevan ('Erivan'), the capital of Russian Armenia, en route to Mount Ararat where, according to Genesis (8:4), Noah's Ark rested in the seventh month on the seventeenth day of the month. Bryce described the scene:

> to see people sitting and sleeping on the flat roofs, or talking to one another in the gate through which a string of camels is passing, to visit mosques and minarets and bazaars, watch the beggars crawl into the ruined tomb of a Muslim saint, and ramble through a grove of cypresses strewn with nameless half fallen gravestones, to stand by the baker or the shoemaker as he plies his craft in his open stall, and listen to the stories told by the barber, even when he does not understand a word , with the sacred mountain of the Arc looking down upon all, this seems like a delightful dream from far-off years.[116]

On 7 September they travelled another 24 miles (38.6 km) to the frontier station of Aralyk on the right bank of the Araxes River, from where the twin peaks of the Ararats are accessible: the great Ararat, a huge broad-shouldered mass capped with a dome, is 17,000 feet (5,180m) high, while the lower is an elegant cone at 12,840 feet (3,914m). Remarkably the snowline here was at 14,000 feet (4,267m) due to the low rainfall and the isolated position of Ararat in the centre of the cauldron of hot air that continually rises up its sides, melting the snows which are deposited there. Due to this phenomenon the mountain top is usually clouded after early morning. Bryce observed the zone of climate and vegetation 'from the sweltering plain to the cap of dazzling silver suspended in the sky'. It was first climbed in 1829 by a Dr Parrot of Dorpat. At 8 a.m. on the morning of 11 September Bryce and Mackay set out from Aralyk to ascend the mountain in a party of nine persons, six soldiers of a Cossack detachment who had been provided by the local Russian commander and an interpreter. They were all on horseback and the climbers were armed with pistols and ice axes. When they reached the Well of Sardarbulakh, the only high permanent camping ground at 7,514 feet (2,290m), the difficulties began. The horses could go no further and the Cossacks proved unhelpful, and so the climbers secured help from some Kurds after slow and tedious bargaining. They started out as soon as the moon rose at 1 a.m., after a supper of boiled mutton and milk and a short sleep. Bryce wrote, 'The silence of the mountain was astonishing. No calling of torrents to one another, no rippling of rills or rustling of boughs, not even the noise of falling stone, only the whistling of the West wind, the home wind over the pass.'[117]

However, he found making progress with the Cossacks and Kurds difficult, as they insisted on stopping and smoking every ten minutes. They breakfasted at 12,000 feet (3,658m) and here Mackay, who was not fit, decided to quit. Bryce decided to go on: 'It was an odd position to be in: guides of two different races, unable to communicate either with us or with one another, guides who could not lead and would not follow, guides one half of whom were supposed to be there to save us from being robbed and murdered by the other half, but all of whom, I am bound to say, looked for the moment equally simple and friendly, the swarthy Iranian as well as the blue eyed Slav.'

Bryce was having some difficulty on a broken lava scree slope where he questioned his ability to reach the summit: 'whether with knees of lead, and gasping like a fish in a boat' he should be able to find his way. He decided he must reach the summit before 3 p.m. to give him time to return to the bivouac site before darkness. Altitude affected him in a way he did not expect, and at times he found himself slipping down nearly as much as he went up. The scree slope gave way to a better ground, but in the mist he still was uncertain how far he was from the top. The angle eased and he was walking on snow in the thick mist following a gentler though still upward slope, trailing the point of his ice axe to assist his return journey. Suddenly the ground began to fall away. He stopped, and a puff of wind drove off the mist on the opposite side from the way he had just come. He was on top of Ararat; it was 2.25 p.m. Soon it was clear on the other side. From up here he records that he found the view rather stern, grim and monotonous. He reflected, however:

How trivial history and man the maker of history seemed. This is the spot which he reveres as the supposed scene of his creation and his preservation from destroying waters, a land where he has lived and laboured and died, ever since his records begin, and during ages from which no record is left . . . The landscape is now what it was before man crept forth on the earth; the mountains stand about the valleys as they stood when the volcanic fires that piled them up long ago extinguished. Nature sits enthroned, serenely calm, upon this hoary pinnacle, and speaks to her children only in the storm and earthquake that level their dwellings in the dust.[118]

He quoted a Persian poet:

> When you and I behind the veil are passed,
> O but the long while the world shall last,
> Which of our coming and departure heeds
> As the Seven Seas should heed a pebble cast.

In 1877 Bryce drafted an important legal document, the *Trademarks Registration Act*, and wrote his historical travelogue, *Transcausia and Ararat*. His father also died that year. His interest in history inspired him to follow the track of Suvaroff's 1799 march on his famous Alpine campaign: from Airolo over St Gotthard; from Altdorf over the Kinzig Kulm to Muota Tal, where he found the gorge leading to the Schwyz blocked by the French; by the Pragel Pass to the Linth valley, where he was checked by another French force at Näfels; and finally over the Panixer Pass to Ilanz. When Bryce wrote about this in his *Memories of Travel* (1923), he described the route from the perspective of Suvaroff and his men.

Bryce was in the Tatras in Carpathia in 1878, where he climbed the Schlagendorferspitze, Lomnitzerspitze and the Gerlsdorferspitze, visited the Ice Cave of Dobschau and made a descent of the Dimojee Rapids. He was elected to membership of the Alpine Club in 1879, proposed by C. E. Mathews and seconded by Douglas Freshfield.[119] His qualifications listed the Schreckhorn, Monte Rosa, Pelmo and Marmolata in the Alps, Maladetta and Vignemale in the Pyrenees, and Hekla and Ararat. Freshfield said he could have added more as he had been to the Appenzell, the Engadine, the Todi and St Gothard districts.

In his political life Bryce was a Liberal, elected to parliament in 1880 for the Tower Hamlets constituency in London and returned for Aberdeen South in 1885, the seat that he held until 1907. He became a valuable member of the Liberal party, his intellectual ability and energy being recognised. Gladstone appointed him Under-Secretary of State for Foreign Affairs in his short-lived government of 1885. In 1892, again under Gladstone, he was appointed Chancellor of the Duchy of Lancaster and a member of the Privy Council. He served as President of the Board of Trade in Lord Rosebury's short administration of 1884 to 1885.

In 1884 Bryce introduced the first Access to Mountains (Scotland) Bill.[120] He was concerned by the increasing exclusivity on sporting estates at the time, commenting: 'Eighty years ago everybody could go freely wherever he desired over mountains and moors. Scotland is the only country in the world where an attempt is made to interfere with the right of people to walk freely over uncultivated ground.'[121]

As a political ally and academic friend to Gladstone, Bryce supported home rule through conviction.[122] He tried to create a liberal Protestant pressure group (the Committee for Irish Affairs) to mediate between the Parnellites and the government after 1881; most of the committee's propaganda was directed at taming the Ulster Liberals. In 1884 he appeared to change tack in a pamphlet entitled 'England and Ireland', in which he proposed a subordinate legislature for Ireland. But when Gladstone decided on a much stronger measure in autumn 1885, Bryce quickly reconciled himself to it, causing tension with many of his Ulster relatives and academic friends, some of whom became Unionists. His suggested modification to Gladstone's 1893 Government of Ireland Bill (the retention of a reduced number of Irish MPs at Westminister) provided the basis for winning back some Irish Liberals to the fold.

In 1883 he visited the USA and made a partial ascent of Mount Rainier, reaching 10,000 feet (3,048m) on the Willis Glacier. He moved on to the Hawaiian Islands where he ascended the active volcanoes Mauna Loa (13,675 feet/4,168 m.) and Kilauea (3,900 feet/1,189m), spending a night in a hut on the edge of the latter's great crater. He returned often to America while he researched his greatest work, *The American Commonwealth* (published in 1888), which examined the institutions of the United States historically and constitutionally. He compared his findings with de Tocqueville's *Democracy in America*, a study written fifty years earlier. He described a dynamically growing population that had doubled in forty years (from 20 to 40 million) and lauded the progress of the American educational system, which had raised the standard of elementary education to a far higher level than that of Europe and afforded increasing numbers of students entry to the very best universities. However, he also found a growth in inequality, with a greater number of 'gigantic fortunes' than in any other country of the world and more poverty than was in evidence in de Tocqueville's earlier study. The book became an instant classic and had gone to 101 editions by 1950. Bryce comprehensively revised it three times himself in 1889, 1893–5 and 1910.

The year 1889 was another busy and important one for Bryce's personal life; he was instrumental in the foundation of the Cairngorm Club based in his own Aberdeen constituency. It is the oldest, and today one of the largest, hillwalking and climbing clubs in Scotland. He became its first president. On 23 July in the same year, at the age of fifty-one, he married Elizabeth Marion Ashton, twenty years his junior. They lived in a town flat in London and in a country house in Sussex. She apparently brought with her a substantial income. They had no children. He was described as dressing in the somewhat bohemian manner of the Pre-Raphaelites: reefer jackets, loosely knotted bright blue ties and fold-down collars. He liked to smoke a pipe and to roll his own cigarettes.[123]

The couple toured the Dolomites, the eastern Alps, Croatia, Carinthia and Carniola, also visiting Venice. Elizabeth was his companion in all his subsequent travels, which included: an 1890 visit to Yellowstone Park in the USA and to Canada; an 1891 cruise throughout Scandinavia; an 1893 tour of France and Spain; and an 1895 cruise to Cape Town, South Africa, where Bryce climbed Table Mountain (1,084m) and Makheka (3,463m), the second highest mountain in the Drakensberg Range in Lesotho. He again visited South Africa in 1897 and published *Impressions of South Africa*, which criticised British repressive policy against Boer civilians and condemned the systematic burning of farms and the imprisonment of old people, women and children in British concentration camps. From 1899 until 1901 he was President of the Alpine Club; in 1903 he visited Sicily and climbed Mount Etna.[124]

When the Liberals were next back in power under Sir Henry Campbell-Bannerman in 1905, Bryce was made Chief Secretary for Ireland. This was another brief and largely unsuccessful appointment. He tried to carry an Irish council bill in parliament, as a partial step towards Irish home rule, but saw it dismissed out of hand by John Redmond and the Irish Party who regarded his proposals as backsliding on the position of the previous government. He had more success when the commission he convened on Irish university education resolved some disputes between the Catholic Church and the movement for higher education reform, an issue which had long plagued successive British governments. He also managed to get himself out on Irish hills while in office. Freshfield wrote: 'As Irish Secretary he was wont to lead his panting subordinates up the steep sides of Croagh Patrick or Croaghaun.'[125] However, he had become long-winded and was unsure and unhappy with the economic policies being adopted by his colleagues in the Liberal government; the solution found was to appoint him British Ambassador to the United States of America. One of his colleagues cynically remarked: 'I realised he would be greatly appreciated in America as knowing more of the history and constitution than most Americans. He had also the quality of liking to make long speeches on commonplace subjects which I knew to be a trait that would be possible with the American masses. He also had a charming and agreeable wife.'[126]

This was a posting to which he was better suited and he did much to improve relations between what Bryce called the 'two great English-speaking commonwealths' during the term of three American presidents: Theodore Roosevelt, William Howard Taft and Woodrow Wilson. Douglas Freshfield once spent a fortnight with him as a guest at the Washington Embassy and recalled: 'Bryce was more of a popular figure than in his own country. The average American citizen – and it was greatly to his credit – discovered in the British Ambassador a simplicity of character, an honesty, a breadth of outlook, a readiness to adapt himself to, and sympathise with, his surroundings, which shone out perhaps the more conspicuously in a country where "politician" has been used as a term of reproach.'[127] True to form, Bryce used his time there to do some travelling. He was reputed to be the only man in Washington to have been in every state of the Union. From September to November 1910 he took three months leave to tour South America, which he followed with his book *South America: Observations and Impressions*. He took the same dispensation from May to September 1912 to visit Tahiti, the Cook Islands, Australia and New Zealand.

After his retirement as ambassador in 1913, he was raised to the peerage as Viscount Bryce of Dechmont in Lanarkshire the following year and became a member of the House of Lords. At the outbreak of the First World War Asquith asked him to report on alleged German atrocities in Belgium. The report was damning of German behaviour towards civilians. He was also outspoken about the circumstances of the Armenian genocide in the Caucasus in 1905.

He died on 22 January 1922, aged eighty-four, at Sidmouth, Devon, and was cremated at Golders Green Crematorium. *Memories of Travel*, the book he was working on at the time of his death and which related tales of his many travels, was published in 1923. His wife died in 1939. Freshfield summed up his career succinctly: 'In Lord Bryce's career we rejoice to recognise a type of a full and complete life. Fortunate in his marriage, he found a wife who shared his tastes and his travels. Acknowledged by all a fine scholar, a sound lawyer, a great historian and a brilliant writer, as a statesman he was esteemed and trusted by his political colleagues.'[128]

11

Valentine Ryan:
The Ryan-Lochmatter Phenomenon

I have long believed that your cousin was by far the greatest British mountaineer in the early part of this century which ended with the first world war and since I became editor of the *Alpine Journal*, it has been one of my hopes to publish an appreciation of his great climbing career.

Professor T. Graham Brown in a letter to Group Captain Ryan, 1949[1]

THE IRISHMAN who has left the finest legacy of Alpine achievement is Captain Valentine Ryan, whose family had deep roots in County Tipperary. They were well-established Catholic landed gentry whose land had been purchased in the seventeenth century from Cromwellian grantees. The family also had a long tradition of military service. Ryan, whose family resided for much of the year on the continent, was inspired by the climbing and writing of Alfred Frederick Mummery (1855–1895), particularly Mummery's ability to find aesthetic, bold, new lines up previously climbed mountains.

Mummery was a political economist and a mountaineer whose family ran a tannery at Dover, providing him with the means to devote his leisure time to climbing and economics.[2] With the guide Alexander Burgener he completed some of the most innovative climbs in the Alps between 1879 and 1881, including first ascents of the bold Zmutt Ridge on the Matterhorn, the Aiguille Verte from the Charpoua Glacier, and hard rock routes on the Aiguilles du Charmos and du Grépon. Despite his growing reputation, Mummery's election to the Alpine Club was blocked by a snobbish coterie for reasons that remain unclear, but seem to relate to the fact that he was a mere merchant. He applied again and was elected in 1888 after he made the first ascent of Dykh-Tau in the Caucasus. He remained an outsider in the Club, which was dominated by gentlemen educated at public schools and universities. Despite the petty jealousies of the committeemen, He progressed to climbing without the use of guides and with partners who included J. Norman Collie and William Cecil Slingsby, and often his wife, Mary, and her friend Lily Bristow.

Mummery wrote a book, *My Climbs in the Alps and Caucasus*, in which he advocated 'the essence of the sport lies not in ascending a peak, but in struggling with and overcoming difficulties', and suggested that all mountains pass through three stages: 'an inaccessible peak – the most

V. J. E. Ryan, 1882–1947

- Son of Tipperary-born Major General Valentine Ryan, who owned an estate at Inch, County Tipperary
- Educated at Stonyhurst College and Woolwich military academy
- Captain in the Royal Garrison Artillery
- Inherited an estate at Thomastown, County Tipperary, in 1905
- Combined with Joseph, Franz and Gabriel Lochmatter to make many important first ascents in the Alps 1905–06
- Returned to Alps in 1914 to make new ascents
- Wounded in his left hand in an artillery accident during the First World War
- Left Ireland at the commencement of the Irish Civil War
- Died in London 1947 and is buried at Meelick, County Galway

Facing page: Valentine Ryan. This snapshot by a German climber was given to T. G. Brown by Ryan's widow in January 1950. (Brown papers, National Library of Scotland)

difficult ascent in the Alps – an easy day for a lady'. The latter being a reference to his celebrated climb of the difficult Grépon with the very competent Lily Bristow. He attempted Nanga Parbat in Kashmir with a small party in 1895, reaching 21,000 feet (6,401m) when he and two Ghurkhas who were supporting him disappeared, presumed killed by an avalanche.

After Mummery's death the early years of the twentieth century saw the British dominance of Alpine climbing in decline, when Austrian and German climbers moved increasing into the western Alps. The visitors brought with them skills learned in their local steep limestone ranges in the eastern Alps and a new philosophy of self-sufficiency that tended towards harder rock climbing and guideless ascents.[3] There were two notable exceptions to this overall trend: one was an Englishman, Geoffrey Winthrop Young (1876–1858), who climbed with the St Niklaus guide Joseph Knubel; the other was the younger Irish artillery officer Captain Valentine Ryan with his guides Joseph and Franz Lochmatter, also of St Niklaus. According to Young (who considered Ryan his only rival) Ryan climbed with 'feverish energy and daring for a few remarkable seasons'.[4] Young explained, 'there has been no great climber about whom so little is known'. In fact, in the normal way, his name would have faded out of all but the climbing journals were it not for the staggering list of new ascents made by his team among the Chamonix Aiguilles and the Pennine range, ascents which have since come to be accepted as marking the beginnings of a new era of difficult climbing.

Valentine John Eustace Ryan was born in 1882, the son of British Army Major-General Valentine Ryan. Inch House (now a hotel and restaurant) and Castle Fogarty, both near Thurles, County Tipperary, were the family's ancestral homes. The latter is a ruin since it was burned down in 1922. For much of his childhood Valentine lived abroad and was educated first by the Jesuits at Stonyhurst College, Lancashire, and later prepared for a military career at the Royal Military Academy, Woolwich (London), where military engineers and ordnance officers were trained. He passed out into the Royal Garrison Artillery, an arm of the Royal Artillary tasked with manning the guns of the British Empire at forts, fortresses and coastal batteries, and in particular the heavy gun batteries attached to each infantry division. In this capacity he served in Malta, Halifax (Nova Scotia), and Ceylon (now Sri Lanka), where he was promoted in 1902 to full lieutenant.

It is unclear when and where Ryan started climbing. Young tells us that Ryan's mother first took Valentine to the Alps and that his younger brother Lionel, who also served in the British Army, was a very talented climber as well.[5] In 1898, when he was just fifteen years old, Valentine climbed two small peaks and a pass in the St Gotthard area of the Lepontine Alps, which border Switzerland and Italy. It is likely that the family were on summer holiday there. The routes he completed were Pizzo Lucendro (2,959m), Pizzo Fibbia and Passo dei Scorsi. His next recorded routes were centred on Arolla in 1900, when he climbed the Aiguille de la Za (2,415m), Pic d'Artzinol (2,998m) and the Ulrichhorn (3,925m) and turned back when close to the top of the Nadelhorn.[6] In 1901 he made just one ascent when he climbed the mighty 4,545m-high Dom in the Mischabel group.

It was his brother Lionel who first made an impact in the Alps as a talented young climber. He engaged the Valais guide Joseph Lochmatter from the village of St Niklaus in 1901; from this first engagement the Ryan and Lochmatter brothers became historically entwined among the pantheon of great Alpine climbing teams. The *Führerbuch* of Joseph Lochmatter for a three-week period in

August 1901 concisely records how Joseph and Lionel Ryan – Swiss guide and Irish client – spent their time in the Pennines and Chamonix districts.[7] The climbs recorded were ascents of some of the best and boldest mixed and rock routes in both areas, including Dent du Géant, a traverse of the Zinal Rothorn, Grand Cornier, Aiguille Verte by the Moine Ridge, traverses of both the Grand and Petit Drus, Aiguille du Grépon and several unnamed passes. At the end of this blitz, the youthful Lionel lavishly praised Joseph's capability and knowledge as a guide, his magnificence as a rock climber and his obliging and agreeable manner.

On 10 January 1902, during a family holiday to Lausanne, Lionel (again guided by Joseph Lochmatter), his brother Rafael and their uncle Alois Pollinger combined to make the first winter ascent of the Weisshorn. Young Lionel commented that Joseph proved himself as competent and agreeable as ever. This first notable winter ascent was reported in the London *Daily Mail*.[8] During the same holiday the two brothers visited Chamonix for a week and climbed Aiguille de l'M and the Petit Charmoz, and also attempted the Grand Charmoz. Lionel was back in Joseph's company again the following August for a short time when they climbed the Dent du Requin in Chamonix, crossed the Moming Pass and ascended the Ober Gabelhorn in the Pennines. During the same period Valentine's ascent list was more modest: he climbed the Aiguille du Moine and made an attempt on the Aiguille du Plan, which was stopped high up by bad weather.[9] There are no details of guides employed by Valentine and Lionel (but it is assumed they hired local guides on these ascents). However, T. Graham Brown, in correspondence with Tom Longstaff (President of the Alpine Club in 1949), was informed that in 1902 Lionel had made three guideless climbs in the Alps – two with Longstaff and L. W. Rolleston. The pair met with Lionel in Chamonix on 19 August 1902. All three travelled to Argentière by carriage on 20 August and carried full sacks up to Lognan, climbing the Tour Noir on 21 August and the Aiguille d'Argentière on 22 August. Longstaff wrote: 'I never saw anyone move so perfectly as L. F. Ryan'.[10] He added: 'I never met V. J. E. Ryan but he was climbing about then and we considered him to be the finest rock climber of his day.'

Lionel's last Alpine outings were in November of that year when he climbed the lower peak of the Gabelhorn, the Dent Blanche and the Gässispitze, and crossed the Augstbordhorn and Ginroz Passes. Soon afterwards Lionel journeyed to meet his regiment in India, where tragically he took ill and died in April 1903. He was clearly a very skilful young climber with great potential. Referring to Lionel's climbing talents, Valentine later told his wife that his younger brother, the one who had died soon after joining his regiment in India, 'was better than me'. His wife also remarked later that Valentine had lived for climbing at that time.[11] At about the same period, when Valentine himself was serving in Malta, he wrote to his mother, 'I always said I would serve for ten months in Hell if I could climb for the other two and Malta is not nearly that.'[12] With the letter he enclosed a photograph to his mother of a colleague named Jackson leading a rock climb in Malta.

It was not until May 1903 that Valentine's name first appears in the *Führerbuch* of Joseph Lochmatter, one of the famous brothers with whose name he will always be associated. He was twenty years old. His routes for May 1903 were climbed with the older brother, Joseph (then thirty years old): Aiguille du Midi, the Grépon, the Charmoz traverse, the Dent du Requin and the Riffelhorn by the Matterhorn couloirs. Bad weather in early June limited him, in company with Franz Lochmatter (then twenty-three years old), to just two ascents: the Aiguille d'Argentière and the Aiguille du Plan.

East Ridge of Aiguille du Plan (Gaston Rébuffat, *The Mont Blanc Massif*)

In 1904 Ryan appears to have spent all his military leave in the Alps, during which he completed a most impressive list of the outstanding climbs of the period. He engaged both Joseph and Franz for the two months of June and July, and his entries in Joseph's *Führerbuch* are as follows: Rimpfischorn; Charmoz traverse; Aiguille Verte with Joseph only; Grépon and Blaitière in one day; Mont Blanc du Tacul; traverse of the Drus from 'the little to the big'; Dent du Géant; an attempt at Grandes Jorasses from Col des Grandes Jorasses (reached top of great Gendarme close to Pointe Marguerite); Aiguille sans Nom; Ober Gabelhorn and Wellenkuppe 'in one day'; Rothorn traverse; Täschhorn by Teufelsgrat; Mominghorn traverse; Trifthorn traverse; Weisshorn descending by north ridge over Bieshorn to Zinal; Dent Blanche by Viereselgrat; Dent d'Hérens; Lyskamm traverse; Matterhorn traverse; Col du Géant; Grand Charmoz from Mer de Glace.[13]

Regarding Franz, Ryan wrote, 'I consider him one of the best guides in the Alps, he is a magnificent rock climber and a wonderful rapid step cutter. He is always cheerful and good natured under all circumstances.'[14] It is interesting to note that the traverse taken from the Petit to the Grand Dru was a difficult new route; Young later characterised it as a subtle 'mantelshelf' traverse across the southerly face, on the opposite side of the peak to the usual route. Not included on Ryan's list was an unsuccessful attempt they made on the north face of the Dru.

He resigned his army commission in Ceylon in June 1905, when his maternal uncle Frederick Philip Bennett died and left him his estate at Thomastown Park, near Birr in County Offaly. He told Young it was 'to have more time to climb'.[15] Free to do as he liked, he went straight to the Alps, where from 25 June until 1 October he climbed alternately with three of the Lochmatter brothers. Franz was only available for five weeks from the end of June until the end of July. Ryan then climbed with Joseph and, on occasion, the third brother, Gabriel, joined the party. He was with Joseph at Pontresina and in the Dolomites during a period when the weather was generally bad. Ryan complimented Joseph's great skill in finding the way in a district unknown to him. The list of ascents was even more impressive than in the previous year, as he was then intent on repeating most of his great hero Mummery's rock routes.

Joseph and Franz set out with Ryan for the Écrin range on 25 June 1905. Starting with an ascent of La Meije, they then climbed Pic Bourcet and Tête de Charrière, from where they moved to Chamonix 'having been driven out of the Dauphiné by the vileness of the weather', as Ryan wrote in the fragments of a draft book he started, which was found at Thomastown after his death in 1947. They set out to make a new route up the Aiguille du Grépon from the Mer de Glace, which Ryan had long contemplated. The first difficulty presented itself at the bergschrund: Joseph noticed that the frozen snow of the cornice projected over the rocks to the right, and seemed firmly attached to them. He gave Ryan his rucksack and, by embedding the pick of his axe in the frozen snow, he succeeded in getting a foothold on the snow-covered slabs. Franz joined his brother and then pulled the remainder of luggage, 'animated and inanimated', after him. Ryan wrote: 'The first chimney required care, but the others presented no great difficulty, tho' they could not exactly be called easy. Our halting place for the Charmoz was soon passed and at 6-15 we halted some 300 feet higher up for breakfast.'[16]

Here Ryan expressed a wish to climb the mountain directly to its summit and to avoid the Mummery Crack: 'Indeed I felt that going up the Crack would be rather shirking the climb.' They resumed their climb up the Grépon side of the couloir, working their way diagonally up the face towards the highest point. Ryan's hopes began to rise as they made good progress up to the level of the Charmoz. The guides were not so optimistic. After a direct traverse to the left, the real difficulties began. For the most part they were now on large slabs; the handholds were none too plentiful, and very small, generally only large enough for the tips of the fingers. Now and then a very difficult chimney varied the climbing:

> We were of course, only moving one at a time; Joseph being generally propelled upwards by Franz's axe. As soon as he was in position of tolerable security he assisted Franz up, who in his turn pulled me after him . . . At last Joseph got up a slab with considerable difficulty, and found himself on a small platform, above which it was impossible to get. He wanted me to come up too and see for myself, but I was quite satisfied to take his word for it.

It was 9.30 a.m. and the day was very hot. Joseph wanted to lighten the rucksack by drinking the champagne, but the other two felt it should be kept to celebrate victory only. They traversed to the right and down towards the Charmoz couloir, until they reached a narrow rock couloir leading to the gap between the Charmoz and Grépon. Following it was easy at first, but then it became difficult after turning to the left at a little col between a crag and the main wall of the Grépon. They were about 100 feet (30m) from the bottom of the Mummery Crack. Ryan wrote: 'all attempts to push Franz up with an axe having failed, we abandoned the craft of rock-climbing for the science of engineering.' Franz, after a couple of unsuccessful attempts, managed to throw a rope over one of two projecting knobs of rock that lead to easier rocks above. Trusting entirely on the rope, Franz reached safety and pulled up Ryan. Both of them traversed to the foot of Mummery Crack, but chose to cross back on the Mer de Glace face over a large flake that had split away from the mountain. Joseph, with the benefit of a top rope, came directly to them. They were now at the foot of large slabs where they found a wooden wedge driven in by a previous party. Franz climbed up, with the help of Joseph's shoulder; Joseph himself stood on the head of his axe, which he wedged in a crack. Ryan was left to bring up the axe and rucksack, and 'very much more than the moral support of the rope was required', he honestly wrote. Small handholds became bigger, finally bringing them out onto the summit ridge at the top of the arch of the Kanones Loch where it joined the ordinary route. At five minutes past two they reached the summit and spent the next forty minutes contemplating their route over the bottle of Bouvier. It had taken them 12 hours and 40 minutes. They were back at Montanvert at 6.30 p.m. Ryan considered this climb the most difficult he had made up to that date.

They followed their success with ascents of La Nonne from the Charpoua Glacier and the Aiguille du Moine from La Nonne. They repeated Mummery's route on the Aiguille du Plan, which prepared them for a new route on Aiguille des Grands Charmoz. This new rock route took a ridge from Montanvert to the Petit Charmoz ridge and Montanvert face. They continued to pick off new routes with another new route up Aiguille de Blaitière from Mer de Glace, which was followed by a traverse of Aiguille du Chardonnet. From 26 July to 8 August Ryan climbed with Franz, when they made an ascent of Col des Hirondelles and an attempt at a new route on the Grandes Jorasses from Col des Hirondelles. Their attempt was stopped by storm when they were close to the crest. They then climbed the north ridge of the Dent du Géant and the Col du Géant and finished their mini tour by climbing the Aiguille Verte from the Charpoua Glacier.

Franz being booked for the remainder of the season, Ryan resumed his partnership with Joseph. Valentine later told his wife, 'Joseph Lochmatter was a great and cautious guide', but he liked Franz better 'for his adventurousness'; she added that he commented that 'he and Franz were like brothers'.[17] The season resumed with an ascent of the Dom from Saas, returning over the Täschhorn and the Mischabeljoch; they then climbed the Südlenzspitze and Nadelhorn starting from Saas and finishing at St Niklaus.

Ryan, with Joseph and Gabriel Lochmatter, met up with Geoffrey Winthrop Young for the first time at the end of August 1905 at the Schwarzsee Hotel. He agreed to join ropes with Young and his regular guide, Joseph Knubel, to climb the Matterhorn from Furggenjoch. This was one of Mummery's bold routes. The Knubel family, like their neighbours the Lochmatters in St Niklaus, were a famous guiding family. Joseph's father and two brothers had died in 1877 while traversing the Lyskamm when the party broke through a serac and perished with their two English clients. Lochmatter also knew Young, who had engaged him as a guide previously. 'You are going for the Furggen Ridge I suppose?' Ryan enquired of his rival, who was six or seven years older. 'So am I', he told the Englishman, a former schoolteacher who was employed at Eton for a number of years.[18] Interestingly, one of Young's climbing companions in the Alps that year was the economist Maynard Keynes who was a student of Young's at Eton. Regarding Ryan, Young wrote later: 'There was satisfaction for both of us in coming across someone else who was playing the rigour of the game, in that slackwater period.'[19] He described Ryan as:

a soldier, tall, lean, hawk like, disdainful swinging past with an Indian gait. His aquiline face with a small black moustache, was bronzed, taut, and impassive, and his eyes sloping and arrogant; they seemed to be observing everything – and with dislike. He smiled seldom and his laugh sounded surprisingly from the dark immobile features. But his tenor speaking voice was high bred and pleasing . . . The Gods who showered on him all worldly gifts, withheld the power of ever appearing to be happy or even in harmony with his surroundings.

They agreed to explore in company, but to keep to their own parties, joining up if things got fierce. The intention was to climb the Furggen Ridge to a high saddle, then traverse left to the Italian Ridge to gain the summit. They raced up the edge of the face, unroped for most of it, stopping at the white saddle from where they observed continuous rockfall down their intended Italian route. Young reported: 'Ryan's impatience with our hesitation to start up those bombarded shelflets over Italy had a rasp in it. He was very much the young officer ordering the charge. But in the end he accepted without resentment our unanimous opinion against the attempt.'[20] The party took the shorter traverse right to the summit via the Hörnli Ridge. Young watched 'Ryan's agile and swift climbing up the Furggen cliffs with delight', and then 'with unqualified admiration saw him walk off the corner in balance across the high angled slabs, with a superlatively flexed foot on light nail-holds.' They descended from the summit together by its east ridge and above the shoulder the two of them unroped and, 'both in their riotous twenties', raced each other down the slopes to the Schwarzsee, leaving the guides to descend at their ease. Young remarked, 'it was delightful, as one waterfall'd under control down the crags, to find someone else who could really go the pace and safely. We were very much in sympathy as we drifted on and down into the valley in company.' Young claims he remarked to Ryan as they looked out from the summit, 'I suppose you have thought of the South face of the Weisshorn too?'

The parties moved to the Weisshorn hut where bad weather confined them inside and Young made do with small tins of jam from Lausanne, which looked sparse compared to the 'old order' tastes of Ryan, who enjoyed plenty of cold fowl and eggs. They talked climbing all day as they played three games of chess. Young said the reserved Ryan never once revealed anything regarding his own life or tastes and that he (Young) felt he had moved higher in Ryan's estimation when he won one game of the three. When the weather improved they climbed the Weisshorn's southeast face by a new route, ascending in the same order as on the Matterhorn, with Joseph and Gabriel Lochmatter and Ryan leading the way, and Young and Knubel following close behind.[21] They climbed unroped northwest, upwards across the eastern bay of the Schallenberg Glacier, threading crevasses at a high level to reach a breach in a great split buttress. They followed a left-handed diagonal snow slope to reach the mouth of the 'Mathews' couloir, which they passed under to reach a rib that descended from the east ridge of the Weisshorn. They pursued this rib until it crossed another rib that led them westwards – and then they were just 900 feet (275m) below the summit. Here 'the angle of the face steepened deterrently' and 'the rocks smoothed out their good frictional wrinkles and snow and ice-salve had been brushed over them with a lavish hand.' They roped up here in their respective parties and climbed carefully up a rib and overlapping rocks into a shallow depression where they were confronted by a steep wall. Minute, well-spaced and hidden holds unlocked an upwards traverse until they reached a broken column of rock that brought them out on the summit crest. It had taken them six and a half hours. They choose Tyndall's East Ridge to descend, taking full advantage of the strong following wind. They were soon in Randa.

Young reflected on Ryan's climbing behaviour: 'He never carried a sack – his guides were there for that; and I never saw him carry an ice axe – the guides, he said, were there for that too, and it bored him. It was another idiosyncrasy that he never cared to lead on rocks himself, or to cut the steps. But he could walk up or down steps in ice or snow at any angle in balance. He had daring, initiative, endurance, and a bold eye for a new line.'

Ryan continued the season with both Joseph and Franz, making the following ascents in the Bernese Oberland: Bietschhorn, up by the west and down by the north ridge; Schienhorn direct by the west face; Aletschhorn; Faulhorn direct from Concordia; Finsteraarhorn by southwest ridge and southwest face; and Kamm traverse of two peaks from the Faulhorn Col. Then he climbed with Joseph on his own for the remainder of the season at Bernina and in the Dolomites, with ascents of Piz Scercen and Piz Bernina; Pomalagnon by its south (Cortina) face; Croda da Lago by its west face and lastly Tofana I by its south face. When Franz's *Führerbuch* is added to Joseph's in 1905 they combine to yield for Ryan an astonishing list of routes, many of which were first ascents or attempts at new routes across the whole range of the Alps, including the Écrin, Chamonix, Oberland, Pennines, Bernina and Dolomites.

In his writings Young was at pains to point out that Ryan, in company with the Lochmatter brothers, were the only competition he and his partner Joseph Knubel had at that time for 'new big climbing' and, since Mummery was dead and Slingsby, Collie and Conway were occupied upon distant exploration, 'English pioneer effort had died down to a steady and centrist repetition of "classic" routes.' Young wrote that 'such prodigies could only upset comfortable traditions', so that 'the placid annual backwater in the Alps was ruffled rather than pleased.' It was difficult for the standard alpine crowd to 'understand the startling effect of a young climber suddenly ranging up and down the whole range of the Alps making only the most difficult ascents many of them new and some of them postulating a standard of rock technique altogether unprecedented'. This was how Young described the malaise that existed in the Alpine Club at that time.

The winter and spring of 1905 to 1906 was a life-changing period for Valentine Ryan; he was then a wealthy young man with a substantial income and climbing was his main passion; he was urged to join the Alpine Club and he began to arrange his own Himalayan exploration. He dined, when passing through London, with his new-found friend Young and was introduced by him to other climbers and explorers. Among those he met was Norman Collie, who had climbed with his hero Mummery and had experience of expeditions to the greater ranges. They discussed climbing in the Himalaya. Ryan went about planning his own expedition; he wrote to Young on 28 January 1906 to invite him to join himself, Joseph and Franz for a trip to the Nubra district of Ladakh in India from May to October of that year.[22] He added that he hoped to get a letter of introduction to the Viceroy. He also applied to join the Alpine Club and prepared a qualifications list dated 6 February 1906, with an unsurpassed list of ascents.[23] Ryan had no reason to suspect his admission would be denied. Despite his young age (he was just twenty-two years old), his 'qualification list of climbs', covered seven years of activity and included many new and all of the previously boldest routes climbed to date in the Pennine, Dauphiné and Mont Blanc ranges. It must have been the strongest list of climbs in support of membership made up until that time. His application was proposed by J. H. Wicks (then vice-president of the Club) and L. W. Rolleston, and his supporters included Claude Wilson (a future president in 1929), J. Melville Beachcroft, and Geoffrey Winthrop Young (another future president in 1941). Despite the fact that his climbing was raising the standards, in the same fashion as had Mummery's before him, he was blackballed by a majority of those attending the Club meeting where his membership was voted on. The record shows simply 'Passed: Feb. 20 1906' and 'Rejected: Mar 6 1906'. It remains a stain and embarrassment on the reputation of that illustrious Club that he was refused entry. His blackballing was, according to Tom Longstaff, 'on the grounds of incivility in the Alps to some older members'.[24] An article entitled 'Failed A.C.' by T. S. Blakeney in *The Alpine Journal* discusses his rejection: 'In 1906 came the rejection of V. J. E. Ryan, with an unsurpassed list of ascents; here again, personal factors are known to have operated against him.' He further states that 'Ryan's rejection caused considerable criticism then and after and it was not clear who was responsible.'[25] Naturally stand-offish, Ryan had obviously made enemies (he was said to have been rude to a party of senior members in a hut) and out of spite they conspired to shut him out.

At about the same time Ryan became engaged in London to Miss Louisa Florence Gully who was, remarkably, twice his age; they were married in London in March 1906. She had been born in India to which her family appeared to have returned. The couple lived at Thomastown; however, there were difficulties as the marriage was not received very well by Valentine's family. His wife later commented that 'Ryan's family did not like his marriage to her a Protestant (Church of England) and regarded him as a bad Roman Catholic and there were therefore family difficulties, and the family would have little or nothing to do with them.'[26]

Ryan abandoned his proposed Himalayan expedition and the couple went on a long honeymoon to the Alps, where Ryan and the Lochmatters went on a climbing tour-de-force over three-month period. A family source said that Louisa 'was quite a climber herself although she hated it'.[27] Valentine, Joseph and Gabriel resumed their Alpine conquests on 6 June with an unsuccessful attempt to climb an imaginative new route up the east face of Aiguille du Plan from the Mer de Glace. The party then climbed Dent du Géant. With Franz

East Face of Aiguille du Plan: 31 is the line of the Ryan-Lochmatter route (Lindsay Griffin (ed.), *Mont Blanc Massif Volume II Selected Climbs*, Alpine Club Guide Books (1991))

replacing Gabriel, they climbed Aiguille de Blaitière by the Chamonix ridge. Strengthened when Franz returned to the party, they went back to the Aiguille du Plan and made the first ascent of the spectacular East Ridge, which has since become one of the classic rock climbs of the Chamonix Aiguilles. Ryan wrote in Franz's *Führerbuch* that 'it was the hardest climb I have ever done, except the Täschhorn, when a snow-storm exaggerated the difficulty.'[28] During July they climbed a series of classic ascents: first, starting at the Col de la Fourche, they climbed Mont Blanc by the Brenva

Captain V. J. E. Ryan during the First World War. (*The Climbers' Club Journal* Vol. IX, courtesy the Alpine Club archives)

ridge; next the Aiguille Rouges d'Arolla, traverse of three peaks; then Dent Perroc, traverse of both peaks; Grande Dent de Veisivi with Franz only; Ferpècle ridge of the Dent Blanche; Zmutt ridge of the Matterhorn; and the Dent d'Herens from Col Tournenche. They continued with the Jägerhorn; Cima di Jazzi and Monte Rosa from the Jägerjoch.

They then moved to the Täschhorn where the party was joined by Young and Knubel to make an ascent described by Ryan in Joseph's book as follows: 'straight up the centre of the face from the glacier above Täschalp.'[29] In Franz's book for the same climb he wrote, 'On the Täschhorn we got into great difficulty & only Franz's courage & skill saved the entire party.' The story of this ascent in Young's book, *On High Hills*, has become the stuff of mountaineering legend as Young recalls the brutal detail of their intense struggle in cold conditions up steep and exposed slabs and icy chimneys. He wrote of the Ryan and Lochmatter team: 'the Comet of the Alps – into their tail – if they had one – little Josef Knubel and I were willingly swept in somewhat conjunction'. He continued: 'Franz Lochmatter's mountain feat was the greatest I have witnessed, and after a number of years I can say the greatest I can imagine.'[30]

Ryan had long contemplated the route and had previously looked down the wall from above and noted the two couloirs that forked out left and right below the summit pyramid and formed a diamond, the top half of which was shaped by the summit.

On 11 August 1906, in the dark and cold of early morning, the party set out for this aesthetic line, heading up the Weingarten Glacier to its snow rim under the south face of the Täschhorn. A steep buttress on the west of the great central couloir provided access to the great wall. They breakfasted at 7.30 a.m., standing on a snow-laden rock bracket and enjoying what would prove to be their last opportunity to share the same standing room for the entire ascent. From there Joseph Lochmatter, on the end of the leading rope, was forced up into a diagonal rightwards traverse 'without the vestige of a good hold' or ledge to belay from. The promise of a better stance above the next wall repeatedly ended in disappointment, but led them on until they were deeply committed and retracing their steps had become even less inviting.

As their situation became more precarious, Ryan suggested to Young that he should tie his rope onto Franz. The proposal was accepted readily by Young, 'due to the insidious character of the climbing', which 'had already succeeded in hustling their mountaineering discretion'. He was 'reassured by the pleasant moral' and 'the psychic value of [Franz's] rope', as the buttress merged seamlessly into the steeper face. Young sensed from the guides' humour there was grave work in prospect even before their eyes had discovered it. 'Ryan was, however, as always, bent upon the immediate "forward"; and his imperious staccato sentences, as little modified as his own fearlessness by any hush of breathless circumstance had their usual effect upon his high-mettled team.' The leading party's pace up the thin slabs, sloping 'like desk lids which joined steep to steep', was tremendous until the difficulties of the steep walls and their lean-to roofs became more awkward and hands and feet grew numb clinging to rounded, cold and slippery ledges. Young called up to Franz to watch his rope as he was about to move upwards. Franz indicated the precarious nature of the whole party's situation when he replied: 'You must do what you can; here we can no longer help one another.' Franz was preoccupied in watching his brother, whose struggles and scrapings (far up in a 'black, repulsive corner') were audible but invisible to Young. It was, however, becoming increasingly clear to Young that each one of them was unprotected and that a slip by any one of them would imperil the rest.

Joseph had traversed via a decrepit mantelpiece around a corner into the couloir, since the series of terraces they had used for their ascent up until that point had run out. Precariously, they all safely worked their way into the couloir and spread out along a slim, shattered ledge. Escape by following the couloir above them needed no second look. Neither was there any hope of further traverse at their stopping place. Forty feet (12m) beneath them lay a chasm, which slanted steeply outwards into space. The only hope was to find a lower-level shelf to continue their traverse. Ryan fed out the rope as Joseph tried to find a lower exit across icy slabs to restart the traverse; but he did not look as if he would ever cross the slabs and said, 'it won't go'. 'But it must go,' responded Franz, and he soon was roped into his brother's place and working his way onto and up a steep, sloping shelf vanishing in a diagonal upward direction. Ryan followed immediately, then Joseph who took in Young's rope. Knubel followed with all their sacks and axes. The traverse continued, easier at first and then becoming more steeply inclined and outwardly sloping just as the day grew darker and the snow, which had started as a mere sprinkle, increased in density. They reached a chimney in which they found some stances on ice-covered chockstones. But the chimney petered out through an exit onto a blank cliff, and they found themselves 600 feet (180m) beneath the summit in the middle of the rock diamond observed by Ryan from below.

A great roof of rock hung above them; if they could reach it, perhaps there was a way through. They joined up their ropes to give Franz 200 feet (61m) of possible run-out. The rope ran out slowly and minutes crawled like hours as Franz, spider-like, edged his way upwards. Young suddenly heard 'the unmistakable scrape and grit of sliding boot nails and clothing' and, looking up, observed Franz's legs shoot into space above the edge of the roof. He was sure that Franz was off, and imagined that the swirling rope would soon drag him from his own feet before it tightened on the doubtful belay. However, the boots again disappeared above the ledge and the rope began to move up the slanting gable end of the roof as Franz worked his way through a flaw in the join of the cliffs above the roof. The rope now hung down, well away from Franz's belayers, who held on to its end as it dangled inside the recess. Joseph followed up first so as to aid his brother in pulling up the others. When Young joined Ryan at the belay, Ryan asked him what he thought their chances were of escape. Young answered, 'about one in five'. In the memorial article he wrote for Ryan, Young recalls: 'I remembered that he remarked in his ordinary staccato voice and manner, that the year before he would not have cared a damn which way he went, live or die, but that this year he had married, and he left it at that.'[31]

V. J. E. Ryan with three Lochmatter brothers at Montanvert (thought to be taken in 1914). (L–r): Gabriel, Franz, Ryan and Joseph. (*The Climbers' Club Journal* Vol. IX, courtesy the Alpine Club archives)

When the rope dropped down Ryan tied himself into it. He reminded his guides that his hands had little power as they were frozen. He ascended towards the right, using handholds up to the roof and, as he did so, the rope coming down from Franz pulled him directly upwards. But before he reached the roof a leftward pressure from the rope pulled him off the wall and his full weight fell on the end of the rope, which tightened about his chest and squeezed the air from him. He called out as he dangled on the rope, 'I am done', but with the great efforts of Franz and Joseph hauling together, he was dragged, inch by inch, to the edge of the overhang where he was able to recover and assist their efforts. He soon joined his two gallant and loyal guides above. Young, a heavier man, had the same experience: the rope inexorably pulled him off, however, he had tied the end of his rope into a chair and chest harness, which saved him from suffocating and he was better able to aid his belayers as they pulled him up to and over the overhang. Knubel, who carried all the sacks and axes with great skill, soon joined the party on the top of the dome where Franz had found his stance. Although the snow had stopped, the route had not yet yielded and they continued their way up more icy slabs, which were as difficult as the previous. Franz led the way following 'a devious upward line through the upheaving of giant slabs without a halt or a false attempt'. They arrived on the southeast ridge, just 60 feet (18m) below the summit pyramid. As they relaxed, lunching on sardines and snow, Young remarked to Franz, 'you will never do anything harder than that, Franz', to which the great rock climber answered, 'no', he said reflectively 'man could not do much more'.

When they reached Randa, Ryan, concerned that his wife would be worried, parted with his guides and started to walk towards Zermatt with Young to meet a horse and trap for which they had wired ahead. It seems Ryan, who was staying at the Monte Rosa Hotel, had told Louisa to expect him back that evening. He did not give his new wife any great cause for concern despite his later than expected arrival. This most difficult of all the Ryan-Lochmatter routes would wait another thirty-seven years before it was was repeated by a strong Swiss party, led by André Rock, who used pitons to overcome its challenges.

Professor T. Graham Brown, editor of *The Alpine Journal* from 1949 to 1953, became engaged in active research on Ryan's career shortly after Ryan's death, with a view to crediting the Tipperary man's achievements. His thunder was stolen when an article on Ryan by Geoffrey Winthrop Young was published in the *Climber's Club Journal* for 1949–51. Young had consulted some manuscript notes written by Valentine Ryan and bequeathed to the Alpine Club library by the inheritor of Ryan's Thomastown Estate, his cousin Captain R. Ryan. Young used these notes, as well as copies of both the Lochmatters' *Führerbücher* and his own reminiscences of the climbs they had made together, to construct his article. Brown's personal papers show that he went to extraordinary efforts, researching not only Ryan's climbing record, but also scouring Young's records for the same period.[32] He wrote to Ryan's cousin and to his father who lived at Inch, County Tipperary, seeking information and any other writings or diaries that Ryan might have kept. He was referred to Ryan's widow and he met her several times, particularly questioning her about the Ryan/Young relationship. She said that her husband did not blame Young or any of his backers for his blackballing by the Alpine Club, but another whose name she could not remember. She said that her husband's Himalayan project had been abandoned as a result of his inheritance of Thomastown and his marriage to her in 1906. Regarding the Täschhorn, Louisa Ryan said, 'Young and Knubel were a serious drag, they had not been asked and Ryan did not know they were coming; and at the bad bit Franz tried several times in vain and finally said: "you may as well die in the attempt, as die otherwise we must"; at which point Joseph despaired that, "we are all dead".[33]

Brown was not convinced that Young's article told the true story of the Täschhorn ascent and was actively looking for evidence that he and his guide Joseph Knubel had gatecrashed on Ryan and the Lochmatter brothers' greatest achievement – the remarkable first ascent of the south face of the Täschhorn considered to be the hardest new route climbed in the years previous to the Great War. His suspicions were supported when he found a note in the 1906 climbing journal of W. E. Davidson, dated Tuesday 14 August: 'Had a long talk with Ryan and to Franz Lochmatter, & gathered that both Young and Knubel went very badly on the Täschhorn. Franz said outright that G.Y. was very good when he could use his arms but he couldn't climb slabs like Herr Ryan.'[34] Brown also observed in a letter written to Sydney Spencer: 'the routes climbed by the Lochmatter brothers between 1907 and 1913 – the years that is when they were not climbing with Ryan – were not very enterprising up to 1906 and again in 1914– but that they were unbelievably enterprising when with Ryan up to 1906 and then again in 1914. So I suspect that the novelties must in large part have been due to Ryan.'

Brown was of the opinion that the motivation, selection and planning of new routes by the party was driven by the determined and competent Ryan. There is absolutely no doubt but that Franz Lochmatter was technically a brilliant climber on both rock and ice. He was daring, agile and very skilful. With Ryan's eye for potential new lines, allied to Joseph's overall skill, experience and mountain craft, they collectively became a very formidable team. It seems Brown and Young did not get along; indeed, Brown's tenure as editor of *The Alpine Journal* was eventually terminated as a result of disquiet among influential members, including Young, when he wrote an article in the 1949 *Alpine Journal* featuring the climbing of H. O. Jones.[35] Brown added copious footnotes and references to the climbing season of 1911, during which Jones had climbed with Young and Knubel.[36] The article undermined, by omission, innuendo and exaggeration, the contribution made by Young and Josef Knubel to what Young considered to be 'the record season of my life'. Jones, who died in 1912, had been considered a rising star. Young and Knubel had found and recovered the bodies of the Jones party, which included his wife and guide. Brown was not re-appointed as the *Journal* editor in 1954, following letters from Young and Arnold Lunn of the Ski Club of Great Britain to the president of the Alpine Club requesting his removal and advising that they would not forward any articles to the *Journal* as long as he was editor.[37] In fairness to Young (who may have been guilty of 'writing up' his own role in planning the Weisshorn and Täschhorn ascents), it is he who has bequeathed us more detail than any other writer on the subject of Ryan and his climbing. It seems, after an examination of Brown's papers, that the article he was so desirous of writing about Ryan was really intended to undermine Young's reputation further.

In any event, Ryan's season of 1906 continued unabated; there were further ascents of the Nesthorn by its east ridge (accompanied by Joseph and Franz), the Sattelhorn and Mönchsjoch (with Franz alone), and a traverse of the Schreckhorn (both guides). Ryan did not climb in the Alps in 1907; in 1908 he made just one climb with Joseph from the Mer de Glace, when he ascended the Petit Muverin on 1 May. In 1909 he made only two (unnamed) climbs before illness stopped his climbing.[38] He wrote to Young from the Hotel Montanvert on 11 July:

I have done nothing – we have had snow and rain since June 2nd. The mountains are in awful conditions, and it is snowing hard here at the present moment. I do not think anything difficult will be done this year; there is a mass of snow on the rocks. I have been laid up for the last three weeks with blood poisoning in my left hand. I had to get a surgeon up from Sallanches. I am almost right now, but the cut is still open, so I could not climb now even if the weather were good. We are going to Vevey on the 13th so I shall not see you here, unless we met in London as I expect to be there about the 20th on my way back to Ireland.

We had lively times there a year ago, but so far I have held my own, and the Fenians leave me pretty well alone now.[39]

Another letter (written from Thomastown Park, Birr, on 29 April 1912 to Young in answer to a request for information) yields only sketchy details of his 1905 routes on the Grépon, Charmoz and Blaitière and his 1906 ascents of the Plan from Mer de Glace, as well as variations he made on routes on the Dru and Blaitière. He congratulated Young for his ascent of the Grandes Jorasses the previous year, which he had read about in the daily papers and, in concluding his letter, made the following political comment: 'When your friends pass Home Rule and I am sent into exile, I may perhaps go back to Montanvert, but I fear my climbing day are over.'[40]

Ryan did return in 1914, rock climbing with both Franz and Joseph in June and July among the Chamonix Aiguilles. Soon new, hard rock routes were falling, as the Ryan-Lochmatter comet burned brightly once more. The routes were climbed in the following order: Wellenkuppe; Aiguille du Moine by one of its several west ridges; Dent du Requin by the Mer de Glace face, starting at Mer de Glace and arriving at the col between Capucin and Requin, then to top by the east-northeast ridge; Aiguille de l'M by its face; a new route on the Grépon by the Nantillons face; attempt on Grande Charmoz from Trélaporte; Aiguille de Blaitière by a new route from Mer de Glace, finishing by the Aiguille du Fou; Grépon by Young's route and down by his own Nantillons route; Grépon by Rolleston's route from Col Dunod; Aiguille de Requin from Glacier d'Envers de Blaitière, striking east-northeast at the col by the Capucin; Grand Cornier traverse; and a Dibona traverse.[41] Young did not cross paths with him, but heard of their great climbing feats from Franz. He remarked, 'after his years of inaction, a flaring up once again of the once consuming fire.'[42]

When war was declared in 1914 Ryan rejoined the Army and served until he was demobilised at the rank of captain in 1918. He was wounded in the wrist, which affected the power of his grip in the fingers of his right hand, after which he was unable to do any more serious climbing. He resumed life at Thomastown in 1919, leaving again in 1921 because of the outbreak of civil war in Ireland. He never returned there alive because his wife 'hated Ireland'. He, it seems, had an equal dislike of England, so the couple moved to Jersey where he built a beautiful house in a land which 'they both hated'.[43] Young (who had lost a leg in an explosion during the war) met Ryan once again at Grindelwald in 1929, when Young was trying some small glacier climbing with one leg in the company of his small son. He said Ryan (who had been on a hard climb) showed great interest in the boy and was, for a short time, his best self. During the Second World War Ryan became active as an air-raid warden and was planning to revisit Ireland once again. Before he did, however, he died in London on 21 September 1947 and was buried in Meelick on the Shannon in County Galway.[44] He left the house in Jersey to his wife. He had already bequeathed, many years before his death, 'his Thomastown home which he cherished so much' to his second cousin, Group Captain Richard S. Ryan of the RAF.[45]

The reason we know so little detail about Ryan and his own perspective on his great achievements is because he seems to have been a very private man who was shy of publicity, shunned photography and, because he disliked writing about his exploits, kept few notes. His wife told T. Graham Brown that her husband had a deep attachment to the history of his own family and Young wrote that he had amassed a collection of early English and gold coins and was a fanatical chess player. Uncovering any detail of his exploits was not helped when his main climbing guide, Joseph Lochmatter, died following an accident soon after his last season climbing with Ryan; his younger brother Franz seems also to have had no interest in keeping records. As a consequence, his rival Young is our main source of information; he declared after Ryan's death that he felt sufficiently strongly about his great contemporary 'to put on record what little has been recoverable of his mountain writing, and of my recollections of our joint climbs'.[46] As a result of Young's writings, Ryan has evolved within mountaineering mythology as an 'untypical type of Irishman, with a reputation for being reserved, proud, excitable, dissatisfied; without any share of the more sociable Celtic qualities, the wit, the humour or the ready human sympathy'.[47] Yet, strangely, Ryan's letters to Young and the latter's reports of their interactions were friendly and do not fully reflect these harsh words from Young. There is no doubt, however, about the quality of his relationship with his guides, whose names are now entwined with those of Valentine and Lionel Ryan, an intrinsic part of the folklore of Irish and Swiss alpinism.

Joseph (1871–1914) and Franz (1878–1933) Lochmatter

Born at the village of St Niklaus in 1871, Joseph was the second son of Joseph Marie Lochmatter, one of the best guides of his day, who (with his eldest son and Mr W. E. Gabbett) was killed on the Dent Blanche in 1882. J. M. Lochmatter was the guide to Robert Fowler on his ascents of the Matterhorn and the Dent Blanche in 1871. St Niklaus, which sits in the Mattertal valley and lies between Stalden and Zermatt, is surrounded by high mountains including the Dom and the Weisshorn. The village has produced some of the Alps' most famous guiding families including the Lochmatters, the Knubels, the Pollingers and Summermatters. Despite the tragedy of their brother and father's deaths the young brothers, Joseph, Rudolf, Franz, Raphael and Gabriel, all followed the same calling, and together they earned for their family a reputation as guides not surpassed by any in the Alps. While Franz was known as an outstanding rock climber, Joseph earned equal respect as one of the most trustworthy and careful guides involved in some of the most adventurous expeditions in the Alps. Their reputations grew when they became the chosen guides of Valentine Ryan, the leading British and Irish climber of the period before the Great War. Joseph was employed by Ryan as chief guide in 1903, with Franz as his porter, and in subsequent seasons Joseph and Ryan made some of the most difficult new rock climbs of that period, executed across the length and breadth of the whole Alpine range. For the more difficult of these expeditions Joseph was careful to make sure of the companionship of his brother Franz. This was undoubtedly due to the supreme confidence each had in the other and, as a consequence, no mishap occurred despite the incomparable list of new routes or variations they completed with Ryan: crossing of the Drus in 1905; Mer de Glace face of Aiguille du Grépon; east ridge of the Aiguille du Plan; north ridge of the Northend summit of Monte Rosa; south face of Täschhorn; full traverse of Dent d'Herens, all climbed in 1906; and the many new hard rock routes completed in the Chamonix Aiguilles, including the east face of Aiguille de Blaitière.

Joseph was killed not on the mountain but while in the service of the Swiss military when he was mobilised and quartered at Zermatt in August 1914. At night he accidently struck his head against a horizontal bar that had been lowered without his knowledge. He died two days later at Brig and was buried at St Niklaus. Franz progressed to the Himalaya on Meade's British Kamet Expedition and later to the Karakoram with the Dutch expedition led by Philips Visser. He died in August 1933 when he fell 400 feet (120m) while descending by Tyndall's east ridge of the Weisshorn, which overlooked his home at St Niklaus.

12

Charles Howard-Bury:
Leader of the First Everest Reconnaissance

The most abiding joy of travel will always lie in retrospect.

Charles Howard-Bury, *Mountains of Heaven*, 1914

Charles Howard-Bury, 1883–1963

- Born in London, son of an Irish heiress who was daughter to the third Earl of Charleville
- As a child lived at and inherited Charleville Castle, Tullamore, County Offaly
- Educated there with governess and later was sent to Eton College, from where he progressed to the Royal Military College, Sandhurst, for two years
- Posted to India as captain with the 60th Rifles, he went travelling and big-game hunting, learning many oriental languages and dialects. Inherited Belvedere House in County Westmeath in 1912
- Travelled widely in Tien Shan, Siberia and eastern Europe
- Fought in the First World War as the commander of a battalion at Arras, the Somme, Passchendaele and Ypres, and was awarded the Distinguished Service Order
- Was successfully involved, on behalf of the Royal Geographical Society, in seeking approval for the Everest Reconnaissance Expedition from the Indian Office and in negotiation with Tibetan authorities
- Was appointed leader of the expedition, which mapped the approaches and reached the North Col of Everest in 1921

COLONEL CHARLES KENNETH HOWARD-BURY (1883–1963) was not an experienced mountaineer, yet circumstances led to his appointment as leader of the First Everest Reconnaissance Expedition in 1921 by the joint committee of the Royal Geographical Society and the Alpine Club. The expedition achieved the goals of surveying and mapping Everest and its approaches and finding the most feasible route to the summit. This route has become known as the Mallory route after the legendary English climber who died in a summit bid in 1924. It is interesting to note that this was the route taken when the first Irish ascent was made on 27 May 1993, by Belfast man Dawson Stelfox. The route today is the most frequented route to the world's highest summit. So, despite the fact that it took thirty-nine more years for two Chinese and a Tibetan to complete the North Col and northeast route to the summit, it is now clear that Howard-Bury and his team got it right first time.

Charles was born in London on 15 August 1883, although his parents' normal residence was at Charleville Castle, County Offaly (then known as King's County), Ireland.[1] He was the only son of Captain Kenneth Howard (1856–1885) of the Royal Horse Artillery and his Irish heiress wife,

Previous page: Lt Col. Howard-Bury who served at Arras, the Somme, Passchendaele and Ypres in the First World War was mentioned in dispatches seven times and awarded the Distinguished Service Order in 1918. (Courtesy Marian Keaney)

Lady Emily Alfred Julia (1856–1931), youngest daughter of Charles William Bury, third Earl of Sharpeville. His father (a grandson of the sixteenth Earl of Suffolk) took the surname Howard-Bury when he married in 1881. His parents had met on a botanical expedition in Algeria; his father was a botanist and watercolourist who had travelled extensively in India, Canada, Australia and liked to engage in big-game hunting. When Charles was born his father wrote to his sister that 'the brat is enormous and ugly and it squalls like hell.'[2] Charles' sister, Marjorie, was born a year later. His father's health had so deteriorated by that time that he took the precaution of writing a final letter to his son:

> My Darling Boy,
>
> I am afraid there is no chance of my being permitted to live long enough for you even to remember me, and this I need not tell you is a very great grief to me, as I had had been so looking forward to having you for my companion in my walks, and telling you all about the birds and plants, flowers and fishes like my father did when I was a little boy, and I want you to grow up a manly boy, fond of all these things as well as your books.[3]

On the death of Captain Howard in 1885, James Keith Petty Fitz-maurice, Lord Lansdowne (at that time Viceroy of India and also Charles' cousin) was appointed to be Howard-Bury's guardian. A German governess was employed at Charleville Castle to educate Charles and his sister, Marjorie. In the summer they visited Lord Lansdowne at Dereen House, Kenmare, County Kerry, or their grandmother at Hazelby in Berkshire, and sometimes their flamboyant Italian art-loving cousin, Charles Brinsley Marlay, who resided at Belvedere House near Mullingar. Charles was sent to Eton College, from where he progressed in 1902 to the Royal Military College, Sandhurst for two years. He spent some of his holidays at this

Charleville Castle, Tullamore, County Offaly, the first home of Charles Howard-Bury. (Courtesy David Hicks/ *Irish Country Houses*)

Belvedere House and gardens near Mullingar, County Westmeath, was inherited by Howard-Bury in 1912 and became his primary residence. (Author's photo)

time at his mother's chalet in the Dolomites where he learned to love the mountains and hillwalking. When fully grown he stood 6 feet 2 inches tall.

Howard-Bury graduated from Sandhurst with the rank of captain and joined the 60th Rifles in 1904; he was posted to India, where he travelled and went big-game hunting. He secretly entered Tibet in 1905, for which he was rebuked by Lord Curzon. Shortly after this he obtained the necessary permits (through the offices of Lord Lansdowne) from Russian authorities at St Petersburg to enter the Pamirs and Turkestan region. A military report in 1908 records his suitability as an intelligence officer: 'a splendid candidate for diplomatic or intelligence work, or for any missive of secret service requiring a clever brain and active body.'[4] His diaries indicate that he had keen powers of observation and an encyclopaedic knowledge of natural history, as well as good linguistic abilities. His photographic work also displays a particular expertise for recording plant life. Charles became an extensive traveller, both on duty and on leave. He spent a lot of time extending his language skills to Indian and other oriental languages, thus facilitating his ability to converse with a wide range of people. He was particularly interested in recording religious practices, and loved to visit holy places in order to meet the lamas, high priests and guardians of shrines and sacred waters.[5]

In 1912 he inherited Belvedere House, near Mullingar in County Westmeath, from his cousin, Charles Brinsley Marlay. He was in the Tien Shan mountains for six months that year, travelling by the Trans-Siberian Railway to Omsk, by steamer through newly settled Siberia, and then for nine days by bone-shaking horse carriage to Kuldja. He then travelled on horseback into the mountain hunting grounds of the Kazaks and Kyrgyz. He added a small bear, named Agu, to his travelling party, allocating the bear a pony for travel. He brought the bear home safely to Ireland when the trip was over and is reported to have regularly wrestled with the animal at Belvedere. On his return from journeying he prepared a draft book from his diaries, which unfortunately he never got to the publisher due to the outbreak of the First World War. The book, *The Mountains of Heaven,* was posthumously edited by Marian Keaney of Westmeath County Library, who included a short biographical introduction.[6]

Resuming his army duties in 1915, he commanded the 7th and 9th Battalions of the King's Royal Rifles, for which he was mentioned in dispatches seven times and was awarded the Distinguished Service Order in 1918. He served at Arras, the Somme, Passchendaele and Ypres where he was captured and held as a prisoner of war at Fürstenberg until May 1919. There were only about fifty survivors in his battalion. He tried to escape once and was caught after eight days while he was asleep, waking up to find a German tracker dog sniffing about his ear. On his return to Ireland he became a Justice of the Peace and was appointed High Sheriff for King's County in 1921.

After the war the Royal Geographical Society, in conjunction with the Alpine Club, proposed an attempt on Mount Everest, which had been identified in 1849 as the world's highest mountain. With the South Pole reached by Amundsen in 1911, Everest was seen as the 'third pole', in terms of the earth's features that still remained unexplored. Political opposition from Tibet and from the British government in India had prevented the expedition first proposed in 1905 by Lord Curzon to Douglas Freshfield, a former president of the Alpine Club who was also an important influence within the Royal Geographical Society. It appears that fears of contravening an Anglo-Russian convention regarding Tibet had worried the Indian Secretary of State at that time. At the

Howard-Bury's photograph of camping in the Tien Shan Mountains in 1913.
(Courtesy Marian Keaney)

close of the Great War attempts to revive proposals for an expedition continued to be resisted by the India Office. At this time Tibet seems to have been seeking a half dozen machine guns and ammunition in return for its cooperation on certain disputed issues, such as the establishment of a British representative in Lhasa and permission for an Everest expedition. Howard-Bury, at his own expense, travelled to India and lobbied government officials and the Viceroy. He spent two months in the region, skilfully negotiating with political and air force authorities for permission. Efforts to have an aerial survey conducted by the Flying Corps came to nothing, as they did not have the appropriate machinery and permission for such activities.

On 7 August 1920 Howard-Bury set out with porters and mules to seek out political officer Charles Bell, who was working in his capacity as a trade agent for Tibet. He found Bell on 13 August at Yatung, just over the Tibetan border, having crossed the 14,390-foot (4,386m) Jelep La Pass. Bell did not favour the expedition until the differences between India, China and Tibet were resolved; he disagreed with the Foreign Office's opinion that once the arms issue and that of an agent at Lhasa had been settled, then the Tibetan government might be approached. He did agree to ask the Tibetan authorities to grant leave for the expedition and felt they would, but was concerned that future negotiations might be prejudiced as a result. It is worth noting that in a postscript to his communication following this meeting, Howard-Bury passed on Bell's recommendation that the Sherpa Bhotias would prove the best coolies for high mountain work, as they were less independent than Tibetans. This is the first identification of the special role that Sherpas would fill in relation to supporting most subsequent expeditions to the Everest region. He was also advised that at Khamba Dzong and Tingri Dzong plenty of mule and yak transport was available. Following their meeting Bell travelled to Lhasa to confer with the Dalai Lama.

The result of Bell's dialogue in Lhasa came in a reply from the India Office on the 20 December

Howard-Bury's photograph of the east slopes of the Saritur Pass (12,000 feet/3,650m approx.), Tien Shan Mountains, 1 July 1913. (Courtesy Marian Keaney)

1920, which confirmed that the Dalai Lama had given his consent to the expedition to travel through Tibet to Everest for exploration. A letter from Sir Francis Younghusband, President of the RGS, to Colonel Howard-Bury, dated 12 January 1921, conveyed the appreciation of the society for the valuable services he had rendered in securing this consent.[7]

Due to the unavailability of Captain Bruce, an experienced Himalayan climber who was the favourite for leadership of the expedition, Howard-Bury was rewarded for his tactful efforts in India by his appointment as leader of the 1921 reconnaissance expedition, which was charged to thoroughly reconnoitre all approaches to the mountain and identify the most feasible route. Bruce, who had recently taken up a post with the Glamorganshire Territorial Association, was expected to lead the expedition in the

Sir Charles Bell (left) with his Holiness the Thirteenth Dalai Lama (right). Bell's advice and assistance helped Howard-Bury secure an agreement with Tibetan and Sikkim authorities for an Everest reconnaissance expedition. (www.erbzine.com/dan)

following year that would make the final ascent of the mountain. The committee chose Howard-Bury for his knowledge of the people of the region and his recent experience of travel there, since this would enable him to resolve any problems the expedition encountered. He was also a very experienced leader of men, having commanded troops in battle, and (not insignificantly) he was prepared and able to pay his own travel and equipment expenses. The expedition was funded by contributions from members of the Alpine Club and the RGS, as well as press and photographic rights agreed with *The Times*, the *Philadelphia Ledger* and the *Graphic*. The total cost is estimated to have been between £3,000 and £4,000.

The team included surveyors, a geologist, a doctor and experienced climbers. Remarkably, the average age of the team was forty-four and a half years.[8] Their brief was to make a thorough reconnaissance of the mountain, with permission to go as high as possible if they identified a favourable route. The mountaineers were chosen by the strong-minded J. P. Farrar, a former president of the Alpine Club, who selected Harold Raeburn to lead the climbers. Raeburn, a Scot, was one of the most distinguished climbers of his generation; he usually climbed guideless and had made the first solo traverse of Meije in the French Dauphiné; he had also made nine first ascents in the Caucasus range and had reached 21,000 feet (6,400m) on Kanchenjunga in the

The 1921 Everest Reconnaissance Expedition. Back row (l–r): Sandy Wollaston, Charles Howard-Bury, A. M. Heron, Harold Raeburn; front row (l–r): George Mallory, Oliver Wheeler, Guy Bullock and Henry Morshead. (Courtesy Marian Keaney)

Himalaya. However, Raeburn was fifty-six years old. The second climber selected was another Scot, 53-year-old Dr A. M. Kellas, a university chemistry lecturer who had become an expert on the physiological effects of high altitude as a result of his Himalayan mountaineering experience, which included ascents of Pauhunri (23,180 feet/7,065m) and Chomiomo (22,430 feet/6,837m). In 1920 he attempted Kamet (25,447 feet/7,756m) and, but for a dispute with the local porters, he would very likely have achieved the summit. He was involved in climbing Narsing and was camped at over 6,000m in northern Sikkim in the spring of 1921, where it appears he had severely stretched himself. He was regarded as an obstinate character by many who climbed with him. He arrived in Darjeeling only a week before the expedition's departure in poor physical condition after an exhausting year of climbing.

Also selected was George Leigh Mallory, the son of a parson from Cheshire who went to school at Winchester where he came under the influence of one of his masters, Graham Irving, a keen alpinist who founded the Ice Club at the college. He progressed to Magdalene College, Cambridge, where he read history and became active in the college rowing club. Mallory was very athletic and had a deep love of mountains; he completed many routes with Geoffrey Winthrop Young, one of the finest and most influential British alpinists of his era and an adviser to Farrar. At the time of the Everest reconnaissance, Mallory was working as a teacher at Charterhouse, an English public school, and was married with three children. Other members of the team included G. H. Bullock, a genial character who had been at Winchester with Mallory and who had climbed with him in the Alps. The team doctor, naturalist and botanist was Dr A. F. R. Wollaston, a member of the Alpine Club who had visited the Ruwenzori Mountains in Africa and had got to within 400 feet (120m) of the summit of the Carstensz Pyramid in New Guinea before retreating. Wollaston had much in common with Howard-Bury. Both were wealthy, covering their own expedition expenses, and both were also keen naturalists and photographers; as a result they became close friends on the expedition.

The surveyors were chosen by the Surveyor General of the Survey of India, C. H. Ryder; he picked men who were both experienced surveyors and mountaineers. The first, Major Henry Morshead, had been to 21,000 feet (6,400m) on Kamet with Kellas the previous year. He was well liked by all, despite his physically very tough exterior. He had a staff of three native surveyors, two of whom accompanied the expedition; the third was left in Sikkim to revise maps that had been found to be inaccurate as the team passed through. The other surveyor was a Canadian, Major Edward Oliver Wheeler, a member of the Canadian Alpine Club and son of Arthur Oliver Wheeler from Maddockstown, County Kilkenny, who had emigrated to Canada in 1877.[9] His father had trained as a land surveyor on arrival in Canada and had surveyed the Rockies and the Selkirks for the Canadian government. For this work he employed photographic surveying techniques, which required that photographs be taken of the surrounding landscape from the highest points. In the course of his work Wheeler made many first ascents in both ranges, which led to his interest in mountaineering and co-founding of the Canadian Alpine Club. His son, Edward Oliver, had joined him in his surveying work at the age of twelve and it was in his company that Arthur Wheeler made the ascent of an unclimbed 8,300 foot (2,530m) peak, later named Mount Oliver. Oliver (as he was always called) was commissioned into the Royal Engineers in 1910 and served in France, Mesopotamia and India during the Great War. He joined the Survey of India after the war. He was chosen for the expedition for his abilities in photographic surveying and his mountaineering experience. Wheeler was married in Darjeeling just a few weeks prior to the expedition's departure. He and Morshead played a major role in achieving their team's reconnaissance objectives. The Indian government also provided an official geologist, Dr A. M. Heron, who was employed by the Geological Survey of India. His mission was to conduct a study of the age and structure of the mountains in the region.

The expedition assembled in Darjeeling in May; Morshead set out first with his surveyors, mules and fifty coolies, following the Teesta River and over the Serpo La Pass into Tibet from Sikkim in order to connect the new survey with the India Survey. The main party followed in two groups of fifty mules and twenty coolies, each group setting off one day apart. This was because the accommodation and camping en route was very limited. They followed a longer but easier route than Morshead's team had taken, via the Jelep La and the Chumbi Valley to Khamba Dzong. Howard-Bury left with the last group and did a double march to join up with the first party. All parties would meet at Khamba Dzong in June. They carried with them the precious passport with the seal of the Prime Minister of Tibet that Howard-Bury had worked so hard to secure. It read:

To: *The Jongpens and head-men of Pharijong, Ting-ke, Khamba and Kharta.* You are to bear in mind that a party of Sahibs are coming to see the Cha-mo-lung-mo mountain [Everest] and they will evince great friendship towards the Tibetans. On the request of the Great Minister Bell a passport has been issued requiring you and all officials and subjects of the Tibetan Government to supply transport, e.g. riding ponies, pack animals and coolies as required by the Sahibs, the rates for which should be fixed to mutual satisfaction. Any other assistance that the Sahibs may require either by day or by night, on the march or during halts, should be faithfully given, and their requirements about transport or anything else should be promptly attended to. All the people of the country, wherever the Sahibs may happen to come, should render all necessary assistance in the best possible way, in order to maintain friendly relations between the British and Tibetan Governments.

Dispatched during the Iron-Bird Year

Seal of the Prime Minister[10]

It took them a full three weeks to reach their meeting point due to the complete collapse of their main mode of transport, the 100 mules lent to them by the supply and transport corps of the Survey of India. Several mules had to be left behind after each day's march; they were replaced by locally hired mules that were clearly fitter and always first to the next destination. Finding replacement mules was very time-consuming, and Howard-Bury eventually reluctantly sent back the remaining government mules, after he had been reduced (only five days into the journey) to fourteen out of the original fifty animals. The rain fell steadily and leeches sucked blood from both man and beast as they crossed the Jelep La Pass (14,390 feet/4,386m) to cross over the Sikkim–Tibet frontier into the Chumbi Valley, arriving at the garrison village of Yatung. In compensation for the poor weather and the debilitating effects of altitude, Howard-Bury observed 'rhododendrons with flowers of every shade of orange and red. Then came rhododendrons of every colour – pink, deep crimson, yellow, mauve, white or cream coloured . . . every yard of the path was a pure delight.'[11]

As he travelled through Tibet he visited many Buddhist monasteries, nunneries and the hot springs at Kambu, where medicinal waters of five kinds flowed from the rocks. At the village of Phari Dr Kellas, who was feeling unwell, retired to bed on arrival. Next day he was unable to ride and was carried in an armchair all day. During the following days he was transported on a litter. Much of his discomfort was put down to the bad cooking; Raeburn and Wheeler were also suffering stomach cramps. Howard-Bury, an old soldier who knew the importance of marching on a well-fed stomach, therefore turned his attention to the cooking routine and tried to identify which of the four cooks was doing the most damage, all the while hoping that the veteran climber would recover before they reached the mountains. Howard-Bury arrived at the limestone gorge at (Fort) Khamba Dzong and was exchanging reports with Morshead and his surveying party, when a man came running up to him in an agitated state and informed him that Dr Kellas had died on the way. Wollaston diagnosed heart failure, arising from his weak condition while being carried over a high pass. They buried him on the slopes of a hill that looked out on three great peaks, Pauhunri, Kanchenjhow and Chomiomo, all peaks that Kellas alone had climbed. Howard-Bury read a passage from Corinthians.[12] One hundred miles away to the west could be seen the snowy crest of Everest, still unclimbed, towering far above all the other mountains; it seemed a climb too far.

The expedition had lost its most experienced Himalayan climber, arguably killed by his own enthusiasm and non-stop activity. Raeburn was also still suffering badly from stomach pains and his condition was not helped by a couple of falls from his pony. Clearly unwell, he was sent back to Lachen in Sikkim to be cared for by the lady missionaries there. Wollaston, who accompanied him, hoped to rejoin the team at Tingri. He later met up with the party again at Kharta but played

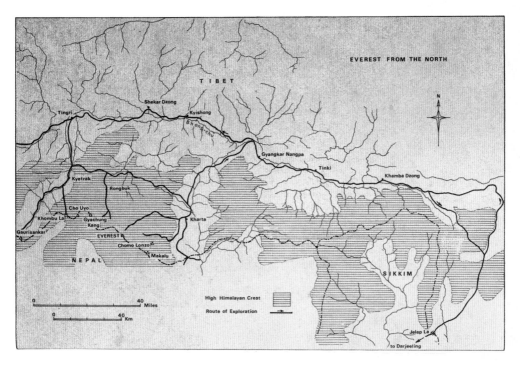

A map showing the 1921 Everest Reconnaissance Expedition's approaches to Everest.
(Courtesy Marian Keaney)

no realistic role in the rest of the expedition. The specialist climbing group was from that point reduced to Mallory and Bullock – and the party had yet to reach base camp.

From Khamba Dzong the route led to Tingri, which was the gateway to the Rongbuk valley and glacier on the north side. It took another eleven days to cover the ground, due mostly to difficulties locating and organising pack animals and visiting the impressive Buddhist monastery at Shekar Dzong, where Howard-Bury formally met and photographed the head lama. The monastery, which housed over 400 monks, was spectacularly perched on a steep, rocky mountain ridge. Copies of this photograph were the most treasured present Howard-Bury could give local people. Travel for the last 20 miles (32 km) to Tingri took two days, due to the absence of a proper bridge to cross the Bhong-chu River; it had taken them four weeks to arrive here, their first base for reconnoitring the northern and northwestern approaches to Everest. They settled themselves into an old Chinese rest house where Howard-Bury set up his darkroom and managed to get 'quite gassed' from sulphur fumes, losing his voice for several days. Wollaston set up his naturalist and botanical kit and deployed the porters to collect local species of fish, animals and spiders.

From Tingri four different parties moved out to explore, survey and map the valleys and passes to the north. Mallory and Bullock set out immediately for the Rongbuk with a group of Sherpas, intent on teaching them climbing techniques, to reconnoitre the north and northwestern slopes for a feasible route. Wheeler and the geologist, Heron, went east of them to Kyetrak, from where Wheeler started his photographic survey. Howard-Bury rode out with a Tibetan named Poo and climbed a 17,000-foot (5,180m) peak on the way to Kyetrak to photograph towards Everest and Cho-Uyo. Next day they rode to the (19,000 feet/5,800m) Khumbu Pass, which leads to the Khumbu Valley in Nepal; they were told that the pass was viable year-round, although it could be dangerous in blizzard conditions. Leaving the pony behind with a porter, Howard-Bury set off with another porter up a slippery moraine; when the porter's boots disintegrated on the glacier, Howard-Bury took the big camera on his own shoulder and carried it to the top of the pass, photographing down into Nepal. Wheeler was later to spend a week and a half photo-surveying this country. Next day Howard-Bury and Heron crossed the Pusi Pass, which descended into a narrow but fertile valley to the village of Tasang where green barley fields flourished. They camped overnight there and were provided with eggs and vegetables by the locals who told them that the good trail ended in a steep gorge on the Tibet–Nepal border where only a coolie could go.

Yaks ascend the Rongbuk Glacier with Changtse and Mount Everest in background. Irish Changtse Expedition 1987. (Author's photo)

Taking yaks, they made their way back and crossed several passes to the Rongbuk Valley to find Mallory and Bullock, whose base camp was near the Rongbuk Monastery at 16,500 feet (5,000m). At the monastery they were told that a reincarnated high lama was in meditation and was not allowed to see anyone. Mallory and Bullock were camped 7 miles up the valley from the monastery and were found to be training their porters at the alpine campsite. Six miles away Everest towered above the glacier with some 10,000 feet (3,000m) of immense ice cliffs. Howard-Bury decided that as Mallory and Bullock were well established there, he should select a new site in the Kharta Valley for a base camp from which the northeastern approaches could be explored. In a period of bad weather Mallory and Bullock made a number of excursions to the end of the West Rongbuk

Edward Oliver Wheeler and his surveying team during the 1921
Everest Reconnaissance Expedition. (Wikipedia)

Glacier before finally being given a clear morning that showed them the glacier was not connected with the Khumbu Glacier on the south side of the mountain. They had also eliminated any practical route in the saddle between Pumori and Lingtren, two magnificent individual peaks. At one point Mallory put camera plates into the camera the wrong way round and the photos that had been so hard won he later discovered could not be developed. He set about retaking many of these failed shots; meanwhile Bullock, with some porters, journeyed to the top of the main Rongbuk to the Lho-La vicinity to discover that no practical passage existed to the Western Cwm. It later transpired that the two climbers had passed the narrow entrance to the East Rongbuk Glacier, where it branched left as a small stream into the main glacial river. This would have led them directly to the base of the North Col. Fortunately the presence of this glacier was picked up by Wheeler in his first rough map. Mallory and Bullock, with support from their Sherpas, climbed a 22,500-foot (6,800m) peak, which they called Mount Kellas; however, following geographical practice the peak now appears on maps under its local name, Ri-Ring. They found their 5,000 feet (1,500m) of climbing effort to be slow and their breathing to be fast and deep. It was, however, the first peak to be climbed in the region and a significant achievement in itself.

Meanwhile, Howard-Bury and Heron had reconnoitred the route from Rongbuk to the Kharta Valley on the eastern side and, with great cooperation from the local 'jongpen' (leader), had located an excellent site for a comfortable base camp that had a house for a darkroom and a store, as well as a garden of poplars and willows for camping. When they completed their work at Tingri the entire team reassembled there. This base camp was at 12,300 feet (3,750m) in a green valley with a clean water supply, an abundance of fresh vegetables and other food, and it was at a low enough altitutude to provide real relief for resting climbers and coolies coming down from higher ground. Once they were fully installed at the camp, they kept up the same frenetic pace as before; following a series of tough outings they surveyed and eliminated a number of possible alternative routes to the elusive glacier, while discovering many exciting valleys and peaks. Mallory and Bullock crossed the Langma La Pass at 18,000 feet (5,486m) and, when the clouds lifted a day later, they saw the grandeur of the Everest landscape to the east. The panorama included the Kangshung Glacier, Everest, Lhotse Shar, Pethangtse, Chomo Lonzo and Makalu, which they discovered was also known to the porters as Chomolungma (also the local Tibetan name for Everest). This confusion cleared up, further exploration led them to the Karpo La (20,000 feet/6,100m), where they eliminated the thought of any feasible route to the North Col from the east. When they climbed to the summit of Kartse (21,000 feet/6,400m), Mallory was also able to rule out any safe possibilities by Everest's northeast ridge. On return to camp, Mallory was unwell and Bullock continued the survey with a search up the Kharta Glacier without success. They both then reasoned that a pass in the direction of Changtse must lead to the elusive glacier.

On 20 September Mallory, Bullock and Morshead, in company with a Sherpa named Niemba, cut through soft, powdery snow with huge physical effort to reach the Lhakpa La Pass, which finally provided the climbers with the alternative access route to the East Rongbuk Glacier that they had been seeking. It was during this passage through soft snow that Howard-Bury unwittingly acquired the threads of an old Tibetan tale that would transmit the myth of the Yeti to Europe. He asked the Sherpa about some large footprints they found in the snow and later, back home, repeated the stories he had been told; the British press had a field day printing these stories of 'wild hairy men who were driven into the wastes for the crime of murder and who preyed on isolated travellers'.[13]

When they reached the Pass they established camp, landing eleven loads of stores there, with two more loads left just 800 feet (245m) lower down; they then retreated back down the Kharta Glacier to their base camp below to ensure a better night's rest at a lower altitude. They were now ready for an assault on the North Col (Chang La in Tibetan) and they mustered all the team. Two days later Mallory, Bullock and Wheeler (with Howard-Bury, Morshead and Wollaston in reserve) and most of their trained Sherpas camped at the Lhakpa La. It was a very cold night and all suffered miserably. It was decided that only a small, strong party should attempt the climb to the North Col accompanied by three competent porters. Mallory, Bullock and Wheeler were chosen and their porters trudged the 2½ miles (4 km) in soft snow: first they dropped 1,200 ft (360m) onto the East Rongbuk Glacier and then walked uphill to 22,000 feet (6,700m), to the base of the North Col where they set up camp to give them a better chance next morning. They had a meal of soup, dried fruit and cocoa and experienced another extremely cold night as a violent wind shook their tents continuously.

When the three climbers and three Sherpas set out to climb the North Col the following morning they were all tired from cold and lack of sleep. They first moved up to the right of avalanche debris and then made a long leftward traverse to reach the Col. They were led remarkably well by two of their Sherpas, Ang Pasang and Lagay. The climbing proved to be easy, except for the last stretch which was very steep in softer snow. It took them four and a half hours. They rested for a while on a lower shelf on the west side of the Col before climbing to the higher shelf where the full blast of a westerly wind revealed its icy fury and eliminated any thoughts Mallory may have had of going higher. He wrote:

> On the col beyond it was blowing a gale. And higher was a more fearful sight. The powdery fresh snow on the great face of Everest was being swept along in unbroken spindrift and the very ridge where our route lay was marked out to receive its unmitigated fury. We

Camp at Lhakpa La at 6,750m on the 1921 Mount Everest Reconnaissance Expedition. (*L'Illustration*, 26 November 1921)

could see the blown snow deflected upwards for a moment where the wind met the ridge, only to rush violently down in a frightful blizzard on the leeward side. To see in fact was enough; the wind had settled the question; it would have been folly to go on. Nevertheless, some little discussion took place as to what might be possible, and we struggled a few steps further to put the matter to test. For a few moments we exposed ourselves on the col to feel the full strength of the blast, then struggled back to shelter. Nothing more was said about pushing our assault any further.[14]

It was decided that camping on the Col (7,100m) to await a change in weather was unsustainable as they had not sufficient rations with them. The weather seemed, if anything, to be worsening and the prospect of sleeping a thousand feet higher (given that the party had suffered when camping at lower altitudes) was not attractive. Mallory decided that 'it would be bad heroics to take wrong risks; and fairly facing the situation one could only admit the necessity of retreat'.[15]

This signalled the end of the Everest quest but Howard-Bury and Wheeler were not about to give up. On 26 September, with Wollaston, they set out to climb the ridge between Makalu and Everest, ascending via the Karpo La (20,300 feet/6,190m). The ascent was steep and tricky and they camped overnight on the edge of the Kangshung Glacier. The next morning they crossed that wide and complex glacier via a rock spur; finally, with two porters carrying the cameras, Howard-Bury crossed yet another glacier to find himself on the ridge that connects Everest to Makalu, the world's fourth highest peak. The photographs taken were the Irishman's final contribution to their mission. How fitting it was that he and Wheeler's solid surveying work contributed so much this first Everest reconnaissance.

On their return from the expedition, he and Mallory wrote *Mount Everest: the Reconnaissance*,

Everest Northeast Ridge and the North Col (Chang La) from the Lhakpa La.
(Courtesy Marian Keaney)

1921, which was later translated into French and Dutch. A variety of white primula (primrose) that had been discovered during the expedition was named after him, *Primula buryana*. Further recognition followed: the RGS awarded him their founder's medal and he also received gold medals from the French Geographical Society and the Club Alpin Français. Reading their accounts of the expedition one is struck by the relentless activity and motivation of the members, and the way in which each group took ownership of its assigned responsibilities. Despite the death of Kellas and the incapacity of Raeburn, all of the team members worked tirelessly and collaboratively. Mallory and Bullock, although they missed the entry to the East Rongbuk Glacier, through great effort and fortitude found another way to reach the North Col. Howard-Bury was clearly capable of coordinating with a light touch, pulling all the efforts of the surveyors and climbers into a great cohesive push that set the foundations for subsequent expeditions. Sir John Hunt, leader of the first successful Everest Expedition in 1956, listed not least among the accomplishments of the 1921 party the establishment of a happy rapport with their Bhotia Sherpa porters and the way in which the great contribution these men could make to mountaineering in the Himalaya had been confirmed.

Oliver Wheeler returned to work as a surveyor with the Survey of India, and was appointed a director in 1938 and Surveyor General from 1941 until his retirement in 1947.[16] He was made an honorary member of the Alpine Club in 1956, a rare distinction that had previously also been awarded to his Irish-born father in 1908. It was not until December 1922 that Howard-Bury was balloted for and elected in the normal way as a member of the Alpine Club.[17] The Alpine Club Register records his election on 11 December 1922; his proposer was Dr Wollaston and his seconder was Norman Collie. At the same AGM it is interesting to note that his successor on the next Everest reconnaissance expedition, Brigadier General Bruce, was elected President of the Alpine

Club. One suspects that Howard-Bury was seen by members of the Alpine Club as an RGS man and not a real mountaineer. Bruce's leadership of the follow-up expedition was announced before Howard-Bury left India, and this must have been a disappointment to the Mullingar man. He knew it implied failure and reflected badly on him. But the Alpine Club clearly wanted a climber from among its own membership to lead the way to what might be its greatest achievement; and it is known that Bruce, now free from his military commitments, actively sought the job from Younghusband.

In 1922 the public acclaim that followed the Everest reconnaissance enticed Howard-Bury into politics. He ran as a Conservative candidate and was elected MP for Bilston in Wolverhampton. He was appointed parliamentary private secretary to the Under-Secretary of War from 1922 to 1924, when he lost his seat. He was elected again as MP for Chelmsford in 1926, but retired in October 1931, when he inherited his ancestral castle at Charleville on the death of his mother. He served as deputy lieutenant and Justice of the Peace in Westmeath from 1927 to 1932 and was honorary Colonel to the 85th East Anglican field brigade of the Territorial Army. He resigned from the Alpine Club in 1939.[18] During the Second World War he was appointed an assistant commissioner of the British Red Cross and set up a small hospital at his home at Belvedere for wounded soldiers.[19]

Howard-Bury met Rex Beaumont (1914–1988) around 1940. Beaumont was an actor with the Royal Shakespeare Company who was then serving in the Royal Air Force. He was to become his close friend and, as Howard-Bury never married, his heir. After the war they restored Belvedere House and its gardens and built a villa at Dar al-Oued, Hammamet in Tunisia. They entertained their explorer, writer, clerical and political friends there, where the tall Howard-Bury was known as 'Monsieur Le Colonel'. He died at Belvedere House on 20 September 1963, aged eighty. He was buried in his family vault in St Catherine's Church, Tullamore. He left Charleville Castle to a cousin and Belvedere House and estate to Rex Beaumont. After Beaumont's death the house was taken over by Westmeath County Council and it was opened to the public in 2000;[20] many of the exotic plants collected by Howard-Bury on his travels may be still be seen there.

Charles Howard-Bury's record as the leader of the first Everest reconnaissance expedition is a proud record of achievement. His team discovered some 'magnificent and un-dreamt of valleys where primeval forests existed' and deep glens filled with rich semi-tropical vegetation where many beautiful flowers were observed and listed. They produced an original survey of 12,000 square miles (31,080 km²) and a detailed photographic survey of 600 square miles (1,554 km²) in the environs of Mount Everest, in addition to the revision of another 4,000 square miles (10,360 km²) of existing mapping. And, last but not least, the most feasible route to the summit of Everest was discovered – a route that would make Mallory its chief scout immortal and provide the path to success for the first Irish team to summit in 1993, when team leader, Belfast-born Dawson Stelfox, became the first Irishman to ascend the mountain and the first British climber to climb Everest from the north side.

When John Hunt's expedition climbed Everest in 1953, Howard-Bury happened to be in London for the coronation of Queen Elizabeth II. There was a brief press embargo on the Everest news until after the conclusion of the coronation ceremony. Word was released in advance to only two people, the Queen Mother and Colonel Charles Howard-Bury.[21]

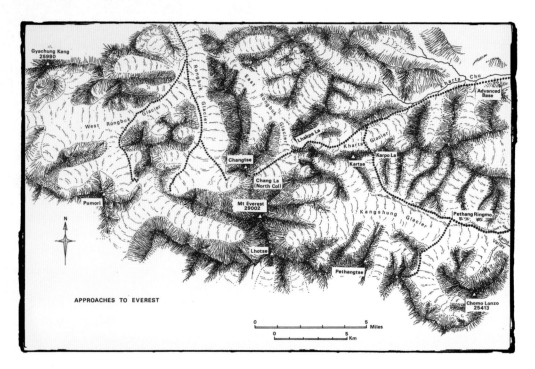

The 1921 Everest Massif map showing approaches via the Rongbuk, Kharta, and Kangshung Glaciers in *Everest Reconnaissance* by C. Howard Bury and G. L. Mallory (1991). Courtesy Marian Keaney.

13

A Legacy of Achievement

It was mainly the quality of not knowing when to yield; of fighting for duty even after they had ceased to be animated by hope. Such thoughts had a dynamic value, helped lift me over the rocks.'

John Tyndall on the ascent of the Weisshorn, *Mountaineering in 1861*

How should we evaluate the collective Irish contribution covered in this history of early Irish alpinists? The author's motivation for researching and gathering their individual stories and achievements was to connect with them, to highlight their individual adventures and achievements, and to record them together in a single volume for posterity. Their tangible achievements are significant in terms of geographic exploration, first ascents and new routes on peaks (not just in the Alps but further afield in New Zealand, Canada and the Himalaya), plus the many maps surveyed and drawn, and guidebooks and scientific reports published. John Ball, John Tyndall, Elizabeth Hawkins-Whitshed (under each of her three married names), William Spotswood Green, James Bryce and Charles Howard-Bury all wrote published accounts of their expeditions and achievements, which fuelled the passions of following generations of alpinists.

Ball and Tyndall were giants of the early Alpine Club; both were public intellectuals possessed with extraordinary ability and a strong work ethic. Ball's seamless integration of mountain exploration with his disciplined recording of flora and scientific observation provided members of the new Club with a role model of how the twin objectives of the Club might ideally be achieved. Picked as the first President of the Club, Ball edited *Peaks, Passes and Glaciers*, which became the template for *The Alpine Journal* that followed shortly after he left office; it has continued to be published ever since. His series of pocket-sized climbing guidebooks, which covered the entire range of the Alps, provided both a useful service to members and a tangible *raison d'être* for the Club from its infancy. Tyndall's fame as an experimental physicist, public lecturer and author, combined with his studies of the glaciers of the Alps, his first ascent of the Weisshorn and his serious attempts to make the first ascent of the Matterhorn made him an early alpine star. In contrast, young Charles Barrington without any previous alpine grounding or experience in a single act of boldness on the Eiger achieved international mountaineering immortality. The climbers who could be considered a part of the Irish diaspora were also leaders and organisers in their adopted lands. Russell was a founder of Société Ramond in the Pyrenees and the Club Alpin Français in France, while A. O. Wheeler was co-founder and leading member of the Canadian Alpine Club.

This history reveals who these pioneers actually were and outlines their story against the background of Anglo-Irish political strife, sketching their wealth, education, professions and social standing, as well as their involvement in Irish and British society during the Victorian and Edwardian period. It is immediately striking that with one notable exception (Tyndall) they all came from wealthy backgrounds; and all but one (Elizabeth Whitshed) were very well educated in the universities of Ireland, Britain and Germany. There were no opportunies for below-deck heroes, such as Tom Crean or Patsy Keohane, as was the case in Polar exploration. The equivalents to Crean and Keohane in alpinism came from among the natives of the Alpine valleys, who became the guides and porters to the visiting travellers. Climbing was a tourist activity requiring both time and money.

Seven of the nineteen climbers were intellectuals or scholars whose work was held in the highest esteem in their individual field of expertise. The most common attribute of all of them was their dogged steadfastness in pursuit of their goals. This industriousness and persistence is very much the hallmark of the Anglo-Irish Christian tradition. They exemplified in their lives

Previous page: Dawson Stelfox going hard for the summit of Everest from the north side to make a first Irish ascent of Everest and the first British ascent of Everest from its north side on 27 May 1993. (Author's photo/*Everest Calling* (2013))

expressions of individual freedom and responsibility in pursuit of sublime majestic summits and science. For Adams-Reilly it was a labour of love to survey and map at his own expense the Mont Blanc massif in France, Switzerland and Italy and to repeat the process on Monte Rosa across the borders of Italy and Switzerland. He revelled in the mountain grandeur and tried to transfer his pleasure to his sketchpad. He stopped at every viewpoint and tried to describe what he saw, understanding the inadequacies of language and his skill as a writer. He found for himself a purpose when he discovered the shortcomings of the maps describing the region around Mont Blanc. He learnt the rudiments of surveying and spent three years of his life addressing the deficiencies of the existing map: his purpose drove him to the detailed exploration and survey of the unclimbed mountains covered in the region. His companions were the greatest stars of the golden age, Croz and Whymper, guide and client. The journey and companionship that ensued was as exquisite as the map it produced; a labour of love completed by steadfast men with artistic talents and generous hearts. The essence of mountaineering is surely the fusion of the physical bodily effort with the challenge and demands of the heart and mind to reach for the aesthetic – the body and soul in perfect unison in the midst of mountain grandeur.

Their Irishness or identity with the land of their birth or rearing varied greatly. Alpinism was not available to the poor or working classes. In the main they were Protestant, from planter forebears with strong family links to Ireland, their families being domiciled and intermarried in Ireland for many generations. Most of them accepted and supported the Act of Union; many fought in the British Army and opposed Home Rule for Ireland. Russell was from dispossessed Irish Catholic stock whose family's military traditions placed them among the ranks of the Irish Wild Geese who fought in the armies of Europe. If Irishness means being targeted for abuse in the Irish political situation, then Ball, Tyndall, Ryan, Bryce and Cullinan surely qualify. They came from the same forebears as Charles Stewart Parnell, Sir Ernest Shackleton, Edward Carson and indeed Oscar Wilde, Oliver Goldsmith and Edmund Burke. Ball referred to himself as an *Irlandais* in Zermatt in the 1840s; Barrington put his address at Fassaroe, County Wicklow, in the *führerbuch* of Christian Almer when he climbed the Eiger. Tyndall identified himself as an Irishman with the politics of 'the Orangemen'. Captain Valentine Ryan, a Catholic landlord who inherited an estate in Ireland, left it with his English wife just as Ireland was poised on the brink of independence, never setting foot on Irish soil again while alive, yet was buried in an ancient Catholic graveyard on the banks of the Shannon after his death.

Ball, educated by the Jesuits, was a remarkably independently minded Catholic who was mauled by the electors of Limerick on the urging of the priests who did not like his open support for a unified Italy. Bryce, another intellectual and Alpine Club president, represented the formidable Scots-Irish Free Presbyterian tradition of Antrim, which also produced Henry Joy McCracken who was hanged following the 1798 rebellion. Green wrote an Irish historic novel about Grace O'Malley, or Grainne Waile, set on the western seaboard he knew intimately. Green, Barrington and Hart all lived and died in their native places and were comfortable and content in their surroundings in counties Kerry, Wicklow and Donegal respectively. All three knew and were familiar with Irish hills and coastlines. Indeed Hart's first rock-climbing guide to Ireland included Ireland's sea cliffs as well as its mountain crags. Scriven wore the green jersey with its shamrock emblem and the captain's armband for Ireland in epic rugby matches with England and Scotland.

The guidebooks, mapping, scientific observation of glaciers, flora and fauna undertaken and the discoveries made by so many of these Irishmen in conjunction with their climbing contributed in no small way to the promotion of climbing as a recreational activity, as well as to our understanding of natural science and the environment. The studies of Hart and R. M. Barrington on Irish mountains, islands and coastlines, as well as off the west coast of Scotland, made a great contribution to Irish and Scottish naturalism. Green's contribution to the development of Irish fisheries was unique and he, in particular, remains unfairly unsung among the people he served so well. His retirement and death came just before the emergence of Ireland as a political entity, independent of Britain; this new independence, exacted as it was by insurrection and guerrilla war, left many great servants of the old regime such as Green lost and forgotten while the new heroes of the Easter Rising took centre stage in the history books of the new state. The neglected grave of this talented and patriotic Cork man in Sneem, County Kerry, is poor reward for his contribution.

Lizzie Hawkins-Whitshed's poor health initially took her to the Alps and saved her from an early death from consumption, raising her up instead to a unique place in mountaineering history. She was a very competent mountaineer, who made many fine and notable first ascents in the Alps and Norway, as well as many first winter ascents in the Alps. Lizzie had the same indefatigable spirit and stamina as her countrymen and, perhaps most importantly, was able to communicate with authority that women *should* climb. Her championing of the world of winter sports has left a remarkable, if perhaps less visible, mark on our modern lives; many of us could not now imagine a winter holiday without access to the varied joys and activities of the mountain slopes. In calmly ignoring the criticism heaped upon her for engaging in unwomanly activities and focusing instead on reaching for her own high standards of excellence, she paved the way for women adventurers and pioneers of the future.

Perhaps the most important Irish contribution to modern lovers of mountain and crag came from James Bryce, who introduced the Access to Mountains (Scotland) Bill in 1884.[1] How pleased he would have been to have seen the Land Reform Act 2003, which comprehensively codified into Scots law the ancient traditions of the right to universal access to the land in Scotland. The Act first moved by him in the nineteenth century was passed in 2004.

How should we regard them? In the author's opinion, exactly as we regard their Irish contemporaries who excelled in the field of polar exploration. They stand alongside Francis Crozier, who served with Ross in the Antarctic, with Parry and Franklin in the Arctic, and with McClintock and McClure who went in search of Franklin. Indeed, Henry Hart was a member of the scientific party on board *Discovery* in the 1875 North Pole Expedition with Nares. The Irish alpine pioneers set out with the same desire as their polar peers: to be useful in endeavours that explored new territory and knowledge. They acquitted themselves admirably.

While searching for the grave of Valentine Ryan at Meelick in County Galway in November 2012, the author observed nearby a plaque recording the opening in 2010 of a new long-distance walking trail along the banks of the River Shannon. The trail was opened by Joss Lynam, a life-long member of the Alpine Club and a founding member of the Irish Mountaineering Club (IMC) in 1948. His link to the pioneers mentioned in this book was the first president of the IMC, the naturalist Robert Lloyd Praeger, who was a close friend of Green, Barrington and Hart. The author went with Joss to the Himalaya in 1987 as a member of the Irish Changtse expedition to the Tibetan side of Everest, first mapped by Howard-Bury's reconnaissance team. A series of Himalayan expeditions followed, which culminated in the first Irish summit success on Everest in 1993 via the North Col. Howard-Bury's dream became reality when Dawson Stelfox made the first ascent from the north side by a climber from either Britain or Ireland. The legacy still bears fruit.

Appendix

Chronological list of attempts on the Matterhorn to second ascent (1858–1865); from Whymper, *Scrambles Amongst the Alps in the Years 1860–69*

Attempt Number	Date	Names of Climbers and Guides	Route taken and high point reached	Remarks
1	1858–90	**J. A. Carrel** J. J. Carrel	Breuil side to the Chimney 12,650 feet/3,856m	Several attempts
2	July 1860	**A., C. & S. Parker**	Zermatt, east face. Highest point unrecorded	No guides
3	Aug 1860	V. Hawkins **J. Tyndall** J. Bennen J. J. Carrel	Just above the foot of the Great Tower 13,050 feet/3,978m	
4	July 1861	**A., C. & S. Parker**	Zermatt, east face 11,700 feet/3,566m	No guides
5	29 Aug 1861	**J. A. Carrel** J. J. Carrel	Breuil side to Crête du Coq 13,230 feet/4,033m	
6	29–30 Aug 1861	**E. Whymper**	Breuil side to the Chimney 12,650 feet/3,856m	Camped out with unnamed Oberland guide
7	Jan 1862	**T. S. Kennedy** P. Perrn P. Taugwalder	Zermatt, east face 11,000 feet/3,353m	Winter attempt
8	7–8 July 1862	R. J. S. Macdonald **E. Whymper** J. Taugwald J. Kronig	Breuil side, arête below the Chimney 12,000 feet/3,658m	
9	9–10 July 1862	R. J. S. Macdonald **E. Whymper** J. A. Carrel Pession	Breuil side, Great Tower 12,992 feet/3,960m	
10	18–19 July 1862	**E. Whymper**	Breuil side, Cravate 13,400 feet/4,084m	Alone

Attempt Number	Date	Names of Climbers and Guides	Route taken and high point reached	Remarks
11	23–24 July 1862	**E. Whymper** **J. A. Carrel** C. Carrel L. Meynet	Breuil side, Crête du Coq 13,970 feet/4,258m	
12	25–26 July 1862	**E. Whymper** L. Meynet	Breuil side, Cravate 13,460 feet/4,103m	
13	27–28 July 1862	**J. Tyndall** J. J. Bennen A. Walter **J. A. Carrel** C. Carrel	Breuil side, the Shoulder to the foot of the final peak 13, 970 feet/4,258m	Tyndall made no further attempts. The minor peak was named Pic Tyndall
14	10–11 Aug 1863	**E. Whymper** **J. A. Carrel** C. Carrel L. Meynet	Breuil side, Crête du Coq 13,280 feet/4,048m	
15	21 June 1865	**E. Whymper** M. Croz C. Almer F. Biener L. Meynet	Southeast face 11,200 feet/3,414m	
1st Ascent	13–15 July 1865	**E. Whymper** Lord F. Douglas D. Hadlow C. Hudson M. Croz P. Taugwalder Snr P. Taugwalder Jnr	Zermatt, Hörnli Ridge 14,692 feet/4,477.5m	First ascent, all reached summit. Croz, Hudson, Hadlow and Douglas died on descent
2nd Ascent	16–18 July 1865	**J. A. Carrel** J. B. Bich A. Gorret J. A. Meynet	Breuil route 14,692 feet/4,477.5m	Second ascent, all-Italian party. Only the first-named reached the summit

Glossary

À cheval: Astride a sharp ridge, as if riding a horse.

Alpenstock: Stout stick, fitted with a forged metal point to aid walking and climbing in snowfields and glaciers.

Arête: Sharp ridge or rocky edge on a mountain.

Bergschrund: Crevasse that separates a glacier or snowfield from a rock outcrop or mountain face.

Brocken spectre: A ghostly illusion that appears when a low sun is behind a climber who is looking down from a ridge into mist below. It is the magnified shadow of the climber surrounded by a rainbow-coloured glow and shimmering rings, which is projected forward by the sun. The name derives from sightings of the illusion on the Brocken, a peak in the Harz Mountains of Germany.

Couloir: Gully above the snow line, usually filled with snow and often subject to rockfall later in the day.

Crampons: Metal shoes with sharp projecting spikes that are strapped to boots while climbing on hard, frozen snow or ice. Early crampons were heavy and cumbersome and difficult to keep tight or rigid on the boots.

Crevasse: Fissure or gap in a glacier or snowfield caused by constant ice movement and gravity over uneven mountain bedrock.

Führerbuch (pl. Führerbücher): Comments book presented by a mountain guide to each client at the end of an engagement. The book was used to record the climbing achievement (peaks and passes climbed) and the competence and behaviour of the guide. Prospective clients could ask to see the book to ascertain the guide's experience and the satisfaction or otherwise of previous clients.

Glissade: Controlled sitting/standing, sliding descent down soft snow slopes using an ice axe or alpenstock as a braking tool.

Grat: German term for a mountain ridge, rock edge or arête.

Guide: Professional climber, usually operating in a specific mountain locality and with local knowledge and experience; qualified to lead and look after paying clients who wish to safely climb peaks and passes.

Ice axe: Type of slater's axe, modified for cutting steps on a glacier. One end is forged into a pick shape and the other into an adze. Early axes had long wooden handles to facilitate step-cutting below the guide's feet.

Massif: Prominent range or group of mountains.

Mattock: Agricultural tool with an adze and chisel on opposite ends of the head (adapted for use as an ice axe by early mountain guides).

Morraine: Ridge or mound of hard-packed mud and rocks carried and deposited by a glacier to its edges and to its end or terminal.

Névé: Hard frozen compacted snow capable of supporting the weight of a climber which therefore usually provides ideal climbing conditions.

Pass: The way across a mountain ridge from one valley to another, often over glaciers and high cols and at considerable altitude.

Porter: Assistant or aspirant guide engaged to carry baggage and provisions or otherwise assist a guide with multiple clients.

Snow bridge: A bridge of hard snow often spanning a crevasse or wide gap in a glacier and providing a way across. They require judgement to assess their trustworthiness for crossing particularly later in the day in places where the snow has softened after exposure to the sun.

Serac: The upper edge or exit point of a snow slope, usually comprised of hard-packed or frozen snow or ice at the top of a snowfield or glacier. Seracs are shaped by wind and are often overhanging. Seracs sometimes have to be chopped through or tunnelled under in order to gain access to upper mountain ridges and rocks.

Endnotes

Chapter 1: The Origins of Alpinism

1   G. R. de Beer & T. G. Brown, *The First Ascent of Mont Blanc* (Oxford, Oxford University Press, 1957).

2   James D. Forbes, *Travels Through the Alps of Savoy and other Parts of the Pennine Chain, with Observations on the Phenomena of Glaciers* (Edinburgh, A & C Black, 1843), p. 6.

3   Ronald Clarke, *The Victorian Mountaineers* (London, B. T. Batsford, 1953), p. 20.

4   J. D. Forbes, *Travels*, p. 20.

5   *Ibid.*, p. 10.

6   *Ibid.*, p. 6.

7   H. F. Montagnier. 'Early Records of the Col de Théodule, the Weissthor, the Adler and other Passes of the Zermatt District', *The Alpine Journal*, 32 (1918–19), pp. 42–67.

8   Charles Edward Mathews, *The Annals of Mont Blanc* (London, T. F. Unwin, 1898), p. 171.

9   Cited in H. F. Montagnier, 'A Bibliography of the Ascents of Mont Blanc from 1786 to 1853', *The Alpine Journal*, 25 (1910–1911), pp. 637–8.

10 *Daily News*, London, date August 1851.

11 Owen Dudley Edwards, 'Wilde, Oscar Fingal O'Flahertie Wills (1854–1900)', *Oxford Dictionary of National Biography*, 58 (Oxford, Oxford University Press, 2004).

12 Guido Rey, *The Matterhorn*, translated by J. E. C. Eaton (London, Unwin, 1907), p. 41.

Chapter 2: John Ball: *Encyclopaedia Alpina*

1   W. A. B. Coolidge, 'In Memoriam: John Ball', *The Alpine Journal*, 14 (1889), pp. 469–470.

2   Foreword by Lord Conway in John Ball, *Peaks, Passes and Glaciers*, third series, edited by A. E. Fields & S. Spencer (London, Longman, Green & Co., 1932).

3   C. E. Mathews, in C. T. Dent (ed.), *Mountaineering* (London, T. F. Unwin, 1892), p. 353.

4   Sir J. D. Hooker, 'Mr John Ball, F.R.S.' (obituary), *Proceedings of the Royal Geographical Society*, 12 (1890), pp. 99–108.

5   *Ibid.*, p. 100.

6   A galvanic pile is better known as a battery which consists of multiple electrochemical cells that derive electrical energy from spontaneous redox reaction taking place in each cell. The name is derived from Luigi Galvani who discovered in 1780 the reaction in experiments which used frog legs in a circuit between two different metals. The solar spectrum is the extent of the sun's electromagnetic radiation including radio waves, microwaves, visible light, ultraviolet rays, X-rays and gamma rays.

7   Hooker, *op cit.*, p. 100.

8   *Ibid.*

9   John Ball, 'Botanical Notes of a Tour in Ireland, with Notices of Some New Plants', *Annals and Magazine of Natural History*, 2 (1838), pp. 28–36.

10 John Ball, M.R.I.A., 'Notice of the Former Existence of Small Glaciers in the County of Kerry', *Journal of the Geological Society of Dublin*, 1848–50 (Dublin 1851), 151–154.

11 John Ball, *A Guide to the Western Alps* (London, Longman, Green & Co., 1866), p. 344.

12 *Ibid.*, p. 347.

13 A. L. Mumm (ed.), *Alpine Club Register,* vol. 1, 1857–1863 (London, E. Arnold, 1923), pp. 12–26.

14 Ball, *Western Alps*, p. 344.

15 John Ball, *Peaks, Passes and Glaciers* (London, Longman, Green & Co., 1859), p. 481.

16 *Ibid.*, pp. 155–192, for Ball's account of the passage of the Schwarztor.

17   Letter from John Ball to E. T. B Twistleton (Poor Law Commissioner), 12 April 1846 (Mullingar), *National Archives of Ireland*, File RLFC3/1/1535.

18   Letter from John Ball to E. T. B. Twistleton, 17 April 1846 (Tralee), *NAI*, file RLFC3/1/1694.

19   John Ball, *What is to be Done for Ireland?* (London, John Ridgway, 1849), p. 7.

20   *Ibid.*, p. 63.

21   *Ibid.*, p. 86.

22   *The Champion*, 18 July & 22 July 1848.

23   *Ibid.*, 15 July 1848.

24   The Stockport Riots: the 1850 re-establishment of the Catholic hierarchy in Britain was followed by growing, irrational fears about the Catholic population in areas where there were large numbers of Irish immigrants; these fears were often fuelled by the pronouncements of Protestant clergymen. In June 1852, three weeks before the general election, the Tory government of Lord Derby was felt to be fomenting anti-Catholic bigotry with a proclamation that forbade Catholics to walk in procession through the streets with the symbols of their religion. There was a short-lived period of increasingly violent protest and demonstration on both sides, culminating in attacks on Protestant and Catholic churches, homes and schools.

25   Editorial, *The Carlow Sentinel*, 24 July 1852.

26   From Grimsel to Grindelwald; the passage of the Strahleck, in Ball, *Peaks,* pp. 255–282.

27   Mumm, *op. cit.*, vol. 1, p. 12.

28   Hooker, *op. cit.* p. 102.

29   David Murphy, 'John Palliser (1817–1880)', *Dictionary of Irish Biography*, vol. 7 (Cambridge, Royal Irish Academy & Cambridge University Press, 2009). Palliser's house was burned down on 18 February 1923 by the IRA who gave his niece, Miss Caroline Fairholme (an old lady of sixty-eight years), five minutes to leave before setting fire to the oil they splashed about the place. The story is told in Irene Spry's 'On the Trail of Palliser's Papers', *Saskatchewan History*, 12, 2 (1959), pp. 61–71.

30   Irene Spry, 'Captain John Palliser and the Exploration of Western Canada', *The Geographical Journal*, 125, 2 (1959), pp. 149–84.

31   *The Sligo Champion*, March 21 1857.

32   The parallels between his own career and the sad career of Sadleir could not have been lost on Ball. John Sadleir had been appointed a junior lord of the Treasury in 1853 by Lord Aberdeen, but was rejected by the Carlow electorate in the same year, apparently as a rebuke for breaking 'the pledge'. Like Ball he went on to stand for election in Sligo and, within months of the Carlow defeat, he was returned for the Borough of Sligo – amid serious allegations that many of his votes were bought. He was eventually forced to resign his ministerial position in 1854 when found guilty of being implicated in a plot to imprison a depositor of the Tipperary Joint Stock Bank (which he owned) because the individual in question had refused to vote for him when he was seeking re-election to Carlow in 1853. In February 1856 that bank was found to be insolvent, owing to Sadleir's personal overdraft of £280,000. During the same month, while still the Whig MP for Sligo, he committed suicide on Hampstead Heath by drinking prussic acid.

33   Editorial, *The Sligo Champion*, 15 August 1857.

34   Robert Gore-Booth was the father of Henry Gore-Booth, an accomplished Arctic sailor and explorer, and grandfather of Constance Gore-Booth, better known as the rebel Countess Markievicz who fought in the 1916 rebellion in Dublin and was the first woman elected to the House of Commons in 1918, when she represented Sinn Féin.

35   John Ball, *A Guide to the Eastern Alps* (London, Longman, Green & Co., 1868), p. 525.

36   'Obituary for Mr John Ball, FRS', *The Times*, October 23 1889

37   *Limerick Chronicle*, 26 April 1858.

38 William Longman, 'Modern Mountaineering and the History of the Alpine Club', *The Alpine Journal*, 8 (1878), p. 85. A fragment of the work was printed as an appendix after the index.

39 G. C. B. Shuster, 'Tyndall as a Mountaineer', in A. S. Eve & C. H. Creasey, *Life and Works of John Tyndall* (London, Macmillan & Co., 1945), p. 386.

40 *Ibid.*

41 Peter Hansen, 'Wills, Sir Alfred (1828–1912)', *Oxford Dictionary of National Biography*, vol. 59 (Oxford, Oxford University Press, 2004).

42 James Quinn, 'John Ball (1818–1889)', *Dictionary of Irish Biography*, vol. 1.

43 Clarke, *op. cit.*, pp. 95–98.

44 Longman, *op. cit.*, p. 88.

45 R. L. G. Irving, *A History of British Mountaineering* (London, B. T. Batsford, 1955), p. 77.

46 Clarke, *op. cit.*, p. 113.

47 Longman, *op. cit.*, pp. 90–91.

48 *Ibid.*, p. 91

49 Lord Conway in Ball, *Peaks*, p. v.

50 *Ibid.*

51 Longman, *op. cit.*, p. 93.

52 John Ball, *A Guide to the Western Alps* (London, Longman, Green and Co., 1866).

53 The paper he delivered was published as 'Discussion on the Origin of the Flora of the European Alps', *Proceedings of the Royal Geographical Society*, 6 (1879), pp. 564–589.

54 W. Mathews, 'John Ball', *The Alpine Journal*, 15 (London 1889), pp. 16–19.

55 C. D. Cunningham and W. de W. Abney (eds), *The Pioneers of the Alps* (London, Samson Low, Marston, & Co., 1887), pp. 81–83.

56 John Ball, 'Val di Genova and the Pisgana Pass', *The Alpine Journal*, 1 (1864), pp. 1–11.

Chapter 3: John Tyndall: the Race for the Matterhorn

1 W. T. Jeans, *Lives of the Electricians* (London, Whittaker & Co., 1887), p. 1.

2 *Ibid.*, p. 3.

3 During his term as Chief Secretary for Ireland (1812–18), Robert Peel masterminded Act 54 (George III), which was passed on 25 July 1814. Using clause 131 of this legislation, he formed the Peace Preservation Force (PPF; later the Royal Irish Constabulary), which was used in any area 'Proclaimed' as disturbed. The PPF forces were often deployed during periods of intense agitation as a result of hunger or general discontent. See Herity, J., *The Royal Irish Constabulary: A Short History and Genealogical Guide* (Dublin, Four Courts Press, 1997), p. 29.

4 Jeans, *op. cit.*, p. 5.

5 From an essay that was to have been the first chapter of a planned biography of Tyndall by his widow, Louisa; cited in Eve & Creasey, *op. cit.*, p. 3.

6 *Ibid.*, pp. 10–11.

7 *Ibid.*, p. 10.

8 *Ibid.*, p. 11.

9 *Ibid.*, p. 17.

10 Shuster, *op. cit.*, p. 341.

11 *Ibid.*

12 Tyndall's first memoir to be published in the *Philosophical Magazine* (1850), co-authored with Knoblauch, was entitled 'On the Magneto-optic Properties of Crystals and the Relation of Magnetism and Dia-magnetism to Molecular Arrangement'; the 1851 memoir was 'Diamagnetism and Magne Crystallic Action'.

13   Sabine was an artillery officer who had been to Spitsbergen in the Arctic and to tropical Africa measuring gravity with pendulums and finding the shape of the earth. He had also been with Ross and Parry to the Arctic looking for the North-West Passage and had established the 'eleven-year period' for magnetic storms and sunspots.

14   John Tyndall, *Glaciers of the Alps* (London, Longmans, Green and Co., 1860), p. 9.

15   John Tyndall and Thomas H. Huxley, 'On the Structure and Motion of Glaciers', *Philosophical Transactions of the Royal Society*, (London, 1857) vol.147, pp. 327– 346.

16   John Tyndall, 'A Day among the Séracs of the Glacier du Géant', in *Hours of Exercise in the Alps* (London, Longmans, Green and Co., 1871), p. 333.

17   Tyndall, *Glaciers*, p 79–81, for the account of the climb.

18   George Yeld, 'Professor Huxley and Professor Tyndall', *The Alpine Journal*, 20 (1901), pp 332–3; citing T. H. Huxley, *Life and Letters*, vol. 1 (London, Macmillan, 1900), p. 46.

19   Tyndall, *Glaciers*, p. 86.

20   Letters concerning the formation of Alpine Club (1857), Alpine Club archives, CL File B65

21   Jeans, *op. cit.*, p. 38. Faraday used the term 'regelation' for the property that ice possesses, causing the freezing together of two pieces of ice by simple contact and slight pressure.

22   J. S. Rowlinson, 'Tyndall's work on Glaciology and Geology', in W. H. Brock, N. D. McMillan & R. C. Mollan (eds), *John Tyndall: Essays on a Natural Philosopher* (Dublin, Royal Dublin Society, 1981), p. 117.

23   The pamphlet by J. D. Forbes, 'Reply to Professor Tyndall's Remarks on his Work on the Glaciers of the Alps, relating to Rendu's "Théorie des Glaciers", Edinburgh 1860', is reprinted as Appendix A in J. C. Shairp, P. G. Tait & A. Adams-Reilly, *Life and Letters of James David Forbes F.R.S.* (London, Macmillan & Co., 1873).

24   Rowlinson, *op. cit.*, p. 123.

25   John Tyndall, *Glaciers*, p. 104.

26   *Ibid.*, p. 106–9.

27   *Ibid.*, p. 112.

28   *Ibid.*, pp. 159–160.

29   Shuster, *op. cit.*, p. 359.

30   Tyndall, *Glaciers*, p. 178.

31   *Ibid.*, p. 191.

32   John Tyndall, *Hours*, p. 57.

33   Eve & Creasey, *op. cit.*, p. 83.

34   Tyndall, *Hours*, p. 58.

35   *Ibid.*, p. 2.

36   *Ibid.*, p. 18–26.

37   *Ibid.*, p. 26.

38   Shuster, *op. cit.*, p. 387.

39   *Ibid.*, pp. 387–8.

40   *Ibid.*, pp. 388–9.

41   *Ibid.*, p. 390.

42   Stephen, Rev. L., 'Ascent of the Rothorn', *The Alpine Journal*, 2 (1866), pp 67–79.

43   Stephen, Rev. L., 'The Bietschhorn and Blümlis Alp', *The Alpine Journal*, 1 (1864), p. 41.

44   Shuster, *op. cit.*, p. 389.

45   Shairp et al., *op. cit.*, pp. 492–566.

46   J. D. Forbes, 'Historical Remarks on the First Discovery of the Real Structure of Glacier Ice', *The Edinburgh New Philosophical Journal*, 34 (1843), pp 133–52; the article is also reprinted as Appendix B in Shairp et al., *op. cit.*

47   Tyndall, *Hours*, p. 72.

48   For Tyndall's account of the ascent of the Weisshorn, see Tyndall, *Hours*, p. 91–113.

49 Mr Vaughan Hawkins, cited in Cunningham & Abney, *Pioneers*, p. 149.

50 *Ibid.*

51 *Ibid.*

52 Edward Whymper, *Scrambles Amongst the Alps in the Years 1860–69*, edn 4 (London, John Murray, 1893), p. 77.

53 *Ibid.*, p. 89

54 Tyndall, *Hours*, pp. 122–3.

55 Whymper, *Scrambles*, p. 84.

56 *Ibid.*, pp. 91–3.

57 Edward Whymper, 'Camping Out', *Alpine Journal*, 2 (1866), pp. 1–11.

58 T. S. Kennedy, 'Zermatt and the Matterhorn in Winter', *The Alpine Journal*, 2 (1864), p. 82

59 Whymper, *Scrambles*, pp. 113–14.

60 Tyndall, *Hours*, p. 157.

61 Letter from Whymper to the editor: 'Professor Tyndall's Attempt on the Matterhorn in 1862', *The Alpine Journal*, 5 (1872) pp., 329–336.

62 Tyndall, *Hours*, p. 161.

63 *Ibid.*, p. 163.

64 *Ibid.*, p. 164.

65 Whymper, *Scrambles*, p. 134.

66 Whymper letter, 'Professor Tyndall's Attempt', p. 331.

67 Rey, *op. cit.*, p. 311.

68 Whymper, *Scrambles*, p. 116.

69 *Ibid.*, p. 121.

70 Tyndall, *Hours*, p. 174.

71 Whymper, *Scrambles*, p. 280.

72 Whymper letter to *The Times*, reprinted as 'The Fatal Accident on the Matterhorn', *The Alpine Journal*, 2 (1864), pp. 148–153.

73 Letter from Joseph McCormack to the editor of *The Times* (London), reprinted in *The Irish Times*, Tuesday 15 August 1865.

74 Tyndall, *Hours*, p. 280.

75 *Ibid.*, p. 283.

76 *Ibid.*, p. 285.

77 Obituary notice for Mrs Tyndall, *The Times* (London), 20 August 1940.

78 Eve & Creasey, *op. cit.*, pp. 279–80.

Chapter 4: Anthony Adams-Reilly: Mapmaker of the High Alps

1 Carte Nationale de la Suisse (1:50,000), No. 5003: *Mont Blanc–Grand Combin* (Wabern, Office Fédéral de Topographie, 1977)

2 Henry F. Montagnier, 'Early Extracts from the Travellers' Book of the Hotel at the Eggishorn', *The Alpine Journal*, 32 (1920), p. 226.

3 J. P. Farrar, 'Historical Documents III, including a Facsimile Copy of the Führerbücher of Johan Zumtaugwald', *The Alpine Journal*, 31 (1918), p. 226.

4 Hamel's party was swept away in an avalanche killing three local guides. This was the first fatal accident to occur on Mont Blanc. Source: J. J. Cowell, 'On Some Relics of the Guides Lost on Mont Blanc', *The Alpine Journal*, 1 (1864), pp. 332–9.

5 Mumm, *op. cit.*, vol. 1, pp. 268–71.

6   A. A. Reilly, 'The Two Routes to the Summit of Mont Blanc', letter to *The Times* (London), 29 August 1861.

7   Note of the presentation by Mr Alexander Mortimer of notebooks and some diaries of the late Mr Adams Reilly to the A.C., *The Alpine Journal*, 32 (1920), p. 109. Four of the six 1861 diaries maintained by A. Adams-Reilly are in the Alpine Club's archive; they were received from the next occupant of his London home, which Reilly shared for a long time with C. E. Mathews (who would later write his obituary and attend his funeral in Ireland).

8   Anthony Adams-Reilly, *Diary 2* (1861), Alpine Club archives, File D1 74, pp. 10–11.

9   An ancient hostel maintained for the safety and comfort of travellers using the mountain pass road, which connects the cantons of Berne and the Upper Valais.

10   Adams-Reilly, *Diary 2* (1861), p. 38–39.

11   Adams-Reilly, *Diary 2* (1861), p. 41–7.

12   For the Reilly account of the ascent of the Jungfrau, see Adams-Reilly, *Diary 2* (1861), pp. 49–71.

13   Adams-Reilly, *Diary 3* (1861), Alpine Club archives, File DI 75, pp. 1–8.

14   *Ibid.*, pp 26–27.

15   *Ibid.*, pp. 29–30.

16   Rev. Leslie Stephen, *The Playground of Europe* (London, Longmans, Green and Co., 1871), p. 76–7.

17   Adams-Reilly, *Diary 3* (1861), pp. 36–7.

18   *Ibid.*, pp. 41–2.

19   *Ibid.*, pp. 43–68.

20   Adams-Reilly, *Diary 4* (1861), Alpine Club archives, File DI 74, pp. 6–13.

21   *Ibid.*, p. 59

22   Adams-Reilly, *Diary 6* (1861), Alpine Club archives, File DI 78, p. 21

23   Mumm, *op. cit.*, vol. 1, p. 269.

24   Ball, *Western Alps*, pp. 231–2.

25   A. A. Reilly, 'A Rough Survey of the Chain of Mont Blanc', *The Alpine Journal*, 1 (1864), pp. 257–74.

26   *Ibid.*, p. 258.

27   *Ibid.*, p. 262.

28   Whymper, *Scrambles*. p. 221.

29   Edward, Whymper, *Four letters from Whymper to Adams Reilly, 1864–5*, Alpine Club archives, London, File B14.

30   A. A. Reilly, 'A Rough Survey', pp. 257–74.

31   Adams-Reilly, *Diary labelled* 'Chain of Mt Blanc 1864'; Alpine Club archives, London, File DI 70.

32   Whymper, *Scrambles*. p. 229.

33   Adams-Reilly, *Diary Chain of Mt Blanc* p. 18.

34   Whymper, *Scrambles*, pp. 248–9.

35   Summary of New Expeditions, *The Alpine Journal*, 1 (1864), p. 374.

36   Adams-Reilly, 'A Rough Survey', p. 269.

37   Whymper, Four letters, 22 April 1865.

38   *Ibid.*, 1 May 1865.

39   *Ibid.*, 20 June 1865.

40   C.E. Mathews, 'Recollections of a Mountaineer', in C. T. Dent (ed.), *Mountaineering* (London, T. F. Unwin, 1892), pp. 354–356.

41   *Ibid.* , p. 353.

42   *Ibid.*, p. 355–356.

43   William Mathews, cited in Cunningham & Abney, *Pioneers*, pp 154–7.

44   Whymper *Scrambles*, p. 247.

Chapter 5: Charles Barrington: Eigerman

1 'The Alpine Club had scarcely been formed when the Eiger was added to the list of conquered mountains. The successful climber was thought an Englishman, did not belong to the club and no account of the ascent has appeared in England. It may therefore fitly conclude our record. The climber was a Mr Harrington, an Irishman; the guides were the well-known Christian Almer and Peter Bohren, who about this time first stand forward as the leaders in every venturesome undertaking. The ascent was made on August 13 1858 by the route still followed up the buttress overhanging the little Scheideck.' Source: W. Longman, *op. cit.*, Appendix 'Modern Mountaineering', p. 81.

2 C. D. Cunningham & W. de W. Abney, *Christian Almer's Führerbuch, 1856–1894* (London, Samson Low, Marston, & Co., 1896). Each guide maintained a *Führerbuch* or logbook into which his clients were asked to write their comments regarding the mountain climbed and the guide's performance.

3 Amy Barrington, *The Barringtons: a Family History* (Dublin, private publication, 1917), p. 282.

4 'Charles Barrington' (short obituary), *The Freeman's Journal*, 23 April 1901.

5 'The First Ascent of the Eiger', a letter from Charles Barrington to his half-brother Richard Manliffe Barrington, accompanied by a note from Richard to the editor of *The Alpine Journal*; *The Alpine Journal*, 11 (1878), pp. 172–4.

6 Richard Barrington's note to the editor, published with his brother Charles' letter; *The Alpine Journal*, 11 (1878), pp. 172–4.

7 Copy of pages 61 and 62 from the *Führerbuch* of Christian Almer. Courtesy of the Alpine Club archives

8 Minutes for 14 August 1860, Society of Friends, *Dublin Monthly Meeting Proceedings, 1858–1877*, p. 86 (minute 8).

9 Diarmaid Ó'Muirithe, 'Charles Barrington (1834–1901)', *Dictionary of Irish Biography*, vol 1.

10 The Society of Friends, *Database/Book of Disownments and Resignations*; D52-1820-71-entry 13531.

11 *Thom's Irish Almanac*, 1869, 1873–5 & 1877 (Dublin, Alexander Thom & Co.).

12 See the Irish Mountain Running Association website for details: https://www.imra.ie/events/view/id/376/.

13 Diarmaid Ó'Muirithe 'An Irishman's Diary', *The Irish Times*, 3 April 2004.

14 Report on the funeral of Mr C. Barrington, *The Irish Times*, 22 April 1901.

15 *The Freeman's Journal*, Wednesday 24 April 1901.

Chapter 6: Count Henry Russell: Wild Goose of the Pyrenees

1 Unattributed article, 'The Russells of Killough', *The Clongownian*, 3, 3 (1909), pp 20–6.

2 *Ibid.*, pp. 20–1.

3 Clongowes Wood College, *Students Ledger*, 1850–1864.

4 *Notes par Voies et Chemins à Travers le Nouveau Monde* par Henry Russell (Des Barons D'Ulster) (Bagnères-de-Bigorre, Dossun, 1858).

5 Henry Russell, *16 000 Lieues à Travers l'Asie et l'Océanie. Voyage Exécuté Pendant les Années 1858–1861*, 2 vols (Paris, Hachette, 1864). Reissued by Amyot, 1866, without the map and the panorama.

6 Bert Slader, *The High Pyrenees: Los Encantados – The Enchanted Mountains* (Belfast, Quest Books, 2005), pp. 240–8.

7 Henry Russell, 'In Memorial Charles Packe', *The Alpine Journal*, 18 (1896), p. 238.

8 H. Russell, 'On Mountains and on Mountaineering in General', *The Alpine Journal*, 5 (1871), p. 241.

9 W. P. Haskett Smith, 'Henry Russell' (obituary), *The Alpine Journal*, 24 (1909), pp. 501–4.

10 *Ibid.*, p. 503.

11 *Ibid.*

12 Henry Russell, *Souvenirs d'un Montagnard, 1858–1888*, edn 2 (Pau, Imprimerie Vignancour, 1908), pp. 660–72.

13 *Ibid.*, pp. 241–2.

14 Haskett Smith, *op.cit.,* pp. 502–3.

15 Mumm, *op.cit.* vol.1 'Count Henri Patrick Marie Russell-Killough (1864–1909)', p. 305.

16 Mumm, *op. cit.*, p. 305.

17 Charles Packe, A Review of *Souvenirs d'un Montagnard*, 1858–1888, par Cte. Henry Russell', *The Alpine Journal*, 14 (1889), pp. 255–7.

18 Rosemary Bailey, *The Man Who Married A Mountain* (London, Bantam, 2005) pp.15–17.

19 Paul Clements, 'Henry Russell: Eccentric Pioneer of Climbing in the Pyrenees', *The Irish Times*, 9 February 2009.

20 Henry Russell, 'In Memoriam: Charles Packe,' *The Alpine Journal*, 18 (1896), p. 239.

Chapter 7: Robert Fowler: Climbing Landlord

1 Mumm, *op. cit.*, vol. 2, pp. 137–8.

2 *Ibid.*

3 Report of Robert Fowler's funeral, *Meath Herald* and *Cavan Advertiser*, 13 November 1897.

4 H. F. Montagnier, ' Early Extracts', p. 240.

5 Ball, *Western Alps*, p. 299.

6 Mumm, *op. cit.*, vol. 2, p. 137.

7 H. F. Montagnier, ' Early Extracts', p. 224.

8 Robert Fowler, 'Narrative of Ascents of the Aiguille Verte and the Chardonnet in the year 1865', *The Alpine Journal*, 4 (1870), pp. 140–7.

9 *Ibid.*, p. 208.

10 Extracts from the *Führerbuch* of Peter Knobel, in A. L. Mumm (ed.), typed continuation of *The Alpine Club Register* (1891–1957), Alpine Club archives, London.

11 J. P. Farrar, 'The *Führerbuch* of Peter Knubel of St. Nicolas', *The Alpine Journal*, 32 (1919), pp. 98–9.

12 *The Times* (London), 22 September 1871.

13 Mumm, *Supplementary*, 14 September 1871.

14 Obituary, *The Irish Times*, 26 October 26.

15 Report of the death of Robert Fowler, *Meath Herald and Cavan Advertiser*, 13 November 1897.

16 On one occasion, while out with the Meath Hunt, the stag and the hounds (with the Empress in close pursuit) found themselves in Maynooth Catholic Seminary. The president of the college greeted her and gave her his cloak when she complained of the cold. She returned for Mass there the following Sunday.

17 Cunningham & Abney, *Pioneers*, pp. 101–2.

Chapter 8: Elizabeth Hawkins-Whitshed: 'Women Should Climb'

1 Mrs Aubrey Le Blond, *Day In, Day Out* (London, Bodley Head, 1928), p. 27.

2 Michael Alexander, *The True Blue: The Life and Adventures of Colonel Fred Burnaby 1842–85* (London, Rupert Hart-Davis, 1957), p. 123.

3 Le Blond, *Day In*, p. 28

4 *Ibid.*, p. 87

5 *Ibid.*, p. 91

6 *Ibid.*, p. 90.

7 E. A. F. Burnaby, *High Life and Towers of Silence* (London, Samson Low & Co., 1886), pp. 54–71.

8 Cited in Rebecca A. Brown, *Women on High: Pioneers of Mountaineering* (Boston, Appalachian Mountain Club Books, 2003), p. 86.

9 Marcus Tindal, 'The Champion Lady Mountaineer', published in *Pearson's Magazine c.* 1902; copy in Mountaineering Pamphlet T 526 (London, The Alpine Club), pp. 355–6.

10 E. A. F. Burnaby, *The High Alps in Winter; or, Mountaineering in Search of Health* (London, Samson Low & Co., 1883), p. 130.

11 Markus Britschgi, 'The Appeal of the Unknown: Photographer Main, A Pioneering Sensation', in M. Britchgi & D. Fässler (eds), *Elizabeth Main (1861–1934): Alpinist, Photographer, Writer* (Lucerne, Dioper-Verlag, 2003), p. 10.

12 Tindal, *op. cit.*, p. 358.

13 Burnaby, *High Alps*, pp 157–65.

14 W. A. B. Coolidge, 'Reviews and Notices', *The Alpine Journal*, 11 (1882–1884), p. 307. Coolidge (1850–1926) was a young American sent to recover poor health in the Alps, He went on to climb over 1,700 routes and became editor of *The Alpine Journal* and a series of climbing guidebooks.

15 W. A. B Coolidge, 'A Day and a Night on the Bietschorn', *The Alpine Journal*, 6 (1872–1874), pp. 114–24.

16 Burnaby, *High Life*, pp. 124–40.

17 *Ibid.*, pp. 98–106.

18 *Ibid.*, pp. 107–10.

19 Les Swinden & Peter Fleming, *Valais Alps East: Selected Climbs* (London, Alpine Club, 1999), pp.103–6.

20 *Ibid.*, pp. 102.

21 Ibid., pp. 189–90.

22 *Ibid.*, pp. 194–5.

23 Ursula Bauer, 'The Three Lives of Elizabeth Main', in M. Britchgi & D. Fässler (eds), *Elizabeth Main (1861–1934): Alpinist, Photographer, Writer* (Lucerne, Dioper-Verlag, 2003), p. 10.

24 E. L. Strutt, 'In Memoriam, Mrs Aubrey Le Blond (1861–1934)', *The Alpine Journal*, 64 (1934) pp. 382–4.

25 Cecily Williams, *Women on the Rope, the Feminine Share in Mountain Adventure* (London, George Allen & Unwin, 1973), p. 64.

26 Burnaby, *High Alps*, p. ix.

27 Frank Harris, *My Life and Loves* (Paris, 1938), cited in Alexander, *op. cit.*, p. 123.

28 Le Blond, *Day In*, p. 86.

29 Katherine Richardson (1854–1927) was from Yorkshire; she first visited the Alps at the age of eighteen and made 116 major ascents in her career, including six first ascents (amongst which the first ascent of Aiguille de Bionnassay) and fourteen first ascents by a woman (including the Meije). She lived and climbed in France with the famous French climber Mary Paillon.

30 Strutt, *op. cit.*, p. 383.

31 Brown, *op. cit.*, p. 88.

32 Burnaby, *High Life*, p. 117.

33 Bauer, *op. cit.*, p. 13.

34 *Ibid.*,

35 Brown, *op. cit.*, p. 88.

36 Le Blond, *Day In*, p. 124

37 Mrs Aubrey Le Blond, *Mountaineering in the Land of the Midnight Sun* (London, T. Fisher Unwin, 1908), pp. 14–16.

38 *Ibid.*, pp. 27–8.

39 *Ibid.*, p. 75.

40 *Ibid.*, pp. 99–102.

41 The Lyceum Club was a women's organisation established in 1907 by women members of the Writer's Club in London to support women interested in the arts, sciences and social concerns to progress in the professions.

42 Note by B. McAndrew, included in Stewart Erskine, 'In Memorium: Mrs Aubrey Le Blond', *Ladies' Alpine Club Yearbook* (1935), p. 20.

43 Bauer, *op. cit.*, p. 15.

44   McAndrew note, in Erskine, *op. cit.*, p. 20.

45   Cunningham & Abney, *Pioneers*, pp120–3.

Chapter 9: William Spotswood Green: a Passion for Mountains and Fishes

1   Christopher Moriarty, *The Reverend W. S. Green: Explorer and Fishery Scientist* (Dublin, Royal Irish Academy, 1994), p. 2.

2   *Ibid.*

3   *Ibid.*

4   Arthur E. J.Went, 'William Spotswood Green', *The Scientific Proceedings of the Royal Dublin Society*, series B, vol. 2 (1967), p. 1.

5   W. S. Green, Note of a week (not dated) spent in a fishing trawler in Irish Sea with school colleague referred to as 'L.', *Journals*, transcribed by Belinda Baldock, Alexander Turnbull Library, Wellington, New Zealand, MS 6637 (1869–1882).

6   William Spotswood Green, *The High Alps of New Zealand or a trip to the Glaciers of the Antipodes with an Ascent of Mount Cook* (London, Macmillan & Co., 1883), p. 4.

7   Green, Switzerland with Lyle and Swanzy, 28 June to 6 August 1871, *Journals*, MS 6637.

8   Green, Lofoten Islands, Norway, 28 June to 6 August 1871, *Journals*, MS 6637.

9   Lake Lucerne in central Switzerland.

10   Ed Webster, *Climbing in the Magic Islands: A Climbing & Hiking Guidebook to the Lofoten Islands of Norway* (Henningsvar, Nord Norsk Klatreskole, 1994), p. 9.

11   Belinda's father, James Butler, was Green's uncle by marriage so she was not a blood relation.

12   Green, the West Indies and Orinoco, 3 January to 29 March 1877, *Journals*, MS 91/241 (1877).

13   Alex Palman, *Aoraki-Mount Cook: A Guide for Mountaineers*, (Christchurch, New Zealand Alpine Club, 2001).

14   Green, *High Alps*, p. 5.

15   *Ibid.*, p. 5–6.

16   *Ibid.*, p. 7.

17   *Ibid.*, p. 9.

18   *Ibid.*, p. 9.

19   *Ibid.*, p. 9.

20   R. L. Praeger, *The Way that I Went* (Dublin, Hodges Figgis & Co., 1937), p. 345.

21   S. L. Gwynn, *Duffer's Luck: a Fisherman's Adventure* (Edinburgh, Blackwood & Sons, 1924), p. 253.

22   Green, *High Alps*, p. 103.

23   *Ibid.*, p. 140.

24   *Ibid.*, p. 166.

25   *Ibid.*, pp. 233–234.

26   *Ibid.*, p. 237.

27   *Ibid.*, p. 238

28   *Ibid.*, p. 23–40.

29   *Ibid.*, p. 243

30   *Ibid.*, p. 244.

31   *Ibid.*, p. 251.

32   *Ibid.*, 250.

33   New Zealand, Department of Conservation, 8 May 2007.

34   Green, *High Alps*, p. 266.

35   Copy of telegram sent 11 March 1882 by W.S. Green at Albury to Dr Julius Haast, Christchurch in MS 2308 (1847–1919), Folder 68. Item 3.

36 Green, *High Alps*, p. 292.

37 *Ibid.*, p. 326

38 *Ibid.*, p. 346.

39 *Ibid.*, p. 308.

40 *Ibid.*, p. 335.

41 W. S. Green, cited in Cunningham & Abney, *Pioneers*, p. 97.

42 Green, Green/Haast letters, *Journals*, MS papers 2308.

43 This is a reference to the Irish Land League agitation in County Cork, which occurred in 1882 against Captain Boycott and his family who were socially isolated ('boycotted') in the local community in retaliation for his punitive actions against his tenants. His name added a new word to the English language and a cruel but effective political tactic to the repertoire of protesters the world over ever since.

44 Precursor to the University of London, founded in 1806 to make scientific education more widely available.

45 W. S. Green, *Among the Selkirk Glaciers* (London, Macmillan & Co., 1890), p. 4.

46 R. W. Sandford, 'William Spotswood Green – Tourist Explorer' in the introduction to W. S. Green, *Among the Selkirk Glaciers*, facsimile edn. (Calgary, Aquila Books, 1998).

47 Paper published: W. S. Green, 'Explorations in the Glacier Regions of the Selkirk Range, British Columbia, in 1888', *Proceedings of the Royal Geographical Society*, 11,3 (1889), pp. 153–70.

48 Green, *Selkirk Glaciers*, pp. 74–5.

49 *Ibid.*, p. 81.

50 Sandford, introduction to Green, *Selkirk Glaciers*.

51 Green, *Selkirk Glaciers*, p. 88.

52 *Ibid.*, pp. 157–58.

53 Sandford, introduction to Green, *Selkirk Glaciers*.

54 Went, *op. cit.*, p. 31.

55 Moriarty, *op. cit.*, p. 10.

56 Went, *op. cit.*, p. 38.

57 Petrel Fulmar, *Grania Waile: a West Connaught Sketch of the Sixteenth Century* (London, T. Fisher Unwin, 1895).

58 Extract from *The Dublin Express*, 18 January 1915, reprinted in 'Alpine Notes' under the heading 'Retirement of Rev. William Spotswood Green C.B.', *The Alpine Journal*, 24 (1915), p. 83.

59 W. S. Green cited in Cunningham & Abney, *Pioneers*, pp. 96–7.

Chapter 10: R. M. Barrington, Hart, Cullinan, Joly, Carson, Scriven, Parnell & Bryce: Wealth, Education & Discipline

1 Amy Barrington, *The Barringtons: a Family History* (Dublin, private publication, 1917), opposite p. 301.

2 Richard Manliffe Barrington, Diary for January to March 1864, *Journals and unpublished papers*, Barrington family private archive.

3 Praeger, *The Way*, pp. 44–9.

4 C. B. Moffat, 'Richard Manliffe Barrington'(obituary), *The Irish Naturalist*, 24 (1915), pp. 192–206.

5 R. L. Praeger, *Some Irish Naturalists* (Dundalk, Dun Dealgan Press, 1949), p. 33.

6 Barrington, Diary for 28 May to 15 June 1872, *Journals*.

7 Barrington, Diary for 1–10 August 1872, *Journals*.

8 Barrington, Diary for 26 April 1874, *Journals*.

9 Barrington, Diary for 28 June 1874, *Journals*.

10 T. Stirton, *Farm Competition: Leinster 1890 Report* (Dublin, Royal Dublin Society, 1891). Under the terms of the Act tenants could buy their holdings by borrowing the purchase price from the government and paying it back in monthly instalments.

11 Patricia M. Byrne, 'Richard Manliffe Barrington (1849–1915)', *Dictionary of Irish Biography*, vol. 1.

12   C. B. Moffat, *op. cit.*, pp. 192–206.

13   Richard M. Barrington, 'The Ascent of Stack-Na-Biorrach (The Pointed Stack), St Kilda' *The Alpine Journal*, 27 (1913), pp. 195–202.

14   Rev. H. Swanzy, 'Across the Rockies', *Montreal Daily Star*, 16 October (1884).

15   Barrington, Diary 7 September to 1 October 1884, His walk across the Rockies with the Rev. H. Swanzy, *Journals*.

16   'Cunningham, C. D., & Abney, W. de W. (eds), 'Copy of the Führerbuch of Christian Almer', *The Alpine Journal*, 14 (1889), p. 250.

17   *Ibid.*

18   *Ibid.*

19   Barrington, Copy of the Last Will and Testament of Richard Manliffe Barrington, 11 August 1909, *Journals and unpublished papers*, Barrington family private archive.

20   W. P. Haskett Smith & H. C. Hart, *Climbing in the British Isles, Volume II: Wales and Ireland* (London, Longmans Green, 1895), pp. 175–9.

21   In 1976 Niall Rice and Eddie Gaffney completed the route in 17 hours and 39 minutes. In July 2004 Bob Lawlor, a member of the Irish Mountain Running Association, ran the route solo in 16 hours 21 minutes.

22   R. M. Barrington, 'Henry Chichester Hart' (obituary), *The Irish Naturalist*, 17 (1908), p. 250.

23   Mumm, *op. cit.*, vol. 3, pp. 150–2.

24   Barrington, 'Henry Chichester Hart', pp. 248–54.

25   *Ibid.*, p. 250.

26   Mumm, *op. cit.*, vol. 3, pp. 14–15.

27   Barrington, 'Henry Chichester Hart', p. 251.

28   Edward Hull, *Reminiscences of a Strenuous Life* (London, H. Rees, 1910)

29   *Ibid.*, p184.

30   Mumm, *op. cit.*, vol. 3, p. 152.

31   Charles Pilkington, 'The Black Coolin *[sic]*', *The Alpine Journal*, 13 (1888), pp. 437–46.

32   Norman Collie, 'The Isle of Skye', *The Alpine Journal*, 32 (1918 & 1919), pp. 163–75.

33   Copy of H. C. Hart's original candidature form, the Alpine Club archives, London.

34   Barrington, 'Henry Chichester Hart', p. 250.

35   Cunningham & Abney, *Christian Almer's Führerbuch*, entry 250.

36   Haskett Smith & Hart, *op. cit.*, pp. 129–193.

37   *Ibid.*, p. 129.

38   *Ibid.*, p. 139.

39   *Ibid.*, p. 155.

40   *Ibid.*, pp. 183–4.

41   *Ibid.*, pp. 175–9.

42   Barrington, 'Henry Chichester Hart', p. 150.

43   Haskett Smith & Hart, *op. cit.*, p. 175.

44   Praeger, *Irish Naturalists*, pp 33–5.

45   Divorce case report, *The Irish Times*, 19 June 1897.

46   Gerald Fitzgerald, 'In Memoriam: Sir Frederick Cullinan K.C.B.', *The Alpine Journal*, 28 (1914), pp. 194–5.

47   Mumm, *op. cit.*, vol. 3, pp. 84–5.

48   Mumm, *op. cit.*, vol. 2, pp. 85–6.

49   Fitzgerald, *op. cit.*, p. 195.

50   'New Expeditions, August 1878', *The Alpine Journal*, 9 (1880) pp. 109–10.

51   F. J. Cullinan, 'The Aiguille de Talèfre', *The Alpine Journal*, 10 (1882), pp. 25–31.

52   *Ibid.*

53   Lindsay Griffin, *Mont Blanc Massif, Vol 1: Selected Climbs* (London, The Alpine Club, 1990), p. 190

54   D. W. Freshfield, 'Alpine Notes', *The Alpine Journal*, 9 (1880), pp 381–2.

55   F. Cullinan, R. Bagwell, J. Fagan, M. Inglis & J. Mulhall, *The Employment of Children During School Age, Especially in Street Trading* (Dublin, Her Majesty's Stationery Office, 1902).

56   Hugh de Fallenberg Montgomery (1844–1924) was a substantial landlord in Counties Fermanagh and Tyrone and a strong pro-unionist politician. He was an early member of the Ulster Unionist Council in 1904. He was a member of the Alpine Club during his university years at Oxford (1864–1869) when he climbed mainly in the Swiss and Italian Alps. (Ref. Mumm's Alpine Club register vol 1, p. 243–4.)

57   Henry Synnott (1871–1924) from Glenageary County Dublin was a Trinity College Dublin graduate and solicitor. He was a member of the Alpine Club with a strong list of ascents in Switzerland from 1895 to 1897 which included a Matterhorn traverse and ascents of Dent Blanche and the Ober-Gabelhorn. Ref. Typed continuation to Mumm's register (AC Archives London) p. 149.

58   George Yeld ed. 'Alpine Club Dinner in Dublin'in Alpine Notes, *The Alpine Journal*, 23 (1907), p. 173.

59   Fitzgerald, *op. cit.*, p. 195.

60   Patrica M. Byrne, 'Joly, Charles Jasper (1864–1906)', *Dictionary of Irish Biography*, vol 4.

61   Patrick N. Wyse Jackson, 'Joly, John (1857–1933)', *Dictionary of Irish Biography*, vol. 4.

62   H. H. Dixon & I. Falconer, 'Joly, John (1857–1933)' in *Oxford Dictionary of National Biography*, vol. 30.

63   Copy of H. C. Hart's original candidature form, the Alpine Club archives, London.

64   Alpine Club Register (London, Alpine Club, 1891–1957), p. 104.

65   Scriven, 'C. J. Joly', p. 58.

66   *Astronomical Observations and Researches made at Dunsink, 1870–1900* (Dublin, Hodges Foster & Co., 1870–1900).

67   F. E. Dixon, 'Dunsink and its Astronomers', *Dublin Historical Record*, 11, 2 (1950), pp. 33–50.

68   Kenneth C. Bailey, *A History of Trinity College, Dublin, 1892–1943* (Dublin, The University Press and Hodges Figgis & Co., 1947), pp. 211–12.

69   Dixon, *op. cit.*, p. 47.

70   P. A. Wayman, 'The Andrews Professors of Astronomy and Dunsink Observatory, 1785–1985', *Irish Astronomical Journal*, 17, 3(1986), pp. 167–84.

71   C. Comyns Tucker, 'In Memoriam: Thomas Henry Carson K.C.', *The Alpine Journal*, 31 (1918), pp 341–4.

72   *Ibid.*

73   R. N. Rudmore, 'Freshfield, Douglas William (1845–1934)', *Oxford Dictionary of National Biography*, vol. 20.

74   Tucker, *op. cit.*, p. 341.

75   Thomas H. Carson, 'Reminiscences of François Joseph Devouassoud', *The Alpine Journal*, 31 (1917), pp. 202–8.

76   Tucker, *op. cit.*, p. 342.

77   Douglas W. Freshfield, *The Italian Alps* (London, Longmans, 1875), pp. 151–2.

78   Carson, 'Reminiscences', p. 207.

79   Tucker *op. cit.*, p.341.

80   Edward MacLysaght, *The Surnames of Ireland*, edn 3 (Dublin, Irish Academic Press, 1978).

81   Mumm, *op. cit.*, vol. 3, pp 261–3.

82   Bailey, *op. cit.*, p. 114.

83   J. C. Conroy, *Rugby in Leinster* (Dublin, Leinster IRFU, 1979) p. 42.

84   Edmund Van Esbeck, *One Hundred Years of Irish Rugby* (Dublin, Gill & Macmillan, 1974), p. 48.

85   *Ibid.*, p. 50.

86   *Alpine Club Candidates Book*, AC3S/8, p. 57.

87   M. Conway, *Mountain Memories* (place, publisher, year), pp 76–81.

88   George Scriven, 'The Dolomites of San Martino di Castrozza', *The Alpine Journal*, 14 (1889), pp. 291–302.

89   George Scriven, 'Prevention of Snow Burning and Blistering', *The Alpine Journal*, 13 (1888), p. 389.

90   'New Expeditions in 1889', *The Alpine Journal*, 15 (1891), p. 151.

91   R. F. Foster, *Charles Stewart Parnell: The Man and his Family* (Sussex, Harvester Wheatsheaf, 1976), p. 70.

92   *Ibid.*, pp. 51 & 223.

93   *Ibid.*, pp. 119–20.

94   *Ibid.*, p. 216.

95   *Ibid.*, p. 102.

96   T. P. O'Connor, *Charles Stewart Parnell: A Memory* (London, Ward Lock, Bowden & Co., 1891), p. 25.

97   Sherlock Thomas, *The Life of Charles S. Parnell M.P.*, (Boston, Murphy & McCarthy, 1881), p. 61.

98   John Howard Parnell, *Charles Stewart Parnell: A Memoir* (London, Constable & Co., 1916), p. 11.

99   Foster, *op. cit.*, p. 224.

100 *Ibid.*, p. 222.

101 T. S. Blakeney, 'Failed A.C.', *The Alpine Journal*, 68 (1963), pp. 269–84.

102 D. F. O. Dangar, 'The Führerbuch of Alexander Burgener', *The Alpine Journal*, 58 (1952), pp. 181–91.

103 Rev. Cecil E. B. Watson, entry in 'Alpine Notes', *The Alpine Journal*, 9 (1880), p. 492.

104 Gladstone's words at Leeds: 'The resources of civilisation against its enemies are not yet exhausted'; cited in O' Connor, *op. cit.*, p. 124.

105 Foster, *op. cit.*, p. 223.

106 Emily Dickenson, *A Patriots Mistake: Reminiscences of the Parnell Family by a Daughter of the House* (London, Simpkin Marshall, 1905), pp. 49–62.

107 Foster, *op. cit.*, p 224

108 Charles Mosely (ed.), *Burke's Peerage and Baronetage*, edn 107, vol. 1 (Delaware, Burkes Peerage and Gentry, 2003), p. 876.

109 Mumm, *op. cit.*, vol. 3, pp. 39–48.

110 *Ibid.*, pp. 41–2.

111 H. A. L. Fisher, *James Bryce: Viscount Bryce of Dechmont, O.M.* vol. 1 (New York, Macmillan Co., 1927), p. 59.

112 Douglas W. Freshfield, 'In Memoriam: Lord Bryce', *The Alpine Journal*, 34 (1922), pp. 303–9.

113 James Bryce, 'Stray Notes on Mountain Climbing In Iceland', *The Alpine Journal*, 7 (1876), pp. 50–3.

114 *Ibid.*, p. 50.

115 James Bryce, *Transcaucasia and Ararat* (London, Macmillan, 1877), p. 69.

116 Fisher, *op. cit.*, p. 160.

117 Bryce, *Transcaucasia*, p. 258.

118 *Ibid.*, p. 282–3.

119 Freshfield, 'In Memoriam', p. 305.

120 www.caledonia.org.uk/land/rambler2.htm

121 Comment by James Bryce MP during the House of Commons Mountain Access debate, 4 March 1892; cited in Alan Blackshaw, 'An Historical Approach to the New Outdoor Access Legislation', *Scottish Affairs*, 62 (Institute of Governance, University of Edinburgh, 2008).

122 Christopher Harvie, 'James Bryce (1838–1922)', *Oxford Dictionary of National Biography*, vol 8.

123 *Ibid.*

124 Mumm, *op. cit.*, vol. 3, pp. 46.

125 Freshfield, 'In Memoriam', p. 305.

126 Sir Charles Hardinge, cited by Harvie, 'James Bryce', ODNB.

127 Freshfield, 'In Memoriam', p. 303.

128 *Ibid.*, p. 309.

Chapter 11: Valentine Ryan: The Ryan-Lochmatter Phenomenon

1   Letter from T. Graham Brown (editor of *The Alpine Journal*) to Group Captain Ryan, 22 November 1949; Brown's V. J. E. Ryan file, *Papers and letters*, National Library of Scotland, Edinburgh, Acc. 4338.

2 Peter H. Hanson, 'Albert Frederick Mummery (1855–1895)', in *Oxford National Dictionary of Biography*, vol. 39.

3 Walt Unsworth, *Hold the Heights: the Foundations of Mountaineering* (London, Hodder & Stoughton, 1993), p. 134.

4 G. Winthrop Young, 'A Great Climber: Valentine J. E. Ryan', *Climbers' Club Journal*, 9 (1951), pp. 20–48.

5 *Ibid.*, p. 22.

6 Ryan's AC qualification list, 6 February 1906, in Brown's V. J. E. Ryan file, *Papers and letters*.

7 Copy of the *Führerbücher* of Joseph Lochmatter in Alpine Club Library, London

8 Kevin Higgins, 'Valentine Ryan: The First Celtic Tiger', *Irish Mountain Log*, 85, Spring (2008), pp. 32–35.

9 Ryan's AC qualification list in Brown's V. J. E. Ryan file, *Papers and letters*.

10 *Ibid.*

11 Notes of an interview by Professor T. Graham Brown with Mrs Ryan, widow of J. V. E. Ryan, Friday December 30 1949; Brown's V. J. E. Ryan file, *Papers and letters*.

12 Young, 'Great Climber', p. 22.

13 *Führerbuch* of Joseph Lochmatter, pp. 136-37 signed by V. J. E. Ryan on 27 July 1904 at Chamonix; Alpine Club archives, London.

14 *Führerbuch* of Franz Lochmatter, pp. 46-47 signed by V. J. E. Ryan on 27 July 1904 at Chamonix; Alpine Club archives, London.

15 Young, 'Great Climber', p. 23.

16 V. J. E. Ryan, extract from fragments of draft book, cited in Young, 'Great Climber', pp. 38–9.

17 Notes of an interview by Professor T. Graham Brown with Mrs Ryan, widow of V. J. E. Ryan, Friday December 30 1949; Brown's V. J. E. Ryan file, *Papers and letters*.

18 Young, 'Great Climber', p. 30.

19 *Ibid.*

20 Young, 'Great Climber', pp. 30–1.

21 *Ibid.*, pp. 31–2.

22 *Ibid.*, pp. 32–3.

23 T. S. Blakeney, 'Failed A.C.', *The Alpine Journal*, 68, 2 (1963), p. 271.

24 Alan Hankinson, *Geoffrey Winthrop: Young Poet, Mountaineer, Educator* (London, Hodder & Stoughton, 1995), p. 88.

25 Blakeney, 'Failed A.C.', pp. 271 & 282.

26 Notes of conversation with Mrs V. J. E. Ryan, 6 December 1949, in Brown's V. J. E. Ryan file, *Papers and letters*.

27 Letter from Group Captain Ryan, 28 November 1949, in Brown's V. J. E. Ryan file, *Papers and letters*.

28 Copy of *Führerbücher* of Franz Lochmatter, Alpine Club Library, London, pp. 53–5.

29 Copy of *Führerbücher* of Joseph Lochmatter, Alpine Club Library, London, pp. 163–5.

30 Geoffrey Winthrop Young, *On High Hills* (London, Methuen, 1927), p. 274.

31 Young, 'Great Climber', pp. 33–4.

32 Detailed notes on the individual Alpine climbing records of H. O. Jones and G. W. Young and J. V. E. Ryan; Brown's *Papers and letters*.

33 Notes of an interview by Professor T. Graham Brown with Mrs Ryan, widow of J. V. E. Ryan, Friday December 30 1949; Brown's V. J. E. Ryan file, *Papers and letters*. Judging by his line of questioning, Brown was clearly looking for information regarding the Young/Ryan relationship and joint climbing expeditions.

34 Copies of a letter from Sydney Spenser to Brown (19 January 1949) and a letter from Brown (20 January 1949), both enquiring if either of the Lochmatter brothers had ever commented on the alleged gatecrashing by Young and Knubel of the Ryan/Lochmatter party during the Täschhorn ascent; in Brown, *Papers and letters*.

35 Jones, a brilliant Welsh rock climber, was killed in 1912 attempting Mont Rouge de Puteret with his new bride while on their honeymoon in the Alps. Their guide, Truffer, slipped on easy but exposed ground and pulled the rest of the party with him to their deaths.

36 Hankinson, *op. cit.*, pp 325–6.

37 Lord Tangley, *Papers*, Alpine Club archives, London, File B59

38 1914 entries by Ryan in the Alpine Club Library copy of J. Lochmatter's *Führerbücher*.

39 Young, 'Great Climber', p. 36.

40 *Ibid.*

41 Listed in both Franz and Joseph Lochmatters' *Führerbücher*; copies in Brown, *Papers and letters*.

42 Young, 'Great Climber', p. 37.

43 *Ibid.*, p. 22.

44 Letter from Ryan to Brown, 28 November 1949, in Brown, *Papers and letters*.

45 *Ibid.*

46 Young, 'Great Climber', pp 20–1.

47 *Ibid.*, p. 21.

Chapter 12: Charles Howard-Bury: Leader of the First Everest Reconnaissance

1   Marian Keaney, 'Charles Howard-Bury (1883–1963)', *Oxford Dictionary of National Biography*, vol. 9.

2   Charles Howard-Bury, *Mountains of Heaven: Travels in the Tien Shan Mountains*, edited by M. Keaney (London, Hodder and Stoughton, 1991), p. 20.

3   *Ibid.*

4   *Ibid.*, p. 21.

5   Charles Howard-Bury and George Leigh Mallory, *Everest Reconnaissance: the First Expedition of 1921*, edited by M. Keaney (London, Hodder and Stoughton, 1991), p. 17.

6   London, Hodder & Stoughton, 1991.

7   Howard-Bury & Mallory, *op. cit.*, p. 43.

8   Walt Unsworth, *Everest: the Mountaineering History*, edn 2 (Oxford, Grafton Books, 1991), p. 44.

9   Kevin Higgins, 'Arthur Oliver Wheeler, 1860–1945', *Journal of the Irish Mountaineering and Exploration Society*, 2 (2005), pp. 7–11.

10 Howard-Bury & Mallory, *op. cit.*, p. 48.

11 *Ibid.*, p. 56.

12 Unsworth, *Everest*, p. 48.

13 Howard-Bury & Mallory, *op. cit.*, p. 19.

14 *Ibid.*, p. 228.

15 *Ibid.*, p. 229.

16 Higgins, *Wheeler*, p. 9.

17 Report by editors George Yeld and J. P. Farrar, *The Alpine Journal*, 35 (1923), p. 125.

18 Alpine Club Register (London, The Alpine Club 1891–1957) p. 195.

19 Rob Bohan & Linde Lunney, 'Bury, Charles Kenneth Howard (1883–1963)', in *Dictionary of Irish Biography*, vol. 2.

20 *Ibid.*

21 Howard-Bury & Mallory, *op. cit.*, p. 21.

Chapter 13: A Legacy of Achievement

1   www.caledonia.org.uk/land/rambler2.htm

Bibliography

Primary sources

Adams-Reilly, *Diaries (1861, 1864, 1865, 1866)*, Alpine Club archives, London, Files DI 70–78

Almer, Christian, *Führerbuch*, Alpine Club archives, London.

Ball, J., *Letters to the Poor Law Commissioner, E. T. B. Twistleton*, National Archives of Ireland, Dublin, File RLFC3/1/1694

Barrington, R. M., *Journals and unpublished papers*, Barrington family private archive

Brown, T. G. (editor of *The Alpine Journal*), V. J. E. Ryan file, *Papers and letters*, National Library of Scotland, Edinburgh, Acc. 4338

Lochmatter, F., *Führerbücher* (copy), Alpine Club Library, London

Lochmatter, J., *Führerbücher* (copy), Alpine Club Library, London

Green, W. S., *Journals*, transcribed by Belinda Baldock, Alexander Turnbull Library, Wellington, New Zealand; MSS 6637 (1869–1882), 91/241 (1877) & 2308 (1847–1919)

Tangley, Lord E. H., *Papers*, Alpine Club archives, London, File B59

Whymper, E., *Four letters from Whymper to Adams Reilly*, 1864–5, Alpine Club archives, London, File B14

Archives

The following archives were consulted: the Central Registration Office, Dublin; the National Archives of Ireland; the National Library of Ireland; Royal Irish Academy Library; Public Records Office, London; the Society of Friends, Proceedings of Dublin Meetings; and the student registers and ledgers of Clongowes Wood College.

Books & Articles

Adams-Reilly, A., 'A Rough Survey of the Chain of Mont Blanc', *The Alpine Journal*, 1 (1864)

— 'Some New Ascents and Passes in the Chain of Mont Blanc', *The Alpine Journal*, 2 (1865)

Alexander, M., *The True Blue: The Life and Adventures of Colonel Fred Burnaby 1842–85* (London, Rupert Hart-Davis, 1957)

Astronomical Observations and Researches made at Dunsink, 1870–1900 (Dublin, Hodges, Foster & Co., 1870–1900)

Bailey, K. C., *A History of Trinity College, Dublin, 1892–1943* (Dublin, The University Press and Hodges Figgis & Co., 1947)

Bailey, R., *The Man Who Married A Mountain* (London, Bantam, 2005)

Ball, J., *What is to Done for Ireland?* (London, John Ridgway, 1849)

— *Peaks, Passes and Glaciers* (London, Longman, Green & Co., 1859; edn 5, 1860)

— *A Guide to the Western Alps* (London, Longman, Green & Co., 1866)

— *A Guide to the Eastern Alps* (London, Longman, Green & Co., 1868)

— 'Botanical Notes of a Tour in Ireland, with Notices of Some New Plants', *Annals and Magazine of Natural History*, 2 (1838), pp 28–36

— 'Notice of the Former Existence of Small Glaciers in the County of Kerry', *Journal of the Geological Society of Dublin*, 1848–50 (Dublin 1851)

— 'Val di Genova and the Pisgana Pass', *The Alpine Journal*, 1 (1864)

— 'Discussion on the Origin of the Flora of the European Alps', *Proceedings of the Royal Geographical Society*, 6 (1879)

Ball, Rev. W. B. W., *Ball Family Records: Genealogical Memoirs of Some Ball Families of Great Britain, Ireland and America* (York, Yorkshire Printing Co. Ltd., edn 2, 1908)

Barrington, A., *The Barringtons: a Family History* (Dublin, private publication, 1917)

Barrington, R. M., *The Migration of Birds as Observed at Irish Lighthouses and Lightships (Embodying Migration Reports 1888–1879)* (Dublin, E. Ponsonby, 1900)

— 'Henry Chichester Hart' (obituary), *The Irish Naturalist*, 17 (1908)

— 'The Ascent of Stack-Na-Biorrach (The Pointed Stack), St Kilda' *The Alpine Journal*, 27 (1913)

Bauer, U., 'The Three Lives of Elizabeth Main', in M. Britchgi, & D. Fässler (eds), *Elizabeth Main (1861–1934): Alpinist, Photographer, Writer* (Lucerne, Dioper-Verlag, 2003)

Beer, de G. R., & Brown, T. G., *The First Ascent of Mont Blanc* (Oxford, Oxford University Press, 1957)

Britchgi, M. & Fässler, D. (eds), *Elizabeth Main (1861–1934): Alpinist, Photographer, Writer* (Lucerne, Dioper-Verlag, 2003)

— 'An English Lady Discovers the Engadine Alps', in M. Britchgi & D. Fässler (eds), *Elizabeth Main (1861–1934): Alpinist, Photographer, Writer* (Lucerne, Dioper-Verlag, 2003)

Brock, W. H., McMillan, N. D. & Mollan, R. C. (eds), *John Tyndall: Essays on a Natural Philosopher* (Dublin, Royal Dublin Society, 1981)

Brown, R., A., *Women on High: Pioneers of Mountaineering* (Boston, Appalachian Mountain Club Books, 2003)

Burnaby, E. A. F., *The High Alps in Winter; or, Mountaineering in Search of Health* (London, Samson Low & Co., 1883)

— *High Life and Towers of Silence* (London, Samson Low & Co., 1886)

Bryce, Viscount J., *Transcaucasia and Ararat* (London, Macmillan, 1877)

— *Memories of Travel* (London, Macmillan, 1923)

— 'England's Real Attitude on Ireland', *Current History*, 12, 6 (1920)

— 'Stray Notes on Mountain Climbing in Iceland', *The Alpine Journal*, 7 (1876)

Carson, T. H., 'Reminiscences of François Joseph Devouassoud', *The Alpine Journal*, 31 (1917)

Clarke, R., *The Victorian Mountaineers* (London, B. T. Batsford, 1953)

Collie, N., 'The Island of Skye', *The Alpine Journal*, 32 (1918 & 1919)

Conroy, J. C., *Rugby in Leinster* (Dublin, Leinster IRFU, 1979)

Conway, M., *Mountain Memories* (London, Cassell and Company, 1920)

— Foreword, *Peaks, Passes and Glaciers*, third series, edited by A. E. Fields & S. Spencer (London, Longman, Green & Co., 1932)

Coolidge, W. A. B., 'A Day and a Night on the Bietschorn', *The Alpine Journal*, 6 (1872–1874)

— 'In Memoriam: John Ball', *The Alpine Journal*, 14 (1889)

Corcoran, T., *The Clongowes Record, 1814–1932* (Dublin, Brown & Nolan, 1932)

Cowell, J. J., 'On Some Relics of the Guides Lost on Mont Blanc', *The Alpine Journal*, 1 (1864)

Cullinan, F., 'The Aiguille de Talèfre', *The Alpine Journal*, 10 (1882)

Cullinan, F., Bagwell, R., Fagan, J., Inglis, M., & Mulhall, J., *The Employment of Children During School Age, Especially in Street Trading* (Dublin, Her Majesty's Stationery Office, 1902)

Cunningham, C. D., & Abney, W. de W., *The Pioneers of the Alps* (London, Samson Low, Marston, & Co., 1887)

— (eds), *A Facsimile of Christian Almer's Führerbuch, 1856–1894* (London, Samson Low, Marston, & Co., 1896)

— 'Copy of the Führerbuch of Christian Almer', *The Alpine Journal*, 14 (1889)

Dangar, D. F. O., 'The Führerbuch of Alexander Burgener', *The Alpine Journal*, 58 (1952)

Dickenson, E., *A Patriots Mistake: Reminiscences of the Parnell Family by a Daughter of the House* (London, Simpkin Marshall, 1905)

Dixon, F. E., 'Dunsink and its Astronomers', *Dublin Historical Record*, 11, 2 (1950)

Erskine, S., 'In Memorium: Mrs Aubrey Le Blond', *Ladies' Alpine Club Yearbook* (1935)

Eve, A. S. & Creasey, C. H., *Life and Works of John Tyndall* (London, Macmillan & Co., 1945)

Farrar, J. P., 'Historical Documents III, including a Facsimile Copy of the Führerbücher of Johan Zumtaugwald', *The Alpine Journal*, 31 (1918)

— 'The *Führerbuch* of Peter Knubel of St. Nicolas', *The Alpine Journal*, 32 (1919), pp. 98–9.

Fields, A. E. & Spencer, S. (eds) *Peaks, Passes and Glaciers*, third series (London, Longman, Green & Co., 1932)

Fisher, H. A. L., *James Bryce: Viscount Bryce of Dechmont, O.M.*, vol. 1 (New York, Macmillan Co., 1927)

Fitzgerald, G., 'In Memoriam: Sir Frederick Cullinan K.C.B.', *The Alpine Journal*, 28 (1914)

Forbes, J. D., *Travels through the Alps of Savoy and other parts of the Pennine Chain, with Observations on the Phenomena of Glaciers* (Edinburgh, A & C Black, 1843)

— 'Remarks on the First Discovery of the Real Structure of Glacier Ice', *The Edinburgh New Philosophical Journal*, 34 (1843)

Foster, R. F., *Charles Stewart Parnell: the Man and his Family* (Sussex, Harvester Wheatsheaf, 1976)

Fowler, R., 'Narrative of Ascents of the Aiguille Verte and the Chardonnet in the year 1865', *The Alpine Journal*, 4 (1870)

Freshfield, D. W., *The Italian Alps* (London, Longmans, 1875)

— 'In Memoriam: Lord Bryce', *The Alpine Journal*, 34 (1922)

Fulmar, P., *Grania Waile: a West Connaught Sketch of the Sixteenth Century* (London, T. Fisher Unwin, 1895)

Green, W. S., *The High Alps of New Zealand or a trip to the Glaciers of the Antipodes with an Ascent of Mount Cook* (London, Macmillan & Co., 1883)

— *Among the Selkirk Glaciers* (London, Macmillan & Co., 1890; facsimile edn, (Calgary, Aquila Books, 1998)

— 'Explorations in the Glacier Regions of the Selkirk Range, British Columbia, in 1888', *Proceedings of the Royal Geographical Society*, 11 (1889)

Griffin, L. G., *Mont Blanc Massif, Vol 1: Selected Climbs* (London, The Alpine Club, 1990)

Gwynn, S. L., *Duffer's Luck: a Fisherman's Adventure* (Edinburgh, Blackwood & Sons, 1924)

Hankinson, A., *Geoffrey Winthrop: Young Poet, Mountaineer, Educator* (London, Hodder & Stoughton, 1995)

Hart, H. C., *Some account of the Fauna and Flora of Sinai, Petra, and Wadi Arabahi* (London, Palestine Exploration Fund, 1891)

Haskett Smith, W. P., 'Henry Russell' (obituary), *The Alpine Journal*, 24 (1909)

Haskett Smith, W. P., & Hart, H. C., *Climbing in the British Isles. Volume II: Wales and Ireland* (London, Longmans Green, 1895)

Herity, J., *The Royal Irish Constabulary: A Short History and Genealogical Guide* (Dublin, Four Courts Press, 1997)

Higgins, K., 'Arthur Oliver Wheeler, 1860–1945', *Journal of the Irish Mountaineering and Exploration Society*, 2 (2005)

— 'Valentine Ryan: The First Celtic Tiger', *Irish Mountain Log*, 85, Spring (2008)

Hooker, Sir Joseph D., 'Mr John Ball, F.R.S.' (obituary), *Proceedings of the Royal Geographical Society*, 12 (1890)

Howard-Bury, C. H., *Mountains of Heaven: Travels in the Tien Shan Mountains*, edited by M. Keaney (London, Hodder and Stoughton, 1991)

Howard-Bury, C. H. & Mallory, G. L., *Everest Reconnaissance: the First Expedition of 1921*, edited by M. Keaney (London, Hodder and Stoughton, 1991)

Hull, E., *Reminiscences of a Strenuous Life* (London, H. Rees, 1910)

Irving, R. L. G., *A History of British Mountaineering* (London, B. T. Batsford, 1955)

Jeans, W. T., *Lives of the Electricians* (London, Whittaker & Co., 1887)

Kennedy, T. S., 'Zermatt and the Matterhorn in Winter', *The Alpine Journal*, 2 (1864)

Laffan, M., *The Barringtons of Glendruid* (Dublin, Foxrock Local History Club, 1990)

Le Blond, Mrs. E. A. F., *True Tales of Mountain Adventure for Non-climbers Young and Old* (London, T. Fisher Unwin, 1903)

— *The Story of an Alpine Winter* (London, G. Bell & Sons, 1907)

— *Mountaineering in the Land of the Midnight Sun* (London, T. Fisher Unwin, 1908)

— *Day in, Day out* (London, Bodley Head, 1928)

— (ed.), *Adventures on the Roof of the World* (London, T. Fisher Unwin, 1904)

Longman, W., 'Modern Mountaineering and the History of the Alpine Club', *The Alpine Journal*, 8 (1878)

Lyons, M. C., *Illustrated Encumbered Estates, Ireland: 1850–1905* (Whitegate, County Clare, Ballinakella Press, 1993)

MacLysaght, E., *The Surnames of Ireland* (Dublin, Irish Academic Press, edn 3, 1978)

Maguire, J. & Quinn, J. (eds), *Dictionary of Irish Biography* (Cambridge, Royal Irish Academy & Cambridge University Press, 2009)

Main, E. A. F., *My Home in the Alps* (London, Samson Low, Marston & Co., 1892)

— *Hints on Snow Photography* (London, Samson Low, Marston & Co., 1895)

Mathews, C. E., *The Annals of Mont Blanc* (London, T. F. Unwin, 1898)

— 'Recollections of a Mountaineer', in C. T. Dent (ed.), *Mountaineering* (London, T. F. Unwin, 1892)

— 'John Ball', *The Alpine Journal*, 15 (London 1889)

Moffat, C. B., 'Richard Manliffe Barrington' (obituary), *The Irish Naturalist*, 24 (1915)

Montager, H. F., 'Extract from Travellers' Book of the Hotel at Eggishorn', *The Alpine Journal*, 32 (1919).

Montagnier, H. F., 'A Bibliography of the Ascents of Mont Blanc from 1786 to 1853', *The Alpine Journal*, 25 (1910–1911)

'Early Records of the Col de Théodule, the Weissthor, the Adler and other Passes of the Zermatt District', *The Alpine Journal*, 32 (1918–19).

'Early Extracts from the Travellers' Book of the Hotel at the Eggishorn', *The Alpine Journal*, 32 (1920)

Montgomery-Massingberd, H. (ed.), *Burke's Irish Family Records* (London, Burke's Peerage, 1976)

Moody, T. W. & Martin, F. X, *The Course of Irish History* (Cork, Mercier Press, 1994)

More, A. G. (ed.), *Cybele Hibernica* (Dublin, E. Ponsonby, edn 2, 1898)

More, F. M., *Alexander Goodman More: Selections from his Zoological and Botanical Writings* (Dublin, Hodges Figgis & Co., 1898)

Moriarty, C., *The Reverend W. S. Green: Explorer and Fishery Scientist* (Dublin, Royal Irish Academy, 1994)

Mumm, A. L. (ed.), *The Alpine Club Register,* vol. 1 (1857–1863), vol. 2 (1864–1876), vol. 3 (1877–1890) (London, Edward Arnold, 1923–5)

— *Alpine Register* typed continuation of Mumm's 'Alpine Club Register' (1891–1957), Alpine Club archives, London

— 'Extracts from the *Führerbuch* of Peter Knubel', *Alpine Register Supplement*, Alpine Club archives, London.

Murray, J., *A Handbook for Travellers in Switzerland, Savoy and Piedmont* (London, Murray, 1838)

O'Connor, T. P., *Charles Stewart Parnell: A Memory* (London, Ward, Locke, Bowden & Co., 1891)

O'Réagáin, L., 'Some Early Mountaineers', *Irish Mountaineering*, 1 (1960)

Matthew, C., & Harrison, B. (eds), *Oxford Dictionary of National Biography* (Oxford, Oxford University Press, 2004)

Packe, C., *Guide to the Pyrenees: Especially Intended for the Use of Mountaineers* (London, Longmans, Green, 1867)

— 'A Review of *Souvenirs d'un Montagnard*, 1858–1888, par Cte. Henry Russell', *The Alpine Journal*, 14 (1889)

Palman, A., *Aoraki-Mount Cook: A Guide for Mountaineers* (Christchurch, New Zealand Alpine Club, 2001)

Parnell, J. H., *Charles Stewart Parnell: A Memoir* (London, Constable & Co., 1916)

Pilkington, C., 'The Black Coolin', *The Alpine Journal*, 13 (1888)

Praeger, R. L., *The Way that I Went* (Dublin, Hodges Figgis & Co., 1937)

— *Some Irish Naturalists* (Dundalk, Dun Dealgan Press, 1949)

Rey, G., *The Matterhorn*, translated by J. E. C. Eaton (London, Unwin, 1907)

Rowlinson, J. S., 'Tyndall's work on Glaciology and Geology', in W. H. Brock, N. D. McMillan & Mollan R. C. (eds), *John Tyndall: Essays on a Natural Philosopher* (Dublin, Royal Dublin Society, 1981)

Russell, H., *Notes par Voies et Chemins dans Le Nouveau-Monde* (Bagnères-de-Bigorre, Dossun, 1858)

— *Souvenirs d'un Montagnard, 1858–1888*, edn 2 (Pau, Imprimerie Vignancour, 1908)

— *Seize Mille Lieues à travers l'Asie et l'Océanie. Voyage Exécuté Pendant les Années 1851–1861* (Paris, Hachette,1864; reissued by Amyot, Paris, 1866, without the map and the panorama)

— 'On Mountains and on Mountaineering in General', *The Alpine Journal*, 5 (1871)

— 'In Memoriam: Charles Packe', *The Alpine Journal*, 18 (1896)

Scriven, G., 'Prevention of Snow Burning and Blistering', *The Alpine Journal*, 13 (1888)

— 'The Dolomites of San Martino di Castrozza', *The Alpine Journal*, 14 (1889)

— 'In Memoriam: C. J. Joly F.R.S.', *The Alpine Journal*, 23 (1907)

Shairp, J. C., Tait, P.G & Adams-Reilly, A., *Life and Letters of James David Forbes F.R.S.* (London, Macmillan & Co., 1873)

Sherlock, T., *The Life of Charles S. Parnell M.P.* (Boston, Murphy & McCarthy, 1881)

Shuster, G. C. B., 'Tyndall as a Mountaineer', in E. & C. H. Creasey, *Life and Works of John Tyndall* (London, Macmillan & Co., 1945)

Slader, B., *The High Pyrenees: Los Encantados – The Enchanted Mountains* (Belfast, Quest Books, 2005)

Spry, I. M., 'On the Trail of Palliser's Papers', *Saskatchewan History*, 12, 2 (1959)

— 'Captain John Palliser and the Exploration of Western Canada', *The Geographical Journal*, 125, 2 (1959)

Stephen, Rev. L., *The Playground of Europe* (London, Longmans, Green and Co., 1871)

— 'The Bietschhorn and Blümlis Alp', *The Alpine Journal*, 1 (1864)

— 'Ascent of the Rothorn', *The Alpine Journal*, 2 (1866)

Stirton, T., *Farm Competition: Leinster 1890 Report* (Dublin, Royal Dublin Society, 1891)

Strutt, E. L., 'In Memoriam, Mrs Aubrey Le Blond (1861–1934)', *The Alpine Journal*, 64 (1934)

Swanzy, Rev. H. B., 'Across the Rockies', *Montreal Daily Star*, 16 October (1884)

Swanzy, Rev H. B. & Green, T. G. H., *The Family of Green of Youghal, Co.Cork* (Dublin, private publication by Alex Thom, 1902)

Swinden, L. & Fleming, P., *Valais Alps East: Selected Climbs* (London, Alpine Club, 1999), p.103–6

Thom's Irish Almanac (Dublin, Alexander Thom & Co.), published biannually from 1860 to 1903

Tindal, T., 'The Champion Lady Mountaineer', first published in *Pearson's Magazine*, circa 1902; copy in Mountaineering Pamphlet T 526, Alpine Club archives

Tucker, C. C., 'In Memoriam: Thomas Henry Carson K.C.', *The Alpine Journal*, 31 (1918)

Tyndall, J., *Glaciers of the Alps* (London, Longmans, Green and Co., 1860)

— *Mountaineering in 1861* (London, Longmans, Green and Co., 1861)

— *Hours of Exercise in the Alps* (London, Longmans, Green and Co., 1871)

— *Principal Forbes and his Biographers* (London, Longmans, Green and Co., 1893)

Unsworth, W., *Everest: the Mountaineering History*, edn 2 (Oxford, Grafton, 1991)

— *Hold the Heights: the Foundations of Mountaineering* (London, Hodder & Stoughton, 1993)

Van Esbeck, E., *The Story of Irish Rugby* (London, Stanley Paul, 1986)

Wayman, P. A., 'The Andrews Professors of Astronomy and Dunsink Observatory, 1785–1985', *Irish Astronomical Journal*, 17, 3(1986)

Webster, E., *Climbing in the Magic Islands: a Climbing & Hiking Guidebook to the Lofoten Islands of Norway* (Henningsvar, Nord Norsk Klatreskole, 1994)

Went, A. E. J., 'William Spotswood Green', *Scientific Proceedings of the Royal Dublin Society*, series B, vol. 2 (1967)

Williams, C., *Women on the Rope, the Feminine Share in Mountain Adventure* (London, George Allen & Unwin, 1973)

Wills, Alfred *Wanderings among the High Alps* (London, R. Bentley, 1856)

Whymper, E., *Scrambles Amongst the Alps in the Years 1860–69*, edn 4 (London, John Murray, 1893)

— *Chamonix and the Range of Mont Blanc* (London, John Murray, 1897)

— 'Camping Out', Hereford B. George (ed.) *The Alpine Journal*, vol. 2 (London, Longman, Green, Longman, Roberts and Green, 1866)

— 'The Fatal Accident on the Matterhorn' (reprinted letter to *The Times*), *The Alpine Journal*, 2 (1864)

— 'Professor Tyndall's Attempt on the Matterhorn in 1862', *The Alpine Journal*, 5 (1872) pp. 329–336

Yeld, G., 'Professor Huxley and Professor Tyndall', *The Alpine Journal*, 20 (1901)

Young, G. W., *On High Hills* (London, Methuen, 1927)

— 'A Great Climber: Valentine J. E. Ryan', *Climbers' Club Journal*, 9 (1951)

Websites

http://www.caledonia.org.uk/land/rambler2.htm

Index

Note: illustrations are indicated by page numbers in bold.

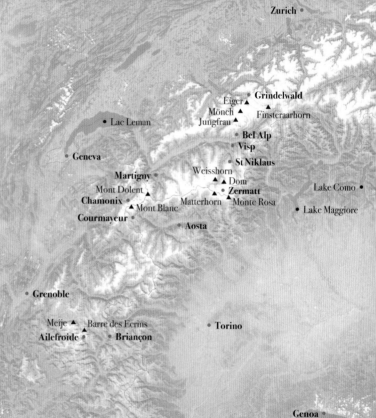

France

Switzerland

Zurich •

Eiger ▲ ▲ **Grindelwald**
Mönch ▲ **Finsteraarhorn**
• Lac Leman Jungfrau ▲
Bel Alp
▲ **Visp**
• **Geneva** ▲ **St Niklaus**
Martigny Weisshorn • Lake Como •
Mont Dolent ▲ ▲ Dom
Chamonix ▲ **Zermatt** • Lake Maggiore
▲ Mont Blanc Matterhorn ▲ Monte Rosa
Courmayeur •
• **Aosta**

• **Grenoble**

Meije ▲ ▲ Barre des Ecrins
Ailefroide ▲ • **Briançon** • **Torino**

France
• **Genoa**

Maritime Alps

• Nice